DON MIL P9-BYV-888

SAUNDERS COLLEGE PUBLISHING

Philadelphia New York Chicago
San Francisco Montreal Toronto
London Sydney Tokyo Mexico City
Rio de Janeiro Madrid

Psychomotor Learning

Robert Kerr

Associate Professor
Department of Kinanthropology
School of Human Kinetics
University of Ottawa

Address orders to:
383 Madison Avenue
New York, NY 10017

Address editorial correspondence to:
West Washington Square
Philadelphia, PA 19105

This book was set in Baskerville by Caledonia Composition.
The editors were John Butler, Carol Field, Salena Kerr, Don Reisman, and Jeanne Carper.
The art & design director was Richard L. Moore.
The text design was done by Arlene Putterman.
The cover design was done by Arlene Putterman.
The artwork was drawn by Ames & Zak, Ltd.
The production manager was Tom O'Connor.
This book was printed by Maple Press.

PSYCHOMOTOR LEARNING   ISBN 0-03-058954-1

234   038   987654321

CBS COLLEGE PUBLISHING
Saunders College Publishing
Holt, Rinehart and Winston
The Dryden Press

Dedicated to my
mother
and the memory
of my father,
Robert Rowan

Preface

By the work know ye the workman

Whether we seek elegance
Whether we seek excellence
Whether we seek skill
Whether we seek fun

We are only who we are
And we can only try
To be what we can.

(Quote expanded by Rowan, 1980)

When we look closely at our lives, from the weekly attempt to clean the apartment, to the end-of-term panic to type major assignments, to the early morning drive into school through rush-hour traffic, to the afternoon pick-up game of tennis, to the nightly practices with the varsity basketball team, and to playing a guitar at the Sunday afternoon picnic, we can see the wide variety of motor tasks that constitute our daily activities and how psychomotor learning has the potential to touch on many aspects of our lives. With this clear potential, the paramount aim in the application of psychomotor learning to our daily lives is not to provide a basis for the production of an Olympic athlete but to bring "skillfulness" into all our lives.

Improving skill means that the performance of any motor task becomes more efficient, thereby reducing the time taken to complete the task and the level of effort required. This increased level of skillfulness could also mean more enjoyment and satisfaction for the performer by increasing the ease with which the task can be completed or by allowing new, more complex skills to be attempted. If by understanding the processes that govern the control of movement we can show the way for all individuals to improve their ability to perform the myriad of motor tasks that they confront, then we can claim to have made a real contribution to improving the quality of life within our society.

If our level of understanding were to advance sufficiently such that the programs fostering these principles of psychomotor learning were capable of moving the general population one step higher on the "ladder" of motor skills, then it would seem reasonable to assume that those individuals with special talents might be able to make even larger gains and those with specific disabilities might be helped to take their place in society. The point of this discourse is simple. Although we at times may seek knowledge for its own sake, it serves us little if at some time we cannot apply that knowledge to help solve real-world problems. Motor performance may only represent one facet of our lives, but because we are not made of stone nor imprisoned in "little boxes," as the folk-singer Pete Seeger once expressed, a full and complete understanding of how we produce and control movement is basic to the betterment of our lives.

The emphasis in this text is on the potentially broad field of application of psychomotor learning and not on the narrow field of sport, within which studies of psychomotor learning originated. Although most psychomotor learning courses are offered to students of physical education and, as such, are taught in the context of sports skills, the limits for the application of this theoretical base are determined solely by the capacity and comprehension of the instructor. The concepts related to learning and performing motor skills efficiently are as applicable to the musician and surgeon as they are to the athlete.

The text is divided into four parts: Learning, Skill Acquisition, Perception, and Motor Control. The first two parts deal with the more traditional applied research that has characterized much of psychomotor learning. In the first part attempts are made to lay a foundation for the text by discussing, in the context of motor skills, certain major learning theories. In the second part some of the main principles that have evolved from the research concerned more directly with motor skills are discussed. Much of the work presented in part two is based on either of the two major theoretical camps—association or cognitive.

The latter two parts of the text, Perception and Motor Control, reflect a change in the orientation of research in psychomotor learning from applied to basic research and to an emphasis on information theory. The information processing approach divides the psychomotor learning area into selective motor learning and motor skill learning. Selective motor learning refers to such factors as feedback, timing, anticipation, and the overall organization of the skill, while motor skill learning is concerned with the execution of the response. However, the selection of the appropriate response also requires knowledge regarding such questions as how much force, how far, and which direction. Therefore, for the purposes of this text, although you can approach the area from either a consideration of the response selection process or the actual execution of the response, the two approaches are not really separable.

In the third part, Perception, the strong link between action and perception is acknowledged. In order to make decisions, react, or modify our actions we must be able to interpret changes in the environment and within ourselves. In the fourth part some of the most recent advances in psychomotor learning are introduced, much of which represents basic research that is still in progress. However, if such research is to be relevant, it must be applicable to the learning of motor skills and analogous to some of the well-founded principles that have evolved from the wealth of earlier applied research.

Researchers in psychomotor learning have sought answers to the question of how we learn motor skills. This search is based on the premise that the more we understand, the better we are able to analyze new situations in teaching and coaching. But, "a little knowledge can be dangerous." Therefore, it is important not to be carried away with one idea that works well in one situation and try to generalize from it. We must recognize that each situation may be different and harbor specific problems. By seeking the reasons why and how the changing circumstances affect the learning and performance of a motor skill, we may find the underlying relationship that pulls together previously unrelated facts.

Consequently, this text has not focused solely on the more recent information processing approach to psychomotor learning but has also attempted to trace the modern development of the field. The information processing approach may not flow easily from the more traditional applied research, but an appreciation of the latter would seem essential if we are to maintain the concepts of information processing in their proper perspective.

Psychomotor learning is an exciting field because it has the potential to touch on so many aspects of our lives. Like most fields of study, there are many new concepts to be grappled with and understood. Because of the gaps in our research knowledge and the complexity of the human machine with which we are dealing, some of the concepts are often difficult to grasp and ill defined. However, if you read the text carefully, re-read what you find difficult, ask questions, and supplement the text examples with illustrations of your own, you may come to comprehend the potential that can be unleashed through an understanding of psychomotor learning.

The preparation of this text involved the tapping of many minds from a wide range of sources, but the resultant synthesis is the product of one individual, the author. If you disagree with any statement, do not dismiss it. Instead try to establish a clear rationale for your disagreement, for in so doing you may be adding your own contribution to our understanding of ourselves and the world in which we live.

Acknowledgments

In preparing this text help has been forthcoming from many sources. Particular thanks goes to the reviewers whose many positive suggestions have added much to this text: Jack Adler, University of Oregon; Keith Henschen, University of Utah; Charles Shea, Texas A&M; John Shea, University of Colorado at Boulder; George Stelmach, University of Wisconsin at Madison; Harriet Williams, University of South Carolina, and Craig Wrisberg, University of Tennessee.

A very special thank you goes out to those friends whose helping hands made the work both possible and enjoyable.

Finally, a personal thank you to the people of Saunders College Publishing who make a complex task seem straightforward.

Salut,
Robert Kerr, Ph.D.

Contents Overview

Table of Contents

Part One

Psychomotor Learning and Learning Theories

Chapter 1
Introduction to Psychomotor Learning

If beginnings mean questions,
Endings never come.
(Rowan, 1980)

A HISTORICAL PERSPECTIVE

Psychomotor learning is in many ways a relatively new field. Some of the earliest work concerned with motor skills was conducted by psychologists at the turn of the century (Woodworth, 1899) and at that time research often involved such motor skills as telegraphy and handwriting, but it was not until the early 1920s that physical educators became involved. These educators began by seeking to measure an individual's motor IQ or general motor ability (GMA). Characteristic of this work is Brace's GMA test (1927). At the same time, researchers were looking at problems related to appropriate teaching methods and practice organization. They turned to the established learning theories, such as Thorndike's theory of connectionism, for a base. Physical education researchers were also active in several other areas, and by 1930 the *Research Quarterly*, the main vehicle for physical education research, was established.

The biggest boost to the overall field of motor skill analysis occurred during World War II, when it became essential to find the most efficient methods to fly planes and fire guns, as well as more effective ways to learn these skills other than by trial and error. Thus, there was considerable financial support from defense departments for research, as there still is today. Emphasis on motor skill analysis has continued through industrial research, in which efficiency of operation is of great importance.

Further impetus was also given by the "latest learning theory" formulated by Hull (1943), who talked about drive reduction, motivation, and fatigue. Hull's theory, particularly the fatigue element, was suited to experiments using motor tasks. The use of motor tasks by the psychologists as a means to an end was a rather back-door boost for motor skill research, but at least it helped "sow the seeds." Following the post-war boom in motor learning research, the subject became an accepted part of most university physical education programs, although it relied heavily on the psychologists for theoretical input.

Motor skill learning supplemented physical education studies because what was being considered was the most efficient way to perform or learn a motor skill. If we think of physical education as skill teaching, then obviously ideas about efficient methods are essential. In physical education, skill has two meanings. It can refer to (1) a particular task (*e.g.*, a basketball jump shot) or (2) a level of proficiency. The early researchers in physical education (in the 1930s and 1940s) tended to limit themselves to the first option, dealing mainly with tasks or skills from particular sports. Thus, the "artificial" laboratory motor tasks of the psychologist became accepted as a means of researching how motor skills were acquired. However, it has since been realized that the acquisition of skill is much the same whether the task involves driving a car, reading, shooting a basketball, or painting. The common denominator for all these tasks is the change in the level of proficiency, or skill, as a result of practice.

What has distinguished physical education researchers has been their attempt to apply research techniques to immediate practical problems. By dealing with specific problems, you get specific answers; what you do not get is a theory which can be generalized. Although this is a very useful approach, it has for many years left the field without any solid theoretical base. More recently, however, there has been a switch in emphasis—from looking at how well we perform a task to asking the question of how we control that behavior. This change in orientation has been facilitated by the growth of cybernetic theory, which was a human/machine analogy. In this approach, persons are seen simply as processors of information who make decisions that in turn set into motion simple or complex motor programs. How a person perceives and processes various types of information, and how these mental operations affect the decisions and the movements produced, is the main concern in cybernetic theory.

Today, we see information about motor skill acquisition coming from a myriad of sources: psychology, sociology, physiology, anthropology, physical education, and many others. However, much of the leading work in psychomotor learning is carried out by the physical educators—kinesiologists

—who are no longer just relying on the psychologists. There are now many scientific journals which emphasize psychomotor learning research, several of which include *Journal of Motor Behavior; Perceptual and Motor Skills; Journal of Human Movement Studies; Motor Skills: Theory into Practice; Research Quarterly for Exercise and Sport; Journal of Experimental Psychology: Human Perception and Performance.* At the moment, psychomotor learning is one of the fastest moving areas in the domain of human performance.

PSYCHOMOTOR LEARNING DEFINED

Before considering how motor skills are acquired, we should first define our area of concern, psychomotor learning. The first step would be to define what we mean by *learning*. This is a fairly common term, and we all have some idea of what it implies. However, producing a precise definition is difficult because of the problem of distinguishing between learning and performance:

> **Learning** is a *relatively permanent change in performance resulting from practice or past experience.*

> **Performance** is a *temporary occurrence fluctuating from time to time: something which is transitory.*

The definition of learning given encompasses two main points: (1) that learning is represented by a *permanent* change in performance and (2) that this change results from *practice* or *experience*, as in simply watching someone else perform. Implicit in our definition is the idea that such changes are measurable in terms of performance scores. This final point leads to a major problem, as we will see later.

Performance, on the other hand, may represent a once in a lifetime event. Performance refers to the actual score achieved on a task, whereas learning refers to a judgment made about the permanence of changes in that performance. We should note that in the definition of learning we do not include those changes which can be attributed to maturation, aging, or temporary physiological changes, such as fitness level.

The next step would be to explain the term *motor*. A simple definition of a motor skill follows:

> *A **motor skill** is any muscular activity which is directed to a specific objective.*

Because the muscular activity defined here is consciously directed toward some goal, all reflex activity and such things as a simple muscle twitch are eliminated. Obviously, such a definition includes a very wide range of activities. In fact, in terms of the overall scope of motor skills we can identify three broad categories:

1. Those developed in early life that are primarily dependent on maturation and are common to all humans (*e.g.*, crawling, walking, talking—the *phylogenetic skills*). The onset and development of these skills are mainly a question of opportunity and maturation. All children acquire these skills as they grow, unless limited by disease, accident, or heredity.

2. Those which are essential for further development in terms of meeting educational needs—*communication skills* (*e.g.*, writing and reading). In speed reading, scanning more than one word at a time involves a large mental component, but it is based on a motor skill.

3. Those learned for oneself—*recreational skills* (*e.g.*, painting or gymnastics).

These latter two categories are sometimes combined and referred to as *ontogenetic skills*, or those skills learned by and peculiar to an individual. Thus, while phylogenetic skills develop naturally, ontogenetic skills require a conscious effort on the part of the learner and, as a result, are developed more by practice and experience than by maturation. In dealing with recreational skills, it is important to recognize that motor skills are not simply manifested by the hockey player but also by the dentist, jeweler, and musician. Thus, we can now state the following:

> **Motor learning** is a relatively permanent change in the performance of a motor skill resulting from practice or past experience.

Finally, we need to explain the addition of the prefix *psycho*. This term implies that the performance of motor skills involves more than just muscular activity. The muscular activity simply represents the external behavior that is observed. Behind this behavior there is a large central control operation that not only supervises the specific muscle commands regarding *how* to move but also supervises the decisions of *why, when, where,* and *how far* to move. Psychomotor learning, therefore, is not just concerned with observable behavior but is also vitally concerned with those central controlling processes that both guide and produce that behavior.

Learning vs performance

Schmidt (1975*a*) attempted to say *what* is changed rather than *how* it is changed when we learn. He distinguished between the physical performance we actually see and how that changes as we learn, and the individual's internal representation of what is being learned. Borrowing a term from psychologists, he refers to learning as a change in *habit strength* resulting from practice. Practice is seen as a necessary, but not sufficient, condition for performance to occur. *Habit* being "some relatively stable internal state," there could be an increase in habit strength without any apparent improvement in performance. An individual might be learning without any observable change in performance. Although a basketball player's technique might be improving slightly, for example, the player may still only score five of ten free throws. If, however, the shooting action was smoother, we can infer that there has been an increase in the habit strength. It would not be accurate to say that nothing had been learned simply because there was no change in the performance score. Schmidt's definition provides a means of acknowledging the qualitative changes that take place as a skill is learned. These qualitative changes may improve the mechanical efficiency of the movement but fail to produce quantifiable changes in terms of performance.

As Schmidt's definition clearly suggests, although we use performance to measure learning, the two terms are not the same. *Performance* is the end product or behavior that we see, while *learning* is represented by an internalized model that allows us to repeat the performance of a skill. Performance is a variable that is much more susceptible to external factors such as reinforcement, as the following experiment by Blodgett (1929) illustrates.

PERFORMANCE ARTIFACTS.   Three groups of rats were timed once per day to see how quickly they could negotiate a short maze. On each day, Group 1 received food as a reward at the end of the maze. Group II did not begin to receive a reward until the seventh day. Group III received a reward on the fourth day. The graph in Figure 1-1 indicates the relative performance of the three groups. It is clear that the differences in performance were removed once the rats were

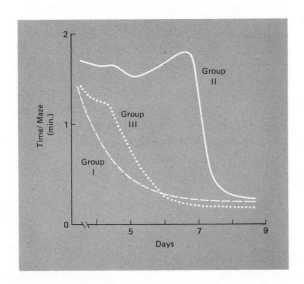

FIGURE 1-1   Maze learning in rats (after Blodgett, 1929).

rewarded. The Group II rats had actually learned the maze but simply had no reason to demonstrate their ability. This phenomenon is referred to as *latent learning:* the idea that learning may have occurred but is not immediately evident in terms of performance. We have defined performance as "a temporary occurrence fluctuating from time to time." As such, it may not represent any change in learning. When a beginning basketball player shoots nine of ten free throws, for example, this performance may just be a "fluke." In the measurement of human performance, we often have problems because of *performance artifacts,* such as plateaus in the learning/performance curve and ceiling or floor effects (Figure 1-2).

If after one hour of practice a player misses all ten free throws, has that player learned nothing? More normally, change is seen as learning progresses. There may be stages in which much improvement is needed to change the performance score. This leveling off in the performance curve is known as a *plateau.* These apparent plateaus in the learning/performance curve are not necessarily indicative of a halt in the learning process. In Schmidt's terms, the change in the habit strength was not sufficient to produce a change in performance; the presence of a temporary performance variable (*e.g.,* fatigue) depressed performance, and, therefore, an inaccurate estimate of habit strength level (*i.e.,* learning) was derived.

A *ceiling effect* exists when there is a maximum performance score for a test (*e.g.,* ten of ten free throws). A *floor effect* exists when there is some minimum time (*e.g.,* zero) beyond which performance cannot improve. Despite these measurement problems and other limitations, performance still provides the only way to assess learning.

All these are performance artifacts in that the scores achieved are not a true measure of learning. This is mainly because of the gross nature of our

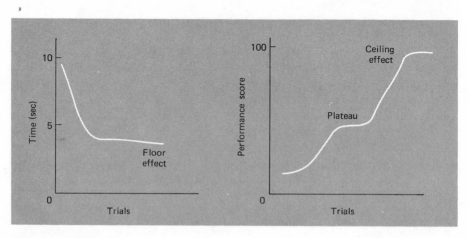

FIGURE 1-2 Performance artifacts.

measurement techniques, which limit our ability to detect changes. A basketball shot is either in or out, but surely ten rim shots are better than ten complete misses. Only by refining our measurement techniques can we reduce these problems.

The learning process

Having defined psychomotor learning, the final step is to consider the main ingredients of the learning process. There are four main ingredients necessary to create a *learning situation:*

1. *A living organism.* By our earlier definition of learning (a relatively permanent change in performance/behavior), all living organisms can learn in some form, although some can learn more than others. Even in humans the capacity to learn, and what affects this capacity, varies.
2. *A desired goal.* The goal represents the consequence or outcome of a particular activity.
3. *A required level of motivation.* This is the result of certain needs or incentives to achieve a particular desired goal. The intensity of these needs or incentives affects the motivation.
4. *An obstacle to overcome.* When the learner is prevented by either lack of knowledge or skill from obtaining the desired goal, then a learning situation is created. If the learner does immediately attain the goal, it suggests that the learning has already occurred (latent learning).

Therefore, in the learning situation it is the motivation that pushes the individual to overcome the barrier and achieve the goal. Characteristic of this process is that the learner will make errors. If there are no errors, there is nothing to be learned. As such, *performance errors are not indications of failure, but of the learning process in action.* How different theorists view this process will be discussed in the next chapter.

CLASSIFICATION OF MOTOR SKILLS

In the attempt to bring order to the area of psychomotor learning, many classification systems have been developed for motor skills. These classification systems, or taxonomies, are important for four reasons. First, they provide a means of bringing some order to the very diverse field of motor skills. The word *taxonomy* implies an orderly classification according to presumed natural relationships. Second, the actual process of identifying these common elements may further our understanding of motor skills. Third, these systems help to focus research efforts on those elements, thereby permitting a greater applicability of the obtained results. Fourth, categorizing motor skills makes it possible to investigate how sample skills from within a category respond to a particular teaching technique. Teaching methods might now be generalized within a class of skills. A technique used in badminton, for example, might be equally usable in tennis but not usable in swimming classes. Two of the more common taxonomies are discrete vs continuous and open vs closed:

1. *Discrete* vs *continuous* (Fitts, 1965). This classification describes a continuum at one end of which we find those skills that have a distinct beginning and end, involving a single effort of short duration (*e.g.*, a baseball throw) and at the other end those skills that involve a continuous or repetitive series of movements with no distinct end points (*e.g.*, driving a car or swimming).

2. *Open* vs *closed*. This idea, proposed by Poulton (1957), divides skills on the basis of environmental predictability. In diving, the environment is "fixed" and the individual can concentrate on internal feedback related to the skill. The skills for diving are therefore classified as "closed." However, in a sport such as tennis the game situation is constantly changing, and thus the individual must respond within an unpredictable environment. Skills for tennis are classified as "open."

Cratty (1973*b*) has offered a third possible division, based on the importance of *internal or external cues* for guiding performance. In a tennis game, noting the direction of your opponent's glance, an external cue, might reveal the direction of the subsequent shot. For the gymnasts, the changing pressure on their hands, an internal cue, may give them cues for the appropriate corrective actions needed to maintain the handstand. All three of these ideas were combined in Cratty's model, which suggested that different skills might contain elements of all or several of the above dimensions (Figure 1-3).

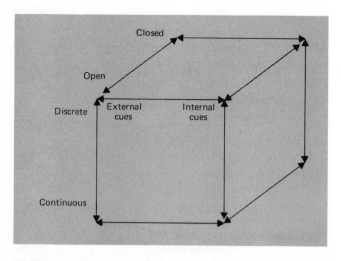

FIGURE 1-3   A three-dimensional model for classifying motor skills (based on Cratty, 1973b).

Because most skills do not lie at the extreme of any single dimension, using three dimensions instead of one allows for a finer discrimination between tasks, *e.g.,* (1) driving a car—continuous/open/external cues; (2) tower diving—discrete/closed/internal cues; (3) boxing—discrete/open/external cues.

In trying to show how a classification system might relate to different teaching methodologies, Knapp (1963) also suggested that skills might be classified on a *habitual-perceptual continuum.* Habitual, or self-initiated, skills would be seen as involving automated stimulus-response chains necessitating repeated practice but requiring little decision-making (*e.g.,* gymnastics). Perceptual skills, in which an individual is reacting to a changing environment, would involve acquiring the basics of the skill and then learning to apply them according to the situation, thereby emphasizing the element of decision-making (*e.g.,* deciding where and how to pass the ball in a soccer game).

Some of the most recent work in the classification of skills has been done by Gentile, Higgins, Miller, and Rosen (1975). When looking at the *open-closed continuum,* they felt that the type of movement involved should also be considered. Thus, there would be two elements: (1) the nature of the environmental control, whether it was open or closed (here defined simply as moving or stationary), and (2) the nature of the movement required for the task. The latter element was subdivided into (a) movements for postural adjustment or total body change of position and (b) movements of limbs for changing or maintaining the position of objects in space.

These ideas were tested experimentally, and eight categories were identified. The open and closed elements were first categorized according to whether there was total body stability or total body transport. These categories were further subdivided, depending on the presence or absence of limb transport or manipulation of objects (LT/M). These categories are illustrated in Table 1-1. You can probably place most sport skills in one of the boxes,

TABLE 1-1
Classification of motor skills based on movement and environment

Nature of Environmental Control	Nature of Movement Required by Task			
	Total Body Stability		Total Body Transport	
	No LT/M	LT/M*	No LT/M	LT/M
Closed: stationary	1 Sit/stand	2 Type/write	3 Walk/run	4 Javelin throw
Open: moving	5 Ride escalator	6 Skeet shooting	7 Walking in moving train	8 Dribbling a basketball

*LT/M, limb transport/manipulation of objects.
Based on Gentile, Higgins, Miller & Rosen, 1975.

from performing a handstand (1), to dribbling a basketball during a game (8), to covering a receiver in football (7).

The question remained, however, of how to classify skills with a moving object which did not vary from trial to trial. In a shooting gallery, for example, the targets move but the movement is predictable for every trial. Also, there are examples, such as the high jump or putting in golf, in which the environment for any given trial is fixed but from trial to trial the environment varies. From this, it appears that the open-closed continuum, rather than being two variations of one dimension (moving vs stationary), actually varies along two different dimensions, the second dimension being *intertrial variability*.

Thus, Gentile and her colleagues proposed a simplified four-category system (Table 1-2), in which open and closed skills were now defined in terms of (1) the nature of the environmental control and (2) intertrial variability. Because the environmental control can be moving or stationary and intertrial variability can be present or absent, there are four possible categories. Categories 2 and 3 probably occur very rarely naturally but are easily produced in a laboratory. This system was tested experimentally by using a dart-throwing task (Figure 1-4). The target was fixed or moving, and its position/movement could be varied according to the height off the ground or the speed. From a biomechanical analysis of the timing and sequencing of the throwing patterns generated within each category, Gentile and co-workers provided support for the distinction between the categories.

Therefore, we now have a description of open and closed skills where

1. Closed skill describes a stationary and stable environment.
2. Limited interaction is when changes occur along only one dimension. The movements resulting from these variations are much closer to those evidenced in the closed skill rather than the open skill category.
3. Open skill describes a moving and variable environment.

An example of category 1 would be attempting a strike in tenpin bowling; trying for the spares which normally follow strike attempts would be an

TABLE 1-2
Open and closed skills based on environment and intertrial variability

Nature of Environmental Control	Intertrial Variability	
	Absent	Present
Stationary	1. Batting off a stationary tee (fixed height)	2. As for No. 1, but height of tee changed for each trial
Moving	3. Batting a ball pitched by machine with a fixed speed and flight	4. Ball pitched by machine but a) speed varied: flight fixed; b) speed fixed: flight varied; c) speed and flight varied

Based on Gentile, Higgins, Miller & Rosen, 1975.

example of category 2. There are few examples of category 3, but one involves the trapeze artist in the circus who works with a trapeze which swings at a fixed speed and angle. The batter in a game of baseball is clearly dealing with an open skill unless, of course, the batter decides ahead of time to treat it like a closed skill and use the same swing each time. The latter strategy would be highly inappropriate because the flight of the ball is not predictable from one pitch to the next.

Structure of motor control

In order to provide a general framework for our later detailed discussions of the major elements of psychomotor learning, this section on the structure of motor control will attempt to define some of the important terms and show their interrelationship.

In psychomotor learning, we are concerned with how motor skills are learned and performed. Because our approach is psychological, we do not deal at great length with the anatomy and physiology of the central nervous system—the brain and spinal cord. Obviously, any assumptions made regarding the functions of various components derived from models describing psychomotor learning must coincide with the physiological potential of

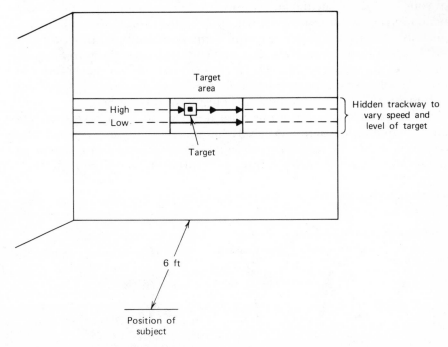

FIGURE 1-4   Variable target display (after Gentile, Higgins, Miller & Rosen, 1975).

the central nervous system. However, while a psychological model cannot hypothesize a working relationship between two components that have no neurological connection, similarly, the existence of a neurological link does not clearly establish a working relationship.

Psychomotor learning, therefore, is concerned with overt human motor behavior and with deriving models of the human motor system that produces that behavior. Once we have an accurate model of how the system works, then we are in a position to determine the best way for new skills to be learned.

At the center of psychomotor learning is a desire to understand how motor skills are controlled. Since we cannot experiment freely on the human brain, the next best way is to observe the responses to various tasks and how these responses change as the experimental conditions are manipulated. Through this process it becomes possible to derive testable hypotheses and, eventually, determine the functions of the various components.

When searching to discover how any system works, one of the questions that quickly comes to mind is, are there different levels of control and, if so, what is their relationship?

HIERARCHICAL AND HETERARCHICAL SYSTEMS. From a rudimentary knowledge of physiology we know that while the brain controls most of our motor responses, some, such as simple reflexes (the jerk of the knee when the doctor taps your leg just below the kneecap with a rubber hammer) can be said to function at the spinal level. Even with this basic example we could talk of higher and lower order levels of control—the brain and the spinal cord.

The idea of a series of levels of control with each succeeding level having control over all the previous levels is referred to as a *hierarchy* (Figure 1-5). Such control systems are common in business, the armed forces, and government. Captain A may have direct responsibility for Sergeants 1A and 2A, but is capable of controlling Sergeants 1B and 2B if necessary. The same principle applies at the next level regarding the relationship between the sergeants and the privates. In a simple model of the human motor system, we could say that while the muscles control the movements of the limbs, the brain

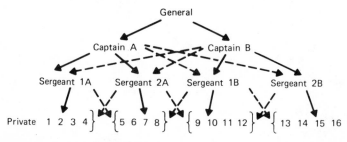

FIGURE 1-5 A hierarchical system.

controls the contraction of the muscles. Each level of control has its own responsibilities. Therefore, while the operation of the system as a whole might be quite complex, the functions of any component are relatively simple.

The army diagrammed in Figure 1-5 provides an example of how a hierarchy functions. The General commands Captain A to lead the attack and Captain B to protect the supply lines. Captain A then commands Sergeant 1A to lead the attack and Sergeant 2A to provide cover. The Sergeants then in turn define the roles of the various privates. The fact that Private No. 1 is involved in the attack and Private No. 15 is protecting the supply lines is a direct consequence of the orders given by the General, but in neither case does the General actually specify the roles of the individual privates. Thus, through some fairly simple commands the General is able to initiate a very complicated battle plan. Of course, if the General so desired he could command all the privates individually, but this would hardly be an effective use of the system for complex maneuvers. Therefore, the complexity of a hierarchical system is more a function of its size than of the diversity of the roles exhibited at any given level.

Overall, hierarchical systems are common because they are simple to comprehend. The line of command is direct and responsibilities are clearly defined and shared through the system. This is not, however, the only system of control.

A heterarchical system (Figure 1-6) may be structured very much like a hierarchy, but there is one important difference. *A heterarchical system recognizes that for a particular response the level of control needed may not be the highest level.* It also recognizes that, unlike the military, the human motor system is not rigid with a unidirectional order of command moving from the highest levels to the lowest. In a heterarchical system it is quite possible for a

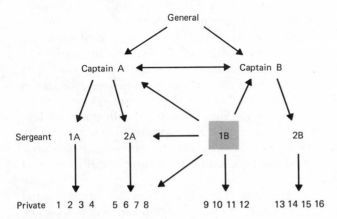

FIGURE 1-6 A heterarchical system.

lower level of control to take a dominant role and both draw from and manipulate higher levels of control. At a busy military airport, the air controller may only be a sergeant but when it comes to deciding who lands and takes off and in what order, it has to be the decision of the sergeant and not that of the captains, who may be flying the planes. In our army example, the movements of the attacking unit led by Captain A may be guided and controlled by one of the privates in the supply squad who is acting as a lookout.

What is important about the idea of a heterarchical system is that it acknowledges the basic flexibility of the human motor system. The human machine is a very adaptable one, and as such the control system must be flexible. Consequently, although the human motor system may function primarily as a hierarchical system, there may be times when it functions more like a heterarchical system, thereby increasing the number of ways in which the components making up the system can be combined and the number of different problems dealt with.

In the context of motor learning, we must recognize that for the system to work we must understand the functions of all the components. As in motor skill learning, we are only dealing with one person and the control system of that individual; we must be able to identify all the elements of the skill and their interrelationships. Then we can build a mini-hierarchy for that skill. In order for the General to implement an attack, the privates must be able to fire their guns. In order for soccer players to be able to pass the ball, they must be able to kick it properly. As the lower levels of control are established and automated, the higher levels of control are able to take over; hence the reason for a lot of basic drill in the army and on the soccer field.

INFORMATION.   In order for the generals, and even the privates, to make decisions, they need information. The sprinter reacting to the starting gun, the violinist taking a cue from the downbeat of the conductor's baton, and the downhill skier judging the distance to the next turn are all making use of information. The term *information* is the modern equivalent of the more traditional psychological concept of stimuli and cues. A stimulus can be almost any item present in our environment. As we sit looking out our bedroom windows, the feel of the glass pressed against our noses, the fumes from a neighbor's motorbike, and the color of the evening sky may all be classed as stimuli. Whether they are relevant stimuli depends on the task at hand. The idea of a relevant cue is somewhat more specific in that it is usually regarded as the stimulus that is used to help initiate some course of action. However, all these terms—stimuli, cues, and information—tend to be used interchangeably.

In psychomotor learning, two of the key types of information are referred to as *feedback* and *knowledge of results*. In its simplest form, feedback may be regarded as information that is produced or results as a consequence of our performing some action. Feedback could range from being aware of what it feels like to lift a heavy barbell to being told that it was a good lift. Knowledge of results refers to one particular type of feedback, knowing the outcome of our effort—whether we succeeded or not in lifting the barbell. For a more detailed discussion of feedback, see Chapter 3. In general we use feedback from our early responses to guide our later attempts at a particular skill. The knowledge of the actual outcome of our effort, whether it was successful or not, is one of the most important pieces of information since this tells us whether any further modifications in our action are necessary.

PERCEPTION.   In order to be able to use any of this information, we must first be able to identify what we see, hear, or feel. In other words, perception involves the ability to identify and distinguish between specific stimuli. We can all see the pitcher deliver the ball, but only the experienced baseball player can easily distinguish between a curve and a slider. *Perception* is more than simply seeing or hearing; it is the interpretation of what we see and hear. While our eyesight cannot be improved, except by artificial means, our visual perception can. We are able to improve our ability to handle the visual information that is available in the environment. Just think, for example, how your ability to recognize another individual improves as your relationship changes from being strangers to being good friends.

Although perception involves all of our senses, the one that is particularly important in motor skills is the *kinesthetic sense*. The kinesthetic sense refers to our ability to know where our arms and legs are without being able to see them; kinesthetic sense is often referred to as body awareness. Although visual and auditory perception are important to motor skill performance, kinesthetic perception may be the key when dealing with the higher levels of motor skill performance.

Overall, psychomotor learning involves an understanding of how we learn to perceive the relevant information from the environment and from our movements and how we then use this information to organize and control subsequent movements.

SUMMARY
In this chapter, we considered both a definition of psychomotor learning and how the activities within that area might be organized. Psychomotor learning was defined as follows:

> **Psychomotor learning** *is a relatively permanent change in the performance of a motor skill resulting from practice or past experience.*

This definition has two implications. First, we measure learning in terms of performance—was it a good handspring or a bad handspring, a home run or a fly ball? The problem is that performance may vary as a result of factors other than the amount learned. Does our drive off the first tee or the 18th tee best represent our skill level, or is it somewhere between the two? We must be very cautious when using performance scores to assess learning. In particular, we must be aware of performance artifacts owing to the measuring techniques or standards employed (*e.g.*, ceiling, floor, and plateau effects).

Secondly, our definition of psychomotor learning implies that we control movements with our heads and not our muscles. The movement produced by the muscles is an expression of what is learned and retained by the brain. If the muscles are tired, the performance may deteriorate, but this does not mean the skill is lost. What we learn is represented as "some relatively stable internal state." Associated with this central representation, which Schmidt (1975*a*) refers to as habit strength, is a whole array of decision factors concerned with why, when, where, and how far to move.

In infancy, motor behavior provides one of the clues about the integrity of the central nervous system. The onset of verbal ability does not represent a demotion in motor skills to the level of reflexive behavior but facilitates a greater application of known and yet to be established motor skills.

The organization or classification of various categories of motor skills according to presumed natural relationships provides several useful services. In particular, it may focus research on those factors that characterize or distinguish the various categories. In a practical sense, it can guide program organization in terms of grouping related skills or skills which can benefit from knowledge of similar principles and/or teaching methods. Consider the task of putting names to 40 new faces at a football practice. The task would be made easier if all the defensive players wore green and all the offensive players wore red. The more unfamiliar the information, the more important this organization can be. A Chinese friend of mine once told me "all you occidentals look alike." True. He identified me by the bowties I always wore.

Perhaps the most important step in psychomotor learning research is the redefinition of the open vs closed concept provided by Gentile and her associates. Added to the traditional environmental control continuum was the factor of intertrial variability, giving a total of four categories. A closed skill is now described as one which operates in a stationary and stable environment, whereas an open skill describes a moving and variable environment.

PROBLEM

At the end of each chapter, a question will be raised and a possible answer provided. The answer given is not meant to be the definitive answer; you may perhaps disagree with it. If so, be prepared to support your arguments "against" with well-reasoned ideas.

Question

Using the Gentilian definition of open and closed skills, how might you classify the following sports?

Basketball	Soccer
Bowling (tenpin)	Tennis
Gymnastics	Badminton

Diving

Try to formulate your own answer and then compare it with the following suggestion.

Possible answer

Initially, guided by the traditional interpretation of open and closed skills illustrated in Table 1-1, it would appear reasonable to classify soccer, basketball, tennis, and badminton as open skills (No. 4) and bowling, gymnastics, and diving as closed skills (No. 1). However, when we reexamine the sports in terms of Gentile's four categories (Table 1-2), we find certain discrepancies.

1. In basketball, the free throw involves a stationary environment and no intertrial variability (No. 1); the lay-up may vary from trial to trial, but the essential ingredient in the environment (the basket) is certainly fixed (No. 2).
2. In soccer, when taking a penalty shot you have a fixed environment and no intertrial variability. The situation is similar for set plays at corner kicks (No. 1).
3. In tennis/badminton, the service can be described as a closed skill (No. 1).
4. In bowling, although the first ball represents a closed skill, there is definitely intertrial variability with bowling spares (No. 2).
5. In diving, similar dives may be performed off different height boards, 1 meter or 3 meter (although height is fixed within a competition). However, a springboard can hardly be considered stationary (No. 3).
6. In gymnastics, specific skills are generally performed on fixed apparatus (No. 1), but the rings are certainly moving (No. 3).

Therefore, even though particular skills within a sport may be classified as representative of categories 1 through 4, it is clearly inaccurate to classify whole sports as being either open or closed in nature.

Chapter 2
Learning Theories

When I see I am doing it wrong there is a part of me
that wants to keep on doing it the same
way anyway and even starts looking for reasons
to justify the continuation.
(Prather, 1970)

The intent of this chapter is to introduce major learning theories while concentrating on those aspects of each theory that have implications for psychomotor learning. Those who wish to study these theories in depth are referred to the many excellent psychology texts on learning. The learning theories discussed in this chapter are divided into three sections: association theories, cognitive theories, and man/machine theories.

Although some of the learning theories presented in this chapter are quite old, they still have some influence on education and current thinking about learning. Therefore, before considering the theories individually we should acknowledge two points. First, most of the established theories of learning have dealt with verbal learning (*e.g.*, the rote memorization of lists of words) or animal learning, and therefore their principles cannot always be transferred directly to psychomotor learning. For the purposes of this text, however, these theories have been interpreted by the author in terms of psychomotor learning. The resulting statements are attributable to this author alone and not to the specific theorists involved.

The second point to note was made by Bartlett (1948). He indicated that a motor skill, as distinct from a simple muscle twitch, is characterized by the idea of a *graded response*. A motor skill is not simply a response to a stimulus but *is a response which may be guided and determined by feedback received from the various sensory receptors.* Many of us have perhaps had the experience of reaching quickly for our glasses to make a toast and immediately having to adjust the speed of our movement because the glass was full to the brim. The idea of graded responses underlines one of the important differences between the learning and performance of motor skills and those theories in which learning is viewed as the association between a stimulus and a response. Motor skill performance implies some level of conscious control rather than simply reflexive activity.

ASSOCIATION THEORIES   *Environment*

The first group of theories are sometimes referred to as stimulus-response (S-R) or behaviorist theories and are generally concerned with how two events that an individual perceives as occurring close together in time become associated. Smoke and fire, for example, are generally associated by most individuals. These theories are concerned with the individual's behavior (or response) and the events (or stimuli) that produce that behavior. Each of the association theories has developed various laws or principles to explain how this S-R relationship is developed. The five theories that we will review are designated by the names of their main authors: Pavlov, Thorndike, Guthrie, Hull, and Skinner. We will also consider the more recent S-R concept: the TOTE unit.

Pavlov—classical conditioning

According to Pavlov (1927), learning is the process of building conditioned reflexes through the substitution of one stimulus for another. The actual response would be unchanged. In his most famous experiment, Pavlov placed food before a hungry dog and sounded a bell. Normally, when a hungry dog is presented with food, it will salivate—a reflex. Pavlov found that if this procedure was repeated many times, the sound of the bell alone was sufficient to make the dog salivate. The stimulus that normally produces a given response is called the unconditioned stimulus, whereas the stimulus that is added by the experimenter is called the conditioning stimulus. Thus, classical conditioning is characterized by the pairing of a conditioning stimulus (CS—in this case the bell) with an unconditioned stimulus (UCS—the food) to produce a particular response (R—salivation). After many trials, salivation becomes a conditioned response (CR) to the sound of the bell.

You can try a similar experiment with a cooperative friend. Blow in his or her eyes while simultaneously flicking an empty glass with your finger. Your friend will blink. Forty trials later, if you have the wind and have not broken the glass, your friend may blink to the sound of your flicking the glass. Based on this experiment, can you fill in the following blanks? (For answer, see page 49).

———————————— (UCS) ———⟶ ———————————(UCR)

——————————(UCS) + ————————(CS) ———⟶ ——————(UCR)

————————— (CS) ———⟶ ——————————————————(CR)

Although Pavlov's theory does not provide the basis for an adequate teaching methodology, it does provide a strong warning signal. The point here for psychomotor learning is that individuals can be conditioned without being aware of it. Therefore, the teacher should attempt to create an environment without undesirable conditioning elements. For example, a student who makes a mistake in a field hockey game and is sent for two laps around the field may well associate exercise with punishment, which is hardly a desirable aim.

Allowing players to be careless when they practice can produce incidental learning effects. If you simply give two boys a ball, they will play with it: ball (UCS) → play (UCR). If this is your method of conducting a volleyball practice (CS), the unconditioned response (play) will become a conditioned response. A training session that is designed to practice and refine skills becomes a time to play and fool around. If practices are constantly loose, then that is the style of performance the athletes will associate with that sport. This style will not be lost simply by placing the players in an actual game. The association has to be "unlearned," or a stronger one has to be developed. Thus, although there are times when you may wish to ease up in your practices so that the players are in top shape for the games, you must ensure that these light practices do not mean a dropping of standards in terms of the quality of performance. All the pre-season hard work could slowly be destroyed by "sloppy" in-season practices.

Thorndike—connectionism

Thorndike (1935) was well known and influential in the field of education. He emphasized learning as a strengthening of the bond, or association, between a particular stimulus (S) and response (R). Thorndike, known best for his work with cats in puzzle boxes and mazes, saw learning as a trial and error process, with success and practice building a bond between the appropriate stimulus and response. For example, a hungry cat might be placed inside a box or a cage that could only be opened by striking a lever. Initially the cat would run around the cage until it accidentally tripped the lever and was released. Over repeated trials the amount of random activity and time spent in the cage would be reduced. Eventually the cat would release itself immediately after being placed in the cage. The bond or connection was established.

From his research, Thorndike generated many ideas, including several "laws" that remain with us today.

(a) LAW OF READINESS. If a person is "ready" to respond (learn), then it is pleasant to respond. On the other hand, you cannot make someone learn. The law of readiness refers both to the idea of being prepared (in the mood) to learn and the concept of developmental readiness in children. Children cannot learn to walk or skate before they have the ability to maintain an upright posture. However, once children can walk properly, they are ready to learn complex skills such as skating. Similarly, you cannot begin to teach very young children certain gymnastic stunts on the apparatus if they do not have the strength to lift or hold their own body weight. Some minimal level of strength is essential to the performance of many skills.

(b) LAW OF EFFECT. If the response is satisfying, the subject will repeat the response and consequently strengthen the S-R bond. A successful shot in basketball, even if it is executed from only 2 feet or if the technique is poor, is a positive and satisfying beginning. Similarly, a beginning golfer is encouraged by making good contact with the ball, regardless of the final outcome. Achieving this good contact may mean altering the skill slightly by putting the ball on a tee or shortening the grip on the club, but then the learner will be in the right condition to learn. A second example, involving less change in the basic mechanics of the skill, can be found in archery where the target is placed at a short target distance for the beginner initially and is gradually moved further back as more proficiency is acquired.

Originally, the law of effect was described as a pleasure-pain principle: satisfying or rewarded responses are strengthened but annoying or punished responses are weakened. Thorndike later changed his thinking and emphasized only the strengthening of responses. Unfortunately, this law has sometimes been misinterpreted to read, "encouragement builds but criticism destroys." However, this is not necessarily accurate, because people when criticized may tend to seek alternative responses and not simply give up. The role of the teacher is to adapt the skill to the level of the learner in order to provide a satisfying experience.

(c) LAW OF EXERCISE. (a) Law of *use*—practice strengthens the S-R bond and (b) law of *disuse*—no practice weakens the S-R bond.

Thorndike's concept of learning and forgetting was very straightforward. To learn and maintain a certain skill you must use it; if you do not, the skill will be forgotten. However, the law of exercise does *not* imply that using or practicing a skill has automatic effects. It is in fact closely related to Thorndike's law of effect. If practice becomes monotonous and unsatisfying, the individual will not concentrate on the task but will simply go through the motions, perhaps using poor technique. As such, it would seem likely that this type of practice will do little to strengthen any S-R relationship. Only when the practice is satisfying is the relationship likely to be strengthened.

What are some of the implications that Thorndike's theory would have for physical education? First, do not just drill a team or class but provide them with sufficient rewards to create an effective learning situation, one in which learning is satisfying. Only a certain minimum level of reward is required, involving, for example, the judicious use of praise, not trips to Hawaii. Second, in terms of the learning of a particular skill, we must carefully consider the concept of readiness and individual development, the most common gauge for this being age and a personal knowledge of the child. As such, skill learning would involve a series of progressions to prepare the individual both psychologically and physiologically for what is to come. For this preparation you can use lead-up games. In "learn to dive" programs the child starts by sitting on the side of the pool. Having learned to swim, the child has no fear of water. The fear of height is reduced by increasing the height only when a child can successfully perform a vertical entry at a lower level, or abandon a dive by tucking the head between the knees.

Finally, from Thorndike's theory, it would appear necessary to practice as close to the game situation as is possible because only specific S-R connections are strengthened. According to Thorndike, transfer involves identical elements only when an S-R relationship that is established can be used as part of another response. One of the major reasons why skills and tactics learned in a practice may not transfer to the game situation is that the most commonly ignored variable in practice situations is live opposition. Even the knowledge that an opponent is only a short distance away could cause a player to miss an easy basket.

Guthrie—contiguous conditioning

Guthrie (1952) had a somewhat more radical notion of learning. He emphasized the timing element in the S-R relationship, pointing out that we tend to associate things that happen close together in time or events that are contiguous, such as smoke and fire. Guthrie felt this association of events only took one trial. He saw a skill not as a habit, as did Pavlov, but as a collection of a large number of S-R associations that connect a specific movement with a specific situation. Therefore, it takes many trials to learn a movement because that movement is used in many situations. Each time you shoot a basketball, for example, it is from a slightly different position on the floor. You may associate the events present at that moment in time, but they only represent one of the many specific relationships necessary to learn the skill itself. One of the reasons you may miss a shot in a game is because you have not practiced that particular shot before.

In a complex movement with a chain of associations, there is the possibility for variation at each link in that chain. Thus, in terms of physical education, Guthrie would emphasize a large number of drills to respond to a range of stimuli, with no reward for the response itself but a little general encouragement to maintain the activity. Guthrie disagreed with Thorndike in that he thought forgetting was a function of interference and not disuse. As a result, you do not practice when you are tired, because then you may practice failure or incorrect movements that will interfere with the correct response.

Finally, it is clear that he would envisage no, or minimal, transfer without exact duplication of the movement, as may be seen in basketball free throw routines. Regardless of differences in the floor markings, backboard, crowd, and other features found in the opponent's gym, the basketball player will still bounce the ball twice, take a deep breath, and touch the ball to the forehead before shooting a foul shot.

4. Hull—reinforcement theory

Hull (1943) saw learning as a result of the organism's biological adaptation to its environment. One of the main elements that Hull introduced was the concept of *drive reduction*. People were seen as having certain basic phy-siological needs, such as hunger or thirst, and certain psychological needs, such as the need for security or recognition. The satisfaction of these needs reduced the drive and therefore reinforced the response. We have all known the child who screams and screams for ice cream, and eventually we give in. What have we just taught that child? One of the most famous concepts to develop from the application of Hull's work to teaching is "education according to pupil needs."

In his complex mathematical theory, Hull tried to quantify the various elements involved in learning. This precise formulation stimulated much research. We will see some other aspects of "drive theory" when we consider the relationship of stress and motor skills in Chapter 3. However, in terms of learning, central to the concept of the biological adaptation of the organism and Hull's theory is the role of reinforcement.

Reinforcement may be either primary or higher-order. *Primary reinforce-ment* involves the satisfaction of some basic biological need such as hunger, whereas *higher-order reinforcement* involves the use of some neutral rein-forcer which has acquired its power through learning. We cannot eat money but we can use it to buy food; as such, money can be a very strong (neutral) reinforcer.

Hull's theory differed from the previous association theories in that he did not feel that an identical stimulus was needed to produce a given response. He felt that if a stimulus was similar, an individual could respond as if it were the same. He also questioned the need for constant repetition, arguing that if repetition did not reduce the drive, it might actually inhibit learning (similar to Thorndike's law of effect). Thus Hull, not being as specific as the other associationists, would concede the transfer of common elements in terms of motor skills. For example, you learn the technique of shooting a basketball and then use that technique in different situations, such as shooting from a long or a short distance. Mainly, Hull suggests that if pupils see the value of what they do, the learning will be more satisfying and effective. They need to be shown and understand the relationship between the skill and how it is built. Therefore, practices must be organized to maintain interest and not just to provide a series of drills.

Skinner—operant conditioning

Skinner (1938) is perhaps best known for his work with pigeons and his use of the famous Skinner Box. The Skinner Box was simply a box which contained an animal, a lever, and a device for delivering a food pellet to the animal whenever the lever was pressed. It thus contained the two main elements of Skinner's theory: a controlled environment and a means of presenting a reward (Figure 2-1). Skinner emphasized the rewarding of the response to strengthen the response itself and its probability of occurrence, not the S-R bond as did Thorndike. In operant conditioning, the reward reinforces the response, thereby making it more likely to recur. We control the environment

FIGURE 2-1 It works for pigeons—why not people?

and thereby control the behavior. In this theory the stimulus that was initially involved in producing the response is no longer relevant once the behavior is produced. It is only necessary that the response occur and, by being rewarded, be made to recur.

The term *operant* refers to the set of acts which constitute the response. The term describes the fact that an individual operates on the environment and as such generates consequences. From the behavior emitted by the animal, or individual, operant conditioning simply makes a particular response more probable. Skinner felt that if the environment can be controlled, you can accurately predict or condition behavior. He was not interested in "the inner self" or personal goals. He simply argued that by controlling the stimuli, you can control the response. There is no law of effect because, in Skinner's view, it was not necessary for a person to know the consequences of the response.

Skinner also makes an important distinction between forgetting and extinction: *Forgetting* is the gradual loss of a response over a long period of time; *extinction requires repetitions of the response without any reward.* Forgetting without extinction would take place very slowly, if at all. Skinner also saw extinction as the appropriate method for removing a response rather than punishment. In agreement with Thorndike, he felt that the results of using punishment were neither predictable nor dependable.

However, the responses most resistant to forgetting were those that had been rewarded intermittently. *An intermittent reward schedule implies that not all responses are rewarded; the reward is simply not predictable.* Applied to psychomotor learning, the concept of intermittent reward implies that if we wish an athlete to maintain some desired behavior when outside our control (*i.e.,* in a game), it would be better if the behavior were rewarded infrequently in practice, rather than on every occurrence. Before proceeding further, however, we must distinguish between intermittent reward schedules used to reinforce desired responses and the concept of shaping.

Shaping is central to Skinner's theory and involves the gradual molding of the desired response from the behavior emitted by the animal. The concept of shaping can be illustrated by an experiment designed to make a pigeon turn clockwise circles. First the pigeon is placed in the Skinner Box. Of its own accord the pigeon will move about the box. If the pigeon turns even slightly to the right, the experimenter will open the food tray and reward the pigeon. This procedure will be repeated for a few trials. Having "taught" the pigeon to move to its right before going to the food tray, the experimenter now begins to reward the pigeon only after the longest movements. On trial 1, a five-degree movement would produce a reward, but several trials later only a 90-degree turn would produce a reward. Eventually the pigeon will turn complete circles—the desired response. Intermittent reward of this circle-turning response will firmly establish it in the pigeon's repertoire; lack of reward will extinguish it.

From a practical point of view, if we use the shaping technique and reward each correct response or a large proportion of responses, some type of teaching aid would be needed. Teaching machines have already been developed for the classroom. Although few would be useful for motor skills, the basic technique can be applied. Success is the key, so the skill must be taught in very small steps, with each level being mastered before proceeding to the next step. The active response requirement of Skinner's theory that the response must involve some observable behavior would be fairly easy to meet in physical education. Thus, according to Skinner the teacher should (1) set goals to be achieved; (2) pretest to establish the current ability level; (3) set up the environment so as to remove irrelevant stimuli and center the learner's attention on the task at hand (concept of the Skinner Box); (4) shape—a slow step-like progression of intermediate goals leading toward the final goal; and (5) reinforce correct responses with appropriate rewards at all stages.

The clinical application of this shaping technique is currently very popular and is more commonly referred to as *behavior modification*. In this form, the technique has been used most effectively in schools, prisons, and other institutions to deal with individuals with difficult behavior problems. A simple problem might be children who leave their bedrooms untidy. The goal is to get them to keep their rooms tidy. First you observe their normal behavior. If you find that they occasionally put some books away so that they have room to move, a first step might be to offer some positive verbal reward (praise) whenever this occurs. Each time they go a little further, the "reward" is offered. Should they put all their books away, then repeat the verbal reward but from then on only if all the books are put away. The technique is simply to establish some short-term goal from their behavior, reward it, and then move one step closer to your overall goal.

Obviously it is important in the above example that the children see the "reward" as a reward. This is particularly important when working with humans. Food may be a reward for a hungry rat, but we cannot assume the same relationship for children and praise. In sports, the approval or praise from the coach can be a most effective reward, because it is the coach who decides who plays and when. A field hockey coach wishing to encourage the attacking players to help out on defense may at first praise them for coming back into their own half of the field, then only if they reach the defensive third of the field, and then only if they guard an opposing player.

From Skinner's point of view, the type of reward was not important as long as it was effective and could be administered easily; however, from an educational point of view the type of reward might be very important. Would you rather have children working for external rewards or for self-improvement? Skinner's operant conditioning is not so much a learning theory as an excellent technique for teaching individuals or animals to produce (perform) desired responses or behavior.

One behaviorist who took a position different from the rest was Mowrer (1960), whose theory might be described more as an S-S rather than S-R theory.

Mowrer felt that reinforcement controlled behavior and not learning. The reinforcement would produce behaviors or responses that the individual could already perform. The actual response produced was an attempt to resolve a hope/fear conflict. If a particular response was not effective, it would be dropped because of fear of failing and an alternative response would be sought. If the alternative response showed signs of being successful, this would give rise to feelings of hope and the response would be repeated. Consequently, the motor response becomes conditioned.

Although this theory may indeed reflect the normal operation of our daily lives, it would not seem adequate to explain the acquisition of high levels of motor skill performance. The initial "learning" of a motor skill may involve some interplay of fear and hope, but advanced performance requires many hours of practice. The theory provides some understanding of the basic motivation involved but not of how the skill was learned. Of course this was not Mowrer's intent, but it is ours. As we attempt to develop a theory of psychomotor learning, however, we cannot ignore the important factors underlined by these established theories.

TOTE unit

When an individual performs a skill, some strategy or plan is assumed. The more complex the skill, the more complex the strategy. The TOTE unit (test-operate-test-exit) is important because it is an attempt to explain how complex cognitive strategies may be developed and organized within an associationist framework. The concept of a TOTE unit, proposed by Miller, Galanter, and Pribram (1960), is basically an advanced extension of the S-R approach. The TOTE unit provides a model of how a skill might be organized (Figure 2-2). In the test phase, you test a goal with an element in the environment. If everything is all right (congruous), you exit; if not (incongruity), you transfer to the operation phase (operate).

A simple TOTE unit for hammering a nail is outlined in Figure 2-3. First, in the test phase, you test the nail to see if it is flush with the wood. If the

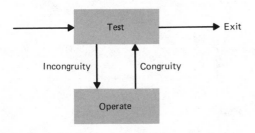

FIGURE 2-2   A TOTE unit (after Miller, Galanter & Pribram, 1960).

nail is flush you exit from the program; however, if the nail is sticking up you proceed to the operation phase (A). Here there are two subunits. You first check the position of the hammer to make sure it is in the up position in order to strike the nail. If it is not up, you lift the hammer and then strike the nail. Once the hammer is down, again you check the nail (test phase). If the nail is now flush you exit; if not you repeat the operation phase. Thus, we see that a skill actually involves a hierarchical structure with single TOTE units embedded within one another. In this case the "lift" and "strike" TOTES are subunits within the main TOTE for hammering. Similarly, as any skill involves a series of options, each of these will be reflected in the overall strategy or structure of the model.

COGNITIVE THEORIES   *Perception*

The difference between the association and cognitive theories is mainly one of emphasis. To the associationists, the environment is the prime source for explaining, predicting, and controlling behavior. The emphasis is on developing the association between a given stimulus and response through repetition, with reinforcement being used to help elicit the response. However, to the cognitivist, the individual's interpretation of the environment is the key, with the emphasis being on the individual's perception of the environment. Therefore, although reinforcement, repetition, and perception are relevant to both concepts, their relative importance differs greatly.

Where the associationists might be described as mechanistic, the cogni-

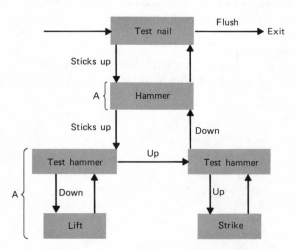

FIGURE 2-3 An example of a TOTE analysis (based on Miller, Galanter & Pribram, 1960).

tivists are nonmechanistic. The associationists have turned to the pure sciences and see the human as a machine that obeys mechanical laws. The ingredients of the situation are quantified, and cause and effect are replaced by stimulus and response. Alternatively, the cognitivist sees the individual as having or seeking some end purpose and maintains that only by fully under- standing this search process can we accurately predict the individual's behavior. For the cognitivist, learning is not a trained response to a stimulus but involves *cognition*—the process of knowing, involving both awareness and judgment. To present the cognitive approach to learning, we will review the Gestalt theory and the work of Lewin and Tolman.

Gestalt theory

The Gestalt theory was, for a time, the main opponent of the S-R theories and had many contributors, including Koffka (1929), Kohler (1925), and Wert- heimer (1959). Basically, the Gestaltists could not accept the idea that the responses of rats and pigeons truly represented the cognitive abilities of humans. The word *gestalt* means an organized pattern or form. Therefore, the Gestaltists were concerned with how an individual abstracted meaningful relationships from the environment to gain the necessary insights to solve problems.

Gestaltists focus on how the learner perceives stimuli in the environment. Collectively, these environmental stimuli are referred to as the field (the background), as distinct from the specific object or figure which might be the focus of your attention. The figure/ground concept is illustrated in Figure 2-4. You see either (1) a vase (figure) against a dark background or (2) a close- up of two people face-to-face (figure) with a light background. According to Wertheimer (1959), children tend to be ground dominant until about 10 years of age, meaning that their perception is swayed by whatever stimuli dominate

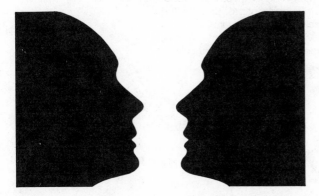

FIGURE 2-4   Two people face-to-face, or a vase?

the perceptual field as a whole rather than by any specific stimulus or particular figure. A much more difficult version of the figure/ground concept is represented in Figure 2-5. Young children would be unlikely to see the face of Christ, but they would be more aware of the overall pattern. Similarly, a cluttered gymnasium wall could adversely affect a young child's catching ability because of the difficulty of seeing the ball (figure) against a background of apparatus and hoops hanging on the wall (ground) (Gallahue, 1968).

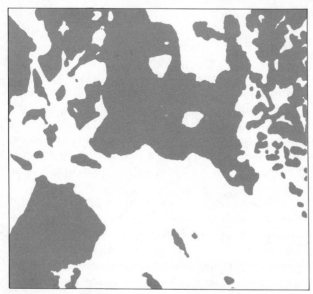

FIGURE 2-5   The face of Christ. According to one source this picture represents a photograph taken by a young Chinese nun in 1940. The photograph was taken during a storm in an attempt to "capture" the lightning. The film was developed, and hidden in the black and white abstract produced by the storm was an image of the face of Christ. This figure is actually based on a painting by Tom Dwyer, "Head of Christ," currently hanging at the Ontario Science Center, Toronto, Canada.

a) Proximity

```
XX   XX   XX   XX   XX
XX   XX   XX   XX   XX
XX   XX   XX   XX   XX
XX   XX   XX   XX   XX
XX   XX   XX   XX   XX
XX   XX   XX   XX   XX
```

b) Similarity

```
X    0    X    0    X    0

X    0    X    0    X    0

X    0    X    0    X    0

X    0    X    0    X    0
```

FIGURE 2-6   The laws of a) proximity, and b) similarity.

In considering the role of perception, the Gestaltists were concerned with how the individual organized the sensory data into objects or units. As a result, several "laws" were developed, including the laws of proximity, similarity, and closure (Koffka, 1929). In Figure 2-6, *a*, we tend to see columns of paired *X*'s rather than rows. This illustrates the *law of proximity,* in which the learner associates, or groups, those stimuli that are close together in time or space. From a teaching point of view, we should attempt to facilitate this process of association by organizing the material we present into "groups."

In Figure 2-6, *b*, we tend to see columns of *X*'s of *O*'s rather than mixed rows. In the *law of similarity* the learner finds homogenous groups easier to identify than heterogenous groupings. The implication is that if we wish to further aid retention, we should try to present logical groups of related information and not a series of isolated facts. In terms of teaching a skill, this law would suggest that rather than present all the points relevant to serving in any racket sport, we might group them. In terms of squash, for example, we might group our teaching points about the service into three categories of before, during, and after the service.

The *law of closure* is demonstrated in Figure 2-7. If asked what we saw, most of us would report the completed figures of HAT and O, or a circle. The learner tends to complete the field or fill in missing parts. The implication of this law is that, dependent on the background or experience of the learner, it may be sufficient to provide only the key points.

In terms of motor performance, the law of similarity may be evidenced in how a beginner compared with an advanced player might view badminton and tennis. To the beginner, they are similar games with a net, a racket, and a rectangular court. The advanced player recognizes more significant differences, such as the use of "wrist" action in badminton compared with a fixed wrist in tennis. When we group the soccer players who guard their own goal as the defense and those who attack their opponent's goal as the offense, we are following the law of proximity. The law of closure, or more particularly kinesthetic closure, might be considered as getting the "feel" of a movement. We may or may not have mastered all the parts of the skill, but with a feel of the total skill we are better able to integrate these parts.

Gestalt theorists saw learning as involving insight, in which the learner thinks about the problem, sees the solution, and then acts (Kohler, 1925). A typical experiment might involve placing a chimpanzee in a cage with two apple boxes, a long stick, and a banana hanging from the roof of the cage. At

FIGURE 2-7 The law of closure.

first the chimp might try climbing the side of the cage and reaching for the banana. This tactic does not work, so the chimp sits and ponders. Suddenly (aha!) the chimp places a box under the banana, takes the stick, reaches for the banana, and misses. The chimp now adds the second box and this time knocks the banana down. The solution is found not by random activity or trial and error but by thinking about the problem. This process might involve a type of mental trial and error in which various solutions are sought but only the "most likely" ones are tried. Many solutions are rejected without being tested because they do not meet the requirements of the situation.

The main concern in regard to teaching, from a Gestaltist viewpoint, is that the learner understands the principles involved and their interrelationships. Important, therefore, is both the capacity and background (experience) of the learner and the effect of these factors on perception and insight. For example, in terms of self-concept, how we perceive ourselves is determined to a large extent by our prior experiences. In turn, how we perceive ourselves affects how we perceive our environment. The more extensive our experiences, the more clearly and firmly we tend to establish ideas and concepts. In fact, one of the major problems for older people in learning new skills is that, because of the extent of their experience, they tend to be more fixed in how they perceive the world around them. This lack of flexibility makes acquiring new skills difficult, but not impossible.

Lewin—field theory

Lewin's theory (1936) is primarily a study of human motivation and not a learning theory. However, as it laid a basis for an examination of the effect of motivation on human behavior, it is very relevant to both sports psychology and psychomotor learning. Basically, Lewin was trying to overcome the problem of relating general learning theory to individual differences. He felt that although the psychological laws might predict the typical behavior of a group, they did not indicate what a particular individual might do in a specific situation. He is noteworthy for his recognition of the important role of internal motivation. Lewin's theory was most original and is more properly called topological and vector psychology, since he borrowed his ideas from the fields of geometry and physics.

In his theory, Lewin was not just concerned with the perceptual field but he was also interested in the individual or, more specifically, in the individual's life space (both internal and external). Lewin emphasized the idea that each individual has their own personal and environmental life space and that the two interact. The concept of life space (Figure 2-8) encompasses both the person and that person's psychological environment and implies we can only understand why a person behaves by studying both together. The psychological environment consists of the perceived objects and events relevant at that time. Embedded in the person are such factors as needs and abilities.

The term *topology* is used here to describe the position of the person relative to particular goals and barriers. A *vector* represents the direction of some psychological force, and *valence* represents the attracting or repelling power of a region of the life space. As in physics, vectors are totaled to determine the final direction of movement. A simplified version of these relationships is provided in Figure 2-8. While the topological concepts can illustrate the organization of the various elements, their dynamics or their tendency to change is represented by the vectors. Thus, learning is a process of differentiating and restructuring, with motivation as the prime force (internal motivation being the most important).

Tolman—sign-Gestalt   *cognitive map-- associated with S-R*

Tolman (1934) attempted to combine some of the elements of S-R and cognitive theory. He saw learning as involving individual S-R associations, but he also felt it was necessary to understand their relationship. Thus, while initial learning is based on a mental trial and error process, the learner then organizes the stimuli to form a cognitive map. This map can also provide cues for future repetitions, in the same manner as a boy scout might "blaze" a trail through the forest. Tolman viewed the learner as being goal directed but guided by certain cues, or signs. This notion is similar to the concept of a set play in which a player does not move until the space to be entered is open.

With its emphasis on mental organization, Tolman's theory underlines the possible importance of mental practice in motor learning. As such, the sign-Gestalt approach would stress the importance of the teacher outlining the main points in a task. In coaching, for example, the coach would point out that player X fakes left then breaks right. Like Guthrie, Tolman saw reward as

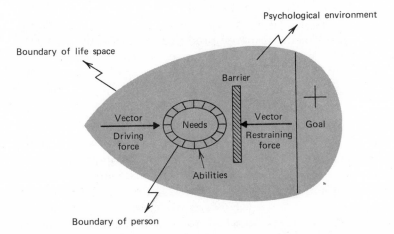

FIGURE 2-8   Lewin's concept of an individual's life space (after Bigge, 1971).

serving only to maintain the learning activity. However, unlike the associationists, he felt that transfer would occur if the relationship was evident. Understanding the general principles of team games would favor transfer, according to Tolman's theory. Finally, when breaking down a skill, we should attempt to provide "wholes" that are within the capabilities of the learner.

Before turning to the final section, we should look at one other concept: *functionalism*. It is not a theory itself but a term utilized by Singer (1969) to describe the approach taken in much physical education research, that of seeking practical solutions to practical problems. Physical education research or functionalism was eclectic in that it drew ideas from all theories in an attempt to bridge the gap between theory and practice. Although this was a reasonable approach to take, it failed to produce any generalizable model. If we observe all the movements that a gymnast can make, we may learn much about the mechanics of movement but little about what makes it work. As a result, much of today's work in psychomotor learning has switched to the area of research described by the next group of learning theories: man/machine theories.

MAN/MACHINE THEORIES

With the rapid growth of technology during and after World War II (particularly the development of computers), there was a wealth of new ideas and concepts. With the use of the man–machine (computer) analogy, many of these ideas were quickly applied to the study of human behavior.

Like the association theories, man/machine theories took a very mechanistic approach; but unlike the former, which were concerned with the presence or absence of certain external stimuli, these theories, like the cognitive theories, were equally concerned with what goes on in the individual's head. Decision making and the factors that influence both that process and the control of the response produced were of central concern. While human behavior is quite flexible, the association theories were fairly rigid. The man/machine theories tried to formulate models which were more adaptable.

Cybernetics   Associated with Feedback (closed loop)

The theory of cybernetics was developed in the post-war era by Wiener (1961). Cybernetics considers the human as a complex machine. Computers have input and output systems plus control and storage systems. Similarly, a person receives stimuli, responds to stimuli, and has a brain to provide the controlling process and storage sytems. However, in cybernetics, the emphasis is placed on the role of feedback, in which some output is isolated and fed back into the system as input. This allows the system to monitor the response and initiate any necessary changes. As you write a check, for example, you concentrate on writing along the lines and within the spaces provided. Thus, in human terms, individuals generate their own motor responses, which in turn give rise to sensory feedback that affects future responses; learning does not involve just an S-R chain.

Cybernetics is a type of closed-loop system in which, characteristically, there is a direct link between output and input based on continual feedback, which may be described as a *servomechanism*. Based as it is on the machine analogy, a servomechanism could function as either a regulator or an adaptive system. A *regulator system* is one which works in relation to a fixed goal, such as a thermostat. If the temperature in a room is below the setting on the thermostat, the heating system is turned on until the room temperature matches the thermostat. Regardless of the number of times that heat is lost through opening doors and windows, the thermostatically controlled heating system will work to maintain a constant temperature. Whereas in an *adaptive system,* there is no fixed goal but one that changes with the situation. In tennis, for example, the placement of the ball (goal) may change with each return. The aim in tennis is not to return every high ball down the sideline and every low ball across the court. A fixed or regulator system would simply not be adequate.

In contrast to a servomechanism is an *open-loop system*. In this case the output or the consequences of that output are not fed back directly into the system. There is no immediate means of obtaining feedback, and each response is separate. If you switch on an electric heater, it will stay on until you switch it off or it breaks down, regardless of the temperature in the room. The relationship of the heater to the temperature of the room is only an indirect one—through your control. In terms of motor skills, when a series of movements are performed so quickly that there appears little time for any corrections to be made between movements, it is suggested that the sequence of movements might be pre-programmed. Such a sequence of movements, which are performed automatically without any apparent thought, is referred to as a *motor program*. Thinking usually precedes response execution, which is then carried out automatically (*i.e.,* without ongoing feedback control). The motor program may be as long as the performance of a tennis serve or as brief as initiating a punch, but the motor program is characterized by its lack of ongoing feedback control.

Information theory   *choice of Infn.*

Information theory, or communication theory, deals with our ability to handle information. Information theory is based on probability theory, in particular the work of Shannon and Weaver (1962) in the late 1940s. These concepts were later applied to motor skills (Kay, 1957). Information theory is concerned with the balance between uncertainty and information.

The basic unit of information is the *binary digit*, usually abbreviated to "bit." One bit is defined as the amount of information that is needed to choose between two equally probable alternatives. For example, in Figure 2-9, if we were to find the position of the X in (a) by asking only one side of a two-choice question, we need ask only one question: is the X above the line? Regardless of the answer, yes or no, we know the solution. To find the position of X in (b) it would take three questions: is the X above the line, is the X to the left of the center line, and is it next to the center line? Thus, one bit is sufficient for two alternatives, two bits for four alternatives, and three bits for eight alternatives. If we had 64 squares, how many bits would it take to find the X?*

If we hear a fire siren, the probability is quite high that the firemen are answering an emergency call. If we actually see the fire engine, the second piece of information (hearing the siren) adds little to our knowledge. Thus, because all events are not equally probable, information theory makes great use of the laws of probability. If this theory were applied to the information contained in this paragraph, both the key and redundant words could be easily identified. Using this idea of emphasizing only the key words, we might rewrite our definition of motor learning (Chapter 1):

> 1. **Motor learning** *is a relatively permanent change in the performance of a motor skill resulting from practice or past experience.*

Motor learning: relatively permanent change—performance—practice—past experience. More than a third of the words in our brief definition might be considered redundant.

Information theory deals with the ability to process information, or the relationship between input and output and the quantity of information that

*Answer: 6 bits (or 2^6).

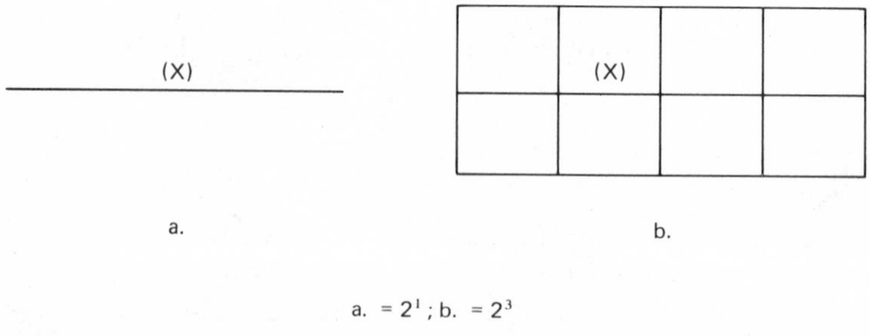

	(X)		

a. b.

a. $= 2^1$; b. $= 2^3$

FIGURE 2-9 Information bits. How many bits of information are needed to find the position of X in a) and b).

can be handled. As the input increases beyond a certain point, so response errors increase. There is too much information for us to handle. An answer to the question of exactly how much information we can handle at one time or store in short-term memory, our channel capacity, was provided by Miller (1956). The idea of *channel capacity* describes the maximum amount of information, or number of items, that we can consciously attend to at one time. Miller suggested that our channel capacity was 7 ± 2 bits.

Try assessing your channel capacity by reading the numbers in Figure 2-10. Most people should be able to read the first number in Figure 2-10 just once (no rehearsal), close the book, and write it down. Some people will find the second number a little more difficult and the third number impossible to remember. However, many will be able to recall the fourth number. The reason for this is that the numbers of the fourth sequence are placed in groups of three and as such the sequence can be treated as four pieces, or *chunks*, of information. Therefore, our limited channel capacity can be partially improved by grouping related bits of information into chunks.

In studying for exams, we have all probably used the technique of selecting a single word in which each letter represents the first letter of a series of words: the word *TEER*, for example, representing the phrase, *T*horndike's laws of *e*ffect, *e*xercise and *r*eadiness. Thus, questions of information storage, retrieval, translation, and rates of transmission are most germane to information theory.

These two man/machine theories (cybernetics and information theory) have now been merged, and certain models have been developed to describe the central processes involved in controlling movement.

Information processing models

Information processing models perform at least two major functions. First, they try to identify the main components involved in processing and illustrate the overall structure of the system. Second, they represent an attempt to derive the various control processes governed or shared by these structural components. For example, finding the X in Figure 2-9 must involve components that recognize the pattern of the rectangle, have knowledge of

a.   2-7-3-8-5-9-1

b.   4-3-5-9-1-7-8-2-6

c.   4-5-2-9-7-6-2-8-1-3-5

d.   528-487-635-191

FIGURE 2-10 Test your channel capacity. Read the first number once, slowly. Close the book and then write the number down. Repeat the process for each number.

probability theory, retain answers as the questions progress, and make choices as to subsequent questions. One structural component we need to propose is memory. Having done this, we need to formulate appropriate control processes that govern the storage and retrieval of information in memory.

The first model (figure 2-11) illustrates the basic man/machine analogy in which a certain input (in this case sensory) is processed by some central mechanism to produce a response—a movement. The model also indicates that any information processing of a specific signal or stimulus occurs against a background of *noise*. Noise in this case refers to any neuronal activity which is going on within the system regardless of whether it is a result of some sensory input (*e.g.*, a sound or a light) or a decision being made. In the same way that it is difficult to identify a friend in a crowd, so there are problems in processing any particular signal when there is constant neuronal activity in the brain. More extended models have tried to show the operations that are performed by the central channel mechanisms.

The human nervous system can be divided into central and peripheral components, and this is paralleled by the information processing models. The central nervous system (CNS) is represented by the brain and spinal cord, and the peripheral nervous system describes all the nerve pathways which connect the CNS with the rest of the body. The peripheral nervous system allows the CNS to collect information and exert its control over the body's functions. The central channel mechanisms, therefore, are equivalent to the CNS, particularly the brain.

In Figure 2-12, we see the three major components identified: the

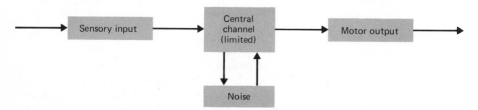

FIGURE 2-11   A basic information-processing model.

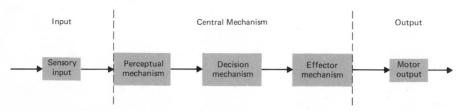

FIGURE 2-12   Functions of the central mechanism.

perceptual, decision, and effector mechanisms. Respectively, these components may be defined as those mechanisms that are concerned with the identification and integration of information, the choice and timing of responses, and, finally, the control and coordination of the response. Therefore, as there is more than one operation to be performed as you move through the system, it is clearly possible to have more than one signal going through the system at the same time, at different stages of processing. As such, the second signal might overlap the first and cause interference. We have perhaps all experienced interference when we tried to watch a foreign movie and read the subtitles at the same time. This is one of the reasons we refer to a *limited* channel capacity (Figure 2-11). When we are performing two tasks, some information may be lost from one or both sources. The implication is that we are limited in the number of signals we can consciously deal with at the same time.

The following composite model, representing one organization (Figure 2-13), includes most of the main ingredients of the system. The first component, the *sensory information store* (SIS), reflects the fact that all incoming sensory information is at least temporarily held so that it might all be available to the rest of the system. The sensory information store also represents one of the three elements of the memory component of the system. The other two elements are the short-term and long-term stores.

As the capacity of the system is limited, the selection of material becomes important. The function of the *selective filter* is to select the information that is to be used. The link with long-term memory suggests that the process of selection may also be affected by past experience. The main ingredients include at least two forms of memory: a *short-term* memory, which can allow

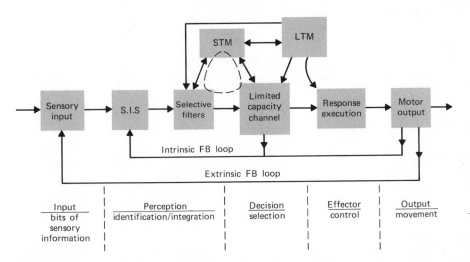

FIGURE 2-13 The main components of an information-processing model.

material to be rehearsed, and a *long-term* memory, which might affect the selection and performance of the response.

In looking at the model in Figure 2-13, we should note that this memory component overlaps the three major divisions of the system: the perceptual, decision, and effector mechanisms. One part of the memory component, the *rehearsal loop,* allows us to focus our attention on a particular item, such as repeating a telephone number several times before dialing. The use of the rehearsal loop, while improving short-term retention, would limit our ability to store and process other material at the same time because of the involvement of the limited capacity channel. Rehearsal is so demanding that it is difficult to deal with more than one task at a time. We may all recall the experience of dribbling a basketball down court while rehearsing a play the coach just gave us, only to discover we have lost the ball. The link between memory and the effector, or response execution, mechanism indicates that past experience might produce a delay in initiating the response. A low percentage shooter in basketball might hesitate when presented with an "easy" shot in basketball because of previous attempts that failed.

The final ingredients in the system of course are the all important *feedback loops,* both internal and external. The feedback loops provide a link between the output and input sides of the mechanism by returning information to the input side derived from the performance of a particular response. This information may be used to modify an ongoing movement or a subsequent response. These feedback loops, other than the direct internal loop from the effector mechanism, are a function of the peripheral nervous system. The internal feedback loop involves both a "record" of the instructions issued by the effector mechanism and the proprioceptive feel of the movement. The external feedback includes all information external to the body, including the degree to which our movement was successful. It is evident from this model that how the teacher supplies information may aid selection and avoid information overload. Recognizing the existence of the limited capacity channel, the less irrelevant information the learner has to process the more efficient the learning process will be.

Adams—closed-loop theory

It is not unusual that as the research orientation changes so do the "laws of learning," Adams' theory (1971) is important because it is the first theory of motor learning that tries to look at the actual process of learning and that is based on direct experimental evidence with a motor skill. Adams felt there was a need for a motor learning theory because not only had prior learning theories been based mainly on verbal skills but also there were clear differences between the retention of motor and cognitive skills.

In outlining his arguments to support the need for a theory based on the learning of motor skills by humans, Adams raised three points. First, he noted that humans do not react to the delay or withdrawal of reinforcement in the same way as animals. While a response may be depressed or even extinguished in animals when the specific reward for that task is removed, humans may continue to respond. The point has often been made in sports that in order to learn a skill the athlete must practice alone for many hours outside of those sessions when the coach is available. Second, Adams indicated that one of the key differences between animal and human learning is a human's ability to verbalize. At the early stages of learning, humans tend to guide their motor behavior with verbal responses, an ability not available to other animals. The third difference underlined by Adams was that humans will not move or make a response until they know they are correct. Animals on the other hand will tend to continue to respond until they receive a reward or some indication that they should stop. The cognitive activity involved in judging the correctness of a response again separates human behavior from that of the animals and, to some extent, learning theories based on their responses. Humans do not simply repeat rewarded responses. They tend to use subsequent responses to correct errors; that is, their responses will vary.

Adam's theory postulates a closed-loop system in which information generated by the production of a response is fed back into the system to help detect and correct any errors in the movement. For Adams, one of the most important pieces of information was knowing the outcome of a particular response: *knowledge of results* (**KR**). If you know that your first pass did not reach your teammate, then you know you have to use more force on the next pass. The alternative system is an open-loop system in which there is no feedback mechanism and the output is based on an analysis of the original input information. Lashley (1917) proposed such as *open-loop system*, the motor program, suggesting that sequences of movement could be controlled centrally and performed without proprioception. Adams criticized this type of idea, giving the example of the traffic light with a fixed timing interval which would snarl traffic at rush hour and impede the flow when traffic was light. Without feedback the system has no compensatory ability.

An early alternative was the S-R chaining notion of James (1890). In the S-R chain, each segment of the response (R) acts as the stimulus (S) for the next segment. Although Adams' theory was similar to the S-R chaining idea, he criticized chaining as not being a true closed-loop system because it had no *error detection mechanism*. Thus, Adams felt that any system required two ingredients:

1. It should be error centered with some mechanism for comparing current performance with previous attempts. This sort of mechanism had already been proposed by Bernstein (1967). Bernstein's mechanism for detecting errors was called a "comparator," but in the Bernstein model the same mechanism that initiated the movement also checked the response to see if it was correct. Adams felt that these functions should be performed by two separate mechanisms because a single

mechanism, such as a comparator, which uses the same model to initiate and check the response, is only in a position to confirm the correctness of its output. The problem is that you may perform correctly the movement you intended, but it may not be the correct movement for that task. As an opponent hits the ball across the net, the tennis player immediately selects the shot that will be used to make the return. If the player had a second mechanism available to check the validity of each selection, then the player would have the capability to detect any error in each choice and to select a new response before the first choice was even initiated.

2. Adams specified quantitative knowledge of results as the most important source of information. Only with precise information regarding the extent to which the (external) goal of the task had been met could an individual make appropriate corrections prior to the next attempt.

Therefore, Adams proposed a two-process closed-loop theory based on a perceptual trace and a memory trace. The memory trace was to serve a *recall* function, to select and initiate the appropriate response, and a perceptual trace was to serve the *recognition* function, to check out each response. As Adams (1971) said in separating these two functions, "Knowing which highway to take is as important as the distance to travel on it."

In order to illustrate Adams' theory, we will describe an experiment in which a subject tries to draw a line exactly 6 inches long while blindfolded, guided only by KR given to him by the experimenter. The experiment will be used to describe both the growth of the perceptual trace and the role of the memory trace.

The *perceptual trace* is assumed to be a record of a given movement based on all the sensory information from previous attempts at that movement. It should be noted that in the experimental procedure on which this theory is based, the subject is first presented with the criterion movement. Aided by the experimenter, the subject draws a line exactly 6 inches long. Then the subject tries to repeat the movement using error KR to guide successive movements. Immediately after each attempt to draw the line the subject has a "memory" of what it felt like to make that movement. The movement on each trial can be said to lay down a trace of sensory information, which then begins to decay (Figure 2-14).

After 10 trials the subject has a good memory of the sensory information (trace) from trials 9 and 10, a weak memory of trials 1 and 2, and some memory of the common elements in the intervening trials. Taken together, these bits of sensory information constitute the perceptual trace. Therefore, the final perceptual trace, which is established after many attempts at drawing the line, is a composite of the distribution of the old and new traces.

Early in learning, the perceptual trace is weak and errors are many as the subject tries to identify the most relevant information. By comparing the perceptual trace with the knowledge of results, the subject can assess errors and help upgrade the perceptual trace such that subsequent movements may be closer to the criterion. If the experimenter indicates that the last line drawn was only 3 inches, for example, the subject knows how the previous movements felt and must now try to draw a line that "feels" twice as long as in the earlier attempt. Adams suggested that once the perceptual trace is strong we can in fact continue to maintain performance and learn without knowledge of results, through subjective reinforcement (Schmidt & White, 1972). Just as a skilled athlete can train without a coach, so we can use a strong perceptual trace to judge our errors.

The _memory trace_ is postulated as the mechanism that simply selects and initiates the response; it does not control a long sequence of movements. The memory trace is really like a short open-loop motor program. Thus, the first part of the movement is automatic, but once the memory trace has initiated the movement the perceptual trace takes over. This mechanism is needed because (1) the perceptual trace cannot check itself and (2) the perceptual trace needs feedback; thus it needs a mechanism to fire the response in the first place. If the movement is slow enough for feedback to be processed before completion of the response, the final part of the movement may be guided (corrected) by the perceptual trace. If we were trying (blindfolded) to draw a horizontal 6-inch line, the memory trace would get us started in the correct direction and then the perceptual trace would take over to guide the rest of the movement. In fast movements the assessment or errors would occur after its completion and affect only subsequent movements.

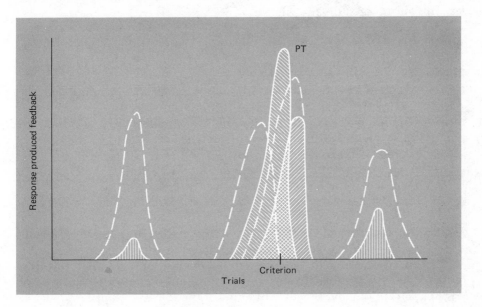

FIGURE 2-14 The growth of a perceptual trace.

Thus, if all our motor skills were collected together in a large dictionary, the memory traces would represent the alphabetical listing of words and the perceptual traces would be the associated definitions. Over time (with practice) the number of words we know increases and also our understanding of their meaning is refined. The strength of both traces is a function of practice, but selection (memory trace) is a function of the number of choices (possible movements) and guiding the response (perceptual trace) is a function of the quality of the feedback. By manipulating these two factors independently (the number of choices vs the quality of the feedback), it has been possible to generate support for this dual process theory.

Adams' theory, although one of the first, was not the only one directly relevant to motor behavior. In the final chapter, when we have established a broader background, we will re-examine the open- vs closed-loop argument, in particular the theoretical positions of Keele and Schmidt and how they relate to Adams' theory.

It should be noted that Adams' theory was based on research with slow positioning movements while many sports skills are ballistic in nature. If, however, the theory is representative of how we learn motor skills, then the principles involved in learning a slow positioning movement should be applicable to other, more ballistic, motor skills. If this is not possible, then the theory should be reformulated. The purpose of research is not to create a new form of learning, *i.e.*, how to learn laboratory motor skills. Consequently, with Adams' theory and with other more recent developments, there will be an attempt, throughout this text, to show how they might be applied to the learning of motor skills in general.

SUMMARY

It is important to note that while psychomotor learning is concerned with the learning and performance of motor skills, most of the learning theories that provided the early direction for psychomotor learning were not based on motor skills. The majority of the learning theories had to be interpreted. Thus, it is important to note the following:

1. Many learning theories dealt with animal learning. Yet humans do not react to the delay or withdrawal of reward in the same way as animals. Also, the ability to verbalize affords humans another advantage.
2. Motor skills may be characterized as a graded response. Feedback is used to guide or even change a response as it is produced.

When considering the traditional association and cognitive theories, most of the major differences arise from the interpretation of the roles of reward, perception, and practice. In terms of the role of rewards, evidence of the phenomenon of latent learning (Chapter 1) would suggest that rewards or reinforcement influence performance more than learning. Therefore, theorists such as Tolman and Guthrie de-emphasized the role of reward. However, as the performance or response is what we wish to produce, Skinner placed a major emphasis on reinforcement. Others like Thorndike felt that the reinforcement lies in the satisfaction gained from the response. In this way, reward is seen as playing an important role in learning by providing the motivation to persevere.

A clearer distinction between the two groups of theories can be made when considering the role of perception. The associationists maintained that it is sufficient if the learner perceives that the stimulus did occur. For the cognitivists, perception is a cornerstone of their work. How the learner perceives the environmental stimuli is essential. It is the learner who decides when and how to move and thereby acts on the environment rather than being controlled by it or simply responding to a stimulus.

All the learning theorists would agree on the need for practice but would differ as to the nature of that practice. The associationists emphasize repetitive practice to groove in the response, although it must be satisfying (Thorndike). The cognitivists see it more as practice in making decisions and place emphasis on organizing and identifying relevant cues in the environment (Tolman).

Briefly, the main theories include the following:

Association

PAVLOV: CLASSICAL CONDITIONING. Unconditioned responses may be conditioned deliberately or accidentally.

THORNDIKE: CONNECTIONISM. The laws of effect, exercise, and readiness were developed. The bond between the stimulus and response is emphasized. Practice is as close to game conditions as possible.

GUTHRIE: CONTIGUOUS CONDITIONING. Things which occur close together in time are associated. Each S-R is learned in one trial only, but each movement is represented by a collection or chain of S-R associations. Each variation must be practiced.

HULL: REINFORCEMENT THEORY. Responses are reinforced by the reduction of primary or secondary drives. Repetitive practice may inhibit learning if drives are not being reduced.

SKINNER: OPERANT CONDITIONING. The environment is controlled and the response is rewarded to make it more predictable. The desired response is shaped in easy steps to provide success.

TOTE UNIT. Illustrates how a motor skill may be organized in terms of a series of S-R associations.

Cognitive

GESTALT THEORY: MANY CONTRIBUTORS. This theory is concerned with how the individual perceives the environment, with the figure/ground concept, with the laws of similarity, proximity, and closure, and with the role of insight. The selection and identification of relevant stimuli and the understanding of principles and their interrelationships are emphasized.

LEWIN: FIELD THEORY. Motivation and the interaction of a person's psychological and environmental life space is studied. The internal motivation in learning is emphasized.

TOLMAN: SIGN-GESTALT (COMBINED S-R AND COGNITIVE THEORY). Mental trial and error lead to formation of a cognitive map to provide cues for future performance.

Man/machine theories

These theories were more concerned with the process by which tasks were learned and controlled rather than with the nature of the response. Models describing this process are seen to involve several major elements or components: components to identify stimuli, a storage or memory system, a central channel where information is gathered to make decisions, components to control the production of the movement, and a system to provide feedback about the response. Each of these components and their specific functions can then be considered separately.

CYBERNETICS: EMPHASIZES THE ROLE OF FEEDBACK. This closed-loop system or servomechanism may work to a fixed goal (regulator system, *e.g.*, thermostat) or may be adaptive with no fixed goal.

INFORMATION THEORY: THE BASIC UNIT OF INFORMATION IS THE BIT. Our short-term memory is limited to 7 ± 2 bits of information. The amount of information stored can be increased by grouping bits of information into chunks.

ADAMS: CLOSED-LOOP THEORY. One of the first theories to address the learning of motor skills, it emphasized the roll of error detection based on knowledge of results, particularly quantitative KR. Two separate mechanisms to initiate and check the response were proposed: the memory trace and the perceptual trace. Once a strong perceptual trace is established, the learner can maintain performance in the absence of KR through subjective reinforcement. The strength of both traces is a function of practice, but selection (memory trace) is a function of the number of choices and guiding the response (perceptual trace) is a function of the quality of the feedback. Although the theory was based on experiments with slow positioning movements, it was thought to be applicable to other types of motor skills.

PROBLEM

Blast of air (UCS)   ⟶   Blinking (UCR)

Blast of air (UCS) ⟶ Sound of glass (CS)⟶ Blinking (UCR)

Sound of glass (CS)   ⟶   Blinking (CR)

Question

What might be some of the characteristics of your teaching methodology if you were to teach a handspring according to each of the following theories: operant conditioning, Gestalt, closed-loop theory, sign-Gestalt, reinforcement theory, and connectionism?

Possible Answer

1. Operant conditioning
   a. Set the goal—what is to be achieved: a handspring.
   b. Pretest—assess the level of gymnastic ability: can the gymnast perform a forward roll, handstand?
   c. Structure the environment—remove irrelevant stimuli (*e.g.*, the trampoline) to allow learner to concentrate on the skill.
   d. Shape the behavior—small steps to allow for success and reinforcement at each stage, for example:
      —handstand against a wall
      —handstand against a wall preceded by a correct approach (hurdle)
      —repeat in open space with support
      —a "walkthrough" handspring, with support
      —running handspring, with support
      —free handspring, with spotter to assist if needed
      —repetition of the handspring to refine style
2. Gestalt
   a. Structure the environment to remove potentially confusing stimuli (*e.g.*, use plain gym mats).
   b. Provide a model or demonstration of the skill in order that the learner can understand the main principles involved and their relationship to the skill. Make sure this description is organized (approach, take-off, landing) and presented at a level appropriate for that person. Do not, for example, use vocabulary that is too complex.
   c. If possible, try to teach the whole movement, depending on the individual. Also, children with poor self-concepts may perceive the skill as very difficult and dangerous, so break the skill down into smaller "wholes" that may be combined later and provide lots of support.

3. Closed-loop theory
   a. Try to provide an "exact" model of the skill to the learner by putting the learner through the correct movement using lots of spotters. This approach can be repeated at intervals to facilitate comparison with later repetitions.
   b. A direct application would be to remove the support and let the learner try the skill and then provide KR regarding the extent to which the skill was achieved.
   c. As this approach may result in many movements which are far removed from the desired (perceptual trace) movement, an alternative that would limit the variations to movements (perceptual traces) closer to the criterion would be desirable. This could be achieved by slowly reducing or withdrawing the amount of support, thereby developing perceptual traces close to the criterion movement.
   d. KR should be given on every trial and before the next trial.
4. Sign-Gestalt
   a. Let the learner see the whole skill and try to develop an understanding of the relationship between the parts of the movement.
   b. Emphasize the main points and provide cues (*e.g.*, shoulders over hands, eyes looking forward).
   c. Encourage mental practice of the skill using these coaching points.
   d. Insist on the need for a lot of practice to establish the movement and provide reinforcement to maintain this activity.
5. Reinforcement theory
   a. Try to create a situation in which the learner wants (desires) to learn the skill, if it does not already exist: motivation.
   b. Make sure the learner understands the relationship between this skill and more advanced techniques. If the learner sees the value, learning will be more satisfying and effective.
   c. Avoid long repetitive drills because they may inhibit learning.
   d. If the skill is too difficult, use progressions to provide success and maintain interest.
6. Connectionism
   a. Law of readiness: use lead-up skills (*e.g.*, forward roll, handstand) to prepare the learner physically and psychologically for the skill. A child who lacks the ability to hold a handstand is not ready.
   b. Law of effect: provide sufficient support/spotters to facilitate successful and, therefore, satisfying repetitions.
   c. Law of exercise: provide sufficient practice to establish the correct movement, but it must be satisfying. This could be achieved by providing encouragement or some variety in the practice session.

In these six theories we have a variety of approaches and, although some of the steps may be similar, each has its own emphasis:

> Operant conditioning—shaping
> Gestalt—understanding
> Closed-loop theory—error detection, model vs self
> Sign-Gestalt—specific cues, mental practice
> Reinforcement theory—satisfying needs
> Connectionism—when ready, exercise effectively

Part Two

Acquisition of Skill

Chapter 3
Selected Practice Factors

If my attention is wandering, there is somewhere
it wants to go, so obviously it does not want to
be where I am holding it in the name of some
self-styled obligation.
(Prather, 1970)

Having considered some of the major learning theories in Chapter 2, we will now turn to a consideration of those factors that in a practical sense directly affect the acquisition of motor skills. In particular, we will look at research that was conducted using the traditional association or cognitive theories as a base. One of the major factors common to both groups of theories is the need to practice. This chapter is concerned with a selection of the main practice factors that should be considered by the teacher, or coach, when organizing a single practice session, a larger unit, or the overall program.

It must be recognized from the outset that these practice factors are neither invariant nor self-regulatory, because in the learning situation it is the teacher who sets up the environment and dictates the number of stimuli, the amount of information, or the number of responses with which the learner must deal. Armstrong and Hoffman (1980) have indicated that experienced tennis teachers are only marginally better at detecting performance errors than inexperienced tennis teachers. Their conclusions may imply that what experience brings is not a superior ability to identify relevant faults but is an ability to maximize effective practice time. The teacher may not be the person learning the skill, but the teacher is the person who controls the learning situation.

For the researcher who accepted either the association or cognitive learning theories as an adequate description of the learning process, the next step was to try and interpret them in relation to motor skill acquisition. A large amount of research addressing the learning of motor skills has been applied research. The problem with applied research on motor skill acquisition has been the difficulty in controlling all the variables. As a result, the findings in regard to the same principle have often been quite diverse. What works for a group of 9 year olds learning to swim in Hawaii might not work in New York. Why? We might find quite large differences in the motivation to learn. Therefore, to gain greater theoretical understanding we must turn for assistance to the more tightly controlled laboratory tasks more commonly employed in psychological studies. In the final step, before we attempt to generate particular principles, we must find the balance between the general trends of the applied research and the specific findings of the laboratory studies. However, "research does not tell the physical education teacher how to teach motor skills—no matter how attentively he (she) listens" (Nixon & Locke, 1973).

When discussing the main topics in this chapter, we need to recognize a few factors. First, most of the information presented here is based mainly on applied research that lacked the guidance of a clearly established theory of psychomotor learning. Only in the later parts of this text will we see the potential basis for the emergence of a theory of psychomotor learning. Second, there is a great diversity not only in the conclusions but also in the definitions of the basic terminology used in these studies. Third, it should also be noted that much of this research was conducted with subjects at the post-elementary level, and yet the largest group of "new learners" is at the elementary level. None of these remarks is intended to negate the value of the research discussed, only to underline the fact that while there are many signposts, there are few hard and fast "laws" in psychomotor learning. Finally, the information presented here represents a personalized description of some of the consistencies within the research and their associated interpretations.

In this chapter, we will consider the selected factors affecting motor skill practice in four major areas: practice organization, transfer, feedback (including knowledge of results), and motivation.

PRACTICE ORGANIZATION

The organization of a practice schedule or a particular training session will be dealt with under three main headings: the distribution of the practice, the structure of the task itself, and the type of practice.

Practice distribution

Whether we are concerned with the scheduling of a certain number of practice sessions over time (referred to as *between* practice distribution) or the organization *within* one particular practice session, essentially we are manipulating the work-rest ratio. By extending or reducing the amount of rest, we have the two options of either *massed* or *distributed* practice. These latter two terms can best be defined in terms of practice trials in a learning experiment, at least for the practice distribution within a given practice session:

> **Massed practice** *is when the rest interval is less than the trial length.*
> **Distributed practice** *is when the rest interval is equal to or greater than the trial length.*

The distinction between massed and distributed practice, in terms of the amount of rest between one practice session and the next (between practice distribution), is somewhat arbitrary but follows the same principle. The possible combinations are illustrated in Table 3-1. Although we refer to massed or distributed between practice distributions as an either/or situation, it is clear that they are described better as being relative points on a continuum.

WITHIN PRACTICE DISTRIBUTION.   We will begin by considering some of the points raised from research on practice distribution within a single practice session. Several distinct phenomena or practice effects have evolved from some of the psychological research. These were mainly derived from experiments involving such tasks as the rote memory of lists of words, but they have found some support in more recent work in physical education. In such psychological experiments, rest intervals between trials would range from 0 seconds to 60 seconds. The three most common effects are reactive inhibition, warm-up decrement, and reminiscence.

Reactive Inhibition (I_r).   This term was coined by Hull (1943) and is defined as the psychological reluctance to sustain work. According to Kimble

TABLE 3-1
Practice distribution

	Within (A Single Practice Session)	Between (Different Practice Sessions)
Massed	Rest interval $\leq$ Trial length	Practice sessions on the same day or consecutive days
Distributed	Rest interval $>$ Trial length	Inclusion of rest or no practice days.

(1949), reactive inhibition is a function of the amount of practice. As the amount of practice increases so does the level of I_r, and, as a result, performance deteriorates. This drop in performance does not necessarily imply an effect on learning, as we will see later. The I_r, dissipates with rest; therefore, under conditions of massed practice I_r will increase.

This is not the case for distributed practice. In such practice situations, the dissipation of I_r during the rest interval will allow practice to be sustained for a longer period of time. If you wish the players on the basketball team you coach to shoot 50 free throws every practice, it would be better to have them shoot five sets of ten, alternating with a partner, than to shoot 50 without a break. However, this concept conflicts somewhat with the next variable.

Warm-up Decrement (WUD).   The WUD concept is based on the idea that mental or physical preparation aids subsequent performance. If a person rests before engaging in physical activity, this warm-up state may be lost, with the amount of loss depending on the length of the rest. Experimentally you wish to avoid this loss of warm-up but still provide rest from the major task in order to maximize performance; otherwise, the state of warm-up must be regained in the early stages of subsequent trials. Therefore, the first few trials after a rest interval actually serve as the warm-up and are often interpreted as a poorer performance. Attempts to avoid such poor performance by keeping the subject physically occupied during the rest interval do not eliminate the problem.

In experiments using a pursuit rotor (following a light around a defined path), it has been shown that just generally tracking around the path with a finger between trials would not be sufficient to overcome WUD. Going through the motions of tracking may give the arm some exercise but places very little demand on the subject to be efficient. The sub-systems involved in processing movement information are therefore not maintained in a state of readiness.

The *activity-set hypothesis* attempts to explain this phenomenon. It suggests that the preparation to perform involves not the specifics of a skill, such as the proper posture, but the preparation of the underlying sub-systems, for example, the level of arousal or the appropriate feedback channels. Therefore, experimentally you should be able to reduce WUD by performing different tasks that involve a similar preparatory set (Murray, 1980). During a force judgment task test performed with the right hand, for example, subjects could try, during the rest interval, a different force judgment task with the left hand. The task would involve processing information and making judgments using a similar type of feedback, thus keeping these "underlying sub-systems" in a state of readiness without affecting the physical fatigue in the right hand. Because the second task is different, it will allow the dissipation of I_r related to the experimental task. Although WUD will be a problem with distributed practice, this will not be the case with massed practice: but what about I_r? One suggestion to accommodate this phenomenon is to use a pre-trial warm-up. Practice ten free throws, stop for instruction, take a couple of jump shots or lay-ups to sight (using the opposite hand), then take ten more free throws trying to correct the fault.

Reminiscence.   The third factor affecting within practice distribution is just as common, perhaps more so, in between practice distribution, but we will discuss it here. *Reminiscence* is the apparent improvement in performance over a period of no practice. The question is whether reminiscence is a true practice effect or simply an artifact. There are three explanations usually offered. First, that such apparent improvement in performance simply represents the recovery from physical fatigue, implying that reminiscence is a performance artifact and not representative of the amount of learning. For example, while practicing the tennis serve, a reduction in the amount of force (due to fatigue) may result in the ball hitting the net, but the overall sequence may become more fluid. After a rest and the resultant reduction of fatigue, this improved fluidity of movement is now evidenced by a large improvement in performance accuracy.

A second explanation is that improvement in performance represents unconscious mental practice. Associated with this interpretation is the idea that within these rest intervals there is greater forgetting of the incorrect, as distinct from the correct, responses (Briggs & Waters, 1958). The learner tends to concentrate on those responses that were closest to the desired perceptual and memory traces (Adams' terms). Third, reminiscence may simply result from the dissipation of I_r.

Although we are discussing within practice distribution, as mentioned earlier, the reminiscence effect has also been evidenced over much longer periods of time (*i.e.*, in between practice sessions). Purdy and Lockhart (1962), working with five novel skills, found evidence of reminiscence in 89% of their subjects in at least one of the skills over a one-year period. However, this study is somewhat of an exception, because no evidence of reminiscence was found in other studies (Fox & Lamb, 1962; Fox & Young, 1962) using shorter "rest" intervals (five and six weeks). Fox and Lamb (1962) did show evidence of reminiscence after 17 weeks.

In addition to the above factors, there is the possibility that reminiscence is related to the learning stage. Reminiscence is found in the early and late stages of learning but not at the intermediate stages. Therefore, in the early stages, it would appear to represent the consolidation or organization of the skill into a meaningful state during rest, that is, during mental practice. In the later stages, reminiscence is perhaps a result of the dissipation of I_r built up from repeated attempts to perfect the skill. One assumes that the advanced performer is physically able to sustain a heavy work load for that particular activity, such that physical fatigue should not be a major factor affecting skill performance. One would seriously question the preparation of a varsity basketball player who did not have the strength to make a lay-up in the last minute of a game.

These were some of the phenomena found during short practice sessions. However, before turning to between practice distribution we might attempt to make a few generalizations about massed and distributed practice. Overall it appears that massed practice within a single practice session has a detrimental effect on performance relative to distributed practice, while there is some evidence to suggest that there is no similar effect on learning (Whitley, 1970). So the answer may be to mass as many trials as possible into a practice. Even though performance may fall off, the learning should be unaffected.

Schmidt (1975a) had drawn slightly different conclusions on this issue. He felt findings from the psychological research were not directly applicable to physical education for two reasons. First, they are based mainly on one practice session, whereas learning in physical education is based on many sessions over a long period of time. Therefore, the effects of massed practice may be entirely different. Second, the poorer performance under massed conditions often involves rest intervals of one second in the laboratory, whereas in class there may be many seconds between repetitions (*e.g.,* shooting foul shots). Therefore, he sees the problem of massed practice within a session as being more a question of physical fatigue than mental fatigue, which is a different problem.

This interpretation would add support to the distinction made regarding the effect of massed practice on learning as distinct from performance. The lack of improvement or deterioration in performance toward the end of a practice session that may result from massed (little rest) practice is not seen to represent a deterioration or a reduction in learning. As was stated in Chapter 1, "the change in habit strength was not sufficient to produce a change in performance." A suggestion made by Goodenough and Brian (1929) may in fact be the most functional for handling a large variety of tasks and individuals. They suggested the use of *massed practice* with pre-schoolers, with rest intervals being introduced when there appeared to be a lack of progress.

BETWEEN PRACTICE DISTRIBUTION. Typical between practice distribution studies would compare massed practice (*e.g.,* practicing on Monday through Friday) with distributed practice (*e.g.,* practicing on Monday, Wednesday, and Friday); the performance of the massed practice group was better after the first three weeks, but no differences were found between the groups after four or five weeks. Therefore, distributed practice is seen to achieve the same level of skill with less total practice time. Put another way, it appears that when the total practice time is held constant, it makes little difference how the practices are distributed through the practice/training period.

Harmon and Miller (1950), in a study with billiards, used a different approach. There were four practice groups:

1. Massed: practice for nine consecutive days
2. Distributed: practice three times a week for three weeks
3. Distributed: practice once a week for nine weeks
4. Additive: practice on days 1, 2, 3, 5, 8, 13, 21, 34, and 55

No significant differences were found between the groups except for the fourth group, and this performance variation did not appear until after the sixth session or third week. These results would seem to suggest a practice schedule in which there is a relative massing of practice at the beginning of learning, with the subsequent spacing of practices in the later stages.

Young (1954), in a study of badminton and archery skills, used either a massed (4 days per week for 6 weeks) or a distributed (2 days per week for 12 weeks) practice schedule. It was found that massed practice was better for archery and distributed practice was better for badminton. This apparent conflict can be resolved if we consider archery as a new or novel skill requiring a lot of organization and badminton as a skill that may have been facilitated by its similarity to other racket sports. Familiarity with other racket sports allows the learner to start at a more advanced stage in the badminton task. Young's results demonstrate the possibility of an interaction between the practice schedule and the type of skill.

Task structure

So far we have considered the overall organization of the practice; now we will turn to its content. The main concern here is whether skills should be taught as a whole or as separate parts. The main problem is in defining the term *whole* in relation to a motor skill. Is it the sport itself, a skill within that sport (the most common notion), or even part of that skill (*e.g.*, teaching the arm action as a separate skill in the sidestroke)? Thus we are left with *part* and *whole* as relative terms, depending on the task at hand. *Part learning* involves practice on the components of a skill, and *whole learning* involves practice on the whole task at hand.

There are four major methods that have evolved:

1. *Whole learning:* practice by performing the whole task.
2. *Pure part:* P_1, P_2, P_3, $P_1 + P_2 + P_3$ . . . . all the components of the skill are practiced independently and then joined together.
3. *Progressive part:* P_1, P_2, $P_1 + P_2$, P_3, $P_1 + P_2 + P_3$ . . . . the components of the skill are combined additively in sequence.
4. *Whole-part:* Whole, P_1, whole, P_2 . . . . alternating practice between each part and the whole skill.

The question is which method is best? Studies using these various methods have produced apparently conflicting results. To look at this question we will outline three studies using different tasks and then try to explain the different results.

1. Barton (1921). For this study the task was maze learning. Barton found that part learning was best, whole learning was worst, and progressive part learning fell in between.
2. Brown (1928). Brown's study involved pianists learning a new score. In this experiment, whole learning was best, whole/part was in between, and part learning was worst.
3. Cross (1937). This study revolved around teaching basketball. The results suggested that whole learning (playing the game) was best for simple skills (*e.g.*, passing), whole/part learning was best for complex skills (*e.g.*, a lay-up), and progressive part (*e.g.*, minor or lead-up games) was best for intermediate skills (*e.g.*, finding a space where you could safely receive a pass).

The apparent conflicts seen here are quite representative of the literature. They were largely resolved by Naylor and Briggs (1963), who considered the nature of the task as the key variable. The nature of the task has two components:

1. *Task complexity* refers to the demands the task places on memory and the information processing capacity: the number of bits of information.
2. *Task organization* refers to both the number of separate components and the inter-relationships of these components within the task: their timing and sequencing.

In a task in which a lot of information has to be retained or processed, even though there are only a few separate components (a high-complexity, low-organization task), the part method should be used. When there are several parts that interact (low-complexity, high-organization tasks), the whole method is appropriate. Thus, the maze task is seen as being complex and learned best by being broken down into smaller pieces that place less demand on memory. The task is then built by reorganizing the bits of information into chunks. The new "score" is not so complex if you are a pianist and, as the main element here involves fitting the components together, it would naturally tend to favor some type of whole practice. The use of terms in the Cross study is slightly different from "normal," but the findings are in keeping with the general model (Figure 3-1).

From the model it is clear that there are at least two other alternatives: a high-complexity, high-organization task and a low-complexity, low-organization task. Possible examples of these might be, respectively, a spike in volleyball and running. Similarly, more sports-oriented examples of the two research tasks mentioned earlier (maze learning and a piano score) might be the return of service in squash and the sidestroke. In the first example (high-complexity, low-organization), although the specific stroke may not involve many components, the player must be prepared to execute several alternative movements, with each choice being tied to a different set of stimulus conditions. In the sidestroke (low-complexity, high-organization), there is little demand placed on memory but the timing and sequencing of the movements will determine the extent to which the individual sinks or swims. Clearly though, bits of information can be chunked to reduce the load on memory, and small components can become integral parts of larger components to reduce the number of organizational units. To the beginner, almost any skill is potentially highly organized and highly complex, but eventually the limitations in terms of skill learning will be determined by the nature of the task itself.

A second way to look at a task is simply by considering its structure or organization. As was pointed out, all tasks may at first seem both highly complex and highly organized to a beginner. However, for certain tasks the nature of their organization may indicate that a whole or part learning procedure would be counterproductive. In terms of task structure we find these three main alternatives:

1. *Serial tasks.* A given set of movements must be performed in sequence to complete the final task (*e.g.*, the pole vault). Here learning the parts of the task either individually or progressively seems to aid the final

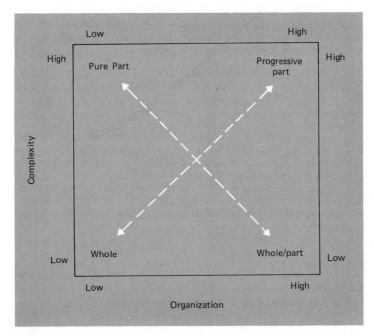

FIGURE 3-1   A model relating the nature of the task and whole/part learning.

performance of the task. However, there may be some instances in which the overall flow or rhythm of the movement is the most important part (as in some individual gymnastic skills), when the whole method might be more applicable. Shay (1934) did find the whole method to be best when learning a kip on the high bar.

2. *Continuous tasks.* These tasks normally involve the repetition of some short sequence of movements (*e.g.*, riding a bicycle or swimming). A (sequential) serial task, however, may be defined as one which has an identifiable starting point and finishing point. In comparison, a continuous task has no such distinct end points. A task such as driving a car might overall be classed as continuous but includes certain sequential movements (*e.g.*, changing gears). The question here that determines the selection of the appropriate method is the interaction of the parts, that is, if manipulating part number one affects part number two, it would be better to treat the task as a whole.

3. *Discrete tasks.* A discrete task has a distinct beginning and end point and is of a short duration (*e.g.*, a straight left lead in boxing). Splitting a discrete task is rather arbitrary and may actually hinder learning.

In a methodological study, Neimeyer (1959) found that part learning was better for volleyball (serial), whole learning was better for swimming (continuous), and either part or whole learning was satisfactory for badminton, at least for the skills that he chose as being representative of these particular activities. Again, these findings generally fit the model in Figure 3-1. Neimeyer went on to suggest that team sports should be taught by the part method, individual sports by the whole method, and dual sports by either method. However, on the basis of what has been discussed already, it should be clear that this study cannot justify such a conclusion. No matter how well controlled a study is, or how clear the results, we must take care before we generalize and we must beware of any research that offers simple solutions to very complex problems. When reading any research article, it is important that you read with care and formulate your own opinions. To be able to interpret research so that it may be of practical value, you must first understand what it is saying. To understand research, you must learn to synthesize, to combine often diverse concepts into a unified whole.

Basically then, in learning skills, one of the main problems is the integration of the separate parts or components of a skill. This integration is done at the same time the task is learned in the whole method but requires an extra effort in the part method after the various parts have been learned. One of the keys necessary when using the part method is in the understanding of the relationship of the parts to the whole, which in turn relates directly to the capacity of the learner. What may be only part of a skill for an adult may represent a whole or separate skill for a child. For example, when looking at the composite drawings shown in Figure 3-2, younger children may only identify specific objects (bat, ball, giraffe). Later they can recognize the whole figure (face or heart), but it may not be until they are 9 or 10 years old that they see both: a face made up of a big ball with two tops for eyes or a heart formed by two giraffes.

As adults it may be very difficult for us to "see" things as a child might. One of the reasons why good players may not necessarily be good coaches for children is that the way they learned or practiced the skills may not be appropriate for children. Pascuale-Leone (1970), in assessing the number of schemes (mental operations or, more simply, bits of information) that a child could handle simultaneously, found a progressive development with age. The 5 year old could only handle one or two schemes, and it was not until they were 15 or 16 years old that they could handle seven schemes—similar to Miller's (1956) 7 ± 2 bits. Thus, whether measured by the number of schemes or bits of information, there are distinct developmental changes in the capacity of the child. Too many people make the mistake of coaching Little League teams in the image of the adult teams.

One final concept, which may explain both the difficulty encountered in obtaining consistent research results and the inconsistent success rate that may accompany some "favored" teaching technique, is the factor of field dependency. Based on the figure/ground concept, it suggests that some individuals are more influenced by the background of stimuli (field dependent) whereas others are more easily able to isolate the figure (field independent). Field-dependent individuals are said to be more holistic, while field-independent individuals are more analytical. This basic difference in cognitive styles will have a large influence on the effectiveness of a given teaching method for a particular child. To conclude this section on task structure, it would appear reasonable to suggest that, generally, although

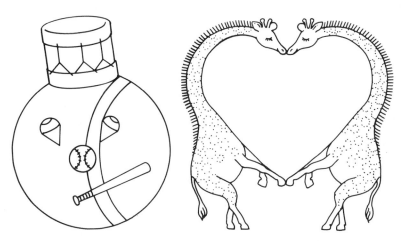

FIGURE 3-2   A child's eye-view of whole/part relationships (after Elkind, Koegler & Koegler, 1964).

noting the various factors that have been outlined, it is better to teach the *whole skill* when possible, or at least as large a part of that skill as the learner can deal with.

Type of practice

When learning motor skills, the most obvious type of practice is physical practice. However, this is not the only alternative. An often ignored supplement to physical practice is the use of mental practice. Here we will concentrate on the role of mental practice or mental rehearsal. Other types of practice could include guided or kinesthetic practice and visual practice. The former would involve guiding the learner through the movement, to give the learner the "feel" of the movement. Alternatively, visual practice would involve practicing the visual movements involved in the task. As vision provides a major source of sensory information, it is thought that orienting the eyes to focus on the appropriate sources of information may facilitate skill learning. In one of the few studies to compare these various approaches to motor skill practice, Smith and Harrison (1962) suggested that both visual and mental practice were effective in improving the efficiency of performance. The first question to ask is how such practice might be used. There are at least four alternatives:

1. A brief review of the skill prior to performance (*e.g.*, the high jumper imagines the approach and successful clearance of the bar) to prepare the performer to establish the overall flow and sequence of movement.
2. Practice between sessions, using imagery to focus on the techniques presented in the previous practice. The learner attempts to isolate the correct response and ignore incorrect responses.
3. Understanding principles, to think about or rehearse strategy, to priorize the various options the player may face at some particular point in the game (*e.g.*, the responses to a dropshot in badminton).
4. Some recent evidence (Ulich, 1967) has revived another role. Electromyographic (EMG) activity recorded in the muscles to be used in the movement suggests that mental practice acts as a sort of subliminal physical practice.

In order to consider the effectiveness of mental practice, we will review one or two typical studies. In one study (Fantasia, 1969), which utilized the overhead clear in badminton, there were nine experimental groups based on combinations of three time patterns (massed/distributed/additive) and three types of practice (physical/mental/physical and mental).

The best combination appeared to be massed-physical practice, and the study seemed to suggest that the effectiveness of learning was more dependent on the time pattern than on the type of practice. However, Jones (1965), looking at the upstart on the high bar (or uneven bars), found that physical practice was not necessary and that mental practice was sufficient to learn this skill. Initially this would appear to be rather an extreme finding, but if you consider the skill itself, and the importance of timing, it is more understandable. The upstart is a fairly elementary gymnastic skill, and the most important element for the learner is to judge the point at which to "kick out." The gymnast must learn to wait; the most common fault is initiating the extension too early. Through observation, the learner may be able to gain sufficient insight, by noting the differences between previously successful and unsuccessful attempts, to perform an acceptable version of the skill on the first trial. For this study involving the early stages of learning a simple skill, undirected mental practice was better than directed mental practice. However, as the complexity of the skill increases, it would appear necessary to give some direction as to the main "coaching points" to be emphasized.

In a study by Twinning (1949) (Table 3-2), more typical results were demonstrated. The task was ring tossing. To assess the differences between the groups, the amount of improvement from the pre-testing to the post-testing score was compared: In Group 1 (control), there was no significant difference (*i.e.*, no reminiscence effect); in Group 2 (physical practice), there was 137% improvement; and in Group 3 (mental practice), there was 36% improvement.

For this skill it is clear that mental practice could help, but not replace, physical practice. Generally, mental practice is found to be more useful when the individual has some background in the skill (Corbin, 1967). Could you mentally practice bowling a "leg break?" Unlikely, but after reading a cricket manual and if you had some experience as a baseball pitcher it might be possible. There is some evidence that mental practice may be more beneficial in the early stages of learning a skill than physical practice (Jones, 1965; Phipps & Morehouse, 1969). These latter studies and that of Corbin (1967) would seem to support an earlier study by Clarke (1960). Clarke found that mental practice was almost as effective as physical practice for experienced players learning a one-hand foul shot, but his finding did not apply for novice players. Experience allows the learner to make more effective use of mental practice.

One suggestion made by Oxendine (1968) is that just as a golfer after a bad shot does a replay to find the correct shot, the replay technique should be used after a good shot. The main point to recognize from this description is that

TABLE 3-2
Practice and testing schedule

Groups	Pretest (Day 1)	Practice (Day 2–Day 21)	Posttest (Day 22)
1. Control	210 rings	None	210 rings
2. Physical Practice	210 rings	70 rings per day from day 2 to 21	210 rings
3. Mental Practice	210 rings	15 minutes per day from day 2 to 21	210 rings

mental practice can play a valuable role by augmenting the gains made through physical practice in the learning situation. However, mental practice is in itself a skill. We all know that relaxation techniques can help improve mental and physical health, but these techniques are not acquired easily. There is no reason to assume that it would be any easier to comply to the instruction "now mentally practice" than "now relax." Indeed, it may take some time before the maximum benefits can be achieved. The fact that physical educators are dealing with physical skills has led many practitioners to ignore what could indeed be a very useful addition to their practice sessions.

Developing a practice schedule

Finally, if we review this section on practice organization, we will find there are certain factors that recur; these are some of the main variables to consider before developing a practice schedule:
1. Nature of the task
   a. Complexity—load on memory
   b. Organization—number of units and their interrelationships
2. Experience of the learner
   a. Age
   b. Level
   c. Ability
3. Specific stage of learning
   a. Beginning or advanced
   b. Learning or refining
4. Purpose of the practice
   a. Immediate gain in learning
   b. For retention

The nature of the task will, to a large extent, determine the teaching method used in terms of whether it can be taught as a whole or must be divided into its constituent parts. This variable may also have some influence on the type of practice. Mental practice could serve to reduce the information load by organizing the information into chunks or to increase the understanding of the interrelationship between the parts. In this regard, Wrisberg and Ragsdale (1979) have found that mental practice facilitates the performance of tasks with a heavy cognitive component more than tasks that are highly motor in nature (*e.g.*, balancing). However, mental practice would also be related to the second variable, experience of the learner. Although there is some evidence to suggest that mental practice is equivalent to physical practice for simple skills, only the more experienced or skilled individuals would appear to gain benefit from the mental practice of more complex skills.

The capacity of the learner to perform a given task would be directly reflected by the age and ability of the learner. In the latter case, this would tend to reflect more the capacity differences within an age-group. The capacity would influence the ability to perceive and handle large chunks of information and would limit the extent of the "wholes" that could be taught. Secondarily, the inability to perceive long-term aims within a learning progression may accelerate the build-up of I_r in the learning of complex skills, particularly when massed practice is used within a given practice session. The level of experience or exposure to similar skills does not necessarily indicate the level of skill, but it will influence the ability to utilize mental practice.

The specific stage of learning will affect decisions regarding practice distribution. Research would suggest a between practice schedule that progressed from massed to distributed as the learner moved away from the beginning stages of learning. For the practice organization within a single session, after considering the nature of the task, Schmidt (1975a) would encourage us to use massed practice. In doing so, we must be aware of the limitation of physical fatigue, specific safety factors, and the danger of I_r; there must be a certain minimum level of motivation. If the learner is attempting to develop a correct model of the skill, the problems mentioned above are factors to be avoided. Physical and mental fatigue are factors that might lead to the practice of incorrect movements and therefore might inhibit learning. However, in the refining of skills it might be quite appropriate to practice performing the skill under these conditions. The change from learning to refining would also suggest a change from part learning to whole or perhaps whole/part strategies.

We must assume that any practice has some overall purpose; to quote Confucius: "Labour without thought is labour lost." The purpose of the practice will exert the final influence on its organization. When the practice is for immediate gain only, the obvious choice is a massed practice schedule. However, when the aim is the long-term retention of a skill, the choice is not so clear; the little evidence that exists is quite contradictory. Perhaps the only guide is provided by Fitts and Posner (1967) when they suggest that the longer a subject is free to rehearse some information, the more likely the subject is to store it permanently. Thus, recognizing the between practice consolidation that distributed practice affords through direct mental practice or simply the forgetting of incorrect responses, distributed practice would seem to be the best alternative.

TRANSFER

As can be seen from the previous section, there are many factors to be considered just in terms of the overall organization of a practice. Practice organization is concerned with the learning of a single skill or of skills within a single sport. However, in any physical education program there are many different sports. Therefore, an important factor is whether the knowledge and skills learned in one activity would aid or hinder the learning of other skills, that is, the possibility of transfer of learning between skills.

Transfer refers to the effect of learning one skill on prior or future learning. In physical education, transfer between skills is often assumed. The question is, should we make this assumption? If we consider the educational viewpoint, the answer is yes. It is assumed that what is learned in school (*i.e.,* knowledge) is usable when entering the "real world," if it is transferable. Indeed, there is a great deal of transfer research to be found in educational psychology journals. The literature is not so abundant in the area of motor skills, and the tendency has been to use fine motor skills (manipulative types of skills emphasizing accuracy, usually eye-hand coordination) rather than gross motor skills (large muscle activities involving movement of the whole body, which includes most sport skills). The difficulties inherent in working with "real world" or sports skills is reflected in the researchers' reliance on laboratory-type motor skills.

There are two basic approaches to explaining the concept of transfer:

1. Thorndike's theory of identical elements (Chapter 2) states that only when the elements within two skills are identical will there be any transfer (*e.g.,* the similarity between the overhead smash in squash and a smash in tennis). This is an S-R approach in which a particular chain, or sequence of movements, may be used in different situations or as an element within a second skill. In transfer studies using the pursuit rotor by Lordahl and Archer (1958) and Namikas and Archer (1960), it was found that transfer was greatest when the speed of the pursuit rotor was identical. Only the radius of the target was changed.

2. Judd's theory of generalized principles emphasizes the transfer of basic movement principles as well as specific skills. Judd suggests that general ideas about how or when to move might be transferred from one situation to another. Here we are looking at the factors controlling movement rather than simply at the mechanics of response production.

Judd (1905, 1908) demonstrated his ideas with two simple experiments. Two groups of fifth- and sixth-grade boys threw darts at a submerged target. The principle of refraction had been explained to the experimental group but not to the control group. Both groups were first tested on a target placed at a depth of 12 inches before they were tested on a second target placed at a depth of 4 inches. From the first study Judd found the following:

1. For the 12-inch target, there was no difference between the groups. Obviously the experimental group needed some practice.

2. For the 4-inch target, the experimental group was much better. They had now recognized the difference.

In a second study involving a more precise analysis of the data, Judd found that knowing the principle aided both the initial learning and transfer (experimental group). Also, the control group subjects often showed sudden insight and subsequently improved their performance. This study implies that when principles are important we should expect to see transfer (*e.g.*, between team sports in which the proper use of space is an essential ingredient). Hendrickson and Schroeder (1941) duplicated this work and produced similar results.

The different approaches taken by Thorndike and Judd reflect the basic difference in the approach to transfer found in the associationist and cognitive camps discussed earlier in this book. However, the Gestaltists, who favor a heavily perceptual theory, have an alternative approach: the transposition theory. Transposition theory emphasizes the identification of a pattern of stimuli by the learner, a holistic approach. Cratty (1962) showed that practice on small patterns facilitated the learning of large patterns in a maze task, thereby giving some support to this theory.

One other approach to transfer, which is worth mentioning because it is a common element of motor skill teaching, is verbal motor transfer. Verbal motor transfer is the verbalizing of instructions or important cues prior to or during physical practice. Both Neumann (1960) and Battig (1956) found support for this idea, but the amount of transfer was reduced as the complexity of the task increased.

To evaluate transfer effects, two main experimental designs have been used:

1. *Proactive transfer:*

      Experimental group ...... learn task A ..... test task B

      Control group .... rest .... test task B

This type of design allows us to look at the effect of current learning on future performance. For example, such a design would allow us to assess the value of particular lead-up games or progressions.

2. *Retroactive transfer:*

      Experimental group ... learn task A ... learn task B ... test on A

      Control group .... learn task A ... rest .... test on A

The question here is how changing activities affects skills that have already been learned. Thus, you can look at transfer in terms of how an "old" skill affects the learning of a new skill (proactive) or how the learning of a new skill can affect the performance of an acquired skill (retroactive). If we desire to build an individual's movement vocabulary (skills), we need to ensure that the foundations are not being eroded. Achieving this objective entails maximizing the opportunities for transfer.

In the area of transfer research, there have been three main sub-divisions, which we will consider individually: (1) bilateral (within-individual) transfer: cross education; (2) intertask transfer; and (3) intratask transfer.

Bilateral transfer

Bilateral transfer refers to transfer from one limb to another or, for example, the ability to learn more easily a skill with one hand after learning it first with the opposite hand. A typical experiment might have the subject (with a stylus attached to the foot) try to follow and learn a maze using the foot. Then the subject might be tested on the task using the opposite foot or hand. Other subjects would follow the reverse procedure, first learning the task with the hand and then being tested using the foot. From such research (Cook, 1933), findings have indicated that bilateral transfer is greatest between hands or feet, next between the hand and foot on the same side, and next between the hand and foot on the opposite side. There have been two main explanations that have been offered for these physiological and psychological effects.

1. While performing the activity with the right hand, there are neuro-muscular signals going to the opposite limb, that is, there is some evidence of EMG activity in the same muscle groups in the resting limbs (Davis, 1942).

2. The key element transferred is the mental organization of the task. In fact, in an experiment in which one group did a transfer task while a second group observed, a similar skill level was found in the observation group (Jones, 1965).

Of course, one other possibility is that performance on the second task (different limb) improves because of subject confidence or familiarity with the task.

Intertask transfer

Intertask transfer involves the possible transfer of learning from one task to a second different task (*e.g.*, as from handball to squash). This type of transfer is perhaps the major concern for the physical educator. One of the problems for the physical educator has been that most of the clear support for transfer is from verbal learning. When we look at physical education, the research picture is a little confused. Without the guidance of any clear theory we find that we have an abundance of applied research, with many uncontrolled and confounding variables. However, the main concern here is whether the effect of one skill on another is positive or negative. In the 1930s, a rough guide was provided by the *Skaggs-Robinson hypothesis* (Figure 3-3), which suggested that the effect of transfer was a function of the degree of similarity between the skills involved. However, although such a curve would appear to suggest that a large proportion of intertask transfer is negative in nature, in fact the opposite appears true in that most intertask transfer is *slightly* positive when the tasks are related.

Research into intertask transfer has focused on the direction (retroactive or proactive) as well as the effect (positive or negative) of transfer and has dealt with the questions of *retroactive inhibition* and *proactive facilitation* and the circumstances under which they might occur.

Examples of retroactive inhibition would be when a beginner at tennis plays badminton and is confused when returning to tennis or the negative effect of a basketball tip-in drill (when the object of the drill is actually to "tip" the ball *over* the basket to a partner) on tip-ins during the game itself. Note that inhibition does not imply that a skill cannot be learned properly. The reverse would be evidenced at a slightly more advanced stage when the learner finds that the quick reflexive movements required in badminton have had a positive effect on the footwork associated with previously learned tennis strokes.

An example of proactive facilitation would be the tennis player who is able to learn squash more easily due to similarities between the sports. A negative progression might be shown by the ice hockey player who tries to learn soccer but cannot overcome the habit of checking the other players instead of playing the ball. It should be noted that one could also refer to proactive inhibition and retroactive facilitation.

Generally, the research on intertask transfer has tended to support the more restricted identical elements interpretation. Many studies suggest that the factors involved in learning a task are specific to that task and are not transferable (Oxendine, 1967; Daniels, 1968). Daniels also indicated that participation in the game (badminton or tennis) does not improve a specific skill, unless that skill is practiced. While most studies show little or no transfer, there are some exceptions. Both Welsh (1962) and Soule (1958) found support for positive transfer between sports. From these findings it would seem that while the teacher continues to teach for transfer, there is little evidence to support this position in regard to specific sport skills.

Thus far, there has been little evidence of negative transfer in the research

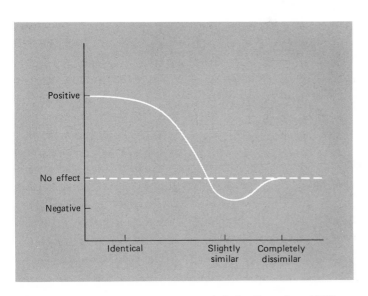

FIGURE 3-3 Skaggs-Robinson hypothesis (after Oxendine, 1968).

conducted (Figure 3-4). Note that negative transfer refers to a negative effect on learning, that is, the final level of skill achieved and not a temporary interference with performance. Such interference may slow the learning process but does not affect the final outcome. There are few studies which have investigated negative transfer directly, and many of those reporting negative transfer were originally designed to look at potential positive effects. Kerr (1970) found significant negative transfer from a fast weighted condition (2-lb weight) to a slow unweighted condition in a horizontal limb adduction task.

A traditional "motor" task that has been used to investigate negative transfer is the card sorting task. Brantly (1938) showed that the degree of similarity and compatibility between the tasks would determine both the amount and the effect of the transfer. If the stimuli on the cards or box were the same (numbers) in the two tasks and the responses compatible—the number three card was placed in the third box in the row—there would be positive transfer. As the amount of similarity decreased, so did the positive transfer; and as the degree of incompatibility between the original and subsequent learning increased, so did the tendency for negative transfer.

One other exception was a study by Lewis, McAllister, and Adams (1951).

FIGURE 3-4 Negative transfer—a sumo diver?

This study involved a three-dimensional tracking task. A joystick controlled the forward/back and left/right movements, and foot pedals controlled the up/down movement. The various experimental groups were given varying degrees of practice on this (standard) task. Next, all the controls were reversed and the subjects practiced on the reversed task. Finally, all subjects were re-tested on the original standard task. The graph (Figure 3-5) illustrates the mean decrement from the last trial of the original learning to the scores of the re-test. The twelve groups are identified by the number of original trials (on the standard task: OL) and the number of trials on the interpolated task (reversed task: IL). There was one group for each combination of OL and IL.

From the graph, it is clear that the greater the original learning, the greater was the negative transfer. Only when the subjects had established a good concept of the original task would the reverse task cause interference and lead to a poorer performance on the re-test. Clearly, in the group with only 10 trials on the original task the subjects were operating at a low level of efficiency; switching tasks for a while could not make them any worse. Also, it can be seen that the amount of negative transfer is a function of the amount of interpolated practice. The groups with 30 and 50 trials on the reversed task performed worse, although only marginally so for the lowest level of original learning.

Unfortunately, this graph does not show a really advanced performer,

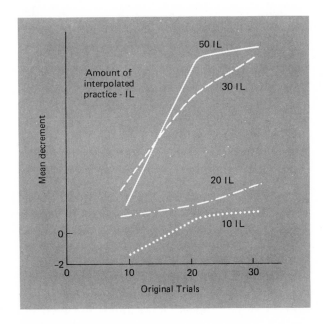

FIGURE 3-5 Negative transfer and degree of original learning (after Lewis, McAllister & Adams, 1951).

that is, 100 to 200 trials on the original task. It is conceivable that at the advanced stage we would see less negative transfer. It would seem more appropriate to suggest that the interference occurs mainly at the intermediate stages, with little interference for the beginning or advanced stages. The intermediate stage here refers to that point at which the learner has begun to come to grips with the task. For example, the forehand shot in tennis now goes in the chosen direction—forward, over the net, and in bounds. We should also note here that in the tracking task described above it took a complete reversal of the task to produce any interference effects, hardly what one would call a slightly similar task (Skaggs-Robinson). Although the stimuli involved in the standard and reversed task were similar, the associated responses certainly were not.

Schmidt (1975a) feels that to overcome these types of problems we need a clearer definition of similarity, because in his experiment (1968), involving knocking over a number of blocks in sequence as fast as possible, he found no inhibition (*i.e.*, increased movement time) on later trials when the block position was changed. From this type of finding, the practical implication for the physical educator is that there should not be an overly great concern about the "dangers" of negative transfer between tasks. It appears that negative transfer is only likely at an intermediate stage and under extreme circumstances. Remember, intermediate skill level refers to what in "lay" terms would describe a beginner rather than a skilled performer, that is, one who is able to perform the task but still lacks precision and consistency. Also, as the amount of the initial learning increases, not only is the original task more resistant to interference but there is also a stronger possibility of transfer to a similar task (Briggs, Fitts, & Bahrick, 1958; Mandler, 1954).

Another point to make from the transfer research relates to the role of mechanical principles. In spite of the findings of some studies (Mohr & Barrett, 1962; Werner, 1972), an understanding of general principles does not always aid *skill* performance as distinct from tactics (Halverson, 1949; Colville, 1957). However, it does not appear to be detrimental to teach mechanical principles, because they may be used at a later stage or may simply act to maintain the interest level or motivate the learner. In fact, it has been suggested that most international divers are "experts" in that part of biomechanics that relates to their sport. The research would appear to justify the presentation of relevant mechanical or analytical information to the learner but certainly does not give the teacher carte blanche to begin each practical session with a long theoretical discourse.

One other interesting point has been made by Logan and Wodthe (1968). They found that giving rules of thumb in an introductory physics course actually interfered with later learning. The problem was that the students tended to overgeneralize the rules. Intertask transfer is not automatic, because people may simply not make the proper connections. Pointing out similarities between tasks, when they exist, as well as indicating the limits of that similarity (Logan & Wodthe, 1968), would appear to be the most prudent strategy for the practitioner.

One important phenomenon not mentioned so far involves the principle of *learning how to learn,* or learning sets, that is, the idea that we may learn a technique for solving a particular type of problem or that we become, by participating in physical activities, better able to assess our own capabilities in relation to the task at hand (Harlow, 1949). Seymour (1957) came to a similar conclusion in a study of engineering skills. The concept of learning sets may be one of the main benefits of movement education. Many people object to the ideas of improved body awareness or kinesthesis but might accept the concept of learning to solve problems in terms of one's ability. After all, by learning techniques to solve simple mathematical problems we are able to establish a method of approaching more complex problems. However, although Lafuze (1951) and Broer (1958) did show some transfer from fundamental movement programs to motor ability tests or sports skills, the more typical finding (Scott, 1967) for movement education studies is no significant transfer.

Intratrask transfer

Intratask transfer refers to the possible transfer between variations of the same task. We generally assume that there is transfer from the simple to the more complex versions of a task (a progressive build-up), but there is some evidence that the reverse may be true. If our aim is to perform a tracking task with the pursuit rotor set at 50 rpm, we might naturally first try at 30 rpm, but not at 70 rpm. Some studies (Baker, Wylie and Gagné, 1950; Gibbs, 1951) have, in fact, suggested there would be greater transfer by starting at the higher speed. In part, this phenomenon appears to be a function of the task. Perhaps what happens is that there are techniques involved in performing the complex skill that are not included in the simple lead-up skills and, therefore, are hard to build into the more complex version. However, an individual may perform the simple skills better if those elements have already been performed within a complex skill.

Perhaps in learning a new or different movement pattern it is best to go directly to it and not use lead-up games, provided of course that the learner is (1) capable and (2) not discouraged. Of course, if the technique or skill involves many special cues (*e.g.,* tactics), it may be better to build it up bit by bit. One suggestion by May and Duncan (1973) is that changes in task difficulty may serve to focus attention on relevant aspects of the task. Thus, just as the factor of similarity could be put on a continuum, so can task difficulty. Tasks with a high cognitive component might be facilitated by changes in difficulty, whereas those with a high motor component might be inhibited.

There have also been some skill learning experiments in which the effects of changing the difficulty of a task by manipulating the equipment have been investigated (Jable, 1965). Jable, in a study using different weight basketballs, showed no difference in learning owing to the weight of the basketball. Working with lighter equipment was found to facilitate learning both in children (Wright, 1967) and adult women (Rhodes, 1963). Also, the use of a smaller ball in water polo facilitated skill learning in children (Pittuck & Dainty, 1979). Therefore, altering equipment to suit the needs of children is not going to interfere with learning and cause problems when those restrictions are removed. Shooting smaller balls at lower baskets simply allows the child to learn the proper technique that much earlier.

A summary of transfer literature by Oxendine (1968) included the following points:

1. Similar tasks allow transfer depending on the definition of identical or similar elements.
2. Response generalization leads to negative transfer, eliciting a new response to an old stimulus. When changing from a car with a standard transmission to one with an automatic transmission you may "change gears" in the second car only to find that you have depressed the brake. Bilateral transfer is likewise an expression of response generalization.
3. Stimulus generalization leads to positive transfer, eliciting an old response to a new stimulus. When we change from a car with one standard transmission to another, the gear lever (stimulus) may be slightly longer but the movements (response) are the same. This form of transfer is based on the classical conditioning type of experiment in which a dog, conditioned to respond to a tone, might salivate to similar tones.
4. Transfer is not automatic.
5. Understanding principles may help, although whether the effect is direct or motivational is not completely clear.
6. Transfer varies according to the difficulty of the skill, the stage of the learner, and the ability or capacity of the learner.

FEEDBACK AND KNOWLEDGE OF RESULTS

Before leaving the topic of practice factors, we should discuss what is considered to be one of the single most important variables in the learning situation, knowledge of results (KR). As Bartlett (1948) said: "It is practice, *the results of which are known*, that makes perfect." First we should distinguish between knowledge of results, knowledge of performance (KP), and feedback. Newell (1977) suggests that KR is some representation of the actual outcome obtained that is normally presented to the performer by the experimenter or teacher as some type of score.

It should be noted, however, that while KR is intrinsic to many "real world" tasks (we see the ball go into the goal), in most research studies that investigate the role of KR this source of (intrinsic terminal) feedback is denied the subject. Instead, KR is given to the subject in some other form, perhaps verbally, by the experimenter. For example, a blindfolded subject attempts to draw a 3-inch line and the experimenter provides the knowledge of the outcome for each trial. Although KR can be either intrinsic or extrinsic, in most studies KR is referred to as an extrinsic source of feedback. It is by relying on experimental procedures in which the experimenter provides the KR that we can investigate the role of KR in learning.

Types of feedback

Feedback refers to the information that the performer receives while performing a task or as a result of performing the task. The various types of feedback, how they are distinguished, and how they relate to KR are illustrated in Figure 3-6. Although there are many ways of labeling the various types of feedback, one simple division is *intrinsic*, that which is a direct consequence of performing the movement, and *extrinsic*, that which is artificially added and is not a direct consequence of performing the movement. Intrinsic feedback refers to all the information we are constantly receiving from our various senses as we move. It is this information that constitutes the perceptual trace, for example, what we hear, see, and feel. This intrinsic feedback can be further differentiated by whether it is evident during the movement (*e.g.*, how

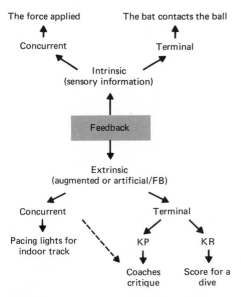

FIGURE 3-6 Different types of feedback.

strongly we push in a tackle), which is called *concurrent* feedback, or at the completion of the response or shortly afterward (*e.g.*, the feel of the grass, which tells you that you missed your tackle), known as *terminal* feedback.

Alternatively, feedback can be artificially augmented in order to high-light one important source of feedback for the learner or simply to provide the learner with additional feedback: this is extrinsic feedback. Again, these extrinsic sources of feedback can be concurrent or terminal. An example of concurrent feedback would be the pacing lights that are sometimes seen in indoor track meets to help the athletes challenge a particular record. Another example of the use of concurrent feedback was provided by Mathews and McDaniel (1962), who reported significant gains when using a "golf lite" in teaching the golf swing. The light when attached to the club would reflect the path of the club onto the floor, where the learner could see it, and concave or convex arcs would indicate to the learner a slice or a hook, respectively.

KR (knowledge of results) and KP (knowledge of performance in which the task analysis is provided by some observer) are classified as augmented terminal feedback. As in KR, some KP may also be inherent (intrinsic) in the task. The beginning skater quickly associates an upright position with a successful performance. KP, however, also represents the most common, and possibly useful, source of extrinsic feedback provided the learner by coaches and teachers. Hence, both KR and KP are identified in their most typical form as extrinsic feedback provided after the completion of the movement.

KR is concerned with the extent to which some external goal was achieved. Did you hit the bull's-eye and if not, by how much did you miss? However, *KP is concerned with the quality or efficiency of the pattern of movement produced.* Was the back overly arched in the handstand? One study by Howell (1956) found that subjects shown force-time graphs of their sprint starts showed greater improvement than a group instructed by conventional methods. This extrinsic terminal feedback about the movement itself repre-sents KP. KP could also include concurrent extrinsic feedback (*e.g.*, your position in relation to the pacing lights on an indoor running track).

The learning of most motor skills requires both KR and KP. We need KR to know if we were successful at the task and if changes need to be made in the movement we have selected, and we need KP in order to make those changes. We cannot change something if we do not know how we did it in the first place. For example, if we moved too quickly, perhaps too much force was applied. By knowing how the movement felt (the sensory consequences), the amount of force applied on the next trial could be reduced proportionately.

The type of information—visual, kinesthetic, or verbal—that would be most useful will depend on the task. Gentile (1972) argued that KP was more useful than KR to the performer, particularly in closed skills. In a sport such as diving, in which the performer is required to reproduce a particular movement, a single score (KR) gives minimal information on the success of performing the movement compared with a previous attempt and, in particular, how it may be improved. A videotape replay of the dive (KP) might be much more useful.

The utility of any particular type of augmented feedback varies with the task, as well as with the degree to which essential information is inherently available in that task. Failure to consider the appropriateness of the type of feedback to the task has led to many conflicting and non-significant findings in the literature. Clearly there are many ways to break down the information that may be made available to the learner. However, here we will deal mainly with KR.

Role of KR: frequency, precision, timing, withdrawal

KR has been described as one of the most potent variables in the learning situation, but many questions remain. Can we learn without KR, how often must it be provided, how accurate must it be, when should it be given, and what happens when it is withdrawn or unavailable? These are some of the questions that researchers have tried to answer. Adams (1971) relied on the importance of KR to support his closed-loop theory. To detect errors you must have knowledge of outcomes, so to some extent a description of the role of KR in learning outlines the impact of the error detection mechanism central to closed-loop theory. To consider the KR variable we will look at several questions (Adams, 1971; Schmidt, 1975a).

Question 1—Can we learn without KR?

In order to assess this question we will examine a study by Bilodeau, Bilodeau, and Schumsky (1959). They used a lever positioning task in which the correct response was a 33° displacement of a hidden lever. The experimental groups varied according to the extent to which they received KR. One group received no KR, another received KR after every trial, and two more received KR only after the first two or six trials. The study produced the pattern of results shown in Figure 3-7. In this figure it is clear that when we compare the no KR group to any other group there is no learning without some KR. Also, we note that in the two groups in which KR is withdrawn there is no further increase in learning once KR is withdrawn. Actually a slight drop off is registered. Therefore, the answer to our first question is no. We must recognize, however, that some form of KR is inherent in many motor skills. When we hear the thud of the ball hitting the catcher's glove we may not need to wait for the umpire to call "strike."

Question 2—How often should KR be given?

We have established that you need KR to learn, but if the two KR withdrawal groups in the previous experiment received further KR after the tenth trial, would they still lag behind the KR group? In an experiment using a knob-rotation task (Bilodeau & Bilodeau, 1958), four independent groups received

KR on every trial, every third trial, every fourth trial, or every tenth trial (Figure 3-8). From this study, it was found that errors were only reduced after KR trials, and this effect was the same for all groups (Figure 3-9). These results indicate that it is the *absolute frequency*, or total number of KR trials, that is the key rather than the *relative frequency*, or the number of trials between KR trials. Put simply, only when you provide KR can there be improvement, and the more frequently it is provided the greater the opportunity for improvement. There is no "magic" schedule.

Question 3—How important is the type or precision of the KR?

The question arises whether it is sufficient to describe the performance of a skill as good or bad or fast or slow, or whether it is necessary to be more specific. In a study by Trowbridge and Cason (1932), blindfolded subjects tried to reproduce a 3-, 4-, 5-, or 6-inch line over many trials. There were four groups for which the quality of the KR they were given varied. One group was given no KR and a second group was given a nonsense syllable after every trial. A qualitative KR group was simply told that they were right or wrong ($\pm 1/8$ inch was judged to be correct). The fourth group received quantitative KR (*e.g.*, "plus three" $= +3/8$ inch).

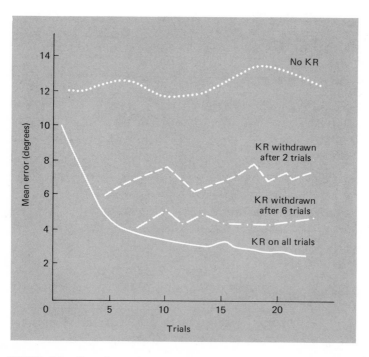

FIGURE 3-7 Can there be learning without KR? (after Bilodeau, Bilodeau & Schumsky, 1959).

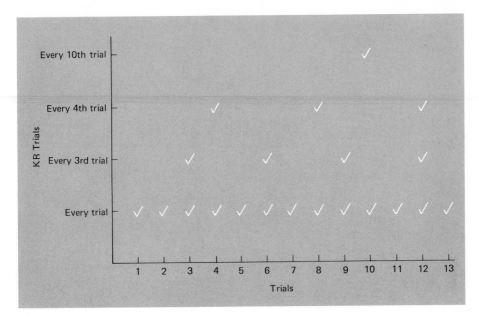

FIGURE 3-8   Frequency of KR (based on Bilodeau and Bilodeau, 1958).

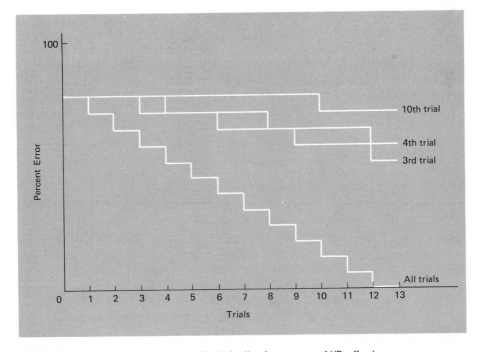

FIGURE 3-9   Hypothetical model to illustrate the frequency of KR effect.

You can try this experiment yourself by working with a partner. Using a blank sheet of paper and a ruler, try drawing an 8-inch line with your eyes closed (don't check the ruler first). Move gradually down the paper and repeat this exercise ten times, keeping your eyes closed all the time. For the next ten trials, ask your friend to tell you the exact length of each line you draw. Finally, do ten more trials without KR. The real subjects would draw over a thousand lines. Now compare your results to those from this experiment.

In the Trowbridge and Cason experiment, the following results were obtained (Figure 3-10). There was no learning in the no-KR group or in the group receiving nonsense syllables. The latter source of KR may even have caused interference as the subjects may have sought meaning from the nonsense syllables. In both the qualitative and quantitative KR groups there was learning evident, but it was much greater for the quantitative KR group. In other words, the more exact the KR the greater the learning, but there are limits to this gain.

Work by Rogers (1974) has suggested that not only may very precise KR produce no additional improvement in learning, it may even inhibit the learning in comparison to somewhat less precise KR. Knowing you are 0.258 inch from a target as compared with ¼ inch might inhibit learning. What is optimal KR in terms of precision would appear to be a function of both the task and the learner (Newell & Boucher, 1974). Knowing certain units of measurement—such as, how many pecks there are in a bushel*—may have little meaning for children.

*four

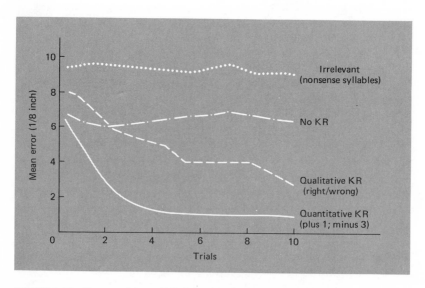

FIGURE 3-10 The precision of KR (after Trowbridge & Cason, 1932).

Question 4—When do we give KR?

We have mentioned that absolute frequency and quantitative KR are necessary elements in making the best use of KR. The question remains, however, of when to give KR during a series of practice trials.

To make this decision we must place KR within a time scale of a series of responses and consider the options (Figure 3-11). By drawing a time line graph to represent a series of free throws and placing KR at some point on that line, we create certain identifiable time intervals: the KR delay, post-KR delay and inter-response intervals. In the KR-delay interval, the subject is thought to store information about the task to use later to compare with KR. In the post-KR delay interval, the subject is thought to evaluate the KR in relation to the prior KR and formulate the next response. Using this model, experimentally, several findings have emerged:

1. Contrary to most animal research, extending the KR-delay interval appears to have little effect on the acquisition of a motor skill (Bilodeau & Ryan, 1960). It appears that instant information is not essential. The coach does not have to be standing behind the athletes in order to provide instantaneous KR after each response.
2. The main exception to the above statement is when the KR delay is longer than the inter-response interval, that is, when the athlete has performed R_2 and R_3 before getting the relevant KR for R_1 (Denny, Allard, Hall, & Rokeach, 1960). If the KR delay is longer than the inter-response interval, there is interference with the learning process. Put simply, KR given about the first throw after performing the tenth throw may be of little use to the learner.
3. The post-KR delay interval is needed to process information. If this interval is too short it could interfere with learning, since the learner may not have sufficient time to initiate the appropriate corrections

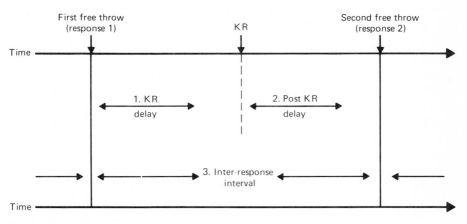

FIGURE 3-11   The three KR intervals.

(Weinburg, Guy, & Tupper, 1964). The optimum interval depends on the complexity of the task.

If a beginner in basketball is constantly missing the basket, the teacher should probably concentrate on form and provide the learner with KP. However, as the outcome of performance that is of primary concern to the learner is no longer immediately available, there is a greater role for KR. The KR could be qualitative, such as the coach saying, "that was correct," or quantitative, such as ranking the quality of the movement on a five-point scale. Thus, at the same time, KR is used to augment the feedback associated with the task and to motivate the learner and provide a means of assessing progress.

Question 5—Can performance be maintained if KR is withdrawn?

We have clearly seen the important role of KR in learning. The next important question is to what extent can performance be maintained when KR is no longer available? Can we do any useful skill training in the absence of a coach?

According to Adams' theory, an individual should be able to rely on the perceptual trace and, through subjective reinforcement, continue to learn after KR is withdrawn. In one experiment (Schmidt & Wrisberg, 1973), subjects were asked to move 20 inches in 200 msec. The first experimental group had visual, auditory, and kinesthetic feedback while performing the task, whereas the second group only had kinesthetic feedback. Vision was obscured with a blindfold, and sound was blocked by the use of white noise. At a certain point, KR was withdrawn from both groups. From the graph in Figure 3-12, we can see two main effects. First, despite having received only limited feedback during the learning phase, the second group was able to learn the task quite well with the use of KR. After KR was withdrawn however, it was clear that the normal feedback group, having developed a better perceptual trace, was able to maintain its performance better. However, they demonstrated no further learning and actually showed a small increase in the size of the errors.

Newell (1974), using a similar task (moving 9.5 inches in 150 msec) with a variety of groups and different numbers of acquisition trials, demonstrated that performance could be maintained for a short while after KR withdrawal. However, as a general conclusion, the decrement in performance after KR withdrawal appears to be an inverse function of the original number of KR trials. The fewer the number of trials, the weaker the perceptual trace and the greater the performance decrement.

One role of KR about which we have said little is its effect as a motivator. KR provides the learner with a means of judging the current level of performance and helps to establish future goals. Locke, Cartledge, and Koeppel (1968) suggested that, by evaluating the current level of performance in relation to some established standard, the learner tends to set very specific and difficult goals. Without KR, the standards tend to be lower and more vague.

Before closing we should note that recent work by Johnson, Wicks, and Ben-Sira (1980), using a transfer design, may lead to some modification in the interpretation of the role of KR. However, after considering the role of feedback in motor skill learning, it is clear that augmenting this feedback can be a valuable aid to learning, whether as a force-time graph (KP) or as a performance score (KR). To be most useful, this information must be as precise as possible, presented as close to the event as is feasible, and given as often as is practical.

MOTIVATION

This section is as short and concise as possible to motivate you to read it.

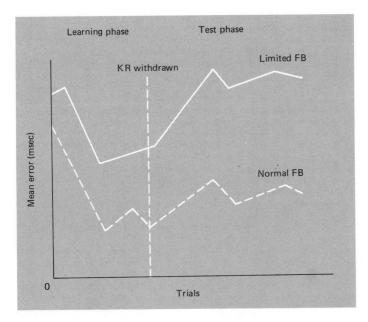

FIGURE 3-12   Withdrawal of KR (after Schmidt & Wrisberg, 1973).

In 1897, Norman Triplett wrote that competition was an activity that served to release "latent energy." He offered no explanation. Now we call that "latent energy" motivation. Sometimes it helps, sometimes it hinders, but without it (generally speaking) there can be no learning. Motivation is the essential ingredient in the learning situation that drives or pulls the learner over the barrier toward the final goal. It is this conflict between the desired goal and the barrier—the inability to successfully complete the task—that helps to create the motivation to learn.

Caskey (1968), looking at the effects of motivation on the performance of the standing broad jump in children, stated that "all other factors being equal, psychologic rather than physiologic factors may determine the limit of performance." Motivation represents a state of being aroused to action, of mobilizing your resources in order to move toward a goal. We have considered many practice factors that affect the learning of a motor skill, but now we will deal with a very personal aspect of learning, and one often not considered in the organization of a practice session—the individual's motivation.

Level of aspiration

As we have seen in Chapter 2, some learning theories are based on the factor of drive reduction or the satisfaction of individual needs. In physical education, the teacher is dealing mainly with secondary or psychological needs, which in turn encompasses the concept of goal setting or level of aspiration, one's personal expectations of performance. Aspiration level is usually related to some specific goal or task, as distinct from the more generalized need for achievement that reflects "life" goals. These are exemplified by what Maslow (1943) refers to as the notions of self-esteem and self-actualization or of feeling adequate and reaching one's potential. Obviously, these more general personality traits will exert an influence over the level of aspiration in regard to a particular task.

The final established level of aspiration is the result of solving a personal equation, an equation that represents the total of all the intrinsic and extrinsic factors impinging on the individual in a given situation. In turn, the level of aspiration becomes a factor in the personal equation that describes the individual's motivation to learn. One of the research problems is that what is stated by the learner may not always represent the true level of aspiration.

The level of aspiration is a personal factor based mainly on the interaction of the individual's self-concept and prior success and failure, particularly the latter. Success and failure mean different things to different people. Just because one class was successful, the teacher would not necessarily repeat the same class the next day. If you throw a discus 120 feet one day, you may feel successful. If you throw it 150 feet on the second day and 120 feet the third day, you may regard the third day as a failure, although earlier, 120 feet was a "success." Frank (1941) indicated that past successful experiences tend to raise the level of aspiration while past failures tend to lower it. Similarly, Gould (1961) suggested that past success can help maintain levels of aspiration when failure is encountered.

The level of aspiration may also change according to how individuals view themselves in relation to the outside world. One's self-concept may or may not be consistent with how the outside world perceives that individual. Generally speaking, a successful performance tends to enhance one's self-concept. Whether this is experienced in a physical education class depends on the standards used to measure success. Often an instructor may set high physical standards such that only the skilled succeed, and as a result many people are discouraged from participating. Instead of encouraging people to participate, standards set by physical education instructors often promote failure. The problem has been characterized as the "winning equals success and losing equals failure" syndrome.

This author had the privilege of attending the United States track-and-field trials for the 1972 Olympics. One of the highlights was to be Jim Ryun's comeback attempt after his failure to win a gold medal at the 1968 Olympics. Ryun entered the mile and half-mile events. In the 880 yards he was in the lead coming around the last bend; the crowd was on its feet; but in the last 20 yards he was passed by three other runners—all in record time. Ryun would not qualify for the Olympics in the 880 yards; the crowd labeled him as a "has-been." He was helped, almost carried, over to the practice field, where he appeared to collapse from his efforts. His last chance was the mile. Again Ryun was in the leading group as they came around the last bend, but this time he was not in the lead. This time it was Ryun who sprinted to the front and won the race. Ryun was full of life at the end of the race, and the crowd knew he would win a gold medal this time. From a loser to a winner, from a record time to an ordinary time: it does not matter how you play the game, it's whether you win or lose that counts. Such was the philosophy at this meet.

In the preliminary heats at the 1972 Olympics, Ryun was tripped by another runner. He fell heavily and, despite a gallant effort to get back into the race, failed to advance. In my book he was still a great miler. Another example is Ron Clarke of Australia, a great long-distance runner. He held, at one time or another, most of the world records for long-distance races, but he failed to win an Olympic gold medal. At all levels of competition, from the Olympics to Little League, there is a need for a realistic attitude toward success and performance. Without this, sports will no longer be positive and fun but will become negative and destructive.

So far we have noted the dangers of very high standards. However, Locke (1968) suggested that subjects faced with hard goals generally outperform subjects with easy goals, even though they attain the goals less frequently. Church and Camp (1965), who found similar results, perhaps found the key in that the goals were based on the subjects' previous performance, that is, they were not unrealistic.

Some of the other factors that affect the level of aspiration are parental standards (Rosen & D'Andrade, 1959) and social factors (Gould, 1961). Overall, when setting goals in physical education, the concepts of progressive goals and success would seem to be the key. We should try to set short-term attainable goals that encourage success.

Level of arousal

Closely related to level of aspiration is the level of arousal for motivation, often thought of as being represented by an increase in the level of arousal.

The inverted U hypothesis suggests a close relationship between the level of arousal and performance (Figure 3-13), with increased arousal leading to improved performance up to some optimal level. For example, when coaching a football team, if the motivational level of the team is low, a pre-game pep talk might be useful, producing high motivation and hopefully high performance. On the other hand, it has been found that wrestlers tend to be highly motivated individuals, so in this case it may be better to have no pep talk immediately prior to competition. It would appear easier to "psych up" a performer than to calm down that same performer (Cureton, 1959), and there is evidence that emotional overstimulation before competition or during rest intervals can hinder rather than aid performance (Harmon & Johnson, 1952). What is suitable appears to depend on (1) the nature of the skill and (2) the stage of the learner. We will now look a little closer at these two factors.

NATURE OF THE SKILL. According to the *Yerkes-Dodson law*, simple skills are facilitated by a high drive, or level of motivation, but for complex skills a low

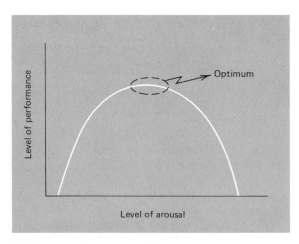

FIGURE 3-13 Inverted U hypothesis.

drive is better. Often in team sports we see apparently skilled athletes execute poorly certain basic passing skills. After the basketball player completes a beautiful reverse "dunk," the next chest pass goes flying over a teammate's head. Too often, skilled, or advanced, athletes believe that simple fundamental skills are below them, producing the events just described. However, the sign of a true professional is that simple skills are executed precisely every time.

Deese (1965) has proposed a more precise way to consider the effect of stress. Stress in this sense may be considered as an extreme level of motivation or arousal. Deese suggested that the various abilities or factors proposed by Fleishman (1954) as representative of separate components within a skill may be affected differently by stress. Fleishman had proposed that motor skills could be analyzed and categorized in terms of the various motor abilities that were necessary to perform that skill. Fleishman (1972a) was concerned with trying to identify what those abilities were. He identified two broad categories: (1) psychomotor abilities (fine motor skills) and (2) physical proficiency abilities (gross motor skills). Some of the psychomotor abilities are arm-hand steadiness, speed of arm movement, and multilimb coordination. In the physical proficiency category are such abilities as explosive strength, dynamic flexibility, and gross body equilibrium. Because any particular skill may involve several of these abilities, the overall effect of stress on that skill will be a composite of the net effect on each of the separate factors (Figure 3-14). For example, if stress increased movement speed but decreased limb steadiness, then high arousal would be great for blocking but the increased tremor would not be so good for putting, assuming that movement speed and limb steadiness were the two major abilities involved in those skills.

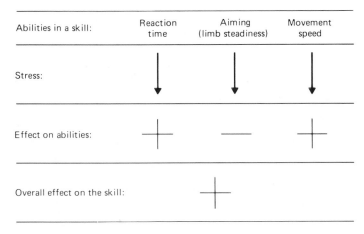

FIGURE 3-14   A model to show the effect of stress on a hypothetical motor skill.

STAGE OF LEARNING. The second factor involved in the idea of arousal is based on drive theory. *Drive theory* suggests that high levels of arousal will tend to elicit the dominant response. In the beginner, the dominant response is the incorrect response; but for the advanced performer, the dominant response will be the correct response. Thus, while the stress of being tested may lead the beginning tennis player to use a loose wrist action, it may result in the professional player placing the backhand passing shot right on the line. Levels of emotional stability that are effective for performance by experienced athletes may inhibit efficient performance in the beginner or non-athlete (Arnold, 1945).

In addition, as Fleishman (1972*a*) has mentioned, the abilities underlying skilled performance may change as the skill is learned. Because there is no nice smooth continuum, it is difficult to generalize. As a practical, easily obtainable indicator of pre-activity motivation, the most useful tool, when compared with established individual norms, is the resting pulse rate (Howell, 1953). Less practical, but more valid, would be the EMG or galvanic skin response.

A possible model

In order to pull together some of these aspects, we will consider a possible model based on the factors involved in motivation. One such model was described by Atkinson (1965). In his attempt to explain the components of need achievement, he proposed the following formula:

$$T_s = M_s \times P_s \times I_s$$

T_s = the interest in the task,
M_s = the motivation to achieve success,
P_s = the subjective probability of success, and
I_s = the incentive value.

As the motivation to achieve success is a personality factor and is fairly fixed, we can only manipulate the subjective probability of success and the incentive value of the task. The subjective probability of success is a function of the task difficulty. If it is too easy or too hard, it will not arouse the individual. Likewise, if a task is not valued, it will not motivate (incentive value). On the other hand, some people are described as motivated to avoid failure. Failing at a difficult task is not as embarrassing as failing at an easy task. For example, athletes may be more concerned with avoiding being cut from the team rather than with achieving success (Deshaies, Pargman, & Thiffault, 1979). It is important to recognize that not everyone seeks success. This in itself may be one argument for ability groupings, although in the past these have tended to fail because of outside labeling (*e.g.*, when students label a group of slow learners as the "dummy" class).

To conclude this section, we will borrow the above formula to recombine the various elements of motivation that have been discussed so far (Figure 3-15) to form a possible composite model representing the main factors.

In assessing a learner's interest in a given task (T_s), the first factor to consider is the motivation to achieve success or avoid failure (M_s or M_f). Whether the individual's drive is based more on internal or external influences is a question of personality. The learner may see certain motor skills as a means of fulfillment (self-actualization), as a means of gaining peer recognition ("glory"), or as a means of maintaining membership in the group or team (to avoid failure). The next factor relates to the subjective probability of success (P_s)—"Is this going to be a very difficult task for me (with my ability level) or very simple?" Whether the answer to this question increases or decreases the level of arousal will to some extent depend on the first factor, the motivation to achieve success or avoid failure. The incentive value of the task (I_s) is the next factor. "I know this task is beyond my present skill level and I will fail on my first try, but I know that in the past by persevering I have eventually overcome some very difficult problems. I think I can, I know I can, and as a first step I am going to. . . ."

Finally, we will consider the on/off switch or the types of motivating

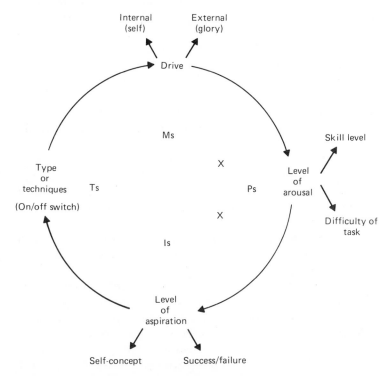

FIGURE 3-15 A composite model for motivation.

techniques used. We will look at one study that, although it is not meant to be all inclusive, does include some of the most common techniques used. Nelson (1962) had ten experimental groups of college students in his study of motivation. All the subjects were students in different activity classes at the University of Oregon. Their task was to exercise to the point of exhaustion on an elbow flexion task (against resistance). Thus, the task emphasized endurance rather than the quality of the performance. They exercised at one-fourth of their maximum lift at a rate of 38 repetitions per minute, to the beat of a metronome. The groups varied according to the instructions/information given to them immediately before being tested for the experiment. The majority, except where stated, were tested in an isolated testing room in the presence of the experimenter.

The experimental groups were divided according to the following factors:

1. Normal (control) groups.
2. Verbal encouragement. The experimenter used some of the coach's traditional vocabulary, the verbal appeal, to keep going.
3. Individual competition. Subjects were tested in pairs, being aware of each other's scores.
4. Group competition. The subjects in this group were told they were competing against the other groups, that is, the other activity classes.
5. Obtainable goal. From the initial testing an above average score was established and given to the subjects as a goal to achieve.
6. Observer's presence. During the testing a man dressed in a suit, carrying a briefcase, and trying to look important would enter the room and observe the testing.
7. Instructor's interest. The instructors from the subjects' activity groups would indicate an interest in the students' participation and anticipated performance prior to the testing.
8. Ego involvement. Subjects were shown test scores of other college students but were told that these were scores for 15-year-old boys.
9. Air Force space program. Subjects were told they were helping to set standards for the United States space program (note the date of the study).
10. Competition with Russians. Subjects were told that there was a duplicate study being conducted at the same time in Russia and that the data were to be compared.

After analyzing all the data, the best performance was found in groups 8, 9, and 3 (ego involvement, Air Force space program, individual competition). An intermediate level of performance was found in groups 10, 5, 4, and 6 (competition with Russians, obtainable goal, group competition, observer's presence), and the lowest performance was found for groups 7, 2, and 1 (instructor's interest, verbal encouragement, control). Overall, group 1 (control) had the poorest performance and group 8 (ego involvement), the highest, but the latter group was also the most variable. All the methods clearly helped performance, with the fictitious settings producing the better results, but obviously they are not really practical.

Competition would seem to be the most effective practical motivator for an endurance task, at least according to this study. Although from an educational point of view, considering some of the previously mentioned dangers evolving from creating too many losers, some might prefer the use of an obtainable goal. Strong (1963), working with children in Grade 6, has indicated that, when compared with self-competition and competition against others, the most effective condition was for the children to set their own goals.

Another common teaching technique is the use of praise or criticism. There is much evidence to show that both types of reinforcement, positive or negative, can be effective. Willcutt and Kennedy (1964) suggested that too much of either would be detrimental to learning and that the most appropriate approach would be a balance between praise and criticism. They also noted that as the learner becomes older and more skilled, the importance of extrinsic motivation decreases. This is interesting in light of the work by Rushall and Pettinger (1969) in which the highly effective use of extrinsic rewards (candy and money) in motivating swimmers 9 to 15 years of age was emphasized. A note of caution was sounded, however, by Deci (1971), who found that the use of extrinsic rewards could reduce the level of intrinsic motivation. Thus, while extrinsic rewards can be very effective in the short term, an over-reliance on such techniques could serve to limit improvement in the long term. The problem is finding a means to develop the level of intrinsic motivation. Perhaps the answer might be found in a suggestion made by Goldfarb (1968): "He who would kindle another must glow himself."

SUMMARY

When considering the effect of selected practice factors on motor skill learning we should recognize that we are primarily concerned with learning and not with performance. Therefore, it is important to distinguish between those variables that affect performance as distinct from learning. For example, the performance decrements seen as a result of physical fatigue or mental fatigue (I_r) within a massed practice and warm-up decrement (WUD) within a distributed practice appear to have little permanent effect on learning. Recovery from performance and WUDs, particularly between practices, is often seen as an example of reminiscence. Similarly, temporary changes in performance may be produced by either the teacher changing the instructions for a task ("when you practice the free throw, don't worry about scoring, just concentrate on the wrist action"), or temporary shifts in the motivation level ("it's been a bad day; you miss your first attempt; you keep trying but your heart is not in it''). Put another way, the human machine is quite flexible and in less than ideal conditions can still produce effective learning.

Practice organization

PRACTICE DISTRIBUTION.   The two main questions here are the organization of the work-rest ratio *within* a practice session and the length of time *between* practice sessions. In either case, practices can be *massed* or *distributed*. Massing practice within a session gives more total practice time on the task but produces performance decrements due to physical and mental fatigue. A distributed work-rest ratio avoids these problems, but there is less total time given to the task. Since, as Adams and Reynolds (1954) suggest, the long-range negative effects of massed practice are usually minimal, the proper recommendation would appear to be to include as much work within a practice session as the learner can handle. In regard to between practice scheduling, the best alternative would appear to be an additive schedule, with the relative massing of practices early in learning and the gradual distributing of practice over time.

TASK STRUCTURE.   Here the main choice is between teaching the whole skill or teaching the separate parts of the skill first or some combination of both. The answer as to which method to use depends on the capacity of the learner and on the nature of the task. Because a child's perceptual and integrative capacities are different from an adult's, one tries to teach the whole skill or as large a part as the learner can handle. However, the nature of the task may dictate the method. The two factors here are task complexity (the demands placed on memory) and task organization (the interrelationships of the component parts). High-organizational tasks require greater emphasis on whole learning, while high-complexity tasks necessitate part learning. The organization of the parts within a task may be serial, continuous, or discrete. Only the former may require a part learning method.

TYPE OF PRACTICE.   One of the often ignored alternatives to physical practice is mental practice. Mental practice can serve to review a skill prior to performance, to rehearse various responses, or to consolidate or organize prior learning by focusing on key elements. In this way, mental practice may be thought of as another source of augmented feedback. Although mental practice alone is seldom equivalent to physical practice, it is always a most useful addition. However, it must be remembered that mental practice is also a skill itself and the learner will need some direction in order to take full advantage of this capability.

Transfer

Transfer refers to the effect that learning one skill has on prior or future learning. The two main approaches to transfer are represented by the S-R identical elements theory and the more cognitivist notion of general principles. In the former, the emphasis is on similarities between how the movements in two sports are produced; in the latter, it is more a case of when to use a particular version of a skill. There is research evidence to support both arguments.

BILATERAL TRANSFER. Sometimes referred to as cross-education, bilateral transfer is the transfer of skill between limbs. This phenomenon has been explained both from a physiological and a psychological point of view. However, it would seem that most of the transfer can be explained in terms of the overall cognitive organization of the task, which muscles to use being only one small part of that organization.

INTERTASK TRANSFER. Intertask transfer is transfer of learning from one task to another. Although the evidence for positive transfer is mixed, there appears to be little evidence of negative transfer between skills. Also, providing mechanical or general principles may not always aid learning, but it certainly would not appear to be detrimental. The practical solution would appear to be to teach for transfer, because the potential benefits far outweigh the possible losses.

INTRATASK TRANSFER. Intratask transfer occurs between different versions of the same skill. There is some evidence to suggest that for skills that emphasize rhythm or flow, going directly to the more difficult version of the skill may be better than the traditional progressive build-up from simple to complex, provided, of course, that the learner is both capable and not discouraged. Also, equipment changes may facilitate the learning process in children without necessitating a complete relearning of the skill when the adult equipment is reintroduced.

A simple model (Blais, 1979) to describe transfer follows. Assuming that the variables that constitute the similarity and difficulty of a task could be measured quantitatively, the amount of transfer would be a function of transfer = similarity + difficulty + other factors.

In the similarity component, we would need to consider such factors as stimulus generalization and response generalization. The difficulty component involves consideration of the amount of practice and the number of tasks practiced at different levels of difficulty. In the "others" category would appear such factors as the capacity of the learner, which might be measured by the number of schemes (Pascuale-Leone) the child could handle. Of course, the influence of any of these factors could be positive or negative, but only by taking all the factors into account can the potential amount of transfer be assessed.

Feedback and knowledge of results

In most learning situations, the learner receives both intrinsic and extrinsic feedback. The intrinsic feedback that the learner receives from all the senses during the performance of a skill and immediately after its termination are what would constitute the major sources of input into the perceptual trace (Adams' theory). In addition, this feedback may be augmented from external sources (e.g., the coach). Into this category fall the two most common types of augmented feedback: knowledge of performance (KP) and knowledge of results (KR). The former is concerned with how the skill was performed in relation to the desired movement, and the latter provides information about the extent to which the desired outcome of the movement was achieved. The more precise, contiguous, and frequent the augmented feedback, the greater the potential gains and the greater the likelihood that the learner can maintain the performance level over a period without augmented feedback. Comparison of intrinsic and extrinsic feedback during the learning phase should facilitate the development of an appropriate error detection mechanism (Adams' theory).

Motivation

Basic differences lie in the individual's personality, whether one is motivated to achieve success or avoid failure, to fulfill one's own potential (intrinsic) or to gain glory and recognition (extrinsic). These factors are difficult to manipulate; more amenable are factors concerned with the levels of aspiration and arousal.

The level of aspiration, or goal setting, is a function of the individual's self-concept and prior success and failure. An atmosphere of failure can severely reduce an individual's aspiration level, even below his or her known potential. The two keys are progressive attainable goals and success.

The level of arousal, when increased, leads to improved performance within certain limits. The limits are set by (1) the nature of the skill, in particular its components, and how it reacts to stress and (2) the stage of the learner. As arousal tends to elicit the dominant response, it could inhibit learning in the beginner.

One of the most common motivational techniques is competition. However, considering the danger of the loser syndrome, an equally effective and more educationally acceptable technique would be setting individual goals. A similar argument applies to the development of intrinsic or extrinsic motivation. Although extrinsic rewards can be very effective in the short term, they may mediate against long-term participation. Intrinsic motivation may not be as easy to develop or as immediately effective, but it does provide a firmer foundation on which to build if we are to achieve lifetime sports participation or advanced levels of performance.

PROBLEM

Question

What are some of the factors to be considered when as a student teacher you are given the job of organizing a six-week games unit (soccer-basketball-volleyball) for Grade 5 children with daily physical education classes?

Possible answer

While not providing the detail to construct daily lesson plans, the following are some of the important factors. First, when considering the nature of the tasks involved, we should look for similarities and differences. For example, there are similar principles involved in the passing skills of basketball and soccer and in the technique of jumping to head the ball (soccer), of spiking (volleyball), and of taking a jump shot (basketball). On the other hand, although there may be similarities in the hand position for a chest pass or a volley, catching and carrying the ball are definitely to be avoided in volleyball. Thus, while there are some possibilities for the transfer of principles and techniques, there is at least one area of possible "negative" transfer. Also, as the majority of the tasks in all these sports are serial in nature, the part method will dominate.

Given the anticipated lack of experience and stage of the learner (beginner), it is likely that you will emphasize the part method (there will of course be regional differences). As Grade 5 children are approaching the adult capacity in terms of the number of schemes or bits of information they can handle at the same time, they should be able to handle some simple "whole" skills (*e.g.*, the chest pass). Also, since you are working with beginners, it is important not to create stress, because the dominant response is likely to be an incorrect one.

In terms of practice organization, it would be additive between sessions and massed within a session, focusing on techniques early in learning and on principles later on.

Daily Schedule: S, soccer; B, basketball; V, volleyball

1-3 4-6 7/8 9/10 11-13 14 15 16/17 18 19 20 21 22 23 24 25, etc.

 S   B   S   B   V   S   B   V   S V B S V B S V

Augmented feedback, such as KR, could be provided by using standard skill tests to assess progress, with the individuals competing against each other or working to some established goal. KP could be provided by using partners to focus on one point of the style—giving more immediate and frequent KP. The precision feedback would come from the ever-mobile teacher.

The role KP or KR can play as a motivator has already been mentioned. Also, to maintain interest within a session, it would be useful to vary the number and type of activities, while focusing on certain specific techniques. Overall, de-emphasize winning and losing in game situations, do not keep score, and encourage personal effort and excellence.

Chapter 4
Retention and Forgetting

This space was reserved
for a quote from Prather,
but I forgot it.

In the first three chapters, we have dealt with the learning process and the practice factors that affect learning. Learning is defined as a relatively permanent change in performance; implicit in this definition is the idea that something is retained or stored. Therefore, in this chapter we will first look at some general points concerned with retention and forgetting and, second, at the main subdivision of memory from an information processing viewpoint. The ability to retain a motor task quite efficiently over a long period of no practice appears to provide one of the distinctions between motor and verbal skills. Purdy and Lockhart (1962), in a study using five novel motor tasks, found excellent retention after 1 year without practice. However, as the main aim of this chapter is to outline some of the major characteristics of retention and forgetting, much of the evidence presented will be based on verbal learning. Motor memory will be discussed in more detail in Chapter 7.

Retention and forgetting would appear, to some extent, to be mutually exclusive. You cannot forget what you have not retained. There are two ways memory can be weakened: (1) the stored information is lost from memory—forgetting or (2) the information fails to enter memory or be stored properly—

retention. In much of the literature, however, the two terms are used inter-changeably.

Expressed simply, *retention is the persistence of a skill over a period of no practice; forgetting* is the reverse, or *the failure to retain information.* Paradoxically, we can investigate the same problem by considering those processes that either increase retention or increase forgetting. In terms of retention, there are two ways of assessing what is retained: (1) qualitative—evaluating style and (2) quantitative—determining the amount retained. Regardless of how we measure retention, over a long period of time the typical retention curve would be represented as in Figure 4-1 on page 100. This curve really represents the rate of forgetting. It is suggested that the curve would not actually reach the baseline if the measurement techniques were sufficiently refined.

When we look instead at short-term retention, there are certain changes found in this curve. Try testing yourself by reading one of the following lists. Read only once and then immediately write down all the items you can recall without looking back at the list.

(a)	(b)	(c)
rock	boot	antler
heart	ball	brail
limb	puck	jangle
belt	goal	realm
ride	foul	lentil
coat	putt	cogent
tree	deuce	decade
house	down	hangar
time	hook	savory
river	slash	tawdry
roof	dive	preface
book	bird	morass
train	skate	engram

The serial position curve in Figure 4-2 illustrates the typical performance in a short-term retention experiment. Compare this curve with your own results. For such a list of items, subjects normally recall best those items presented early in the list and the final one or two in the list and forget many of the items in between. These phenomena are referred to as the *primacy* and *recency effects.* Considering the lists presented here, persons with a back-ground in sports may find list *b* easiest, and list *c* most difficult. The degree of non-familiarity or familiarity with the items can inhibit or facilitate retention, and overall the curve may not be as smooth as one based on a list of nonsense syllables.

Wilberg and Salmela (1973) attempted to duplicate these findings using a motor skill—the movement of a two-dimensional joystick. Their experiment

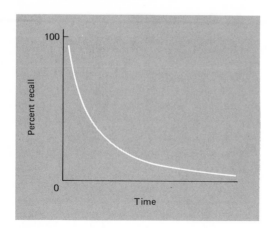

FIGURE 4-1 Typical retention curve.

did not produce the traditional serial position curve, but this curve is commonly found in the verbal literature. Obviously, if we cannot hold onto information even for a short period of time, it is unlikely to enter our long-term storage. So, by extension, the above example might suggest that when teaching or coaching we make our important points either at the beginning or at the end of the session.

At this point, we should note the difference between short-term retention and short-term memory. Experiments in short-term memory are concerned directly with the functions of that store; that is, learn some information and

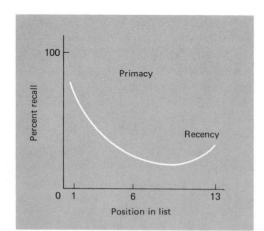

FIGURE 4-2 Serial position curve.

then reproduce it after a filled or unfilled retention interval. Short-term retention is a more general concept and includes intervals of a few minutes that, while short, are greater than the established limits of short-term memory. For example, the primacy effect seen in the short-term retention curve is attributed to information entering long-term memory.

RETENTION

We have defined retention and seen the typical retention curves; next we will examine some of the ways in which we measure retention.

Measures of retention

Recall and recognition represent the two most common techniques for assessing retention. A third alternative is relearning.

RECALL.   Testing for recall is perhaps *the most common method.* A subject learns a list of words and then tries to repeat it. If we are dealing with a motor skill, certain responses are tested. The person is either right or wrong; you know the answer or you do not. Motor skills are in some ways a little easier to score, because even a poor attempt still represents some minimal level of skill (*e.g.,* in throwing a discus 30 feet some part of the skill must be evident). However, in many cases the scoring system still only allows for a hit or a miss (*e.g.,* in basketball).

   Although recall is the obvious way to test retention, it is also *the least precise measure.* As we saw in our discussion of learning and performance, if only a few test trials are given, there is a danger that a "fluke" performance might give a false indication of what has been retained. Thus, if recall is the only method of measuring retention for a particular task, then there should be enough trials to see whether the performance score is consistent.

   Alternatively, it might be possible to be more precise by devising your own scoring system. O'Hara (1977) suggested a scoring system for free throw shooting in basketball that took into account hitting the back, front, left, or right of the rim of the basket. Thus, a basket might now count 4 points; back or front of the rim, 2 points; the side of the rim, 1 point; and only complete misses, zero points. Also, a secondary grading system might be established for style, in which points are given on a scale of 1 to 5 according to use of the wrist, the position of the elbow, and other pertinent coaching points. Functionally, the aim is to devise a test that is precise and within your power to administrate and that measures what you want it to measure.

RECOGNITION.   The most common test of recognition is the multiple choice exam. *The chances of producing the correct answer are somewhat greater, because the correct answer is made available to you.* In sports skills you could provide cues for a particular strategy or set play in the game. Although you may not have perfect recall, you may have retained sufficient information that when given a "clue" you can make the correct decision. For example, you may not be able to list all the factors necessary for a perfect "give and go" situation, but you may still be able to recognize the opportunity to use this play when it occurs during the game. A two-on-one situation involving a defender, for example, will test whether that individual has remembered how to use the various techniques taught.

RELEARNING.   The most sensitive measure of retention is relearning. Even when retention registered zero by recall or recognition methods, relearning techniques may demonstrate retention. This technique was used by Swift (1906), who found that while it took him 55 days to learn to type, it only took him 11 days to achieve the same standard two years later. The relearning technique implies that if you can learn a skill quicker the second time around, then you have saved time. The implication is that you are faster the second time as a result of something you retained from the original learning. Therefore, *retention is measured as the degree of savings (%) economy in the effort to learn.* If it took you 80 trials to reach some criterion performance the first time but only 40 trials the second time, that is a 50% savings.

One problem inherent in the relearning technique is that the learner with a high skill level will tend to achieve the standard much quicker than the low-skilled individual. The low-skilled person who took a long time initially to learn the task is likely to show more improvement on the retest, simply because there is that much more room for improvement. This problem could be avoided by adjusting the standards or criterion according to the skill level. Although relearning is the most precise measure of retention, it is perhaps the least used, simply because of the time required to use such a measurement. However, the less precise our measurement techniques are, the less dependable are our conclusions. Thus, the decision as to what technique to use must be related to the importance of making a precise evaluation.

Theories of forgetting

Having considered briefly some of the ways of measuring retention, we will now review some of the theories of retention or, alternatively, the causes of forgetting. The two major causes of forgetting are thought to be decay and interference. These theories form the two main theoretical explanations of forgetting, and two other theories are information overload and repression.

DECAY THEORY.   Decay theory is based on the law of disuse (Thorndike) or on the idea that in time the "memory trace" decays (Brown, 1958). It is usually much easier to recall information closer to the event. One problem with this theory is that we can sometimes recall "long forgotten" names, perhaps because they burned a deep groove in our memory. There is also some evidence (Murdock, 1960, 1965) to suggest that as the time over which the information is presented increases, so does the amount of information that is retained. Some minimal time does appear to be a factor in allowing the information to be properly registered in long-term memory, but time alone does not appear to be a sufficient explanation for forgetting.

INTERFERENCE THEORY: Interference theory provides the main alternative explanation of forgetting and considers the effect of interpolated activities on learning, that is, proactive and retroactive interference (Guthrie). Strong evidence for this theory is found in verbal learning (Underwood, 1957). As we have seen in the section on transfer, there is little evidence for proactive and retroactive interference in physical education, least of all for proactive interference. However, movement activities performed between the learning and reproduction of a movement have been shown to cause interference in short-term motor memory experiments (Pepper & Herman, 1970). Perhaps the appropriate interpretation would be a combination of these two positions. Thus, we would see the quality of the retained information slowly deteriorating over time and, in the process, becoming more susceptible to interference (confusion) from other pieces of information as they enter the memory system.

There is also some evidence that the act of recall itself may interfere with the stored information (Belbin, 1950). The recalled version of the information, including any errors or distortions, is fed back into the long-term memory store and becomes part of the permanent record. We have all heard the complaint, "the story gets better every time it is told." It would seem a reasonable assumption that the same process would apply to motor skills. If, in the practice session without a coach, a gymnast started throwing back handsprings with a slight twist, it might be a very difficult process to correct this fault. The problem encountered when trying to correct the fault is in identifying the difference between this new "twisted" perceptual trace and the correct perceptual trace that the gymnast has lost. The only answer may be to establish a new correct perceptual trace by starting to learn the skill from the beginning.

INFORMATION OVERLOAD. Information overload relates particularly to the limited capacity of short-term memory. As you increase the amount of information entering short-term memory, you must eliminate some of the information previously stored; therefore, the information is lost and it cannot go into long-term memory. Melton (1963) pointed out that it was not simply a combination of time and a lack of rehearsal that produced forgetting in short-term memory. More important is how close the short-term memory store is to capacity and whether the incoming information can be "chunked." If short-term memory is fully occupied, then little of the new information will be retained in long-term memory because it cannot get past the bottleneck caused by the limited capacity of short-term memory.

REPRESSION THEORY.   The suggestion here is that we repress, rather than forget, unpleasant experiences. Forgetting is not a loss of information but a breakdown in the retrieval process, and, therefore, under shock we may remember those experiences. There is some evidence to support the idea that electrical stimulation of the brain produces lost or forgotten items (Penfield & Roberts, 1959). Also, under hypnosis subjects may recall in great detail apparently trivial events from their childhood. What is most important about the repression theory is the idea that we never actually forget information once it has entered long-term memory. This would require a large storage capacity but certainly one within the capacity of the human brain. It would also suggest that the problem is not one of retention or forgetting but one of storing of information (encoding) and retrieval.

The several theories outlined all reflect some aspect of forgetting, but as yet there is no clear-cut theory, particularly for motor skills. On the other hand, we do have some clear ideas about the factors affecting retention.

Factors in retention

The three most obvious factors are the degree of original learning, the nature of the skill, and attention.

DEGREE OF ORIGINAL LEARNING.   Stated simply, the greater the initial level of proficiency that is achieved in the performance of a skill, the greater is the retention (Fleishman & Parker, 1962). We have already considered the influence of original learning in our discussion of negative transfer in Chapter 3 (Lewis, McAllister, & Adams, 1951).

Closely related to the question of degree of original learning is the idea of *overlearning*, or the continued practice after the skill is learned. The theory of overlearning states that we continue practice once a skill is established not so much to improve the skill itself but to "set" or reinforce the learning. In Adams' terms, overlearning might be seen as establishing a clearer definition of the perceptual trace or, in terms of drive theory, making the correct response more dominant. For example, if it takes 50 attempts to learn a skill such as a vertical entry for a basic dive, 50 additional attempts represents 100% overlearning; others might define this as 200% of the original learning.

In one study (Melnick, 1971), using a balance test, 50%, 100%, and 200% overlearning were found to be equally effective and better than no overlearning when measured in terms of absolute retention scores. In a practical situation, this suggests that 50% overlearning would be the most efficient to promote retention. Melnick also found that 200% over-learning was best for retention when retention was measured as the degree of savings, that is, the amount of time or number of trials "saved" when the skill is relearned.

Before applying the overlearning theory, we should note the limitation referred to earlier in this chapter regarding fast and slow learners. The more trials it takes to learn a skill initially, the greater the number of trials involved in overlearning. Of course you have to be aware of the dangers of fatigue and, as a result, of poor learning technique. Even though you may wish to use a skill when fatigued, there is some evidence to suggest that it is better to practice the skill under "ideal" conditions (Barnett, Ross, Schmidt, & Todd, 1973). There is a tendency when teaching motor skills to learn a skill and move on. The concept of overlearning would suggest that perhaps more time should be given to the consolidation or review of previously learned skills, thereby progressing a little slower but establishing a firmer base.

NATURE OF SKILL.   The nature of the skill is perhaps the other key variable in retention. A study by Purdy and Lockhart (1962) in which they examined the retention of five novel motor tasks revealed 94% retention over a one-year period without practice. We might ask, do we spend *too much* time on reviewing some skills? The answer to this question lies in the fact that motor skills do not always behave in the manner suggested by verbal learning. Why? Some part of the answer may be found in (1) the type of task—continuous vs discrete; (2) patterning—temporal and spatial; and (3) the meaningfulness of the material.

Type of task.   It is often difficult to compare the retention of different tasks. Continuous skills, such as swimming or riding a bicycle, by their repetitive nature acquire more practice of the actual movement in a given amount of time than serial skills. Thus, the factor of overlearning is inherent in these continuous tasks and facilitates their retention. By contrast, serial skills are often judged by their end result and not by the quality of the movement, as in a basketball jump shot or volleyball spike. In this case the method of measuring retention, success or failure, might imply poor retention of the skill when the sequence of movements itself was actually retained quite well but the variation of the movement selected did not produce the desired outcome. Generally, we retain continuous tasks best and serial tasks worst, with discrete tasks in between.

Patterning.   The timing or temporal patterning of the skill and the sequencing or spatial organization of the task are referred to here. It seems that the actual sequence of movements is retained better than the timing. Therefore, we find that we can ride a bicycle after many years without practice, but we wobble a lot. Similarly, in our examples of a serial skill, the basketball shot may look quite good; however, because the timing is inappropriate, we release the ball too early and hit the backboard instead of the basket or we strike the spike too soon and put the ball over the end line. This, in turn, suggests that when skills are reviewed we should concentrate on the timing aspect. Let the skill flow, but provide extra cues for when to spike or when to open up from a double back somersault off the high bar.

Meaningfulness of material. The more organized or structured the material, the better is the retention. Organizing the material allows the individual to fit what is being learned now with any previous instruction or experience. Gagné and Foster (1949) found positive transfer when they used a picture representation to provide greater understanding of a complex motor task. Their findings support the idea that a coach should demonstrate plays in the game situation and not just in isolation. A "give and go" play (basketball) in which there are five pairs of hands (the opposing team) ready to intercept either pass—if their defensive assignments allow them—is more realistic than a two-on-one situation.

ATTENTION. The final factor that may be one of the most important, even more so than the amount of practice, is the quality of the individual's attention during the learning process. James (1890) described attention as ". . . the taking possession by the mind, in clear and vivid form, of one out of what seem several simultaneously possible objects or trains of thought. Focalization, concentration of consciousness are of its essence. It implies withdrawal from some things in order to deal effectively with others."

A subject who is told that he will be tested on a task retains it better than a subject who is unaware of this factor. Such instructions affect the quality or detail of the model that is retained. This is similar to the phenomenon known as the *Von Restorff effect,* which states that if one of the items to be remembered is notably different from any of the other items, this item tends to be retained better (Posner & Rossman, 1965). We often see this technique used in texts in which key words are set in **boldface** type. This method is effective not because it improves memory but because it redistributes attention so more time is given to the key item. As a result, the un-cued or incidental information will be less well retained (Hershberger & Terry, 1965).

The question of attention and, in particular, attention span is most critical with children. The problem is to find the right mix of intense activity, rest, and variety for any given age level. The whole theory behind the traditional, "be quiet, sit up straight, and look at me," was to try to ensure that you had their attention. However, the factor of attention is tied very closely to the amount of motivation the learner has in regard to a particular task.

IMAGERY

We have dealt already with the potential gains to be made from mental practice. Mental practice involves the use of imagery as the learner tries to relearn the skill. Because the learner is trying to rehearse a model stored in memory, this technique is linked closely to retention. Most of the work on imagery is based on verbal literature, but it does have implications for the learning of motor skills. The two main features in imagery are organization and meaning.

Organization

An important topic related to retention is the question of imagery. Although we are dealing with the retention of *motor* skills, one of our prime sources of information is vision. Knowing how we can use imagery may give some insight into the retention of motor skills. Luria (1968) described the phenomenal memory of one subject referred to as S. As long as S was allowed to study the material for 3 or 4 seconds, he was capable of remembering perfectly a list of nonsense syllables memorized 15 years earlier. The key to S's memory was imagery. For example, to memorize a particular list he might imagine himself walking down a familiar street and placing various objects, or words, in places along the way. These places are referred to as loci. In order to recall the list, S had merely to retrace the steps of his imaginary walk. We have often heard the phrase "walking down memory lane." All S did was to turn this into a usable mnemonic technique (*i.e.,* an aid to memory). Although this technique would appear to be a most useful method to improve memory, a highly detailed memory depending on imagery is not necessarily always desirable. In S's case the vivid imagery interfered with his ability to abstract the meaning of a message. He would tend to think about irrelevant details rather than follow the message. However, the technique might be used on a more moderate scale. In order to make the most use of imagery, there are certain guidelines that must be followed (Keele, 1973):

1. The images must be well structured (Horowitz, Lampel, & Takanishi, 1969). For example, the image of a *horse* behind a *man* standing with a *ball* and *polo mallet* at his feet may produce poor recall. Just the word "horse" might be recalled. However, the image of a *horse* being ridden by a *man* swinging a *polo mallet* at a *ball* may well lead to good recall of all four items.

2. The images must be placed within an organized framework that will help to guide recall (*e.g.,* the sequence of places or loci used by S) (Atwood, 1969).

3. The time taken to develop an image is also important. When a student rewrites a set of course notes in order to study for an exam, the process of rewriting is almost as valuable as the time spent studying the notes that were made. By properly constructing images, as in a picture, we make them quite resistant to forgetting. That this should be so is quite reasonable because the whole process necessitates a considerable synthesis of information, which in turn demands a full understanding of that information. The key is in the formation of the image; the retention is a natural outcome.

Meaning

The second factor that is important in imagery is meaning. Most of the time we are not learning lists of words or a series of plays but are trying to abstract meaning from a series of events. In sports, this search for meaning revolves around the choice of when to pass or shoot, when to tackle or hold back. A great deal of work has been done in verbal learning, and one technique for assessing the various shades of meaning was developed by Dawes (1964) (Table 4-1).

The first three relationships represent fairly clear-cut cases. The finer type of discrimination is illustrated by the disjunction (*e.g.*, some, but not all, good tennis players are left handed). If a person remembers a simple relationship such as an exclusion, an inclusion, or an identity as a disjunction, then that person has made a *pseudodiscrimination,* that is, a finer discrimination than warranted. An example of this is when a 7-foot tall player has blocked all the opposition's previous shots (one on one), but the 5-foot tall player still feels capable of shooting when covered by this player. The reverse process, to take a finer discrimination and transpose it into a simpler form, is to *overgeneralize, (e.g.,* all good tennis players are left handed).

The research in verbal learning has shown that most of the errors in recall are a result of overgeneralizations; that is, we tend to simplify relationships. For example, Logan and Wodthe (1968) reported that the poor performance on transfer tasks after teaching "rules of thumb" was due mainly to the misuse or overgeneralization of the rules. Although the Dawes method was applied mainly to the organization of the elements within a written passage, it can be applied to a motor skill, particularly to the principles of motor performance and the factors governing the choice of when or how to use a specific skill. The difficulty, in terms of retention, lies in the degree of organization within the task or motor skill and, in particular, the various relationships associated with the performance of that skill.

To answer the question of how you can improve your memory, the answer might be to organize, rehearse, and image. If a set play has several components, organize them into units, rehearse each of the units, and try to create an image to represent each part of the complete task. Be sure to base this

TABLE 4-1
The logical relationships between elements (based on Dawes, 1964)

Type of Relationship	Venn Diagram	Examples
An exclusion	(A) (B)	No types of soccer ball (A) are types of squash ball (B)
An identity	(A B)	In basketball all free throws (A) are one point (B) and vice versa
An inclusion	(A B)	All soccer players (A) are sportsmen (B)
A disjunction	(A ∩ B)	Some basketball players (A) are over 7 feet tall (B)

image on a successful performance. As you learn a new move, to aid the recall of what you have just learned, organize it with respect to other plays or strategies you have learned and try to make clear all the relationships that exist between the various elements. A mnemonic scheme, such as the method of loci, may help the quarterback or lineman to store the long list of plays that eventually must be recalled very accurately. The process is one of organizing the significant meaningful relationships or elements. For McLuhan and Fiore (1967), "the medium is the message"; for those wishing to increase their retention, "the process is the image."

INFORMATION PROCESSING MODEL

Finally, having reviewed some of the general concepts of retention and forgetting, we will consider the processes involved in terms of the information processing models presented in Chapter 2. From Figure 2-13 we can identify the main *structural components* of memory: sensory information storage, short-term memory, and long-term memory. Forgetting may occur from any of these stores, but the rate at which this occurs and the causes may be different. Norman (1970), like many others, also refers to an intermediate or *operational short-term memory*. Although a short-term store, it is more concerned with information that has been retrieved from long-term memory for use in a current task. For example, we may recall the successful strategy used in a previous tennis match when playing the same opponent for a second time. However, while this is an attractive descriptive concept regarding a functional aspect of memory, there is little supportive evidence to justify its existence as a *separate* short-term memory store.

The structural components of memory should be distinguished from the *control processes* that regulate the information that is selected, rehearsed, and stored. These control processes will be considered in more detail in Chapter 5. To complete this chapter, we will look at the main structural components or "memory boxes" from the information processing model and some of the evidence used to support these divisions.

First, we should define the term *memory span*. Memory span refers to the amount of information that can be handled at one time. When the information processing models were first discussed in Chapter 2, we noted that the number of bits of information that can be held at any one time was limited to 7 ± 2 bits, which represented the channel capacity. Although we can retain only a few bits, the actual amount of information can be increased by chunking. The total amount of information depends on the language used to formulate those chunks. With practice, it may be possible to increase memory span slightly, but it still remains the major limitation to the retention of information. Why this is so can best be illustrated by examining the individual components.

Sensory Information store (SIS)

Sensory information storage refers to the phenomenon that general information provided by the senses is available not only for the duration of the event but also for a short while afterward. For example, a stimulus of short duration such as a flash bulb leaves us with a strong impression of that flash even after it has gone. This afterimage is present at both the receptors and the sensory area of the brain. To test if anything is stored and, if so, how precisely, the following experiment might be performed.

A slide (Figure 4-3) is presented for 50 msec, and the subject tries to recall all the letters from that slide. On some trials the slide is immediately *followed* by a high, medium, or low auditory signal. This auditory signal cues the subject to report only the letters in the top, middle, or bottom row, depending on the tone. Thus, subjects could be required to recall all the letters or just one row (Figure 4-4). At that point the slide would no longer be available.

In such an experiment when subjects are asked to report all the letters (Figure 4-4, *a*), they may average only four. If asked to identify one row only on cue (Figure 4-4, *b*), they show 80% to 90% recall, regardless of the row selected for recall. If the tone is delayed 1 or 2 seconds, recall is again poor. Therefore, if

H	F	X	A
E	V	I	O
K	T	R	V

FIGURE 4-3   A slide presentation with immediate recall directed by an auditory signal (based on Sperling, 1960).

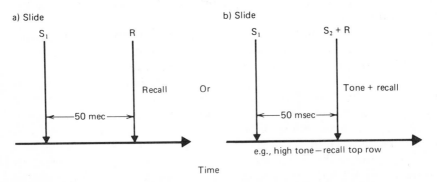

FIGURE 4-4   Experimental paradigm for testing the sensory information store.

we can retrieve a high percentage of the items on cue, this suggests we actually have 80% to 90% of the total information available to us but lose some of it in the process of reporting. Most is lost in the first one-half second. Clearly, we do "store" information for a short duration after it is presented, and the information is precise. There is similar evidence for audition (Darwin, Turvey, & Crowder, 1972). How much is retained depends on the focus of our attention, because the extremely short duration during which the information is available makes it difficult to retrieve all the information. The rare individual with a photographic memory may be the exception. When complex stimuli are presented tachistoscopically (briefly for 50 milliseconds) to subjects, they report with greater accuracy stimuli that they have been instructed to observe. The question remains whether the original perception of incidental features is less accurate than the perception of emphasized features or whether it is the additional time incidental items are held in memory that causes performance to deteriorate as the incidental features are reported last.

To test this hypothesis, Chapman (1932) made use of a before-after design, reasoning that if instructions influence perception, then they can be effective only when given before the presentation of the stimulus. However, if the effect is due to selective reporting of the contents of memory, then the instructions ought to yield the same accuracy of report when they are given shortly after the stimulus. The stimulus, or information presented for recall, varied along three dimensions. The accuracy of the recall was consistently higher when the dimension to be reported was specified before presentation as opposed to after presentation.

Averbach and Coriell (1961) suggested that the decay of the visual memory trace is so rapid that the advantage of the before condition may be due to the speed with which the instructional set can operate on the memory trace and strengthen it, that is, we focus on the information to be recalled. However, the use of before-after techniques has been criticized (Brown, 1960), since it allows differential effects during retention. Instructions given prior to stimulus presentation allow subjects to report immediately, whereas instructions given after stimulus presentation must first be perceived before being acted on. Thus the information must be retained and thereby decay a little before being recalled.

In the experiment by Brown (1960), the subject received two auditory instructions two seconds apart. The second instruction was given at the same time as the stimulus presentation. The critical instruction told the subject what aspect of the stimulus to report, and a neutral instruction told the subject the side of the answer sheet on which to record the response. Either the critical or the neutral instruction could arrive first. The results of the experiment show that the accuracy of recall was greater when the critical instruction came before the neutral instruction, but this was only true when the instruction specified the class of symbols to be named (a digit or consonant). When the critical instruction specified the position or color, no advantage was gained. Brown concluded that a selective process may operate during perception when the subject knows which of two classes has to be reported.

The above studies combined with other work suggest that the duration and accuracy of sensory storage depends on the duration and the intensity of exposure to the stimulus plus the degree of *masking* imposed by subsequent stimuli; that is, if a stimulus is followed immediately by a second more intense stimulus the first stimulus may not be identified. The loss of one stimulus because of the intensity of a second stimulus is commonly referred to as *backward masking*. Marteniuk (1976) felt that the sensory storage was of such a short duration that it did not play a significant role in the learning and performance of motor skills, and therefore he concentrated on the longer duration memory stores. Although there is evidence for the sensory storage of actual information for one or two seconds (Bliss, Crane, Mansfield, & Townsend, 1966), there is little direct evidence for a similar store for kinesthetic information. For example, Norrie (1969) suggested that a kinesthetic aftereffect was present on immediate reproduction but disappeared after 30 seconds. However, in baseball we still see the batter warming up with a weighted bat in order that the normal bat will feel that much lighter when it is time to bat. Although the ritual may help prepare the baseball player psychologically, most of the kinesthetic aftereffect will be gone.

Although the duration of the visual "afterimage" is less than one second, it does provide a very precise picture. Only the information attended to will be retained and be available to aid in decision-making. This situation is very much like the athlete who takes a quick look at the opponent before making the play. All the information necessary to make the decision may be available to the athlete, but if it is not focused on, the athlete can only guess.

One way to facilitate this decision-making process is to use the tachistoscopic experimental procedure, described earlier, and present slides of game situations; in this way, the athlete can learn to focus on the most pertinent cues (Kerr, 1978a). The use of a tachistoscope (T-scope) as a teaching aid has met with some success (Ciszek, 1968; Damron, 1955). In an ice hockey game, one player may receive the puck 20 times and each time that player must make a decision—pass or shoot. Twenty slides of game situations relating to the relevant principles could be presented to that player tachistoscopically in less than two minutes. Tachistoscopic learning could give a hockey player practice in the total number of decisions to be made in a full game, all in less than ten minutes. In the spring of 1979, the National Hockey League All-Stars were embarrassed by the Russian hockey team, losing by a score of 6–0. Clearly, individual talent was not enough. Perhaps some T-scope training on the principles of team play related to some particular system would have helped the All-Stars function as a more cohesive unit.

Short-term memory

Obviously, if the information held in the SIS is to be preserved, it requires attention. If the information is simple and can be rehearsed, it can be stored for a long time; but if you cannot rehearse it, you get different effects. These effects are illustrated by the following type of experiment. A subject is presented with a *trigram* for 1 second and then starts counting backward in 3's from a number given by the experimenter. A trigram is a three-letter nonsense syllable (*e.g.*, XYT). The experimenter presents the nonsense syllable and a number (*e.g.*, 121). The subject starts to count: 118, 115, 112, 109. . . . The experimenter can assess the limits of short-term memory by varying the length of the retention interval. When you prevent the subject from rehearsing, you get results like those in Figure 4-5. Note that within 20 seconds only 10% of the original information is left, with the greatest loss occurring during the first 10 seconds.

When rehearsal is prevented, the accuracy of retention deteriorates rapidly over time. Of course this does not necessarily mean we have lost the information; perhaps it has just faded. You may forget a telephone number that you have just looked up, but only one digit may be wrong. The idea that information has only faded was tested by showing subjects a series of numbers and then asking whether the presented number had appeared before, that is, the subjects were being asked to recognize, not recall (Shepard & Teghtsoonian, 1961). It was found that responses were correct beyond pure chance, which shows that some aspects of the stimulus persisted even on a single presenta-

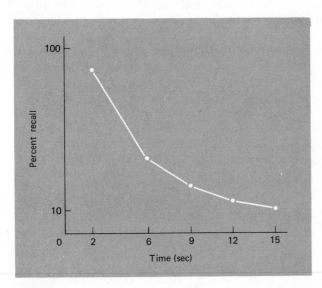

FIGURE 4-5   A curve representing the duration of short-term memory.

tion. (Can you recall the sequence of letters in the trigram just presented?)

Short-term vs long-term memory

To maintain information in short-term memory takes rehearsal, but this is not true of long-term memory. In terms of the information that is transferred from short-term memory to long-term memory, in general, the smaller the amount of information, the more it is rehearsed, or if it is novel or fresh, then the more likely the information is to reach long-term memory. We do forget material from long-term memory, but at a slower rate. We should also note that in many situations long-term memory is applied to describe retention intervals that are only "long" when compared with the few seconds for which information is held in short-term memory. In Figure 4-5, note that 90% of the information was lost within 20 seconds. The implication is that our memory for information presented once is very brief.

Next we will consider some of the evidence used to justify two separate memories. Keele (1973) proposed two lines of argument: spacing and representation. We will add a third line of evidence based on consolidation memory theory. As already noted, while there are definite limitations to the capacity of short-term memory, such is not the case for long-term memory. In itself, this fact suggests two separate memory stages.

SPACING. Keele (1973) suggested that if the two memory states are indeed different we would expect to find different conditions that might facilitate recall at intervals of less than 10 seconds (short-term memory) or at longer intervals (long-term memory). He considered 10 seconds to be the effective limit of short-term memory.

The following experiment, based on Peterson, Hillner, and Saltzman (1962), tests Keele's idea. Subjects were presented a list of word-number pairs (*e.g.*, jug–9). These pairs were presented at the rate of one pair per second, with each pair occurring twice in the list. The two experimental groups differed as to whether they received massed or spaced practice. The massed practice condition was one in which the criterion pairs (the items to be tested later) followed each other in the list (Figure 4-6).

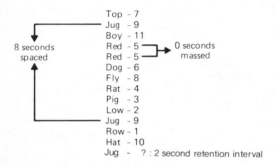

FIGURE 4-6 Part of a hypothetical list of word–number pairs (based on Peterson, Hillner & Saltzman, 1962).

The subject was not aware which pairs were to be recalled and was faced with the task of trying to retain the complete list of word-number pairs. In the spaced practice condition, there was an 8-second interval or eight word-number pairs between the presentation of the criterion pairs (Figure 4-6). The subject's ability to recall the criterion pairs was tested by presenting the word alone after a retention interval of either 2, 4, 8, or 16 seconds. The time interval was measured from the last presentation of the criterion pair. As a result of this procedure, the retention interval was filled with other word-number pairs, thereby preventing rehearsal.

The results of this study are illustrated in Figure 4-7. There is a clear difference in the performance of the two groups. Spacing appears to aid long-term memory, as shown by the superior performance of the spaced practice group over the longer retention intervals of 8 and 16 seconds. The reverse appears to be true for massed practice, suggesting that massing practice aids short-term memory. Although this difference is not as large, the massed practice group did perform better in the two shortest retention intervals. Therefore, these differential effects offer one possible distinction between short-term memory and long-term memory.

REPRESENTATION: A second line of evidence put forward by Keele (1973) was that the nature of the representation in memory is different. The evidence relating to the retention of verbal material suggests that normally verbal information is recoded in an auditory form in short-term memory. This is indicated by the type of experimental errors that are found. These errors show that when subjects are required to recall nonsense syllables they tend to confuse letters by their sound rather than by their shape (*e.g., P* and *V* not *O*

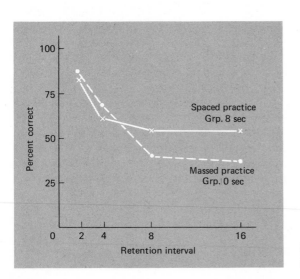

FIGURE 4-7 Retention and the spacing of practice.

and Q). In long-term memory, on the other hand, we find semantic errors. Long-term memory stores meaning and is more abstract. For example, the original item in a list of words to be recalled may be "pail," but when the items are recalled some time later the subject may recall it as "bucket." The word that was recalled has changed, but the meaning is the same; we do not report it as "pale." Therefore, verbal short-term memory is based on sound and verbal long-term memory, on meaning.

Posner and Keele (1968, 1970) have also produced evidence for a similar process of abstraction in relation to the long-term storage of purely visual information. Subjects trained in categorizing distorted dot patterns were able to recall previously unseen prototypes equally as well as the original distortions and better than new distortions. Thus, long-term visual storage also involves a process of abstraction. These abstracted memories are generally preserved very well over time, but there may be some distortion owing to interference between different sensory abstractions of the same event (Davis & Sinha, 1950). Your interpretation of what you heard may be influenced by your interpretation of what you saw, or vice versa. In addition to these two lines of argument, further support for the identification of separate memory states is provided by consolidation memory theory.

CONSOLIDATION MEMORY THEORY. This theory also proposes a separation between short-term and long-term memory. Briefly, it is suggested that information is initially maintained in short-term memory in the form of reverberating electrical activity until a memory trace is firmly consolidated or stored in long-term memory, as a result of some more permanent chemical change. Consolidation theory is actually a three-stage theory. The first stage is the transformation of sensory information into a physiological representation that is briefly stored, the sensory information store. Consolidation memory theory parallels the information processing model presented in Chapter 2. Interference with these short-term electrical events has been shown to disrupt long-term memory, giving further support to the consolidation theory. If you interfere with short-term memory, the information cannot pass into the long-term store (King, 1965).

Some of the evidence for this interference has come from experiments using a step-down procedure with rats. On a daily basis, a rat when placed on a platform will step off it consistently. If the rat experiences an electric shock each time it steps on the floor, it will stay on the platform. However, if the rat's short-term memory is interfered with by passing an electrical current through its brain via electrodes when it steps off the platform, the rat will have no memory of the foot shock and will step down again the next day. A key element is the timing of the shock, because if the time interval between the foot shock and the brain stimulation is increased, the rat will again remember and stay on the platform. The electrical stimulation will not disrupt the long-term memory directly. Similarly, Eysenck (1966) has proposed a two-stage consolidation process in human learning.

The evidence for a chemical theory of long-term memory is somewhat more indirect. One chemical which is purported to play a major role in memory is ribonucleic acid (RNA). Work by Agranoff (1967) on the blockage of protein synthesis would seem to suggest that long-term memory is chemically based and dependent on protein synthesis. Studies by Morrell (1961) have shown an increase in RNA synthesis in learning situations, and Hyden (1965) has also found changes in the RNA base ratios following learning. However, there is some suggestion that RNA is only one factor in the construction of protein "memory molecules." Although there is much work still to be done, there is sufficient evidence to give support to the consolidation memory theory.

So far we have been concerned mainly with verbal information, but how movement information is stored is still not clear. For example, Posner (1973) reported that a touch typist could type the alphabet very quickly and with very few errors. When that same typist was given a blank sheet with an outline of the typing keys and asked to fill them in, the process was slow and there were many more errors. This does not tell us how movement information is stored, but it does suggest that it is not simply stored visually. The evidence for separate memory states for movement information is not as consistent.

Short-term motor memory studies have shown that the rate of forgetting is very rapid (Posner & Konick, 1966), regardless of whether the retention interval is, or is not, filled with potentially interfering activities. In contrast, the long-term retention of well-learned motor skills is very good (Stelmach, 1974). In Chapter 8 we will look at this problem in more detail. For now, it would seem sufficient to say that there is adequate support for the basic structural components that constitute the memory capacity of the information processing model.

Finally, as we started this section by looking at memory span, we will finish by considering the concept of *running memory span*. Few motor skills allow us to perform the party trick of viewing a tray full of objects and then demonstrating our ability to recall those items. This is important because many motor skills involve keeping a running account of changing events in the perceptual field, and therefore involve the continuous presentation and retrieval of information (*e.g.,* typing, playing a violin, reading, or skiing). Consider the following experiment:

If subjects were presented with a long list of unrelated words and then suddenly were stopped and asked to recall the most recent part of the series, we would find that the average score was only three or four items or only half the normal memory span, 7 ± 2 (Pollack, Johnson, & Knaff, 1959). A similar phenomenon occurs in reading, when considering the eye-voice span. The eye-voice span represents the time interval between the word the eyes are reading and the word the voice is vocalizing. It has been found to vary from zero, for unfamiliar words, up to 1 or 2 seconds ahead (Woodworth, 1938). It appears that familiar tasks provide an advantage in that we can chunk information and check it out before responding. Thus, it is important that the basketball player becomes familiar with the opponent's gym or the skier, with the slalom course. By this preselection process of identifying relevant cues, the performer can overcome some of the limitations imposed by the running memory span.

SUMMARY

Implicit in the definition of learning is that something is retained. The focus of this chapter was how, where, and what amount of this "something" was retained. The short-term retention curve typically shows elevated recall for the first and last few items presented in a list: the primacy and recency effects. A long-term retention curve shows no such peaks, but instead it shows a slow decline toward the baseline. If our measurement techniques were sufficiently refined, this curve would never reach the baseline.

Measures of retention

RECALL.   Usually measured on a pass-fail basis, recall is the most common measure because it is simple to administer, but it is susceptible to "fluke" performances. Refining the measuring technique can overcome some of the problems, that is, giving credit for the movement quality itself as well as for the outcome.

RECOGNITION.   Recognition is a finer measure of the amount retained. The learner is given a cue, as in multiple choice exams. Thus, credit is given even though the memory is less precise.

RELEARNING.   Relearning is the most sensitive measure. It is measured as the time saved when "learning" a skill for the second time. The only bias is one in favor of the slow learner, who has more room for improvement. However, the quality of our decisions is limited by the quality of our measurement.

Theories of forgetting
Although not all inclusive, these theories each underline some of the important factors affecting forgetting.

DECAY THEORY.   Over time, the strength or quality of the memorial representation decays. However, because some items are not forgotten, time alone is not a sufficient explanation.

INTERFERENCE THEORY.   Rather than information decaying, it is thought to be distorted as a result of interacting with other stored material. Although there is more support for this theory, a more logical approach would be to combine the two. As the material stored begins to decay, it also becomes more susceptible to interference.

INFORMATION OVERLOAD. This theory suggests that information is lost because of the limited capacity of short-term memory and, therefore, never enters long-term storage.

REPRESSION THEORY. The theory that we repress rather than forget certain memories is the Freudian approach. These memories can be retrieved under hypnosis or by electrical stimulation. The main suggestion is that nothing entering the long-term store is actually forgotten.

Factors in retention

DEGREE OF ORIGINAL LEARNING. The greater the amount of initial learning, the greater the retention. This involves overlearning, or continued practice after the skill is established. Overlearning could also include reviewing "old" skills. Fifty percent overlearning would appear to provide a fairly efficient guideline.

NATURE OF THE SKILL. This can be sub-divided into three areas:
1. Type of task. The repetition inherent in continuous tasks facilitates their retention when compared with discrete or, particularly, serial skills.
2. Patterning. The two main elements in the patterning of any skill are timing and sequencing. Of these, the general sequence of movements is retained better than the timing, so the latter factor should be emphasized when reviewing skills.
3. Meaningfulness. The more structured or organized the material, the better the retention. When possible, demonstrate plays or skills in the game situation.

ATTENTION. The quality or detail of what is retained is directly related to the quality or focus of the attention during learning (*e.g.*, the **Von Restorff** effect in which highlighting material aids retention). This factor is also closely linked to the level of motivation.

Imagery

ORGANIZATION. Images to be effective must be well structured and placed within an organized framework (*e.g.*, the loci method).

MEANING. Retention of any material can be facilitated by identifying the logical relationships between elements (exclusion, identity, inclusion, disjunction). Over time, errors occur more from overgeneralization of these relationships than from pseudodiscrimination.

Information processing model

This model is used to describe the various structural components of memory.

SENSORY INFORMATION STORE. The SIS represents the very brief duration for which sensory signals are available centrally after the original stimulus has disappeared, that is, the afterimage. There is evidence to support this concept for visual, verbal, and tactile information but little for kinesthetic information. Signals followed immediately by a second more powerful stimulus may not be detected (*i.e.,* backward masking).

SHORT-TERM MEMORY. This store has a limited capacity, 7 ± 2 bits, and demonstrates rapid forgetting for unrehearsed material within 20 seconds. Material is most likely to pass into long-term memory if it is in small amounts, is rehearsed, or is novel.

SHORT-TERM VS LONG-TERM MEMORY. There are four sources of evidence for a distinction between the two stores:
1. Spacing. Massed practice favors short-term memory, while distributed practice aids long-term memory.
2. Representation. Long-term stores for both verbal and visual information are more abstract that the short-term representations.
3. Consolidation memory theory. Short-term memory is thought to involve reverberating electrical circuits, whereas the more permanent long-term store is chemically based.
4. Capacity differences. Short-term memory is limited whereas long-term capacity is extremely large. One of these limitations is represented by the *running memory span,* which is almost half the normal memory span. Identifying relevant cues prior to performance can help overcome this limitation.

PROBLEM

Question

Using the logical relationships approach, how would you analyze the principles that govern the role of one position for a particular team sport and ability level?

Possible Answer

This answer is based on the role of a fullback in competitive soccer in the 13- to 14-year age-group. Before giving examples of the relevant principles, it is necessary to preface this answer with a few general remarks. The soccer players in this age-group are certainly old enough to handle the finer type of discrimination described as a disjunction, but for the most part it is still better to give more non-disjunctive relationships. In this way, there should be less danger of misinterpretation. Therefore, the emphasis would be on the non-disjunctive type of relationship, even though in the more advanced form of the game some of these principles would not apply. It is only after establishing some general framework of how to play within the team and subsequently gaining considerable experience that the player can handle the more flexible relationships that govern the advanced game. By giving simple guidelines to help the player, it becomes possible for that player to perform in a difficult game in harmony with the rest of the team. Also, it is important to give as few principles as possible, otherwise there is the danger your players will become confused.

Some sample principles include the following:

Defense—General

1. Always stay between your goal and the ball (*i.e.,* when out of position run in the direction of the nearest goal post until the above condition is met). This represents a simple rule. Without fulfilling this principle, the player cannot play defense.
2. When the ball is on your side of the field, guard the attacking player in your zone closely. When the ball is on the opposite side of the field, leave your player and cover the center of the field. Although this principle is stated simply, it will need some interpretation to deal with the intermediate situations (*e.g.,* the ball in the middle of the field).
3. If in doubt, kick it out. A simple principle which may be retained better because of the novel way it is stated (the Von Restorff effect).

Offense—General

1. When the goalkeeper *gains* possession during play, immediately run the first 20 yards (or meters) out of the defensive zone at a 45-degree angle to the goal. A simple principle, this would put the fullback in an effective position to help initiate the offense.
2. Always pass in the direction you are facing. A principle which is both simple to follow and simplifies the game.
3. When in possession of the ball, pass it to your winger. If he is guarded, kick a long pass inside the opposing fullback for the forwards to chase. Again, the player has some interpretation to do, but, when combined with defensive principle number three, it should avoid the critical problem of the fullback losing possession of the ball in the defensive zone.

When we take the role of a coach, we should try to analyze the principles and their relationship to the game in the same manner that Dawes (1964) analyzed a written passage. Bruner (1960) said, "the foundations of any subject may be taught to anybody at any age in some form." The essence of this idea is that the basic themes of any discipline are "as simple as they are powerful" (Bruner, 1960). All sports can be reduced to their basic elements. This applies not only to the techniques but also to the principles that govern when and how to use those techniques. The coach by analyzing the game and giving specific principles to the player, adjusted to reflect the age and experience of the player, can greatly simplify the overall decision-making process. In turn, this will mean that more people will have a greater opportunity to learn to play the game.

Part Three Perception

Chapter 5
Elements of Perception

Perceptions are not of things but of relationships.
Nothing, including me, exists by itself—this is
an illusion of words. I am a relationship, everchanging.
(Prather, 1970)

The basic information processing model presented in Chapter 2 identifies three distinct elements within the central controlling processes: (1) those that deal with the initial sensory input; (2) those that deal with the decisions made based on an analysis of that input; and (3) those that construct and initiate the motor output or response. These elements that constitute central processes involved in the control of movement represent, as was indicated in Chapter 1, the "psycho" element of psychomotor learning.

The main emphasis of the latter two parts of this book, Perception and Motor Control, will be to look at the acquisition of skill from the viewpoint of what changes take place in relation to the central processes that control movement. The mechanisms that control decisions and responses will be covered in Part Four, Motor Control. This part, Perception, will deal with the input or perceptual aspect, describing how the information gathered by the sensory system interacts with past learning. Any new sensory information is combined with information we have gained in the past in order to build a "picture" of our environment. As we are constantly receiving new information, so our "picture" will be continually modified. To rewrite the last line of the Prather quote at the start of this chapter: *"Perception* is a relationship, everchanging."

Motor skills and information theory

To understand the central controlling processes, we must look at motor skill performance from an information processing point of view, because this is the only model of learning that attempts to describe what these processes might be. In Chapter 1, we defined motor skills as the following:

1. *An organized sequence of activities, implying that a skill is something more than a simple muscle twitch*

2. *Goal directed, as represented by the cybernetic notion of a thermostat.*

Using information theory, we can expand on our earlier definition to include an additional idea:

3. *Motor skills require feedback from three sources of information to achieve goals.*
   a. *Information about what is to be achieved*
   b. *Information from the task itself*
   c. *Information from the results of one's actions (Holding, 1965)*

Information as used here could include (1) verbal instructions about the goal of the movement, (2) tactile information—as you bump into another player—and (3) visual information as you see the ball hit the rim and bounce out. From an information processing point of view, therefore, the emphasis in motor skill performance is on the identification and manipulation of different types of information, particularly feedback. The need for accurate information/feedback alone underlines the important role of the teacher or coach as a provider of relevant information. It is important to provide the learner with information pertinent to the task, rather than just general encouragement.

Having redefined motor skills in terms of information theory, it is now relevant to review the concept of skill acquisition in terms of the learning process. We have indicated above that there are at least three relevant sources of information in the acquisition of motor skills. In order to gain a clearer understanding of the overall learning process and the central controlling processes in the brain that govern the learning process, we must consider both the role of different types of information and how that role may change during the learning process.

Stages of learning

Schmidt (1975a, based on Fitts, 1965) divided the learning process itself into three stages:

1. *Cognitive stage.* In this stage the learner evolves strategies, makes a lot of errors, and often shows large improvements. In the learner's early attempts at serving in tennis, for example, many serves will hit the bottom of the net or clear the boundaries of the court before the learner can land the ball in the serving area with any consistency.

2. *Association stage.* Here the association is made between the correct response and what it feels like to make that movement. This phase emphasizes the organization and timing of the parts of the movement and the use of knowledge of results to decrease errors. By knowing the results of one's actions, it becomes possible to modify either the timing or organization of the movement in order to decrease errors on the next attempt. With practice and experience we improve our ability to assess our errors and modify our actions accordingly. This process of discovering the source of our errors allows us to develop what is referred to as an error detection mechanism. If we throw the ball over the catcher's head, we may have used the wrong angle of release or too much force. Having detected the source of the error, we can now try to correct the fault.

3. *Autonomous stage.* The final stage of skill refinement, in which skills are performed with little conscious effort, requires minimal attention. Many of us when driving home may find ourselves halfway there and suddenly realize that we have very little recollection of the first part of our journey. We may have been driving through some very busy traffic, but because everything was normal we were able to complete the task of driving successfully while contemplating some other task. Our driving responses—stop for red lights, avoid other cars—are almost automatic; we no longer have to look for the turn indicator on the steering column when we signal a change of lanes.

Progress through the various stages of learning—cognitive, associative, and autonomous—can be produced by changes in the perceptual process, as can be seen in the refinement, with practice, of an error detection mechanism for a particular skill.

THE PERCEPTUAL PROCESS

What is perception?

In most instances, a movement is produced as a response to, or in anticipation of, some event. A study of psychomotor learning that considers only how well the movement was produced or how accurately and how quickly the decisions were made has failed to recognize one of the most crucial elements in the overall process: *perception*. Perception precedes decisions and actions. It represents the first step in processing motor skill information, and as such it has a profound influence on the whole central processing system.

Perception is an active not a passive process. It can be contrasted to the passive role played by the sensory receptors, such as the eyes and ears, which is one of receiving and transmitting signals. Some stimulus in the environment "triggers" the receptor, and, as a result, the receptor sends a signal to the brain. The eyes, for example, record the fact that there are several objects in front of you. In a team sport, these "objects" are the teammates and opponents that you must recognize and differentiate between in order to play the game. Sensory receptors simply report the presence or absence of certain stimuli; their role is passive. *Perception, which is a function of the brain itself, is the interpretation of these sensory stimuli.*

Perception, however, goes beyond simple recognition. The brain is not just a passive receiver of sensory information but acts on that information to identify it (labeling a player as "George," for example) and to integrate that information with the other bits of information that are received (such as George's position on the field) to decide how this information can be used (whether George will be the player who receives your pass).

Take a look at Figure 5-1; it would hardly be called a picture. Now look again and imagine a cleaning-woman with a bucket, on her hands and knees cleaning the floor. In Figure 5-1 we have a rear view showing the two feet. Perception is based on the interpretation of the information derived from past experience and therefore involves certain expectations. That the same figure or pattern of stimulation is open to differing interpretations even by the same individual is clearly shown in Figures 5-2 and 5-3.

Figure 5-2 may represent an old woman or a young woman, while in the Necker cube illustrated in Figure 5-3 the small circle may appear to be either on the front or the back face of the cube. In fact, in the latter case, it is impossible to say which choice is correct. Now look at Figure 5-4. Do these

FIGURE 5-1 An object, or just meaningless lines?

drawings represent puddles of water, clouds, or something else? From these examples we see that vision does not provide us with a picture of the world, only information to be interpreted. To the student who asked the question "where's the action, man?" the reply of the second student was "you are the action!" You cannot be involved in any "action" without being active

FIGURE 5-2   An old woman or a young girl? (based on Boring, 1930.)

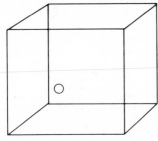

FIGURE 5-3   The Necker cube.

yourself. Similarly, sensory information does not come to you pre-analyzed. The interpretation of perceptual information is not a passive process but involves the interaction between an individual and the environmental stimuli. To what extent we have to *learn to see* is not easily determined.

Perception involves the conscious organization of incoming information, and it is this perceptual organization that provides the basis for learning. By monitoring and reviewing the incoming information, the learner is able to refine the perceptual process and thereby progress through the various learning stages. The beginning soccer player is at first confused by the large number of players on the field and is unable to distinguish relevant from irrelevant information. The result is that the skills practiced earlier in simple drills are forgotten when the game begins and are replaced by harrassed kicks at the ball aimed at moving the ball toward the opposition's goal. In time, the beginner is able to separate teammates from the opposition and tries to pass the ball to a player and not just kick it downfield. Eventually, the player is able to perceive differences in the advantages to be gained from passing to one player as compared with another.

Clearly, the quality of perceptual processing can affect both the quality and validity of a response. Hockey players who are blind to the colors red and green will face some serious difficulties if their team wears red and the opposition wears green. However, as well as such obvious physiological limits, the aspect of quality also reflects the ability to identify the most important cues. When a basketball player jumps to take a rebound or to block a shot, it is important to know which arms belong to whom in order to avoid fouls. The more precise the information that the player abstracts, the greater the chances for success.

Similarly, the speed with which the perceptual process operates can influence the time available to perform that response. Let us assume it takes the tennis ball only one second to travel from the server to the receiver. The player who takes one-tenth second to decide where the ball will land has a significant time advantage in which to decide on and execute the return over the player who takes one-half second just to decide where the ball will land. *These changes in the quality or speed of perception* are some of the changes—products of improvement in the perceptual process itself—that *we identify as learning.*

FIGURE 5-4 Puddles, clouds, a reflection, or an ink blot?

Integration of sensory information

Having defined what we mean by perception, as distinct from sensation, and illustrated its importance to the learning process, the next question to answer is, "how do we handle the mass of sensory information that is constantly being received?" Rappaport (1971) presented a perceptual model that shows how the mass of sensory information can be integrated and reduced to a more manageable size. A simplified version of this model is shown in Figure 5-5. There are five levels through which the various types of incoming sensory information may be processed.

The first level of Rappaport's model is referred to as the *proprioceptive level,* which provides for the initial organization of all incoming information within any sensory modality, such as the visual, kinesthetic, or auditory system. Sensory modalities, such as vision or hearing, respond to certain types of stimuli with their own receptors. The eyes and ears connect via the optic and acoustic (the cochlear branch) cranial nerves to the visual and auditory cortex of the brain. The combination of receptor, nerve pathway, and reception area of the brain represents what is referred to as a sensory modality. The components of the kinesthetic modality are more diverse, as we shall see in Chapter 6, but the main elements of specific receptors, nerve pathways and reception areas in the brain, are present.

At the proprioceptive level, information about movements of the limbs or kinesthetic information can be identified. As you reach the end of a mountain climb, differences felt by the left and right hands (loose or firm outcrops on the rock surface and whether you can pull hard against them) may be important in deciding which direction you will take to reach the top. These limb positions represent cues that would be identified at the proprioceptive level.

Eventually, the bits of information from within any one sensory modality will become organized and distinct enough to be grouped and labeled by the individual. This labeling process occurs at the *preceptual level* of integration in which various bits of kinesthetic or auditory information are recognized as being associated with some event. Therefore, while the proprioceptive level involves labeling each bit of information, the preceptual level involves combining related bits of information within one sensory modality. The take-off for heading a ball in soccer, for example, involves kinesthetic information

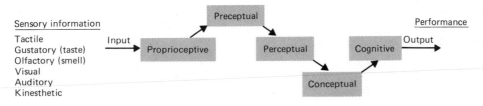

FIGURE 5-5   A model of the perceptual process (based on Rappaport, 1971).

about various leg, arm, trunk, and head positions and movements. Taken together, these bits of information can be labeled by the individual as the kinesthetic precept of the take-off.

To further reduce the total amount of information with which we must deal, we then combine related information from different sensory modalities to form mental images or percepts. At the *perceptual level* we begin to combine what we feel with what we see and hear to form a mental image—percept—of a movement (*e.g.*, heading a soccer ball).

The combination of different types of sensory information would result in a large number of percepts, and therefore we proceed to the next level: *the conceptual level*. Here we categorize and generally organize the percepts to produce concepts. A concept would represent the general group of motor tasks associated with jumping, for example, whether the object of the jump is to perform a lay-up, to spike a volleyball, or head a soccer ball. The specific mental images associated with performing each of these skills would be quite different; however, certain characteristics common to all of them would allow them to be grouped together. In all these jumping skills, the coordination of the leg drive with the thrust of the arms would be most important in order to maximize the height of the jump. Once we can identify the main characteristics of jumping, we can then adapt the technique to the needs of a given situation.

The final level of knowing at which this organized and reduced information comes to have some specific meaning for us is the *cognitive level*. "Knowing" what is involved in heading a soccer ball does not imply that the performer will produce a correct response, only that the learner perceives a certain response as being correct. The cognitive level implies a sense of knowing what the movement feels like and the circumstances under which it is normally produced.

Occasionally, however, this may lead the performer to overlook some small change in the incoming kinesthetic information and thereby produce the wrong response in a particular situation. When heading a soccer ball with a strong wind behind, it may be more advantageous for a player to concentrate on accurately directing the ball toward the goal rather than to emphasize the amount of force with which the ball is struck. The player, having been in this situation before, "knows" the particular aspect of the motor concept (*i.e.*, heading) that should be applied. Unfortunately, the player may overlook the small piece of proprioceptive information that indicates that the wind velocity has temporarily fallen. Misled by the context of the situation and not realizing the wind velocity has dropped, the player chooses the wrong response. The player concentrates on directing the ball to the goal; but because the wind velocity has dropped, the ball now lacks sufficient force to reach the goal.

Being able to function at the conceptual or cognitive level is essential to simplify and speed up the decision-making process. Once the concepts relating to a particular activity have been established, the performer does not have to analyze new situations in detail but has only to check out the key elements in the concept. Many decisions can be made quickly, but this process carries with it the danger of overlooking important details in a given situation. In the example given above, if the player did not notice the sudden drop in wind velocity before heading the ball, an incorrect response might result. A compromise might be to make the "obvious" choice (direct the ball to the goal) but double-check before initiating the response. The wind velocity has dropped, so head the ball hard.

Although Rappaport's model is essentially descriptive, it does illustrate how we might reduce to some manageable size the mass of sensory information that is continually available to us. Only by understanding this process can the practitioner help the learner avoid or identify potential sources of error, thereby achieving a state of "knowing" that is in step with the task at hand. Clearly, with each repetition of a given task, precepts, percepts, and concepts become more easily established. This in turn will help with future sensory analyses. This process can work in either direction. Just as sensory information can be reduced to concepts, so concepts can be used to establish what the major proprioceptive cues will be for a particular task. Working at the conceptual level simplifies the decision-making process in that it allows you to generalize—do I shoot or pass? Working at the proprioceptive level you have to judge the distance to the goal and the distance to your teammates. Which level you actually work at will be determined by your past experience with the task, the demands of the task itself and the sort of analysis required, or the need for fast, accurate decision-making.

When you play your first introductory game at the beginning of a soccer class, you are initially bombarded by new sensory information: the shape of the ball, the markings on the field, the feel of the grass or the ball when you kick it, the cold wind, the referee, the many players running in all directions, and you alone lost in a forest of stimuli. The initial identification of all these stimuli represents the proprioceptive level.

Slowly you identify groups of items, separating what you heard from what you saw: the precepts. Then you sort these different groups of stimuli and combine them to form percepts: the sound, sight, and feel of a shot on goal or the sound, sight, and feel of a tackle. Eventually you formalize some elementary concepts (*e.g.*, how to dribble or pass the ball). Whether the technique to be used is a chip pass or a push pass, you must have some feel for the relationship between the distance the ball must travel and the amount of force to be applied.

Finally, at the cognitive level, you begin to understand what the game itself is all about and how you can use the skills you have acquired to penetrate the opposition's defense. It is this last step, understanding the characteristics of the activity itself, that provides one of the main justifications for requiring physical education students, who are the potential teachers and coaches, to participate in a wide range of activities. By participating in a range of sports you can gain some knowledge of the basic principles associated with each sport. From your personal experience with the difficulties that exist when trying to apply these principles, you can improve your understanding of the sport. Regardless of your personal athletic ability and knowledge of teaching methods, it is only when you have an understanding of the game itself that you can fully appreciate the problems of the learner and provide appropriate guidance. You do not have to play a sport in order to coach it, but your personal experiences do provide a head start as you attempt to understand that sport.

PERCEPTUAL THEORIES

Although Rappaport has presented us with a general model of the perceptual process, it is not the only explanation of perception. There are many approaches to the question of what affects perception. Here we will consider briefly some of the diverse perceptual theories. These do not represent such in-depth explanations as some of the learning theories presented in Chapter 2, but they do represent some of the main attempts to identify the major factors involved in perception. A more complete explanation of perception using elements of all these theories is then proposed.

Core-context theory

The core-context theory (Tichner, 1916) considered perception to be a dynamic rather than a static phenomenon. Relationships between specific sensations are not fixed but are changeable. Sensations on their own are meaningless, (e.g., a flashing light), but these sensations acquire meaning when placed within a given situation (e.g., the flashing light placed on top of a police car or on an instrument panel). The meaning we associate with a particular sensation is derived from the context of the situation in which the stimulus occurs. Consequently, perception is thought to involve two types of sensations: (1) a *"core"* of immediate sensation aroused by the stimulus and (2) secondary sensations based on past experience—the *"context."*

Because the core is fairly stable for different individuals, the variation in meanings derived by different individuals from the same situation is due to differences in their past experiences. The core may be thought of as the size of the image on the retina, but the exact size and distance of objects, as interpreted by the individual, is based on one's relationships with other objects—the context. Assuming both have normal vision, two players looking at the same ball may be in complete agreement as to its size and color, but, because the context in which the stimulus is viewed is different, the attacker views the ball as too far from the goal to score and the defender views it as too close to the goal for safety.

How the stimulus event is interpreted depends on the individual's past experience. Because past experience differs from person to person, so may the resulting judgments. For example, a football coach may be used to seeing a particular opposing team always use a certain defense. The opposing coach may try to disguise a new defense by using the same starting line-up even though the role of each player has changed. The apparent lack of change in the context of the situation (the same players in the same starting positions) may result in the home team coach failing to identify a change in strategy.

Adaptation-level theory

The adaptation-level theory (Helson, 1951, 1964) is based on the importance of past experience in developing meaning. This theory introduced the idea of "pooling" events within a given frame of reference; that is, those events that are related to a particular type of situation are pooled together. Any new information that we categorize in relation to this pool of information is drawn from our past experiences.

Helson's theory goes one step further than the core-context theory in that it separates the object, which is the focus of our attention, from the background in which it exists and produces the three elements that make up the "pool" or triad (Figure 5-6). *Adaptation-level refers to the size, or level, of the difference between the object and its background and the extent to which this difference is influenced by past experience.* In football, when a play is initiated, all the receivers and backs move, even though the play may be designed to get the ball to only one player. The task faced by a linebacker is to

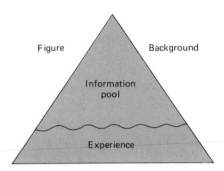

FIGURE 5-6 Adaptation-level theory.

identify the primary receiver (the object) from among all the offensive players (the background) guided at the same time by the opposition's earlier attempts to run that play (past experience).

Changes in the adaptation level are produced by variations in the accompanying stimuli or as a result of different prior experiences. It is differences in the adaptation level that result in divergent interpretations of identical stimuli by the same or different individuals. When you slow down to 35 mph as you enter a small town, after speeding along the highway at 70 mph, you feel as if you are crawling. On the other hand, when you turn out of your driveway into the street, accelerating up to 35 mph seems quite fast. However, to a professional racing driver, even 70 mph might appear quite slow.

Sensory-tonic theory

Here again there are two main elements: (1) *sensory*, the input from the object and its background, and (2) *tonic*, the input from inside the body. The sensory-tonic theory (Werner & Wapner, 1949) recognizes that perception is affected by the state of the individual as well as the visual field.

The theory emphasizes the interaction of the various sense modalities, such as hearing and kinesthesis, with visual perception. Internal signals from the semicircular canals of the inner ear play a major role in the maintenance of equilibrium; if they are disturbed, so will be our vertical perception. You can easily demonstrate this for yourself by spinning around quickly five or six times with your eyes closed and then immediately trying to walk a straight line with your eyes open. The continued movement of fluid in the semicircular canals, after the spinning has stopped, is sufficient to temporarily disrupt all other signals concerned with equilibrium and makes walking very difficult.

In this theory, there is also a concern for a greater recognition of the interaction between the sensory and motor areas of the brain, in particular the relationship between tonus—the general state of muscle tension—and perception. In one experiment, Wapner, Werner, and Chandler (1951) found that by stimulating the postural muscles on either side of the head they could affect the subject's ability to judge the vertical position of a luminous rod in a dark room. One would expect the judgment of the position of the rod to be based purely on external visual information: the rod itself. Clearly, this was not the case, because internal signals reflecting changes in muscle tone influenced this judgment.

A second experiment by Krus, Werner, and Wapner (1953) illustrated a more indirect interaction. Here, motor involvement—exerting pressure on a board for 20 seconds—by subjects viewing pictures that suggested motion was shown to decrease the amount of motion perceived. Although not as dramatic as the effect of rapid rotation, these experiments do underline the sensory-tonic interaction between internal and external sensory inputs.

Transactional theory

Transactional theory (Ittelson & Cantril, 1954) is based on external variables and not internal anatomy. It suggests that we should consider *all* aspects of the event, or transaction, occurring between the person observing a particular event and the object that is the focus of attention. That is, we should concentrate on those *details*, external to but including the individual, that characterize the event, rather than on what the stimuli do to the individual. We cannot separate the immediate perception of one portion of the environment from our overall perception of the environment. In badminton, the doubles players at the net only receive visual information from in front of them; however, their overall perception of the game involves assumptions regarding the position of their partners behind them.

Using transactional theory as its base, research would aim at finding all the discrepancies or similarities in different situations. It is from transactional theory that we have been presented with the famous distorted rooms. A person standing in one corner of the room appears as a midget but grows to gaint proportions by moving to the opposite corner of the room. Only by taking a second look at these rooms do we realize they are distorted. Our assumption that the room was of normal proportions caused us to distort our perception of the site of the people. When we recognize that the person has not changed size, we realize that the floor and ceiling are sloping. This theory illustrates how assumptions based on our earlier experiences are used to deal with recurring or new situations.

While the assumptions we make about our environment simplify the perceptual process, they may also lead us to overlook important details of the transaction. In a game such as basketball, for example, researchers would try to identify the differences between shooting at a basket with a wooden or a clear backboard and the effect of differences in the markings on·the gym wall behind the backboard.

Neurogeometric theory

Neurogeometric theory (Smith & Smith, 1962) looks at the way we handle visual-motor distortions and is based on the concept of feedback. In their experiments, Smith and Smith created distortions by interfering with or delaying the visual feedback received by subjects. A subject might be asked to draw a picture. By only allowing subjects to use a television monitor to view their movements rather than watching their hands directly, the visual feedback from their movements was easily manipulated. The camera angle was changed or a delay introduced into the transmission to the monitor such that movements were viewed one-fifth second after they were initiated. Artificially increasing the time interval between movement of the hand and vision of this movement, normally simultaneous events, Smith and Smith created what they called visual-motor distortions. How subjects were able to deal with these distortions has provided valuable information about the role of feedback control of movement and has led to the formulation of the neurogeometric theory.

The two main elements of the theory were thought to be the spatial relationships involved in making the movement (changes in position) and the associated sensory feedback. The theory suggests a neural mechanism called "detector neurons" that detects differences or changes in spatial patterns or positions. "Detector neurons" are presumed to be similar to the mechanism that allows sensory receptors in the muscles and joints to signal changes in the position of limbs.

There has been some argument over this position (Cratty, 1973a), but neurogeometric theory is noteworthy as one of the few theories to take the approach of emphasizing feedback generated by the subject's own actions and of offering a physiological explanation of its effect on perception. A more detailed description of some of the neural components of motor control will be presented in Chapter 6.

Space perception theory

Held (1965) considered the relationship between perception and self-induced movement. He felt that the development of perceptual organization occurs through active interaction of the individual with the environment.

An often-cited experiment compared active and passive kittens in a controlled environment (a large cylinder) where "active" and "passive" describe the extent to which the kittens were allowed to move. The active kittens were able to move around the cylinder but in the process they would pull the passive kittens around with them. The experimental apparatus was arranged mechanically so that there was no large resistance for the active kittens to overcome. The passive kittens were fixed in a "box" such that they received the same visual information as the active kittens when they traveled around the cylinder, but the passive kittens were unable to move. The results could be summarized as follows. The active kittens, who were free to move, developed normal sensory-motor reactions. However, the passive kittens, whose movements were restricted, did not develop normal sensory-motor reactions until they had been free for some time.

From this and other experiments, Held suggested that perceptual organization was learned, and at the center of this process was self-initiated movement. We assess the environment by its reactions to our movements. Today it is suggested that this is true for some perception but not for all. According to one study (Smith, 1966), movement and manipulation aid the development of depth perception but not distance judgments. Held's emphasis on the relationship between self-induced movement and the development of perception may appear a little tenuous. However, he is not the only researcher to emphasize the role of movement in the early stages of development. Both Piaget (1950) and Bruner (1973) consider the sensory-motor stage (birth to 1 year) to be the first step in the development of intelligence (Piaget) and of motor skill development (Bruner) in the infant. Nevertheless, as children develop so do other means of interacting with their environment (*i.e.*, speech), leaving an important role for movement but not an exclusive one.

Toward an explanation of perception

As stated earlier, each of these perceptual theories emphasizes one aspect of perception. To provide a more complete description of the perceptual process that captures a majority of the factors affecting perception, we would need a combination of all these ideas.

The core-context, adaptation-level, and transactional theories would all appear to revolve around the three elements of object, background, and past experience. Consider an experiment in which the subjects were asked to observe the flight of a ball (the *object*) and judge its point of impact on the ground. Different decisions would be made by one person from trial to trial about the same ball traveling the same flight path because of changes in the *background*. The movement of a white ball would be harder to judge against a white rather than a black background. Transactional theory emphasizes that we pay attention to the detail of the situation. The main cue used by subjects for judging the flight may actually be a crack halfway down the wall that provides a backdrop for the flight path. Only by paying attention to the detail of the situation can we be sure of identifying the most pertinent cues.

In a practical sense, the transactional viewpoint would suggest that it is important for the visiting team to have an extended warm-up in the opponent's gym, arena, or field. Even though the dimensions of the playing surface may be fixed by the laws of the game, small differences will exist. If these differences go undetected, they may adversely affect the player's judgment.

Variability in the judgment of the flight path between subjects could be accounted for by differences in past experience. The individual who has played a lot of tennis may be superior to a swimmer in making judgments about the ball's flight. However, exposing the swimmer to tennis may produce changes in the judgments made by that person. Obviously, between individuals there are physiological differences in perceptual ability that are fairly fixed, and these will also produce differences in how two people perceive the same situation. Consider, for example, the problems to be faced in distinguishing the object from the background by a person who is color blind.

One final factor that can account for variability in perception, both between individuals and within the same individual, is the changing *internal state*, particularly emotional, of the individual. This factor was referred to in the sensory-tonic theory. The "problem" of losing the competitive edge due to sexual intercourse before an important game is often argued by coaches. The problem is concerned equally with the possible negative effects on performance as the result of feeling greatly relaxed and perhaps lethargic as it is with the possibility of burning up vital energy supplies.

While all the perceptual theories mentioned thus far provide a starting point, we need to look more closely at the stages of sensory analysis in order to understand more fully the process of perception. By sensory analysis we refer to the psychological processes of signal detection and recognition and not to the underlying physiological mechanisms—receptors and neural pathways—that facilitate this process.

STAGES OF SENSORY ANALYSIS

Having reviewed some of the perceptual theories, we will now present a more detailed breakdown of the perceptual process. Particular emphasis will be given to those operations that may be performed on the sensory information and that represent both the extent and the limitations of the perceptual mechanism.

The Rappaport model (Figure 5-5) presented a descriptive view of how the mass of perceptual information can be reduced to a manageable size. Now we will examine the main stages in the analysis of the sensory information. These stages progress from the initial detection and comparison of a signal to the recognition of both individual stimuli and patterns of stimuli. This section closes with some notes on the overall influence of perceptual organization in the learning situation.

Detection

All the sensory information detected by the body's receptors (*e.g.*, eyes, ears) is forwarded to the brain, where it is collected and interpreted. The messages of the nervous system are transmitted along nerve pathways. While the spinal cord and the brain represent the central nervous system, the nerve pathways that carry neural impulses to and from the brain and spinal cord constitute the peripheral nervous system.

Regardless of whether the sensory information is visual, auditory, or kinesthetic, it is all transmitted to the brain as nerve impulses. These nerve impulses or signals can be compared to electrical currents moving along wires. Most of these signals are moving at very high speeds—more than 150 meters (or 1½ football fields) per second. Thus, if you imagine yourself as a miniaturized spaceman exploring the human brain you may well find yourself deafened by the sound of electrical charges (nerve impulses) crackling along the wires (nerves). The brain receives over 100,000 signals per second, and for that reason all the neural activity in the brain may be referred to, collectively, as *"noise."*

When a sensory receptor at the periphery of the nervous system fires (consider the speed of the nerve impulse) a signal to the brain, there is no guarantee that because the sensory receptor recorded and reported the change it will be recognized or interpreted accurately by the brain. Remember, the brain constantly receives thousands of signals. Any new signal that arrives in the brain will find itself in the middle of a considerable amount of pandemonium, in which only the "loudest" messages are afforded any attention.

In order to be part of a skill, sensory information must be detected by the brain. To be detected by the brain it must first be within the *sensory capacity* of the individual. We do not necessarily perceive all the available information, however, because there are limits to sensory capacity, notably physiological limits. We cannot detect certain sounds because the pitch is too high or the volume is too low. Similarly, a light may be too dim for our eyes to discern physical details of our environment. In addition, the physical properties of the type of sensory information impose their own limitations, as can be seen when choosing sound or light as a warning signal. Sound tends to be a better warning signal because you do not need to be facing the source in order to hear it. It is only when you hear the siren that you look in your rearview mirror and see the flashing lights that signal the resultant speeding ticket. Even if a stimulus change is reported by a receptor, however, it does not mean that we will become consciously aware of it. Perception, including the conscious detection of a stimulus, is a function of the central processing (*i.e.,* the brain).

As the perceptual theories point out, central perception is not just a record of the stimuli present in the environment at a given moment in time. Information previously processed and related to that event can influence our current perception of that event. This can be illustrated in two ways. When entering a brightly lit room from a dark corridor, you are initially dazzled by the lights but after a few seconds your eyes adapt to the change and you are no longer disturbed by the bright lights. Put simply, we could say that the sensory receptors (the eyes) that signal changes in the level of stimulation (the amount of light) tend to adapt and fire less frequently when the level of stimulation becomes constant after the initial change.

This phenomenon of adaptation is common to all sensory receptors. The same light that is initially perceived as being too bright might later be considered acceptable. As you step out of a quiet downtown bank onto a busy street, you may at first find the noise almost deafening. A minute later, having adapted to the change in noise level, you walk to the bus stop and are hardly aware of the commotion around you. A second way in which our current perceptions are influenced results from the fact that signals are dealt with in the context of other sensory information present at that moment in time. The car headlights that look white on an unlit country road become a pale yellow when seen against a background of bright city lights. You can try this for yourself by striking a match in a dark room and then switching on the lights.

Signal detection theory

Assuming that a signal is within the normal range of sensitivity for a particular sensory receptor, the conscious detection of a signal is a function of (1) the intensity of the signal and (2) a threshold value for detectability, the minimum intensity above which a signal becomes detectable. The precision or acuity of the different senses varies, but there are generally certain limits. Our ability to detect changes in the loudness of a sound, for example, is measured in decibels. A change of 1 decibel represents an increase in the intensity of the sound of about 1.26 times, approximately the minimum change in intensity that we can detect.

Unlike the sensory receptor that may fire off a signal after some minimal change in the level of stimulation, there is no fixed threshold value or fixed intensity above which a sound or a light suddenly becomes detectable centrally in the brain. For example, if you tried to ascertain the threshold volume at which a subject could detect (hear) a particular tone, the graph of your data would look like Figure 5-7. There would be a certain range of intensities below or above which the detectability of the signal would be predictable, but between those two points the level of detectability would be subject to large variations. In fact, the intensity at which the signal is detected varies not only with the type of stimulus but also with the subject's motivation and the instructions given.

The lack of a fixed threshold represents only one of the problems for

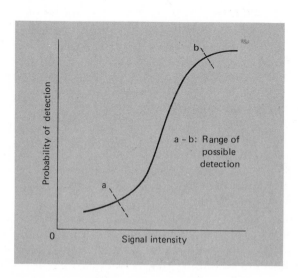

FIGURE 5-7 Signal detection—a threshold.

signal detection. The second problem is that all signals are normally received in the brain against a background of noise that, in turn, may interfere with detection. Here we use noise in its broad sense as referring to a general level of neural activity within any sensory modality, the cumulative effect of which is to produce what we referred to earlier as pandemonium. Background noise itself does not just refer to sound. In the above example of detecting a tone, we were dealing with sound, but the signal (a tone) to which we are trying to attend does not represent the only signal being processed in that sensory modality. Other sounds when represented as neural impulses constitute the background noise (interference). The same idea applies equally well to any sensory modality. Although we may be trying to watch the traffic lights change, other flashing neon signs may interfere with this process. Here, the traffic lights represent the main signal to which we wish to attend and the flashing neon signs are the background noise or interference.

The problems of lack of a fixed threshold value and background noise can be illustrated by a simple experiment. If you hold a wristwatch close to your ear you can easily hear it ticking, but if it is placed at arm's length it may be impossible to detect any sound. However, if you hold your watch far enough from your ear so that you can just hear it ticking, you will note that soon the sound appears weaker or louder or may even disappear. This demonstration, suggested by Woodworth and Schlosberg (1954), illustrates the variable detectability that is characteristic of the perceptual process, resulting from the lack of a fixed threshold value for any signal and compounded by the factor of background noise.

In an attempt to explain this signal/noise problem and the lack of consistency in the ability to detect signals, the *signal detection theory* was proposed based mainly on the work of Tanner and Swets and their associates (Tanner & Swets, 1954; Swets, 1964; Swets, Tanner, & Birdsall, 1961). Signal detection theory is represented by the following two assumptions:

1. Every change in physical energy of the signal gives rise to some change within the organism. When a sensory receptor registers some change in the level of stimulation and sends a signal to the brain, there is, as a consequence, increased neural activity in the brain.
2. The probability of detection depends on the intensity of the signal relative to its background. Simply, the greater the level of background noise, the lower the probability of detecting a specific signal.

Unless a person is dead there will always be some neural activity (noise) in the brain. Any new signal that occurs will add to this level of background noise in proportion to the intensity of the signal. If you draw a graph to represent the level of background noise where X represents the amount of internal activity present at any given moment in time, you will produce a normal probability curve (Figure 5-8). If you monitored the level of neural activity in the brain over a given period of time, only occasionally will the level of background noise be either extremely low or extremely high. Most of the time it will be at some intermediate level. If we add a specific signal to that general noise level, the probability that the signal will produce a given level of neural activity (noise) will vary as a function of the background noise itself. As the signal gives rise to a specific amount of neural activity, the total level of activity (signal plus background noise) will depend on the amount of background noise that was present when the signal occurred. Thus we could draw a second curve for signal plus background noise somewhere to the right of the first curve, depending on the intensity of the signal. The extent of the separation or overlap between the two curves provides a measure of signal detectability.

The greater the distance between the peaks of the two curves (d' pronounced "d prime"), the more likely you are to detect a signal. Put simply, if the signal is very strong, the two curves are totally separate and you will be able to detect all signals when they occur. If the two curves overlap, there is the possibility of reporting a signal that did not occur or of making errors. The greater the overlap, the greater is the chance for errors, because there will be times when the level of background noise alone is higher than some occurrences of low background noise plus signal. Within this region of overlap you may either miss a signal or give a false alarm.

To overcome this problem, people adopt a criterion (C) and report any activity beyond that criterion value as a signal (Figure 5-8). By shifting the criterion, you can either increase the probability of missing a signal (move C to the right) or of giving false alarms (move C to left). Where the criterion is set

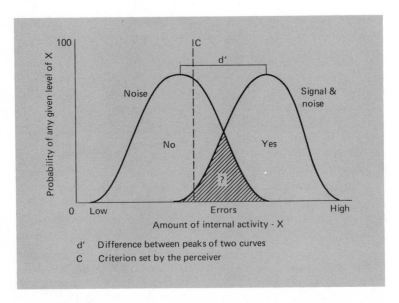

FIGURE 5-8   Relationship between signal and noise: is a signal present?

will depend on the situation or perhaps the motivation of the receiver and on the importance placed on not missing signals or on not giving false alarms. The task of plane spotters during wartime demonstrates our point. It would be imperative to alert the antiaircraft gunners at the first sight of a plane, even though you are not sure it is the enemy. It would be suicidal to wait until the plane is overhead to determine whether or not it actually is the enemy (Figure 5-9).

The computation of d' is based on probability theory and provides a useful tool for assessing sensory capacity. Sensory capacity can be evaluated by recording the number of correct identifications, false alarms, misses, or correct rejections made by a subject when trying to determine the presence or absence of a signal. Results produced by subsequent subjects reflect not only individual differences in sensory capacity but also differences in motivational level or previous experience, all of which might affect choices. Varying the

FIGURE 5-9 Your plane or mine?

rewards and punishments for correct responses or false alarms, for example, can affect the placement of the criterion (Katz, 1964).

Signal detection theory helps us to understand the problems faced by beginning skiers listening to their instructor yell, "hold that snowplow, keep your weight forward, head up and bend your knees" as they head down the slope. Among the mass of unfamiliar kinesthetic information the beginners are experiencing, they probably do not even know where their knees are, let alone whether they are bent. To help the beginner, we must try to decrease this signal detection problem by reducing the amount of interfering stimuli or by providing signals that are so strong that they cannot be missed. The latter situation can be illustrated by the diving coach who calls "now" in order to tell the diver when to come out of a dive. Similarly, for the skier a single instruction, "bend your knees," would be easier to handle. The clear verbal cue now helps the learner detect and focus on the important kinesthetic information.

Comparative judgments

Having established how we may detect that a signal has occurred, the next operation is *to compare the signal with previous information from the same sensory modality* in order to make some judgment about that signal: was it the same as or different than a previous signal? In a typical experiment, a subject is presented with one stimulus, referred to as the standard, and then asked to compare that standard stimulus with a series of similar stimuli. Using weights, for example, the subject would in each case try to identify the new weight (stimulus) as either the same weight as the standard or as heavier or lighter than the standard.

In terms of the visual sense, it has been reported that if the eye is presented with two stimuli—a standard stimulus plus a test stimulus placed side by side—it is able to detect a 2% difference in brightness between the stimuli under good conditions (Fitts & Posner, 1967). This ability to make comparative judgments between some standard and a second signal allows us to distinguish between large numbers of alternatives. The limits of this capacity are expressed as *Weber's law*, in which the smallest amount of stimulus change that can be detected, the just noticeable difference (jnd), is approximately proportional to the size of the standard. This is expressed as a ratio:

$$K = \frac{\text{the just noticeable difference}}{\text{the intensity of the standard}}$$

where K is a constant. For example, if the standard was a 1-pound weight and the jnd was 1 ounce, the Weber ratio would be 1/16 or 0.0625. This means that if you add either 1 ounce to a 1-pound weight or 1 pound to a 16-pound weight, the changes in weight of the standard should be equally detectable. If you can detect a 1-ounce change in a 1-pound standard (15 or 17 ounces) then you should be capable of detecting a 1-pound change in a 16-pound standard (15 or 17 pounds).

Weber's law is important because it provides a simple means of assessing the precision with which judgments might be made in any sensory modality. The Weber ratio varies for different senses and types of comparisons, one of the most sensitive being the discrimination of pitch. The Weber ratios for kinesthetic sensitivity (lifting small weights) and visual brightness are also fairly precise. Both ratios are higher, and therefore less sensitive, than the discrimination of pitch, but at the same time they are lower than the Weber ratio for the judgment of loudness (Woodworth & Schlosberg, 1954). Thus, the kinesthetic sense seems to be equivalent to the other two dominant senses of vision and audition, at least in terms of comparative judgments.

Whether a basketball guard is trying to judge the shortest route to the basket or whether the fullback in football is looking for the largest hole in the defensive line, the ability to make accurate judgments is an essential element of motor skill performance. The technique of measuring Weber's law can be applied to any type of judgment involving a standard. As such, it provides one way of assessing an athlete's ability to discriminate. This technique could be used, therefore, as one element in a test battery for team assignment or selection, depending on the abilities required for each position.

Absolute judgments

Unfortunately, most often when performing motor skills we have to make judgments without having a standard available to help categorize a given stimulus. The quarterback cannot play the game with a playbook in one hand and the ball in the other to make a comparative judgment about whether the players are in the proper positions. In these cases we must use some standard stored in memory; the standard is said to be internal or *implicit*.

Judgments that are made on the basis of some standard stored in memory are referred to as *absolute judgments*. Anyone who has studied music has probably been faced with the task of distinguishing between two tones and judging the interval as a fourth or a third. An interesting and related question might be: when a random number of tones are presented, how many different tones can be identified? Are we limited to distinguishing between two tones, or can we use the implicit standards stored in memory to make judgments about a whole series of tones?

We have met this problem before when we considered the number of bits of information that could be stored in short-term memory, the limit being 7 ± 2 bits. As was the case with Weber's law, there has been a great deal of research on the topic of absolute judgments. A typical experiment usually involves the presentation of a number of tones to a subject who tries to remember them and gives each tone a label in order to identify it. The tones are then presented to the subject a second time in a random order, and the subject is asked to identify each one. Generally, these experiments show the following (Fitts & Posner, 1967):

1. When dealing with absolute judgments of only one sensory dimension of an object such as shape, we are limited in our ability to distinguish values of those dimensional stimuli to only five to ten (Attneave, 1959). Above that maximum, errors appear. If in an experiment we were required to reach through a curtain and distinguish between a series of similar objects only by their shape (tactile information), we could probably distinguish consistently no more than ten.

2. A few individuals have a greater capacity for absolute judgments along some sensory dimensions (*e.g.*, the person who has "perfect pitch" and can easily identify any note on the piano).

3. The limits of our ability to make absolute judgments change only slightly with practice (Hartman, 1954).

4. As the number of dimensions of a stimulus increases, the number of separate stimuli that can be recognized increases, but this number is fewer than would be expected if the dimensions were independent. For example, in an experiment (Pollack, 1952) tones were varied by both pitch and loudness—two different sensory dimensions. A high pitch may have been combined with a low volume. Subjects were able to identify 5 tones (loudness) and 5.5 tones (pitch) when faced by each dimension independently, but the total only increased to 8 (and not 10 or 11) when they were combined. The numbers of identifiable stimuli are not simply additive.

The main problem in making absolute judgments lies in the inexactness of the implicit standard held in memory. Swimmers approaching the end of the pool, for example, must recognize the point at which to initiate the racing turn in order to gain the maximum thrust. Unfortunately, there is no "magnetic field" on the water's surface to identify this point and the swimmers must judge their position in relation to some markings on the pool floor or surroundings. An error in this judgment could result in the swimmer losing the race, so it is most important that a precise standard be established.

The coach of a team sport has a different problem that may interfere with the precision of the standard, and that is the number of different game situations or set plays the player must retain. One practical suggestion for the coach of a team sport might be to limit the number of variations of a particular set play to five or six. In this way the coach can be sure that the number of variations is within the capacity limits of most of the players. This is particularly important when considering the large number of possible variations in some basketball offenses. We will see this problem relating to the accuracy of the retained standard more clearly in Chapter 6 when we look at some of the experiments comparing visual and kinesthetic perception.

Pattern recognition

From the previous section, it would appear that we are fairly limited in our perceptual abilities, at least when we are concerned with specific signals. Generally, however, this is not the case, for rather than deal with signals one at a time it is more normal to be faced with a whole pattern of stimuli. Fortunately, we have in fact a fairly large capacity to respond to patterns of stimuli or relationships.

Just consider your own ability to read various sizes of printed word on a page or to recognize the spoken word even though everyone's voice is different. A human's pattern recognition ability is a capacity matched as yet by few machines in terms of its flexibility. There are machines that can identify voice patterns, shapes, or forces, but the human "machine" can do all these and more.

The important question for pattern recognition is how much distortion can we handle or how precise does the pattern have to be before it is identifiable? The following experiment by Miller, Heise, and Lichten (1951) deals with that question. The subjects were required to pick a word from a number of alternatives when those words were presented against varying amounts of background noise (white noise or static). In this experiment "noise" does refer to sound, as the subjects were trying to hear and recognize one spoken word against a background of static. The spoken word itself was regarded as the signal the subjects were trying to detect. The subjects knew from which list of possible words the signal word was selected. The results of this experiment (Figure 5-10) show that (1) the subject's ability to pick out the correct word increased with the intensity of the signal in relation to the

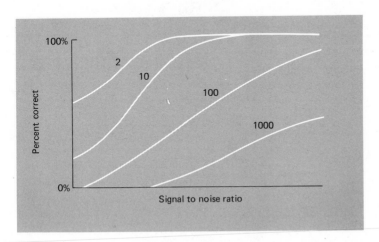

FIGURE 5-10 Recognizing words against background noise (based on Miller, Heise & Lichten, 1951).

amount of background noise (the signal-to-noise ratio) and (2) the ability to identify the correct word decreased as the number of alternatives increased. When the number of words in a list is low (two), the probability that any given word would occur is high (50%). If there are ten possible words that might occur, the probability of any specific word occurring is much lower (10%). Therefore, if an event is highly probable, it can withstand distortion and still be identified, but if it is not predictable then the distortion will greatly affect recognition.

People generally overcome this problem of distortion by using prior knowledge. After many hours of television viewing, you may find that if you know the outline of a particular program, it is easy to follow that program even though you have missed the start. Your previous experience and knowledge of the program helps to make it more predictable. Does the hero of a detective series ever get killed?

In proofreading the reverse situation occurs. We find it easy to make an error because the context or meaning leads us to see the correct pattern even though it is not present. Many an assignment handed in five minutes before the deadline has contained just such "unbelievable" errors as appear in Figure 5-11.

In team sports, players are constantly on the move, making it difficult to locate one particular player. Such is the situation often faced by the quarterback in football. The quarterback must throw the ball before the receiver arrives at the point where the ball will be caught. When looking over

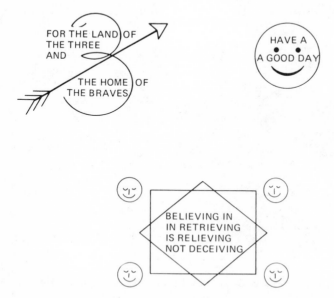

FIGURE 5-11 The proof is in the reading.

the onrushing defensive line, the quarterback may not be able to see the receivers clearly. However, by observing the position of the yardmarkers, the sideline, and the line markings across the field and by knowing the pattern being run by the receivers, the quarterback may be able to identify where to throw the ball. Alternatively, on the first play the defense blitzes and sacks the quarterback. On the second play they line up for another blitz. The quarterback sees this and throws long, only to discover the play was a fake and the ball has been intercepted.

Whether applied to reading or motor performance, pattern recognition helps overcome the problems or limitations associated with absolute judgments by reducing the number of different stimuli with which we must deal. To some extent it is an extension of what we saw in absolute judgments. We saw that by creating a signal that is a composite of stimuli from two different dimensions (pitch and volume) we are able to differentiate between more signals. In pattern recognition, the individual is combining many, rather than just two dimensions. Because of this integration of sensory information from different sources, pattern recognition implies that rather than working at the proprioceptive level (Rappaport, Figure 5-5), we are dealing instead with mental images or percepts. In pattern recognition we are no longer trying to distinguish between and identify separate sensory stimuli (the proprioceptive level). We are concerned with the combination of different sources of sensory information or percepts. Pattern recognition represents a higher level of perceptual processing.

Perceptual organization

The idea of perceptual organization through a process of information reduction—reducing the mass of incoming sensory information to a manageable size—is implicit in the Rappaport model and has previously been referred to in Chapter 2 as chunking (information theory) or grouping (Gestalt theory). The Gestaltists suggested that such organization occurred because of the similarity or proximity of stimuli. It was viewed as part of the natural perceptual organization process that was necessary to bring order to our perception of the environment.

Some sort of organization would seem to be essential even when handling small amounts of information. An organizational structure permits both the handling of large amounts (chunks) of information and the handling of small amounts more efficiently, and thereby facilitates memory. Obviously, how a signal is perceived will affect how it is stored and what is retrieved from memory.

The role of perceptual organization has been researched extensively in the verbal learning literature. Tulving (1965) has demonstrated a clear relationship between organization and performance when subjects are learning lists of words. The same author (1966) also illustrated that prior learning of a portion of a final list of words may actually retard the effective learning of the final list itself. The inference here is that the organization established to handle the partial list was not sufficient for the final list of words. Therefore, the subject must reorganize the previously stored items in relation to the new information. Remembering five countries and five towns may be easy to organize, but adding 20 random nouns to that list would involve a complete reorganization of the total list, rather than the addition of new words to the existing memory structure.

Applying these ideas to perceptual organization in motor learning, researchers have clearly shown that movements are reproduced better when there is some pre-movement organization. When the subject is able to establish the relationship between the movement to be reproduced and other movements previously made, performance is enhanced (Stelmach & Kelso, 1977). Extending this work, Diewert and Stelmach (1978) have shown that experimenter-presented organizations (the experimenter tells the subject the relationship between the movements to be reproduced) and subject-discovered organizations (the subjects create their own organization) are both powerful variables in the retention of movements. The effects are strongest when the subjects themselves establish the organization.

Diewert and Stelmach (1978) also suggest that the factor of perceptual organization may be sufficiently strong that in certain situations learning can occur without knowledge of results. However, it is important to note that the mere presence of an organizational structure within the learning situation is not sufficient in itself. It is not sufficient for the instructor to know that some relationship exists, the learner must be encouraged to actively organize the information. Again, perceptual organization is a dynamic rather than a passive process. It involves understanding and interpreting the organized information, rather than simply memorizing the relationships involved. In a passing drill, the aim of the practice may not be to simply practice the technique of passing but rather to learn when to pass. You pass when the receiver is in a space and not guarded by a defender. The important variables involved in making this judgment are the distance between the receiver and the defender, the distance the ball must be passed, and the speed with which the players are moving. Encouraging the learner to organize this information in order to decide when and when not to pass may be equally important as practicing the passing technique itself.

SELECTIVE ATTENTION

So far we have considered the problems of detecting a signal, how part of a stimulus pattern can be used to recognize the complete pattern, and the influence of perceptual organization on learning and performance. From the previous chapter we know that these operations all require attention. If all these processes do take attention and occupy the limited capacity of the central mechanisms, the question remains as to how the learner can deal with the mass of information that is available. The answer lies in selective attention.

Selective attention refers to the process whereby people can selectively attend to a specific stimulus. In other words, the individual can concentrate on one specific feature while ignoring other simultaneously presented stimuli. This is a situation that is common to most team and dual sports.

Most of the research on selective attention has been concerned with selectivity within a single sensory modality. The three chief types of experimental tasks used are

1. Searching complex visual fields or searching memory
2. Recognizing briefly presented material
3. Attending to a specific auditory message

When considering the role of the sensory information store in the recognition of briefly presented material (Chapter 4), we noted that the precision of this store, in terms of items recalled, was a function of attention. Only when the subject was presented with three rows of numbers and was cued as to which row was important, or when the subject focused attention on one part of the pattern of stimuli, could items be recalled accurately. Also, we noted that one of the possible limitations of recall was the retrieval process itself. The following section will deal with the rate of search and models of attention that have evolved from this work and related experimental tasks.

Rate of search

One of the major characteristics of sports is their speed. Not only must the players make accurate decisions, but they also must make them quickly. The tennis player only has a brief glance over the net to judge the position of his opponent on the court. The offensive lineman has only a second to search his memory when the quarterback changes the play just before the ball is snapped. Whether searching the field of visual stimuli or memory, the one factor that plays an important role in the identification of an item or of a pattern within a large number of stimuli is the rate at which the key element in that visual field can be found. The Gestaltists (Chapter 2) used the term *visual field* to describe the mass of stimuli that we could see in the environment at any one time. Experimentally, when a subject is presented with a sample of these stimuli, by means of a slide, these stimuli are referred to as an array. In visual search tests, subjects are presented with an array of stimuli and required to locate a specific stimulus (the target item) in the array (Figure 5-12). Although not involving motor skills, these visual search tests do revolve around an important element in motor performance: *the rate of visual search.*

The non-target items in the array of stimuli are referred to as field items. Responses vary from (1) indicating whether or not a target item is present, (2) indicating the actual location of the target item, or (3) remembering its identity. *The critical factor in visual search is the delay between the presentation of the array and the onset of the response indicating the subject has located the target item. This time interval is called a latency period.* Visual search tasks usually involve either identification (finding a Z in a list of letters) or relationships, such as determining whether or not a list of words contains a word that is the name of a flower. The important question in such a search task is whether the perception of target items differs in any way from the perception of field items.

Try the following simple experiment yourself using Figure 5-12 and a watch with a sweep second hand. On each trial, start when the second hand reaches the 12 o'clock position and then note the position of the second hand when you find the required item. There are three trials, so complete the first one before you read the instructions for the second trial. For the first trial, you are looking for the letter *h*, not *H*. In the second, you are looking for an *m*. For the third trial you have a question: is there an *a* in the list? Now compare your impressions of this task with some of the conclusions drawn from similar experiments. Findings from experiments using these techniques include the following:

1. Subjects report not "seeing" the irrelevant items; the non-target or field items are passed over in a blur while the target items seem to stand out.
2. Subjects show very little retention of field items when these items are tested subsequently for recognition. Returning to the experiment you

RCDSVX
VECObH
rdCODG
negXVR
UOXNuV
NCDVOT
SWVOdg
HVhNZP
nfWXMG
EgGBYC
SZNIyV
NXhDHY
VEVHGD
HDqSdW
ZOCSDB
FSLYuO
kBbWuN
PYCGNe
RtmFJM   **FIGURE 5-12**   Rate of search.

have just completed, do you recall if there was a p in the list? As you were not asked to search for this letter, or any similar letter, it is unlikely that you could answer this question.

3. The search *for* a given target is faster than the search for its *absence*. If you performed many trials searching for specific items, on the average you would only have to scan half the list. On some trials the target item would be the first item you see; on others, it would be the last. However, checking for the absence of a target item means checking every item in the list on every trial, thereby taking more time. In addition, this difference in the rate of search implies that you spend more time per item analyzing the field items as you endeavor to be certain they are not target items.

4. Similarity between the target and the field items influences the rate of search, with the rate of search decreasing as the degree of similarity between these two variables increases. Searching for a b might be made more difficult by increasing the number of ds in the list.

5. Initially there is a direct relationship between the total number of items in the array and the time required to find the target item. In other words, as the number of items increases, so does the search time.

6. After extensive practice, the speed at which subjects search for targets becomes independent of the number of targets.

On the basis of these results, Neisser (1964) concluded that recognition, at least during visual search, may be described as a hierarchical system of decision processes. A hierarchical system implies that the information is processed through a series of tests that become more refined as the number of items left to be considered is reduced. Imagine the sort of characteristics you would look for while searching for an O or an A in the list in Figure 5-12. Clearly, all non-capital letters would be rejected as non-targets and fail to pass the first low-level test. The basic or low-level tests are those that are used initially to sort out the information. In this case, all non-capital letters are rejected and not considered further, while all capital letters would be analyzed further (Figure 5-13). These simple tests would then be followed by more demanding tests. The hierarchical model suggests that the perception of target items is indeed different from the perception of the field items, in that the field items rejected by the low-level tests are not processed any further, whereas target items receive greater analysis.

With this model, it is now possible to explain some of the results of the visual search experiments. The field items failing the elementary tests are not positively identified, appearing to blur as a consequence, and since they are not fully perceived they are not remembered during subsequent recognition tests. In our simple experiment we were not asked to search for the letter p; consequently we cannot be certain if one existed in the list of letters.

Search for the presence of a target is faster than search for its absence, since when searching for a target the field items are scanned quickly and do not engage the full depth or range of tests necessary to identify the target item. Looking for a capital *A*, the eye searches for a spot where at least two straight lines meet at an angle; other formations are not even considered. Only then are more refined tests applied to determine if it is a target item (Figure 5-13). It does not matter if it is the *A* in the first line or the *A* in the tenth line. However, the more refined processing of other "linear" items, such as an *L* or an *I*, is required in every line when searching whether *A* is absent, in order to be certain that the item is not an *A*.

The similarity of target and field items also calls for a more detailed examination of all the items before their rejection as non-targets. This is necessary since similar items, an *N* or a *V*, will pass some of the low-level tests and there will be a more detailed analysis of these items. As more time is required to analyze each item, the rate of search will decrease.

In the reverse situation, however, if a pattern is highly familiar the number of items has little effect on the rate of search, and the presentation and recognition of the target become increasingly simultaneous. Without this ability, reading would be impossibly slow. Imagine going through the alphabet for each letter in a word. Note, therefore, that these incremental rates—more items, longer search time—only apply to new material.

In water polo, the attacking players with the ball scan the pool ahead to find a player to pass to, the target item. They look for players with the same color cap, who are in a space, and who have a clear path between them and the

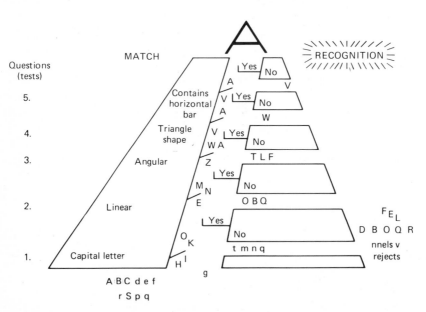

FIGURE 5-13 The search for the letter A.

ball carrier. The attacking players can choose the first player they see. On the other hand, the defensive players are faced with the task of checking all the opposition to make sure they are all properly guarded. In line with our experiment, while the offensive players search for the presence of a target, the defensive players search for its absence. The reduced time required by the offensive players gives them an advantage over the defensive players.

Depth of processing

From the visual search research, it would seem reasonable to accept Neisser's (1964) conclusion that the perceptual mechanism can be represented as a hierarchical series of processing stages, proceeding from the initial sensory analysis, of pitch or brightness, for example, to matching or pattern recognition, through to the extraction of meaning. This hierarchy of processing stages may also be referred to as the *depth of processing*. The alternative description of processing stages we have previously used is illustrated by the information processing model described in Chapter 2. This model identified three separate storage components for memory: the sensory information store, short-term memory, and long-term memory. The information processing approach attempted to identify the various central controlling structures, such as memory, and to assign mental operations, such as rehearsal, to each structure. The depth of processing concept focuses on the actual series of decision processes or mental operations involved. The implication of the depth of processing concept is that information stored at any level can be submitted to more refined perceptual processing.

The depth of processing concept can be viewed in two ways. In general, a greater depth of processing implies a more detailed or refined analysis. However, this can either involve a progression from one processing stage to the next (from pattern recognition to relationships and meaning) or a more detailed analysis within one processing stage (a more detailed sensory analysis). The former idea of a progression of stages was expressed in Rappaport's model, which reduced the information over a series of stages from a mixture of precepts to general concepts. The hierarchical series of tests referred to in the visual search experiments represent the idea of a detailed analysis within one processing stage.

Craik and Lockhart (1972) have suggested that the retention of any information is to a large extent a function of the depth of the perceptual processing. Recognizing the word *work* requires less processing than interpreting its meaning and relating it to other words or concepts stored in memory. Asking a subject to perform this extra analysis would produce a more permanent retention of the information. The deeper or more elaborate the analysis, the more likely the information is to be retained, assuming that the intent of the learner is to abstract meaning from the information.

In order to facilitate the process of abstraction, the information can be recirculated or rehearsed at one processing stage. It was suggested in Chapter 4 that rehearsal or the repetition of information is one of the ways for information to enter long-term memory, but now we see rehearsal as an operation that can be performed at any processing stage, including the processing of semantic information (meaning) that is normally associated with long-term memory. The implication here for motor skill performance is that, although we tell the learner to repeat the technique, we might produce a more permanent understanding by encouraging the learner to make comparisons with similar skills. The learner might relate the overhead smash in tennis to the serve. Even key points in the skill might be retained better if they are related to the events that immediately precede or follow them.

Craik and Lockhart (1972) further distinguish between two types of rehearsal. *Type I* rehearsal serves only to maintain the information at a particular stage of processing. If a subject in an experiment was required to recall some words a few seconds after they were presented, only a low level of processing (identifying the words) would be necessary. If the information were to be retained for a later time, a more elaborate or deeper analysis would be required, defined by Craik and Lockhart as the type II rehearsal. *Type II* rehearsal involves the continued analysis of the information and, as such, requires more attention and puts greater demands on the individual's limited processing capacity. However, only with type II rehearsal—the active organization of the material—can memory be improved. Craik and Lockhart also suggested that the rate of forgetting is related to the depth of processing, with the rate being slower for the deeper levels of processing.

Thus, the approach taken by Craik and Lockhart emphasizes the level of effort or quality of processing involved. The deeper the analysis, the greater the central processing capacity involved. This contrasts to the information processing models, which illustrate a sequence of stages (boxes) and associate specific mental operations with each stage. Such clear-cut divisions do not accurately represent how the human brain functions. Here we see short-term memory (type I rehearsal) treated not as a separate box but as a mechanism that can facilitate continued or repeated processing at various levels or stages. Specific operations may be shared by different components.

To apply the depth of processing concept as a coaching strategy, we must first change the focus of our attention from lists of letters to the stimuli normally faced by athletes, such as the sound of a slapshot, the feel of an armlock, or the sight of the ball entering the basket. The field items would now consist of opposing players, teammates, sidelines, and nets. The task for the learner is to identify the target items such as the goals, the puck, or the finishing line. If we accept the idea that perception involves a hierarchy of processes or tests, it would appear more useful to provide the learner with specific cues regarding what to look for rather than to provide general instructions. We need to provide the learner with some simple low-level tests that can be applied quickly and easily in order to identify the relevant information.

Providing general instructions that require a deeper analysis can only make performance less efficient as more attention is given to the analysis and taken away from the execution of the appropriate movement. A general instruction such as telling a soccer player to pass only to players who are not closely guarded requires that player to check out many players before finding the appropriate player or target. This takes time and increases the chances of losing possession of the ball. It would be more efficient to tell the player to look to the winger first; if the winger is covered try the center forward; and if the center forward is covered, either carry the ball or try a long, through ball.

In a fast-moving game the coach can play an important role in reducing the amount of information a player must handle and thereby improve the efficiency of each player's performance. By reducing the depth of processing that the player is required to perform, the coach frees the player's processing capacity to handle other tasks, such as the execution of the skill itself. On the other hand, only by encouraging the learner to engage in a deeper analysis (type II rehearsal) during training sessions, can the learner begin to understand the relationships between one game situation and another.

Doctrine of prior entry

Before presenting the models of attention, we shall examine some of the experiments that led to their formation. The following experiment, described by Boring (1950), represents an early attempt to investigate selective attention.

In this experiment the subject was instructed to listen for a bell and at the same time watch the sweep second hand of a large clock. The subject's task was to indicate the number the needle was pointing to when the bell sounded. The results from this experiment showed that when the bell sounded with the needle pointing at number 5, the average subject reported that the needle was on the number 4. Why this happens is explained by the *doctrine of prior entry*, which suggests that people are limited in their ability to process two simultaneous signals from more than one sensory source. When signals arrive simultaneously from two different sources, the subject will process them in serial order. One signal is delayed while the other is being processed. In the experiment, subjects were listening for auditory information (the bell) and therefore processed this signal first while processing of the visual information was delayed. The subject had just processed the number 4 when the bell sounded. This auditory signal (the bell) delayed the processing of further visual information and the subject tended to report the number that had most recently been seen (number 4). If the emphasis had been placed on watching the clock, subjects may have reported the number as 6. In both situations, some subjects would report the correct answer, but the errors made would vary according to which source of information was emphasized, the clock or the bell.

Although this is a simple experiment, it does point out some limitations in our ability to deal with multiple signals. However, the ability to attend to and process signals varies in that signals from patterns that are well learned place little demand on attention. In fact, we can process signals simultaneously if they are highly regular or predictable. In an experiment by Bahrick, Noble, and Fitts (1954), subjects were required to react to stimulus lights by pressing response keys while performing simple mathematical problems that were presented orally. For one group the light signals occurred at regular intervals while they performed the mathematics problems. The first group (regular intervals) did the problems efficiently, but the second group (irregular intervals) had difficulty in both reacting to the signal and doing the mathematics. They had problems time sharing or performing two tasks at the same time, both of which demanded attention. In a practical setting, this would be equivalent to giving a team a new strategy in the last minute of a basketball game, certainly an inappropriate time as the players would probably have enough trouble dealing with the opposition while following their prearranged game plan. Adding a new task that demanded attention would make playing the game more difficult.

Another aspect of selective attention relates to the fate of information that is not attended to at any given moment. People constantly receive thousands of different stimuli, but only a few appear to reach consciousness. Even as you sit reading this book you are receiving signals about the room temperature, the sounds in your immediate environment, the pressure of the chair against your back, and the itch on the end of your nose. Meanwhile you read and comprehend. One approach—the selective listening to speech—has direct relevance to selective attention and the fate of the "non-attended to" information and reveals that subjects are able to receive two or more auditory messages simultaneously and listen to one specific message when so instructed.

There are two elements involved in the selective listening to speech: (1) the location of the sound and (2) the discrepancy between the to-be-remembered message and the irrelevant information. These two elements can be investigated by broadcasting two different messages over two separate speakers or by trying to drown (mask) one message with a louder, distracting message. Experiments on the masking of both pure tones and speech have indicated that a signal can be most easily heard in background noise when the signal and the background noise come from physically different locations (*e.g.*, over two different loudspeakers). When there is a distinction between the two messages, such as differences in volume, rhythm, and pitch, it can serve as a cue to aid in listening to a message against an irrelevant background.

In shadowing experiments (Cherry, 1953), subjects wearing headphones listened to two different messages at once (one message was channeled into each ear) and they shadowed (repeated verbally) the message heard in the right ear. At the end of the experiment they were asked what the left ear had heard. Subjects reported having heard very little. Even switches from English to German were missed but subjects did hear their own names and gross changes in physical characteristics of the message, such as switches from a male to a female voice. From such simple tasks, we can perhaps understand why learning a new skill involves so many mistakes. The beginner at tennis must deal with at least three sources of information: the sequence of arm movements, the position of the feet, and the flight of the ball. Successfully dealing with two of these elements can still produce failure. To understand how some of the more experienced performers deal with multiple sources of information, we need to examine the models of attention. In the following section some of the most relevant models will be discussed.

MODELS OF ATTENTION

Broadbent's theory

Broadbent (1958) describes the central controlling mechanisms of the brain in terms of an information processing model. By rearranging the first part of Figure 2-13, we can produce a simplified version of Broadbent's model (Figure 5-14). Information enters the control system through a number of parallel sensory channels (*e.g.,* the eyes or ears), but like the information processing model presented in Chapter 2, there is a limited channel capacity later in the system. The limited channel capacity recognizes that an individual can only consciously deal with a limited amount of information at any given time (7 ± 2 bits). This is much less than the total amount of information that may be available to the individual. Hence, either information must be lost or there must be some form of recoding of the information.

Broadbent proposed a mechanism, the *selective filter,* that would select the channel having direct access to the central limited capacity channel. The selective filter would function much like the channel selector on a television set, except that it is capable of making some basic analysis of the incoming information and determining which information reaches the conscious part

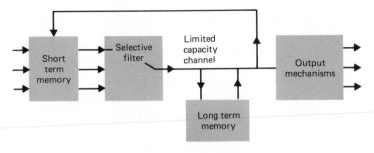

FIGURE 5-14   Broadbent's model (after Moray, 1970).

of the system. The filter could select visual or auditory channels or the particular source of information within one sensory modality. Based on the pitch of the voice and the spatial position of the sound, the filter could help select which message you attend to and which one you ignore. For instance, you may hear the coach's pre-game speech mainly through your left ear, while in your right ear you pick up the beginnings of a joke.

Information in the sensory channels not selected is held in short-term memory but becomes progressively degraded. However, by switching sensory channels the filter can "save" some of the information held in short-term memory. To use our earlier analogy, by changing television channels during the commercials, it is possible to monitor two different programs at the same time. The ability to monitor more than one channel is exemplified by an experiment in which subjects were presented two series of three digits to both ears simultaneously. At a presentation rate of one digit per second, subjects could follow the two series easily, but as the rate increased, subjects tended to report all the digits from one ear first. As switching sensory channels (in this case, ears) became difficult, one series of digits was processed first. However, if a coherent sequence was presented that could be obtained by switching between ears (the left ear is presented numbers 1, 3, 5; the right ear, numbers 2, 4, 6) subjects could handle higher rates of transmission. The subject hears 1–2, 3–4, 5–6. Consequently, the basic element of Broadbent's model was the filter that could select messages on the basis of such factors as their pitch, loudness, or spatial characteristics.

Spatial characteristics refer to the location or the distance between two sources of sound. This can be illustrated by the so-called cocktail party effect (Cherry, 1953), in which you can attend to the conversation of a person who is standing some distance away from you while eavesdropping on a second group of people quite close to you. Sounds from the different sources arrive at different times and do not have the same intensity. Having two ears allows us to separate out and localize the sounds to which we wish to attend. Visiting basketball players when shooting foul shots try to ignore (filter out) the catcalls of the home crowd as they prepare to shoot. The offensive linemen try to ignore both the crowd and the threats of the opposing defensive linemen as they listen to the call being made by the quarterback. Although Broadbent's model could account for these basic situations, other authors felt that further refinements of the model were necessary.

Treisman's model

Treisman (1960) attempted to make more explicit the selection rules governing the filter and the identification of signals on previously unattended channels. The question is, if we are attending to the information from one sensory channel, what happens to all the information being collected by the other sensory channels? If we are watching our favorite television program and the radio is also turned on, would we become aware of the important news flash that interrupts the radio broadcast? In Treisman's experiment, subjects were assigned a shadowing task during which they were required to depress a key on hearing a digit in either ear, whether it was contained in the message being shadowed (repeated verbally) or in the irrelevant message. In addition, they were instructed to repeat the stimulus. Treisman reported that subjects responded only to digits appearing in the selected message, not those in the irrelevant message.

Moray (1970), however, reported that instructions delivered via the unattended ear were noticed significantly more often when they were preceded by the subject's name than when they were preceded by the name of an unknown person. Attempting to accommodate this sort of finding, Treisman (1964) proposed that the mechanism of selective attention is attenuation rather than rejection of irrelevant messages (Figure 5-15). *Attenuation* simply means that the strength of the signal is weakened, rather like adding a muffler to a car's exhaust system. As such, all incoming signals proceed through the selective filter to the next stage of the model, but as weakened signals.

The Treisman model implies a hierarchy of tests in the filter that are carried out on the information entering all channels whether they are attended to or not. This idea is similar to the hierarchy of tests—a series of tests that become progressively more refined—that were associated with searching for a target item (the letter *A* in Figure 5-13), except that this process has now been located in the selective filter. If a subject has been told to listen to a message to the right ear, then all other outputs from what might be termed the "position analyzer" of the filter, representing incoming signals from other locations, will carry only weakened signals. If we assume that the selective filter involves a series of tests, each of which analyzes the incoming information before passing the information on to the next test, then all messages, except the one selected, would be gradually attenuated (muffled). If selection is for a male voice, then the "voice quality analyzer" will attenuate any signals that do not

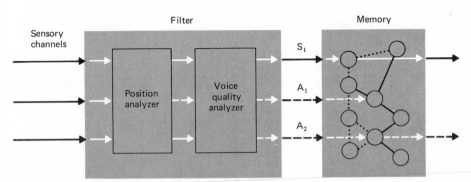

FIGURE 5-15   Treisman's model (based on Moray, 1970).

◯ Dictionary Units in memory, i.e. a description of some item. The lines between the
     units acknowledge that some are interrelated
S_1 Selected message; $A_{1,2}$ Attenuated messages (See p. 164)

meet that requirement. Eventually these attenuated messages and the one non-attenuated (selected) message pass through the system to the higher levels of processing. In this case, the non-attenuated message would involve a male voice heard by the right ear.

These higher levels or tests represent the conscious perception of some word or event. These tests may be biased by the individual's expectancy of certain words or events. If a particular word is expected to appear, then the tests that might be involved in selecting that word are pre-biased (made ready), thereby simplifying the analysis of expected material. When the teacher initiates a game of "Simon says," the first syllable of the word *Simon* may be sufficient for the children to spring into action. This preparation may be more permanent for certain words that are common or important, such as one's name. The threshold value for activation of the item in memory may be permanently lowered, allowing it to be recognized even from a signal that has been weakened after passing through the filter. The *threshold value* might be regarded as the minimum amount of information or stimulation needed to make a positive identification and to activate some item in memory.

For Treisman, therefore, attention is a two-stage process that involves initially all the sensory information passing through the filter where the signals are either selected or attenuated on the basis of particular characteristics or physical cues. The second stage involves the application of more refined tests that lead to conscious recognition based on the threshold values of the stored information in memory. Only when you make a positive identification is an item activated in memory, although the minimum amount of information needed would not be high for items important to the individual.

From Figure 5-15 we see that the selected message (S_1) activates the associated unit of information in memory and this information is attended to. The unit could represent the actual play called by a quarterback although the message (signal) itself was only a series of numbers. Of the two attenuated messages A_1 and A_2, A_1 might be some abusive shouts from the crowd that are ignored; they are too weak to activate any unit in memory and do not come to our attention because they have been weakened by the filtering process. A_2, although a weakened signal, does activate a unit in memory because that unit is your name—a teammate on the sideline is trying to tell you that your shoelace is untied. While the system of filters (analyzers) allows you to focus on the information relevant to the task at hand, it is possible for unexpected, but important, information to gain your attention.

The Treisman model implies that important signals can be identified from unattended channels because of the lower threshold values for recognition associated with those items. The Treisman model avoids the problem of the Broadbent model, in which only information from the attended channel is admitted further into the system. However, as all the attenuated and non-attenuated signals are submitted to further analysis, the actual selection of relevant information occurs much later in the system. This raises the question that, if all this analysis is necessary just to decide which signal or message is attended to, where or what is the benefit of selectivity?

Norman's model

The first two models, which propose either early or late selection, although capturing some aspects of attention, are ultimately inadequate. The Broadbent model is simple and efficient but presupposes a loss of information on unattended channels that does not always occur. The Treisman model provides for a more complex analysis, but this analysis in itself would tend to be inefficient when speed of response was an important factor. Norman (1968), utilizing some of the work of Deutsch and Deutsch (1963), proposed an alternative model based on all of these approaches.

The Deutsch and Deutsch proposal, although derived from that of Treisman, emphasized *response selection*. These investigators saw the filter as being redundant, since this function can be achieved by allowing the incoming signals to have direct access to memory. Once an item in memory is recognized, it will be activated, but the strength with which these stored representations are excited will be proportional to the importance of the signal to the organism and not necessarily to the initial strength of the signal itself. Deutsch and Deutsch saw the perceptual analysis described by Treisman as being performed on all incoming signals regardless of whether they were attended to or not. Consequently, any item in memory for which there is sufficient information for it to be recognized will be activated. The key as to which items are attended to lies in how strongly they are activated. It is the item that is most strongly activated in memory that captures our attention. How strongly an item is activated depends not on the strength of the initial signal but on the importance of that item to the individual. Thus a person's name may be described as having a low threshold value for activation, but, even with this low stimulus, it will be activated strongly because it has a high importance weighting (Figure 5-16). The importance weighting, or importance given to each item, is a function of past experience. For a basketball player, an item representing the favorite fake of an opposing player may have a high importance weighting, at least while that player is in the game.

To summarize, all signals pass through the filter, but it is only that unit that is firing most strongly that is allowed to transmit to the next stage. The strongest unit will continue to transmit until either it is no longer stimulated or until a stronger unit fires. When the neural circuit in the brain that represents some unit of information is activated, it begins to send signals to the conscious part of the brain. Firing strongly suggests that it may send a constant stream of impulses, and not just an occasional signal, to the conscious part of the brain in an attempt to gain our attention. As we have mentioned several times, we are limited in our ability to deal consciously with many bits of information at any one time and some selection process is needed. If we return to our pandemonium analogy, only the loudest or strongest signals will be attended to and these will quickly lose their place if a stronger signal appears. This situation might be likened to the standard comedy routine in which an intense conversation is suddenly halted when an attractive member of the opposite sex walks by.

Temporary changes in importance, and therefore in the items selected, may result from changes in the context (*e.g.*, a new player coming into the game) or in the instructions given to the player (by the coach in this instance). Long-term differences in the importance weighting, which are more permanent, are a result of learning. The output from this selection process is also affected by the level of arousal in that when the level of output is low (during sleep) only the most important signals, items which are activated very strongly (your name), will be attended to and lead to a response. As the level of arousal increases, so more and more signals will lead to some response. The system as a whole becomes more active.

Putting Norman's model into the context of the general information processing model presented in Chapter 2 would produce the model shown in Figure 5-17. There are two main aspects to this model: First, at the stimulus-analyzing level, the selective filter, the main parameters of each signal are identified. This information then activates the associated unit in memory, and

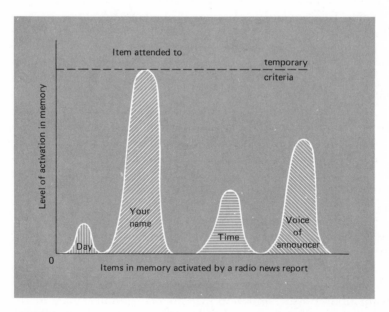

FIGURE 5-16   Elements of the Deutsch and Deutsch model (based on Deutsch & Deutsch, 1963).

the resulting information is temporarily stored in short-term memory. The *sensory analysis* part of the process is thought to be quite automatic and proceeds without creating any demands for attention. This part of the process is the same as that described by Deutsch and Deutsch (1963). As more than one source of sensory information is being processed at the same time, this first element in the operation provides an example of what is referred to as simultaneous or *parallel processing*.

At the same time this first operation is occurring, the second major element is provided and is based on the performer's expectations. Based on either the context of the current situation or on previous experience with the task, the learner activates another set of units in memory based on the particular cues or events that the learner feels are *pertinent* to the task. In a one-on-one situation in basketball the player may want to consider how far behind or ahead is the defender, and whether there is a direct path to the basket. Therefore, if some cues that the learner feels are pertinent to the task are also activated by the sensory analysis, which means the cues are actually present in the environment, these are the items which will be selectively attended to by the learner. Basketball players know that if the defender is one stride behind (an expected or pertinent cue), they can drive for the basket. They see that this situation exists as they approach their opponent's basket as a result of the sensory analysis. The players focus on this item and make the appropriate decision: they drive for the basket and score.

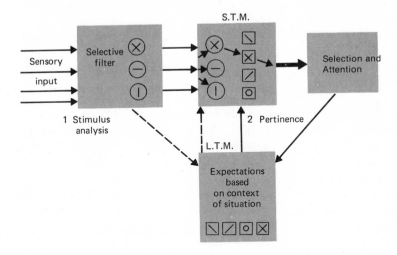

FIGURE 5-17   Norman's model of attention (based on Norman, 1969).

From this model, we can now understand where the experienced performer gains the advantage. As short-term memory has only a limited capacity, it is most important that the truly pertinent items be selected. Increasing familiarity with a given situation may help the learner speed up the sensory analysis element, but it is the ability to select in advance the most pertinent items that characterizes the skilled players. While the beginning tennis player waits for the ball to land in the service court before initiating the appropriate return, the advanced player, by noting the way the server's racket strikes the ball, will have far more time to prepare the appropriate stroke. The two players may be equally swift in completing the sensory analysis of the cues actually present in the environment, but the inability to select the most pertinent cues places additional limitations, particularly that of time, on the beginner.

We should note here that Norman (1976) emphasized that his model was flexible. As the demands of the situation changed, so would the depth of the analysis performed in the selection process. It can vary from an emphasis on the quality of the sensory data to an analysis of the interpretations to be derived from that data. To illustrate this, we only have to consider the different perceptual demands faced by the offensive lineman waiting for the signal to initiate a block in contrast to the linebacker who must analyze and react to the play as it develops. Returning to the Rappaport model (Figure 5-5), we could say that the lineman who must identify only one stimulus, the signal from the quarterback, out of the mass of incoming sensory information is operating at the proprioceptive level. In contrast, the linebacker must relate images of what was seen previously to what is happening in this play. At the very least, the linebacker is operating at the perceptual level (mental images) or even the conceptual level while seeking to identify those characteristics that this play has in common with earlier plays.

Events are constantly changing, and selective attention is an ongoing process. The selected items, which at one moment help choose a course of action, may the next moment be used to update what the performer sees as the pertinent information for the next stage of the task. The selected item represents the end product of the recognition process and a key step in the performance of any motor task.

However, the selection process involves the limited capacity of short-term memory, and this places the responsibility on the coach to point out to the learner the appropriate or most pertinent cues. Even if players can execute a skill perfectly, it will serve little purpose if they cannot recognize the appropriate time to use that skill. Clearly, this applies mainly to open skills in which we face the choice of when to use a skill such as we see in most team sports, but it can also apply to closed skills found in sports like gymnastics in which we are trying to duplicate one particular version of a skill. Gymnasts who cannot identify the correct point to initiate a back somersault after landing from a back handspring may find themselves unable to perform a combination of two skills, each of which they can perform in isolation. Alternatively, the learner must be given more time in which to seek out those cues. In a practice situation, the defender can be required to stand some distance away from the player receiving the ball and to run in to challenge for the ball only after it is received. In this way, the receiver will have more time to think about where to pass before having to avoid the defender.

Not only does the learner have the problem of identifying pertinent cues, but also the performance of the motor task itself may already be occupying a large amount of the learner's attention. For example, when a beginning ice hockey player is skating or stick handling the puck, the short-term memory of that player may be full of things to be remembered about the skill itself; as a result, there is little space in short-term memory for the learner to complete the analysis of pertinent cues in regard to making a pass. Even assuming the learner can identify the most pertinent cues, the items may have to be considered a few at a time and double-checked. Such a situation can only be accommodated by playing games with a small number of players in a fairly large area. The reduced number of players and increased amount of space both simplify the game for the learner and provide the extra time needed to identify the appropriate cues. Fewer players means fewer options to be considered and less information to be processed. The extra space may mean that the beginner can stop performing any skill and simply stand still while trying to analyze the situation. In a closed skill such as gymnastics, the coach could provide physical support for the gymnast by actually lifting the gymnast through part of the movement. As such, any loss of style produced by the gymnast focusing on the changeover point from one skill to the next could be compensated for by the coach, allowing the gymnast to complete the combination succesfully.

SUMMARY

The perceptual mechanism represents the first of the three elements in the basic information processing model. As it precedes both decision and action it can be considered as providing a basis for the learning and control of motor skills. From an information processing point of view, the successful performance of a motor skill requires feedback about the results of one's actions, the task itself, and what is to be achieved. Thus, the teacher or coach may be described as a provider of relevant information.

Within the overall learning process, there are three main stages: (1) the cognitive stage, which is characterized by many errors and large improvements in performance as the learner evolves specific strategies to deal with the task at hand; (2) the associative stage, in which the spatial and temporal patterning of the components of the movement and an error detection mechanism are established; and (3) the autonomous stage, in which the skill is refined. This chapter dealt with the sensory or perceptual mechanism and how changes in this mechanism provide a basis for progress through the stages of learning.

The perceptual process

While sensory receptors report the presence or absence of certain stimuli to the brain, perception is the interpretation of these stimuli. Perception involves the conscious organization and integration of the incoming sensory information. Improvements in either the quality or speed of the perceptual process are essential to learning.

A basic description of the perceptual process is provided by Rappaport's model whereby the original mass of sensory information is progressively organized and reduced. First the information within one sensory modality is labeled, at the proprioceptive and preceptive levels, and then different types of sensory information are combined to form mental images, percepts. Eventually, seeking common characteristics within these mental images leads to the formation of concepts. The final stage of knowing that a response is correct is referred to as the cognitive level. Functioning at the cognitive or conceptual levels avoids the time-consuming process of analyzing the details of every situation, thereby facilitating faster responses.

Perceptual theories

There are various perceptual theories that illustrate diverse aspects of perception:

CORE-CONTEXT THEORY.   Sensations only acquire meaning from the context of the situations in which they occur. While the core of immediate sensations is the same for any individual, differences in the past experiences of these individuals may lead them to formulate different interpretations of a stimulus, based on the context of the situation.

ADAPTATION-LEVEL THEORY.   Perception is based on a pooling of events. The three main sources of information that interact are the object, its background, and past experience. Adaptation level refers to the size, or level, of the difference between the object and its background and the extent to which this difference is influenced by past experience.

SENSORY-TONIC THEORY.   This theory emphasizes the interaction between internal and external sensory inputs. The relationship between tonus and perception is stressed in particular.

TRANSACTIONAL THEORY.   We cannot separate the immediate perception of one portion of the environment from the overall perception of the environment. The emphasis here is on the detail of the identifiable characteristics in a given situation and the resulting discrepancies and similarities between different situations.

NEUROGEOMETRIC THEORY. This is one of the few theories to propose a particular neural mechanism in the brain—similar to the sensory receptors in muscles and joints—to detect changes in spatial patterns or positions involved in movement.

SPACE PERCEPTION THEORY. This theory is concerned with the actual development of the perceptual mechanism and underlines the important role played by self-induced movement in establishing our perception of the world around us.

Stages of sensory analysis

In order to provide a more detailed description of the perceptual process itself, it is necessary to examine the main stages by which the sensory information is analyzed. These include the detection, comparison, recognition, and organization of sensory information.

DETECTION. The main sources of perceptual information are the sensory receptors that feed information to the brain via the peripheral nervous system. These receptors, however, have certain physiological limits. Consequently there are certain signals that people cannot detect without artificial aids. Even within these limits there are no fixed threshold values above which signals become detectable. How people are able to detect signals despite the natural variability of the perceptual system is explained by *signal detection theory*. The main assumption is that all signals occur against a background of noise or neural activity and that it is the signal-to-noise ratio that determines signal detectability. Finally, the performer can superimpose a flexible criterion value when judging whether a signal occurred or not, depending on the need for accuracy, and thereby increase or decrease the number of missed signals or false alarms.

COMPARATIVE JUDGMENTS. Weber's law describes a person's ability to detect stimulus changes within one sensory mode when comparing a signal against some standard present in the environment. As such, the just noticeable difference (jnd) provides a measure of the discriminability of a particular sensory mode.

ABSOLUTE JUDGMENTS. When making absolute judgments, the standard, which is used for comparison with incoming signals, is stored in memory. Whereas we are able to make an unlimited number of comparative judgments, we are limited in our ability to make absolute judgments. Most of this limitation is related to the inexactness of the standard held in memory. Combining different dimensions affords a small increase in our ability to make absolute judgments.

PATTERN RECOGNITION.   The recognition of patterns of stimuli based only on partial information represents one of the more flexible capabilities in the stages of sensory analysis. Prior knowledge or predictable information makes it possible to overcome a great deal of distortion.

PERCEPTUAL ORGANIZATION.   The active organization of the sensory information, whether by the experimenter, the subject, or the learner, provides a powerful tool in the learning of a motor skill. In some circumstances,.it may even be equivalent in its impact to knowledge of results.

Selective attention

Because the processing of information takes time, we cannot attend to all the sensory information we are capable of detecting. Therefore, we must either seek to make the various processing stages more efficient or selectively reduce the amount of information that we must process. Some of the principles of information processing are represented by the rate of search and doctrine of prior entry:

RATE OF SEARCH.   Initially searching for a target item among a pattern of stimuli, or in memory, takes longer as the number of items increases, but it can become automatic with extensive practice. The search rate is influenced by the degree of similarity between items. Research has also shown that the search for an item is faster than the search for its absence. The various operations that describe the stages of sensory analysis, ranging from the simple detection of a signal to the more complex analysis of a pattern of stimuli, including the abstraction of meaning, represent what is referred to as the *depth of processing* capacity. The deeper or more elaborate the analysis, the more likely the information will be retained. The role of the coach is to provide the player with simple tests that can be applied to the incoming sensory information in order to reduce the amount of processing that must be performed and give the player more time to concentrate on skill execution.

DOCTRINE OF PRIOR ENTRY.   One of the limitations of the central processing capacity is illustrated here. When two signals from different sensory modes arrive simultaneously, they are processed serially; that is, one signal is given priority. This represents one example of the time sharing problems involved in performing two tasks at the same time.

Models of attention

The research regarding the question of selective attention has resulted in several models of attention.

BROADBENT'S THEORY.   Broadbent proposed that a selective filter would select the sensory information channel (eye or ear) to which the individual would attend. The information from non-selected sources (channels) would be stored temporarily in short-term memory where it would begin to decay, but some of the information could be recovered by switching sensory channels.

TREISMAN'S MODEL.   In opposition to the notion that only certain information is selected by the filter, Treisman contended that all signals would activate their matching representations in memory; however, selection would be determined by the importance assigned to the stored item. The greater the importance, the lower the threshold value needed for activation of the stored item. Signals on non-attended sensory channels were merely attenuated—weakened. As such, high priority items could be activated by the weakened signals arriving from the attenuated channels.

NORMAN'S MODEL.   Norman tried to blend these two models of Broadbent and Treisman with other work. He proposed that, after an initial sensory analysis, all incoming signals automatically had access to their stored representations in memory that were activated according to their priority (threshold values). Prior to the task, the learner would select those cues or events that were felt to be most pertinent to the task. Selection, therefore, was based on the outcome of this joint activation. In other words, an expected (pertinent) cue that was actually present in the environment would be most strongly activated and selected for further analysis.

The items selected in the manner described by these models of attention represent the final outcome of the perceptual recognition process. The model presented by Norman was felt to be a more flexible one in which the depth of analysis required would vary with the demands of the task, from an emphasis on the quality of the sensory data to an analysis of the interpretations to be derived from that data.

PROBLEM

Question

Considering such factors as signal detection theory and pattern recognition, what are some of the perceptual problems that might be encountered by a high school basketball player when playing in the opponent's gymnasium for the first time?

Possible answer

The major source of problems for the player will be the changes in the perceptual field. Most of the cues with which the player is familiar on the home court are no longer present and will be replaced by an entirely new set of stimuli. Many of the most important cues will be similar, such as the dimensions of the court, but the small variations that exist may be crucial in such a fast-moving sport. The court markings may be narrower and mixed in with badminton and volleyball markings; the backboard may be opaque rather than clear; the walls may be cluttered rather than empty; and the bleachers may be close to the court rather than set back. All these changes may interfere with the player's ability to detect signals and to make quick and accurate judgments during the game.

Let's consider the problem of extra court markings in terms of signal detection theory. The profusion of lines on the gym floor will add to the number of incoming visual signals that will be attended to and processed when the player seeks to estimate the distance to the sideline. With such a level of interference (background noise), only a clear signal—a broad sideline—would be easily detected. Otherwise, there is a clear advantage for the home team who, through experience, will have established a very high priority for the correct line and become very skilled at detecting its presence. The visiting players can only avoid errors by setting a low criterion when trying to find the sideline. To avoid going out of bounds, for example, they can stop before reaching anything that looks like a sideline. This means that the effective playing area is reduced for the visiting team, but they will have avoided one potential source of turnovers.

In a competitive basketball game there is a lot of real noise (sound) present, and not just psychological noise within the individual. Such real noise can also pose a signal detection problem. Obviously, in critical situations with the home crowd chanting "defense," any auditory signals used in the offense will have to be dropped and replaced by visual cues or well-rehearsed plays. The latter option would seem preferable, because this large increase in real as well as psychological noise may make the detection of any cue very difficult.

In the home court, a player may have established many cues that help that player to judge the angle and distance to the basket or the distance from the end line, all without the opponent being aware. The home court player knows there is only 6 feet to the end line because of a poster on the gym wall. Losing these important cues might be disorienting in itself, but the player might compensate partially by identifying other cues which could help with the most important choices. However, if the opponent's gymnasium is of a similar design, the problem might be worse. Just as in proofreading, when the context of the situation may lead the reader to read something that is not really there, so in basketball the player may be drawn into an error. For example, after the red and white lines there may not be a blue line before the proper end line of the basketball court. The discrepancy between the home and opponent's gymnasiums may cause the visiting player to make out of bounds violations.

Therefore, as part of the preparation for the game, all visiting players should carefully inspect the court and the gymnasium. They should run through their set plays and individual moves and look for relevant or irrelevant cues. In this way, criteria can be established to avoid, for example, the out of bounds problem. The other alternative is to minimize these problems when coaching. This means trying to free the players from as many cues as possible that are external to the game, such as taking a positional cue from the timekeeper's bench, and emphasizing cues that are more reliable, such as the top of the key.

Finally, the more organized and coordinated the team play, the more time or processing capacity each player will have available to interpret the perceptual information.

Chapter 6
Selected Sensory Modalities

What use is sight
To one who does not see?
(Rowan, 1980)

In the context of motor learning, selected sensory modalities refer to the two most important senses for motor skills: vision and kinesthesis. Clearly, other types of sensory information may play a role in controlling movement, for example, the sound, the smell, and the movement of air that announces the arrival of a defender behind your back. When vision is present, which is the case in most sports skills, and the visual information is usable, it will tend to dominate the other senses. Visual information may even be used to calibrate information arriving from other senses (Marteniuk, 1976). However, motor skills are concerned with movement, and it is through kinesthetic perception that we get most of the information about our own movements. This chapter concentrates on vision and kinesthesis, not because other sensory information is irrelevant but because these two senses dominate the learning of motor skills.

Some general information regarding the perceptual characteristics of both of these senses will be presented first. Then, in the latter part of the chapter we will review some of the research dealing with the joint role of vision and kinesthesis in the acquisition of motor skills.

VISUAL PERCEPTION

There are many types of information that are processed by the visual system and many visual-perceptual effects that either guide or mislead the learner. In this chapter, however, we will only review a selection of those effects that are particularly relevant to psychomotor learning: spatial awareness, depth perception, perceptual integration, perception of movement, apparent movement, and speed of vision.

Spatial awareness

Spatial awareness is a concept that is often talked about, particularly by those involved in movement education, but seldom defined. Basically, this concept consists of three main elements, each of which represents a stage in the development of spatial awareness in children (Cratty, 1970; Stallings, 1973). Each stage marks an increase in the level of visual complexity that the child can handle and about which the child is capable of making judgments, the final stages being reached by around 9 years of age in the majority of children. The three main elements in the development of spatial awareness are the following:

1. *Spatial relations,* which refers to the ability to discriminate direction with one's self as a reference point
2. *Spatial orientation,* which involves making judgments about the positional changes of objects in space
3. *Spatial visualization,* which represents the learner's ability to mentally manipulate objects in space

One important extension of spatial visualization is the concept of imagery control. We often give coaching tips to athletes that require them to imagine how the skill should look or feel. However, although spatial awareness was expressed as a developmental phenomenon, the manipulation of images is not simply a function of age but a very distinct ability.

Try closing your eyes and visualizing the scenes described below, which are based on the Gordon test of visual imagery control (1949). Do not be surprised if you find it very difficult.

1. Can you see a new car parked on the street in front of your house?
2. Can you now see the same car turned upside down?
3. Can you see it driving along your street?
4. Can you see it turn into the driveway, go out of control, and crash into the house?

If the learner cannot manipulate these images, one would question the effectiveness of a technique that relies on visual aids or visual imagery for the teaching of motor skills in which the learner performs blind. Teaching the front somersault in gymnastics, for example, a teacher might say: "Look, your arms go like this." In fact the teacher may be presenting the learners with an impossible interpretation problem whereby they must try to imagine themselves doing the correct or incorrect movements. If the learner cannot interpret the visual information in terms of the physical skill, then even video replays of their performance are of limited value.

Depth perception

We have already dealt with some of the perceptual laws during the discussion of Gestalt theory. One of the criticisms of the Gestalt laws is that they are only two-dimensional while we live in a three-dimensional world; we see things in depth. As noted in Chapter 2, the Gestaltists suggest that the learner tries to group or organize the sensory data into simple units or objects (Figures 2-6 and 2-7) in a constant search for meaning.

Whether depth perception is in fact learned or innate is still in debate, but it is certainly present by 6 months of age, as indicated by the visual cliff experiment of Gibson and Walk (1960) (Figure 6-1). Human infants placed on a specially constructed table with a top that was half clear plate glass were

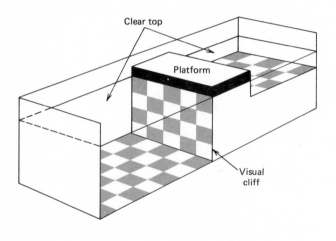

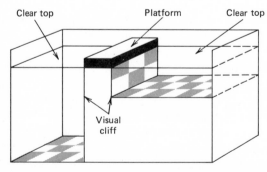

FIGURE 6-1   A visual cliff (based on Gibson & Walk, 1960).

encouraged to move from the "solid" side over an apparent cliff. Their refusal to do so was taken as evidence of some basic awareness of depth perception. While the argument of innate ability vs experience is not directly a concern of psychomotor learning, what is relevant are the cues that we use in depth perception. Normally, we use many cues to give us information about the relative distance of objects. Some of the cues or artist's tricks that are used in depth perception are shown in Figures 6-2 and 6-3.

The type of cues illustrated in Figure 6-2, are often referred to as *monocular cues*, in that they can be used by one eye to judge depth, as distinct from the *binocular cues* in which both eyes work together (Figure 6-3). The most obvious perceptual cues are size and partial overlap (Figure 6-2a,b). If two objects that are known to be equal in size appear as smaller or larger than each other, then we can assume that one is behind the other. The same

FIGURE 6-2   Monocular cues for depth perception.   a) size

b) partial overlap

c) shadowing-cast

d) filled vs unfilled (appears larger)

assumption can be made for partial overlap regardless of size, although most often these two cues work together. Linear perspective represents one of the first cues that we must learn in order to avoid making our drawings appear flat. Similarly, the other cues of shadowing and filled and unfilled spaces are another example of the cues that can be used by an artist to create the impression of depth or solidarity.

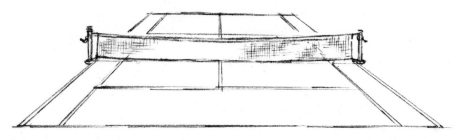

e) linear perspective

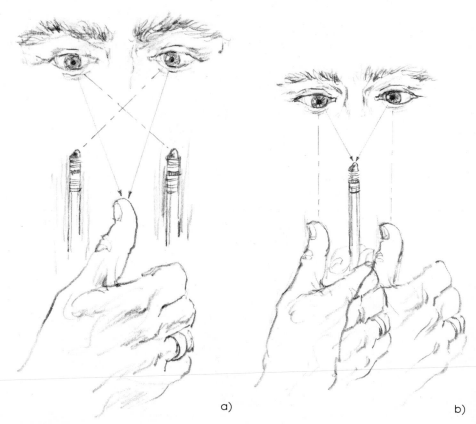

a)   b)

FIGURE 6-3   Binocular parallax, a) crossed and b) uncrossed images.

One of the most basic cues for depth perception—*binocular parallax*—is based on the fact that our two eyes are set approximately 2½ inches apart. As a result of this, two separate images are sent to the brain. Just try to close one eye, stare straight ahead, and make a note of the limits of what you can see. Then repeat this with the other eye and note the disparity of the images. This disparity is what is constantly available to the brain. Similarly, hold your left arm straight out in front of you and make a fist with your thumb pointing up (remember the artist?). Next, holding a pen in your right hand, place the pen halfway between your nose and your left hand and in line with your thumb. Now, by fixating on the thumb or the pen you will discover the phenomenon of *crossed and uncrossed images,* which gives us a further cue about relative distances:

1. Fixate on the thumb. By closing each eye in turn the pen is seen to be on the left of your thumb by the right eye and on the right by the left eye. The images are said to be crossed (Figure 6-3, *a*).
2. Fixate on the pen. The thumb is now seen on the right side of the pen by the right eye and on the left by the left eye. The images are now uncrossed (Figure 6-3, *b*).

The images are really the same, but whether they are crossed or uncrossed depends on whether you focus on the near or the far object, and as such this gives us cues to their relative distances. Also, even though your pen is directly in front of your thumb, you have little difficulty in viewing the details of the lines on the skin. You can, to some extent, see behind near objects. Finally, even with one eye closed you can get cues about depth by moving the head 2½ inches to the side. All of these effects are a function of the separation of the two eyes and constitute what is referred to as binocular parallax.

Perceptual integration

Exactly how much we rely on various cues for depth perception can be illustrated by deliberately manipulating those cues. We can look at Figure 6-4 for hours, but we will never see the number two card as being in front of number one. Despite the fact it actually is or at least could be. Such an effect is

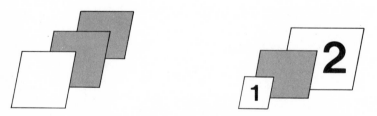

FIGURE 6-4 Problems for perceptual integration (based on Gibson, 1950).

achieved simply by cutting away parts of the number two card and the intervening card to create the illusion of an overlap. Viewed from the correct angle we "see" something that we know is not true; we cannot decipher the illusion.

Gibson (1950) has helped untangle the question of how we perceive objects. Perspective, for example, is established by seeking the invariance within the available information. Once the observer has established that objects are of similar sizes, this information may be used to provide a gradient of size representing different distances. In Figure 6-5, once the rectangles are assumed to be of equal size, the gradient is established and we see a line of rectangles disappearing into the distance. When the gradient is observed, the actual slope, relative to the viewer, is determined by the rate of change in the size of the objects (in this case, rectangles).

Such gradients can be applied to other types of information, such as differences in brightness or volume. When such a perspective gradient has been established, all other information within the visual field tends to be

FIGURE 6-5   Perceptual gradient (based on Vickers, 1971).

scaled in proportion to that gradient. Gregory (1971) illustrated this with the railway lines illusion shown in Figure 6-6. Once the two outside lines are taken to represent a railway line disappearing into the distance, the horizontal line deepest into the ("V") is then viewed as being longer regardless of which way you orient the figure.

The elements mentioned so far relate to the spatial relationships of objects. Welford (1970) also refers to transformations over time; that is, as a person moves then so does the perceptual field. *The items you can see and the angle at which you view them changes as you move through the environment.* Again, the presence or absence of invariance in the positions of objects allows the individual to establish gradients that will provide cues regarding the relative stability or movement of objects. An object appears to get larger in size, for example, indicating you are moving closer to the object. These processes are fairly automatic. It is only as we try to integrate the various bits of perceptual information that our prior experiences come into play.

Welford (1970) describes the process whereby perception is regarded as providing a running hypothesis that enables the learner to compare what is actually present in the environment with expectations based on prior learning or experience. What is perceived is not "seen" all at once; the final perceptual framework is built up in a piecemeal fashion from successive samplings of the environment. The integration of the various bits of information with previously established perceptual frameworks is greatly influenced by familiarity; unfamiliar items may be ignored or identified separately.

Returning to Norman's model of selective attention (Chapter 5), what is pertinent to a given situation may be represented by a previously established perceptual framework. Consequently, familiar items may be quickly identified and attended to. However, recognizing the variability of our environment and the matching flexibility of the perceptual system, the perceptual framework provides the basis for what is only a running hypothesis, which can be modified as circumstances demand.

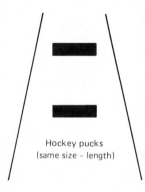

Hockey pucks
(same size – length)

FIGURE 6-6   Two hockey pucks (same size)—based on the railway-lines illusion (Gregory, 1971).

Movement

As we have seen, vision does not provide a static image of our world, but it allows us to observe and make judgments about the relative movements of objects around us. In addition to the factor of perspective gradients, it appears, possibly as part of our evolutionary development, that the edge of the retina is sensitive only to movement.

Look straight ahead and move two pens slowly from in front of your nose to the edge of your visual field. At the point where they disappear, the limit of your peripheral vision, hold still for a second and then move the pens up and down. Although you cannot identify the pens, you may be aware of the movement; you may also find yourself taking a look. Detection of movement was obviously important to man's survival, and it has been suggested that only the higher animals signal anything to the brain in the absence of movement.

The main sensory receptors of the eye are the rods and cones. The rods are primarily used in "black and white" vision, while the cones enable us to see colors. Most of these receptors, however, only signal changes in illumination, and very few give a continuous signal to a steady light. As a result, these receptors may be divided into "on," "off," and "on-off," receptors, according to whether they respond to the initiation or termination of a light signal or both. As these receptors are sensitive to changes in the amount of light, they will respond to the trailing or leading edges of an image but not to stationary images. Consequently, the eyes may be regarded primarily as detectors of movement. Basically we see movement in two ways:

1. Through the relationship between the image and the retina: when the eye is still and the image of an object moves across the retina
2. Through the relationship between the eye and the head: when the head is still while the eye follows an object, with the image remaining still on the retina. Either the movement of the eye or changes in the position of background objects can provide the movement cues.

During normal eye movements, the neural signals from the two systems–the image/retina and the eye/head system–cancel each other out to give stability to the visual world. If this did not happen, our visual world would spin around every time our eyes moved because retinal images run across the receptors whenever we move our eyes. The size of objects also affects our judgment about their movement, because we tend to see large objects as moving slower. The approximate relationship between size and speed is twice the size equals half the speed. In addition, we perceive equivalent speeds as being faster in the horizontal than in the vertical dimension.

Apparent movement

Having considered how we observe movements, it may be interesting to note how we see movement when there is no movement. How do we see movies?

After all, movies are just a series of still pictures. There are two main factors:

1. *Persistence of vision, or afterimage.* From the section on sensory information storage in Chapter 4, we know that there is some sensation of a stimulus centrally for a short time after it has ceased. If you flash a light at an increasing rate, eventually you will see it as a steady light. This is known as the *critical flicker frequency* (CFF) and ranges from 30 to 50 flickers per second, depending on the intensity of the light. Fluorescent lights function in this manner.

2. *Phi phenomenon.* If two lights are sequentially switched on and off in a darkened room in a synchronized manner, the light will appear to move (Figure 6-7).

If the time interval (I) between switching off the first light and switching on the second light is very small (less than 10 msec), the change will appear to be simultaneous. Above 1,000 msec the lights appear sequential. However, from 25 to 400 msec you move away from simultaneity to first partial movement and finally smooth movement. Finally, as you gradually increase the interval, the optimal movement becomes slower until you do not see any movement but simply have a sense of movement itself, a phenomenon referred to as the phi phenomenon. The normal movie film runs at about 24 frames per second, but a special shutter shows each frame three times, thereby reaching the CFF and fusing the image. Without this shutter the films would appear to flicker, as in the old silent movies. Another everyday example of apparent motion is that observed when viewing the lighted signs outside many movie theaters. The light pattern appears to "move" around the sign when in fact all

a) alternating lights

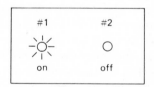

b) timing

FIGURE 6-7 Phi phenomenon, a) light arrangement and b) timing of alternation.

that is happening is the turning on and off of a sequence of lights in rapid succession.

Speed of vision

In the majority of motor tasks, the information or situation is constantly changing and therefore the learner must continuously check and update the current situation, or modify the running hypothesis. In basketball, this could be represented as a quick look between dribbles. We have already mentioned some of the limitations, implied here when the running memory span was discussed, but these are pulled together more when we consider what is referred to as the speed of vision.

Oxendine (1968) separates the speed of vision factor into two elements:

1. The *span of apprehension*, which is based on sensory information storage and represents all you can absorb in a glance. For example, to sum up a situation in a game, you must have some afterimage or brief storage of the sensory information. Earlier we referred to this concept as the running memory span.
2. *Pursuit speed*, which represents the ability to follow or track a target. There appears to be a high correlation between this factor and motor skill performance.

Speed of vision is the ability to monitor accurately a constantly changing environment and is especially important because of the large amount of information that the system can absorb.

Before dealing with the topic of kinesthesis, we will briefly discuss two other items: *peripheral vision* and *audition*. There are varying estimates for the normal range of peripheral vision, but Sage (1977) places it at 170 degrees for both eyes, with the vertical field ranging from 47 degrees above the midline to 65 degrees below. As might be expected, the range of these fields has generally been found to be greater for athletes than non-athletes (Olsen, 1956; Stroup 1957; Williams & Thirer, 1975), underlining the importance of peripheral vision in motor behavior. The most important factor in peripheral vision is not the absolute value but is the extent to which the learner uses the available peripheral vision. Functional peripheral vision tends to be lower than the absolute value. Therefore, it is important in teaching and coaching to encourage the learner to maximize the use of available peripheral vision.

One important source of information related to vision that has gained little attention is audition, in particular, rhythm discrimination. Smith (1970) has suggested that as temporal discriminations are made through audition prior to being made visually by children, training in rhythmic activities involving sound may facilitate later visual judgments. Although there has been some research that illustrated the motivational effects of music (Beisman, 1967; Dillon, 1952), few investigators have tried to look directly at the role of sound in learning and performing motor skills.

KINESTHETIC PERCEPTION

From a psychomotor learning point of view, kinesthesis, and not extrasensory perception (ESP), might be regarded as the sixth sense. *Kinesthesis* is simply the awareness of body position and movement based on proprioceptive information. Excluded from this definition is visual and auditory information about movement, but included is information from the vestibular apparatus of the inner ear (balance). Scott (1955) has suggested that kinesthesis can be partitioned into four main categories that function independently of each other:

1. The ability to reproduce accurately a muscular force
2. Balance
3. The identification of body position or movement precision
4. Orientation in space

Although not a precise breakdown of kinesthesis, Scott's definition does serve to remind us of some of the types of kinesthetic information that we use and the type of task in which kinesthetic information can play a major role. In terms of research with either active or passive movements, we find that people are more accurate in the space directly in front of them, losing accuracy as they make movements farther away from the body. People are also more accurate when using their preferred limbs. Both these findings would seem to reflect a practice variable. If kinesthetic awareness can be improved with practice, this would seem to be an argument in favor of the movement education, problem-solving approach to physical education. The emphasis in this approach is on developing kinesthetic awareness—learning to make full use of the information available by exposing the individual to a vast range of movements. Although there is little direct research evidence to justify this last point, there is evidence that suggests a link between higher levels of athletic ability and kinesthesis (Mumby, 1953; Wiebe, 1954).

Although the role of proprioceptive information or kinesthesis has been rather loosely investigated in the past, there has been a resurgence of interest over the past ten years. In particular, researchers are turning to physiological data to support their models of learning and perception. It is not the intention of this book to be a text in physiological psychology, but it would seem relevant to have a basic understanding of the anatomical and physiological factors of primary interest in the control of motor behavior. Therefore, we will look at the components of the motor system, then consider the main receptors involved in movement, and finally examine how the system may control movement.

The motor system

The major components of the nervous system that are involved in the control of movement are illustrated in Figure 6-8. They constitute the three major levels of the central nervous system: (1) the spinal cord, (2) the lower brain, and (3) the higher brain or cortical level (Guyton, 1971). The spinal cord represents the lowest level of control. The peripheral nerve pathways bring sensory information into the brain via the spinal cord and are referred to generally as *afferent pathways.* In contrast, motor responses are carried from the brain to the periphery by *efferent pathways.* Within the central nervous system, the sensory and motor pathways are referred to respectively as ascending and descending tracts. The name of the tract indicates its anatomical end points (start/finish), and the order indicates the direction of the tract. The corticospinal tract, therefore, is a descending tract from the cerebral cortex to the spinal cord.

Most of the ''subconscious'' activities of the body are controlled by the

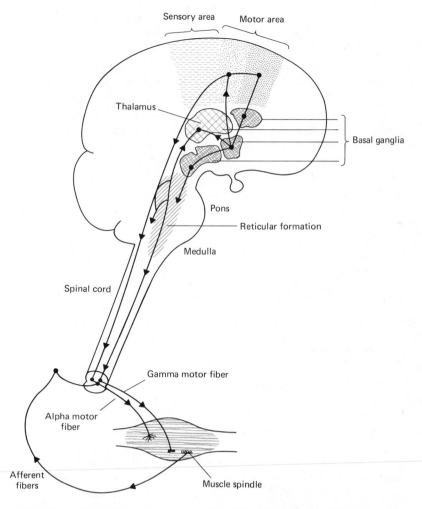

FIGURE 6-8   Major components of the nervous system involved in motor control (based on Guyton, 1971).

components of the lower brain: the medulla, pons, thalamus, and basal ganglia (Figure 6-8). The highest level of control is represented by the cerebral cortex. The cerebral cortex is actually the thin surface layer of the two cerebral hemispheres that dominate the brain. Approximately three-fourths of all the nerve cell bodies in the nervous system are located in the cerebral cortex. The particular areas of the cerebral cortex of interest for motor control are the sensory cortex and the motor cortex, often referred to jointly as the *sensorimotor cortex*. The two areas are closely linked to each other and to other areas of the cerebral cortex. The motor cortex receives both direct stimulation from other areas of the cerebral cortex and from subcortical areas via the thalamus, which is the main point of entry for sensory signals to the cerebral cortex.

Each of the different body parts are represented in the sensorimotor cortex, and connections with each area are provided by two descending pathways (Figure 6-9). One pathway, the corticospinal or pyramidal tract, provides a direct link from the sensorimotor cortex to all levels of the spinal cord and is thought to be involved in the more precise control of individual muscle groups. The second system, the extrapyramidal system, sends fibers to the basal ganglia and the reticular formation of the brain stem (the pons and medulla), thereby providing a less direct means of controlling movement. The pyramidal tract is found only in mammals and is most highly developed in primates. A simplification of the roles of these two tracts would be to associate the pyramidal tract with the control of skilled movements and the extrapyramidal tract with reflex activity and the alteration of response tendencies, ranging from postural adjustments to some elements of motor control.

Each sensory modality has primary and secondary areas in the cerebral cortex that record and organize the sensory information. Accordingly, with help from the cerebellum and the basal ganglia, the sensorimotor cortex, linked closely to the association areas that interpret and provide meaning, is in a prime position to translate sensation into action.

The organization of the four main higher centers involved in the control of movement, the sensorimotor cortex, the basal ganglia, the brain stem and the cerebellum, is represented in Figure 6-9 (Henneman, 1974). The *basal ganglia* are a group of nuclei that occupy a large area of the brain. They receive descending connections from the sensorimotor area, discharge into the brain stem, and appear to have a primary role in controlling or generating slow movements (Evarts, 1973), as well as having a modulating influence on all cortical output.

The *brain stem* is primarily involved with the more automatic or reflexive types of motor behavior involved, for example, in posture and locomotion. The brain stem receives signals from all higher centers and processes them for transmission to the spinal cord. All tracts that descend to the spinal cord, other than the pyramidal tract, originate in the brain stem, which may be referred to as the prespinal integrating system. A major element of the brain stem is the reticular formation, which, via the reticulospinal tracts (*i.e.*, those from the brain stem to the spinal cord), acts to facilitate or inhibit certain reflex movements. These reticular structures, together with the basal ganglia and the descending fibers from the cerebral cortex, form the bulk of the extrapyramidal motor system.

Interconnecting with all levels and functioning as the overall coordinator of motor activity is the *cerebellum*. The cerebellum receives sensory information from most receptors, including the visual and auditory receptors, and uses it to help regulate the fine movements of limbs. It has an extensive cortex of its own and has efferent connections to the thalamus, vestibular nuclei (associated with the balance functions of the vestibular apparatus of the inner ear), and the reticular formation. Through these connections, the cerebellum

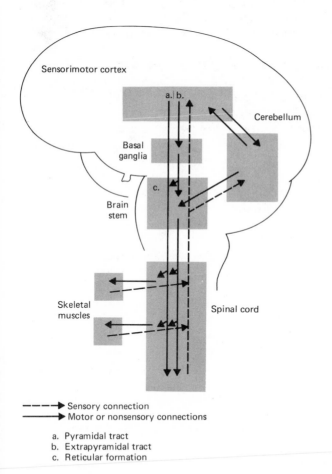

Sensory connection
Motor or nonsensory connections

   a. Pyramidal tract
   b. Extrapyramidal tract
   c. Reticular formation

FIGURE 6-9 Higher centers involved in the control of movement (based on Henneman, 1974).

can exert a strong influence on motor activity at all levels of the central nervous system in fulfilling its role as the coordinator of complex movements. Thus, the overall control of movement is achieved mainly through the functional integration of the motor cortex, the cerebellum, and the basal ganglia, with the cerebellum controlling fast movements and the basal ganglia controlling slow movements.

The proprioceptors

In order for the motor control system to function efficiently, a continuous stream of sensory information regarding the outcome of previous movements and the current physical status, or position, of the various body parts is required. Much of this information is provided by the proprioceptors that constitute the kinesthetic sense, in particular, the joint receptors, the Golgi tendon organs, the muscle spindles, and the vestibular apparatus.

JOINT RECEPTORS. There are three types of receptors that are generally identified: (1) the Ruffini endings, (2) the Pacinian corpuscles, and (3) endings in the ligaments that resemble Golgi tendon organs. The Ruffini endings appear to signal the speed and direction of movement and, because they are affected by muscle tension at the joint, they may also signal the resistance to movement or discriminate active from passive movements (Kelso & Stelmach, 1976). The Pacinian corpuscles probably respond primarily to acceleration and may be capable of detecting very small movements (Skoglund, 1973). The Golgi tendon type of organ in the ligaments is not affected by muscle tension at the joint and, therefore, may signal a more exact joint position as well as direction.

GOLGI TENDON ORGANS. As their name implies, these receptors are situated in the muscle tendons close to the junction with the muscle. They signal the amount of tension in the tendon as a result of muscle contraction and consequently perform a protective function. When the receptor's rate of firing becomes very high, representing high muscle tension, a reflex is initiated that reduces the amount of muscle contraction. Since the threshold for discharge is much lower for active than for passive movements, Goodwin (1977) suggests that the Golgi tendon organs may play a role in the detection of movement during active contractions.

MUSCLE SPINDLES. Muscle spindles are extremely complex receptors, and there has been considerable debate over their function (Smith, 1977). The spindles have both sensory receptors and specialized intrafusal muscle fibers within the spindle itself (Figure 6-10). Muscle spindles are found in most skeletal muscles and lie parallel to the main extrafusal or skeletal muscle fibers. The intrafusal fibers are innervated by their own gamma efferent motor neurons, which are distinct from the alpha motor neurons that innervate the skeletal muscle fibers. There are some intermediate-sized beta motor neurons that may terminate on either type of muscle fiber, but they will not be considered here.

There are two main sets of sensory fibers that have endings in the muscle spindle; these are the Ia and group II fibers. The terminal branches of the Ia fibers are known as the primary endings and are present in all spindles. The secondary endings associated with the group II afferents may be absent from some muscle spindles (10% to 20%). Both primary and secondary endings respond by firing at a rate consistent with the amount of stretch on the intrafusal muscle fibers, with the Ia fibers giving signals related to the dynamics of the stretch velocity and acceleration and group II fibers signaling proportional changes in length.

VESTIBULAR APPARATUS.   The vestibular apparatus is specifically concerned with the position of the head in space. Located in the inner ear, this organ provides the one source of proprioceptive information that is not directly linked to muscle or joint action. The main elements concerned with movement information are the three semicircular canals, the utricle, and the saccule (Figure 6-11). The movement of fluid in the semicircular canals provides information about sudden changes in the speed of movement or direction, particularly rotary acceleration or deceleration. Changes in linear movements are signaled by the utricles and saccules in each ear; the utricles are sensitive to forward and backward movements, and the saccules are sensitive to sideways movements.

The vestibular apparatus is primarily a mediator for the reflexes that maintain a stable head position. By coordinating this sensory information

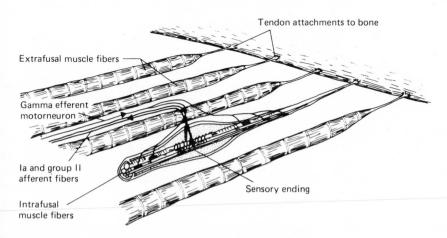

FIGURE 6-10   The muscle spindle (based on Barker, 1962).

with the proprioceptive information from other receptors in the neck and thereby knowing where your head is in relation to the rest of your body, it becomes possible to monitor and regulate body equilibrium. Normally other types of sensory information are available to aid with orienting the body in space, but these proprioceptors are capable of indirectly initiating righting reflexes in the absence of other sources of sensory information. For example, proprioceptive information may help us to maintain our balance when walking down a hill on a moonless night. You cannot see the ground, but changes in body angle and head position give you information about the slope of the ground, thereby allowing you to maintain an upright posture.

Relationship to motor control

The control of movements or motor programs is said to involve two main feedback loops: a short central loop involved in adjusting elements of an ongoing movement and a long loop based on proprioceptive, visual, and other sources of sensory information. We will deal more with the central loop in Chapters 7 and 8.

The extent to which muscle spindles participate in providing sensory information directly to the central mechanisms (the long feedback loop) has been a source of great debate. However, work by Goodwin, McCloskey, and Matthews (1972) suggests that muscle spindles may play a role in the

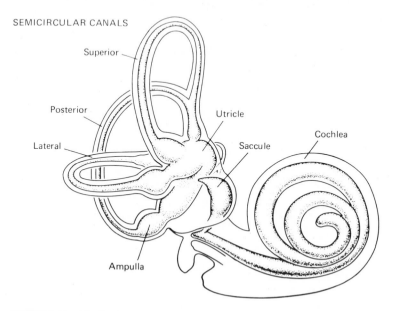

FIGURE 6-11 Vestibular apparatus (based on Langley, Telford & Christensen, 1969).

conscious perception of movement, in that subjects have been found to be able to perceive the movement of an anesthetized finger at the interphalangeal joint or knuckle as long as the rate of movement was above 5 degrees per second. These investigators also found that subjects could mirror quite accurately movements made by the opposite normal finger, suggesting that sensations from the joint receptors were not essential in voluntary movements. Therefore, Kelso and Stelmach (1976) proposed that while research would suggest a more important role for the joint receptors in the encoding of movement, there may be circumstances in which joint information is overridden by muscle information for processing by the higher centers. The Goodwin, McCloskey, and Matthews (1972) data certainly opened the possibility of an important informational role for the muscle spindle in the control of active or voluntary movement.

Certain motor functions are associated with the muscle spindle. These may be illustrated by the stretch reflex, gamma loop, and alpha-gamma coactivation. We should note first that the muscle spindle afferents synapse in the spinal cord with the alpha motor neurons that supply the extrafusal muscles in which the muscle spindles are situated. The stretch reflex of the patellar tendon, the knee jerk, is perhaps the best known. If the muscle spindles are suddenly stretched by an external force, the sensory receptors will fire; this is usually achieved by the doctor delivering a sharp blow to the patellar tendon with a rubber hammer. The resulting afferent discharge stimulates the alpha motor neurons of that muscle (the quadriceps group), which, in turn, causes the muscles to contract and the knee to extend.

A second way that the muscle spindle can "cause" muscle contraction is through the gamma loop. When the gamma motor neurons are stimulated, they produce contraction of the intrafusal muscle fibers, which in turn stimulate the spindle receptors. The resulting spindle afferent discharge can again lead to a contraction of the extrafusal fibers of the same muscle, because these impulses synapse on the associated alpha motor neurons. This loop may have some part to play in the control of slow movements and postural adjustments, but the gamma motor neurons are thought to function mainly in conjunction with the alpha motor neurons. The concept of *alpha-gamma coactivation* and its relationship to the slower proprioceptors is illustrated in Figure 6-12, a simplified flow chart for maintaining or changing limb position.

If a central command is given jointly to the alpha and gamma motor neurons, then as the skeletal muscle contracts so will the intrafusal fibers of the muscle spindle. The result may be conceptualized as taking up the slack, in that a steady-state relationship between the length of the muscle and the amount of stretch on the spindle is maintained. If the movement proceeds normally, nothing further will happen. However, if there is suddenly some extra load on the muscle that stretches the extrafusal fibers, this will stretch the muscle spindle, causing the spindle afferents to fire, and eventually produce extrafusal muscle contraction. With the help of this system, we are still able to complete the tennis stroke despite the gust of wind that nearly knocks us off our feet. In turn, we are able to regain our balance with the aid of the sensory information gathered from the various receptors that have well-established cortical representations, including, possibly, the muscle spindle.

It may be interesting to note that in a quick, forceful movement such as a dive by the soccer goalkeeper, the muscle spindle can be "used" to generate more force in the movement. If the extensor muscles are stretched slightly before contracting in the take-off, the muscle spindle will discharge and the spindle afferents will stimulate the alpha motor neurons at the same time that they receive signals from the higher centers. The effect will be a summing of these two sources and a maximal contraction of the extensor muscles. For the goalkeeper, this could be achieved by stamping the main take-off foot and

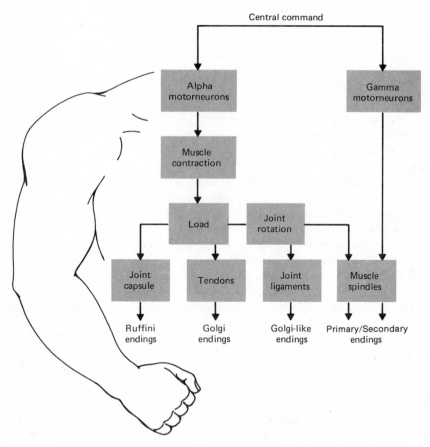

FIGURE 6-12 Proprioceptors involved in maintaining or changing limb position (based on Goodwin, 1977).

stretching the spindles in the gastrocnemius (the main calf muscle of the lower leg) or by letting gravity flex the knees slightly and stretching the spindles in the quadriceps muscles.

To conclude, it would seem reasonable to suggest that while an understanding of the basic physiology of kinesthesis is necessary to properly interpret recent theoretical developments in psychomotor learning, the state of the art is not yet sufficiently advanced to provide a practical model for psychomotor learning. Conversely, when the researchers in psychomotor learning do establish an effective model, they may well have to turn to the physiological psychologists to explain exactly why it works. This is not meant to be a comment on the relative expertise of the two areas but is an acknowledgment of the difficulties faced when taking a physiological approach to the study of learning; human subjects are just not available for any but the most superficial neurological experiments.

CONTRIBUTION TO PSYCHOMOTOR LEARNING

The final part of this chapter will be concerned with the relative roles of vision and kinesthesis in skill acquisition and the contribution of vision and kinesthesis to the learning of a motor skill. This will be achieved in part by focusing on the research of Fleishman and Rich (1963) and Connolly and Jones (1970).

Kinesthetic and spatial awareness

One study that investigated the relationship between vision and kinesthesis was conducted by Fleishman and Rich (1963), who investigated the role of kinesthesis and spatial awareness in the learning of a perceptual motor skill. The task used was a two-hand coordination (THC) task, in which subjects followed a target, necessitating simultaneous movement of two separate controls.

The kinesthetic sensitivity (KS) of the subjects was measured by a weight judgment task in which the subjects were asked to make comparative judgments, thereby establishing Weber fractions. Spatial awareness (SA) was measured by using an air force test involving the judgment of the correct horizon for a given plane position. The forty subjects used in this experiment then performed ten blocks of four one-minute trials on the two-hand coordination task. The performance scores for each block of trials were correlated with the scores on the two pretest measures of kinesthetic sensitivity and spatial awareness. The correlations derived were as follows:

SA vs THC = 0.49 significant
KS vs THC = 0.58 significant
SA vs KS = 0.12 non-significant

Both of the pretest perceptual measures were found to have a significant relationship with performance on the coordination task. The implication is that both perceptual tests measure an ability that can account for a substantial amount of variance in the performance scores on the coordination task. However, as the two perceptual tests correlate very poorly with one another ($r = 0.12$), this means that they are measuring different factors or abilities and are not both measuring some general hand-eye coordination ability. The next step in the analysis of the data was to repeat the correlations between the perceptual tests and the coordination task for each block of trials in order to assess their contribution at different stages of the learning process (Figure 6-13).

From the correlations in Figure 6-13, we can see that as practice continues the relative importance of the two variables changes, as indicated by the size of the correlations. The progressive changes in the correlations indicate that spatial awareness is important early in learning and kinesthetic sensitivity is important later on. The final step was to split the subjects in half according to how they scored on each of the perceptual tests.

For spatial awareness (Figure 6-14), it can be seen that the two performance curves, representing a division of the 40 subjects into two groups of high and low spatial awareness, converge with practice, although the high spatial awareness group appears to have some advantage in the early stages of learning. In Figure 6-15, which represents the performance scores when the subjects are divided on the basis of kinesthetic sensitivity, we see that these curves diverge.

Block	THC vs SA	THC vs KS
1	.36	.03
2	.28	
3	.22	
4		
5		
6		
7		.23
8		.28
9		.38
10	.01	.40

FIGURE 6-13 Block analysis correlations (based on Fleishman & Rich, 1963).

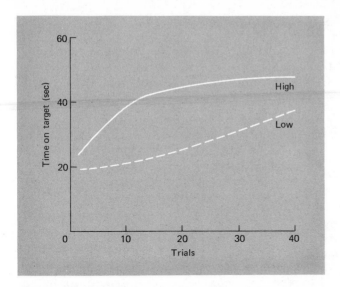

FIGURE 6-14   Spatial awareness (based on Fleishman & Rich, 1963).

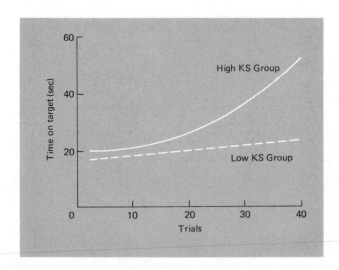

FIGURE 6-15   Kinesthetic sensitivity (based on Fleishman & Rich, 1963).

It would seem reasonable to conclude that initially visual cues are important to guide the learner and that those subjects with higher spatial awareness make faster progress up to a certain level. Beyond this point, finer adjustment is needed; therefore, those with a higher kinesthetic sensitivity will make greater progress. From this, we see how different abilities may contribute to the learning of a specific skill and how their roles may change as the skill is acquired.

As coaches or teachers, it is important to identify the types of information that are of primary concern in the learning of a particular skill and to focus the learner's attention on those elements. Also, we must recognize that those factors that are important in the performance of the final skill may be different from those that are relevant in the initial attempts at that skill. As the skill changes, so must our methods and the points we emphasize.

Intersensory integration

Intersensory integration has been the topic of many studies. In one such study by Connolly and Jones (1970), the authors tried to look at the ability of subjects to make judgments that involved switching from one sensory mode to another, in this case from visual to kinesthetic. The task they used involved judging the length of a line and then trying to reproduce that line. The line was presented either visually or kinesthetically. The subject was then required to reproduce, or match, the same line either visually or kinesthetically. This procedure produced four possible combinations:

1. Visual presentation—visual match (V-V)
2. Kinesthetic presentation—kinesthetic match (K-K)
3. Visual presentation—kinesthetic match (V-K)
4. Kinesthetic presentation—visual match (K-V)

For the visual presentation, the subjects viewed the standard to be reproduced for that trial. After the standard was removed the subjects watched the experimenter slowly extend a metal tape. For the visual reproduction, the subjects were to stop the experimenter when they felt the tape had reached a length equivalent to the previously viewed standard. In the kinesthetic presentation, the subject, who was blindfolded, would move a pointer down a wooden groove until it hit a stop. The kinesthetic reproduction required the subject to move the same distance again but with the stop removed.

These absolute judgments represented the intramodal vision to vision (V-V) and kinesthetic to kinesthetic (K-K) matching conditions. The two cross-modal matching conditions were V-K and K-V. Thus, the method of presentation was the same in V-K as in V-V and the same in K-V as in K-K. The method of reproduction was the same in V-K as in K-K and the same in K-V as in V-V. The results of this study showed that both of the intramodal conditions were more accurate than the cross-modal conditions and that V-V was more accurate than K-K.

To explain these findings, it was suggested that intramodal matching was more accurate because it was simpler to perform and did not require the translation of information between sensory modes, assuming that the process of translation would lead to a reduction in the quality of the information. That V-V was more accurate concurred with earlier work in short-term motor memory studies (Posner, 1967), suggesting that visual storage was more accurate than kinesthetic storage. This latter fact was also used as part of the explanation for the cross-modal asymmetry when K-V was found to be more accurate than V-K. As visual storage appears to be more accurate, it would have been reasonable to expect V-K to be more accurate than K-V.

To account for this asymmetry, Connolly and Jones proposed a model of sensory integration (Figure 6-16). In this model there are separate memory systems for vision and kinesthesis, with translation between the senses being governed by an integrated store. It was also proposed that in cross-modal matching this translation of information between the two sensory modes occurred before storage. This is the key assumption that underlies the following argument. In the V-K condition, as the information enters the visual channel, some of the quality of the information would first be lost in the translation process and would further deteriorate while being held in the weaker kinesthetic store until reproduction. However, in the K-V condition, although some information would be lost in translation, the further loss of information while it was held in the visual store would be small compared with the weaker kinesthetic store. Hence, reproduction would be more accurate in the K-V condition because there is less opportunity for information loss.

The inferiority of the kinesthetic store was confirmed in a second study by Jones and Connolly (1970). By not telling the subjects the method of reproduction in advance, the resulting performance should reflect the storage

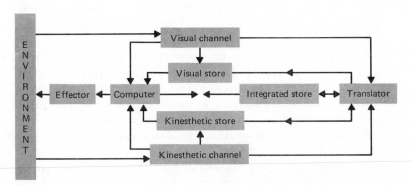

FIGURE 6-16   A model to illustrate sensory integration (after Connolly & Jones, 1970).

characteristics of the mode of presentation. This occurs because the subjects would have to store the information in that sensory mode until told the method of reproduction, and therefore translation is delayed. Under these conditions, V-K should be more accurate than K-V, and this is what they found.

Note at the heart of this model is the integrated store. This is like an English/French dictionary. For any given task you may only need the A to C section of the dictionary, and this should be placed in the translator. Assuming that both languages are needed for the task, your ability to perform the task is a function of the number of words and their equivalents available to you in the second language. During the task you may learn new words and their translations. These bits of information can then be added to the integrated store. Over time, you gradually increase both the size and quality of the dictionary and, therefore, your ability to perform an increasing number of tasks. The Connolly and Jones study was also a developmental one in that it involved groups of subjects ranging from 5 years to 23 years of age. Their study showed an increasing ability with age to perform the cross-modal conditions, providing the basis for the dictionary analogy.

While accepting Connolly and Jones' basic model, Bies and Kerr (1977) questioned whether the ordering of the conditions was a function of using a visually loaded rather than a kinesthetically loaded task. They suggested that the task of judging length was naturally more amenable to visual processing and storage. Even in the kinesthetic reproduction the subject has to pay little attention to how the hand actually reaches the end point. The subject only has to store (imagine?) the end location and does not have to think *how* to move the hand 4 inches. However, a task that requires the subject to pay attention to how the movement is achieved might produce different results.

In their study, Bies and Kerr used a task that required the subjects to move two intersecting wires to one of four locations (Figure 6-17). The wires were moved by turning two concealed dials 3¼ inches in diameter. Obviously, subjects could, and did, count the number of dial turns they made, but to be accurate they had to reproduce the same movement for each turn, their final error score being a function of the variability of each turn. In other words, as there was no handle on the dial to indicate some starting point, the subjects had to calibrate their own movement. This involves trying to turn the wrist a fixed distance each time and then returning to your own starting point for the next turn. The final position of each dial would be represented by a partial turn. To be accurate on the overall task would involve producing precise repetitions of your chosen movement. Otherwise, the experimental design was the same as in the Connolly and Jones experiment (1970).

Bies and Kerr again found that intramodal matching was more accurate than cross-modal matching, but the order of the conditions was the reverse of the Connolly and Jones study, with K-K being most accurate. The cross-modal asymmetry was also reversed with V-K being more accurate than K-V.

These results would suggest that the order of the conditions is more a function of the amenability of the task information to processing in a particular sensory mode than to the qualities of the associated sensory stores.

The second part of the Bies and Kerr study (1977) examined the function of the integrated store. The ability of the subject to perform the task should reflect the quality of the information made available to the integrated store. Subjects placed in four different groups were given practice in one matching condition only (V-V, K-K, K-V, or V-K) with knowledge of results. They were then retested on all four matching conditions. The results were not very strong, but a certain general pattern did appear. The V-V practice group showed no improvement. Because the subjects were university students, it would seem they had had a lot of previous practice in making visual judgments, so the practice of this task gave them little new information. However, the other three groups who received some type of kinesthetic-related knowledge of results did improve, most of the improvement being demonstrated under the K-V condition. The novel part of this task was the movement itself and how it was to be produced. Any information about the movement, in terms of the earlier dictionary analogy, helped to upgrade the quality of the dictionary. Although the results were not strong, the data of Bies and Kerr could be interpreted in terms of this important concept of the integrated store.

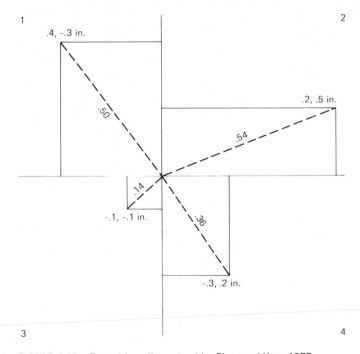

FIGURE 6-17   Target locations used by Bies and Kerr, 1977.

Newell, Shapiro, and Carlton (1979) have also challenged the original Connolly and Jones findings. Specifically, they found no support for the assumption that translation between modalities occurs before storage in the cross-modal condition. Also, the cross-modal asymmetry in which K-V performance is more accurate than V-K was found to occur only when visual information of the surroundings was available. Intramodal matching was, however, consistently superior to cross-modal matching. Newell and co-workers proposed that this may partly reflect the degree of invariance in the stimulus features, suggesting that as the invariance increased the difference between the two matching conditions would be reduced.

Clearly, an overall concept such as the integrated store would suggest the importance of diversification within a physical education program to ensure exposure to a wide variety of skills. As mentioned earlier, this is one of the main aims of movement education. However, just as we try to increase the number of items in the movement dictionary, it is also necessary that the items be properly "defined." In motor learning terms, we do this by paying attention to the skill itself, trying to repeat it and refine it. This process provides one of the main reasons for having a physical education program as contrasted to a free play situation, in that if we can expand the movement vocabulary we may lift the individuals closer to their potential.

We have seen how the role of vision in the learning of a motor skill can change as the level of learning changes. In a perceptual-motor task, vision (spatial awareness) played an important role in the early organization of the task; but in the later stages of refining the task, kinesthesis was more important. Also apparent was how experience with a task and prior learning can affect the quality of information in the integrated store, which in turn relates to the quality of our performance. Both factors have implications for the teaching of motor skills. The former suggests that the elements within a skill on which we should focus the learner's attention change as the learner acquires the skill, and the latter suggests that providing the learner with a broader base of motor skill experiences should enhance the learner's ability to deal with new tasks.

Anticipation

In the first part of this chapter dealing with speed of vision, the importance of visual tracking in motor skill performance was mentioned. Closely linked to this idea is the factor of anticipation. Certain aspects of anticipation have already been covered, including the role of the learner's expectations of what will occur. The implication is that the learner can use these expectations to anticipate events in the environment and thereby make some response to coincide with those events.

Williams (1967, cited in Cratty, 1970) conducted a study in which children had to judge and move quickly to the point where a ball would land after being allowed to observe only the initial arc of the ball's flight. Children from the first two elementary grades, 6 to 8 years of age, tended to react quickly and inaccurately. By 9 years of age the children reacted more slowly but became more accurate. However, only in the later elementary grades were children able to move quickly and make accurate judgments. Therefore, although the younger children in this study had developed accurate visual tracking and locomotor abilities, the integration of these two elements was still a problem.

Similarly, Whiting (1968) used a task in which subjects had to intercept a tetherball as it swung around a pole. Various conditions, including total darkness, were tested by restricting the amount of flight information available to the learner. Whiting found that subjects learned to anticipate the flight based on information received near the beginning of the ball's flight.

Salmela and Fiorito (1979) took the work one step further and looked at a practical skill, goalkeeping in ice hockey. They acknowledged the fact that balls, or pucks in this case, are not normally thrown by machines but are hit by people. These people have to perform certain movements that may even provide cues in advance of flight information. By using films and occluding the frames for one-twelfth, one-sixth, and one-third second prior to the shot, they were able to assess the extent to which the goalkeepers could anticipate the direction of the shot. The results showed that pre-shot information that could facilitate anticipation was both available and usable by the goaltenders. Clearly, goalkeeping can be learned and is not simply a function of fast reflexes.

Perhaps the main role of anticipation is to eliminate feedback delays when we must wait to see the outcome of some event before we can respond further. To summarize, Poulton (1957) has outlined three types of anticipation: effector, receptor, and perceptual anticipation.

EFFECTOR ANTICIPATION. *The performer must predict the time it will take to perform a movement.* Clearly, for your response to coincide with some external event (e.g., hitting a tennis ball), you have to know how long it takes to perform the movement in order to initiate it in sufficient time. We have often seen the beginning tennis player judge the flight of the ball accurately, move to the spot where it will land, but miss the ball because the learner failed to recognize how long it would take to perform the skill.

RECEPTOR ANTICIPATION. In a skill such as tennis, *the player must also assess the duration of certain external events,* such as the flight time of the ball. This knowledge, in conjunction with the known duration of the movement (effector anticipation), facilitates appropriate timing so that the ball is struck with the maximum power in the center of the racket. The integration of effector and receptor anticipation is known as *coincident timing.*

PERCEPTUAL ANTICIPATION. *The performer must identify some regularity in the approaching events in order to predict the occurrence of some particular stimulus event.* This can be particularly important in the timing of a sequence of events in which information from the first part of a movement might be used to initiate a second component. For example, knowing that movement number two is initiated one-half second after movement number one allows the second movement to be cued by the initiation of the first without waiting for proprioceptive feedback to provide this information, in which case it may be too late.

While receptor information involves judging an external event (the flight of a ball), perceptual anticipation involves the situation in which the relevant movement information is not yet available and the learner must rely on past experience to make a judgment (*e.g.,* trying to estimate when a car crossing a covered bridge will reappear at the other side or trying to read the defense before it begins to move). Thus, perceptual anticipation can involve judging both when (temporal anticipation) and where (spatial anticipation) some event will occur (Adams, 1966).

SUMMARY

In Chapter 6 we presented some of the perceptual characteristics of the two major sensory modalities related to motor skill performance: vision and kinesthesis.

Visual perception

SPATIAL AWARENESS. The three main elements of spatial awareness are (1) spatial relations, or the ability to discriminate direction with oneself as the reference point; (2) spatial orientation, or the ability to judge positional changes of objects in space; and (3) spatial visualization, or the ability to mentally manipulate objects in space.

DEPTH PERCEPTION. Although the Gestalt laws provide some useful information as to how we organize our perceptual world, the laws were criticized because they were two dimensional and we live in a three-dimensional world. The main monocular cues to depth are the size and partial overlap of objects, shadowing, linear perspective, and filled or unfilled space. The major cue to depth, however, stems from possessing two eyes that are spatially separated, creating the effect known as binocular parallax. This means that the brain receives two different views of the world, and this disparity can provide cues about the relative depth of objects.

PERCEPTUAL INTEGRATION. Gibson extended our understanding of perception by observing that we establish perspective by abstracting gradients based on the invariant characteristics of objects in the visual field. Once established, these gradients provide a scale by which to judge other objects. As we move through the environment, we gain further cues from the relative stability of objects in space. Finally, perceptual frameworks built from successive samplings of the environment provide a base or running hypothesis to guide our behavior.

MOVEMENT. Built into the eye is a reflex based on the sensitivity of the periphery of the retina to movement. The head moves instinctively in the direction of the movement detected by the retina. Only a few cells in the eye fire continuously in response to a steady light; other cells signify the passage of the leading and trailing edges of some image. It seems that the human eye is primarily a detector of movement. The two main systems whereby these judgments of movement are made involve movements of images across the retina or movement of the eye within the head.

APPARENT MOVEMENT. Although the eyes are our "window on the world," the information "seen" still needs interpreting. There are many movement effects or illusions. Such illusions are apparent in movie films in which there are two elements that create the impression of movement. First, if you increase the flicker rate of a light to about 30 flickers per second, the afterimages will fuse to create a persistent image. This is achieved in films by changing the presentation rate from 24 to 72 frames per second. Secondly, by properly synchronizing the timing of two lights being switched alternately on and off, it is possible to develop a sense of movement known as the phi phenomenon.

SPEED OF VISION. Speed of vision refers to the ability to monitor accurately a constantly changing environment. It is based on the span of apprehension (how much we can take in at a single glance) and visual tracking ability. Also, it was noted that peripheral vision is greater in athletes than non-athletes, giving them a possible advantage in the span of apprehension. It was also pointed out that there is a lack of research into the role of sound, particularly rhythm, in the performance of motor skills.

Kinesthetic perception

Kinesthesis was defined simply as the awareness of body position and movement based on proprioceptive information. Scott proposed four separate divisions of kinesthesis: the replication of muscular force, balance, the identification of body position, and orientation in space. These provide only a rough guide to an understanding of kinesthesis; we need to consider the basic physiology of the system.

THE MOTOR SYSTEM.   The major higher centers of control are the sensorimotor area of the cortex, the basal ganglia, the brain stem, and the cerebellum. Overall control appears to be a function of the integrated effort of these centers, with the exception of the brain stem, which acts more as a relay station and is involved primarily in reflexive activity.

THE PROPRIOCEPTORS.   The joint receptors provide information about the speed and direction of movement, while the Golgi tendon organs perform a protective role in guarding against excess tension. There is argument about the role of the muscle spindle, but it does fire at a consistent rate proportional to the amount of stretch on the spindle, reflecting changes in muscle length. The vestibular apparatus located in the inner ear provides information regarding the position of the head and is particularly associated with body righting reflexes.

RELATIONSHIP TO MOTOR CONTROL.   The major involvement of the muscle spindle is thought to be in alpha-gamma coactivation. By jointly stimulating the alpha and gamma motor neurons, it is possible, based on signals from the muscle spindle, for sudden perturbations in the movement of the skeletal muscle to be detected and corrections initiated and for movements to be completed accurately without higher center involvement.

Contributions to psychomotor learning

KINESTHETIC AND SPATIAL AWARENESS.   The abilities that are important in the performance of a skill can be identified, but their relative importance may change as learning progresses. For coordination tasks, visual cues have been shown to be more important early in learning while kinesthetic cues are more important at the later stages.

INTERSENSORY INTEGRATION.   The work of Connolly and Jones, although controversial, illustrated the need for an integrated store of information in order to facilitate translation when tasks requiring similar judgments in different sensory modalities are performed such as: "how far away is my partner? how hard must I throw the ball to get the ball there?"

ANTICIPATION.   The three main elements are (1) effector anticipation, which involves determining the duration of a movement or response; (2) receptor anticipation of the duration of some external event; and (3) perceptual anticipation or using some predictability in upcoming events to help coordinate a sequence of movements. The former two when taken together are referred to as coincident timing, as demonstrated in the action of catching a moving object.

PROBLEM

Question

You are faced with the task of teaching a young soccer player how to play goalkeeper in soccer. Using Poulton's analysis of anticipation, how would you analyze and define some of the main components of the goalkeeping skills prior to actually teaching the player?

Possible answer

The first two elements of Poulton's model, effector and receptor anticipation, would influence mainly the decisions of when, or if, to use a certain skill. The third element, perceptual anticipation, is more concerned with the actual technique, which in goalkeeping might mean how to avoid giving rebounds or how to avoid dropping the ball using the "wrap around" technique (Figure 6-18).

When faced by an oncoming attacking player with the ball who in turn is being chased by a defender, the goalkeeper must be aware of how long it will take to perform the various defensive maneuvers: (1) running out and trying to fall on the ball at the attacking player's feet; (2) waiting for the shot and moving sideways to catch the ball but remaining upright; (3) as in number two, but diving sideways; and (4) moving out to meet the player to cut down the shooting angle before performing any of the previous options. As the duration of each of the successive options is shorter, options one through three give the goalkeeper increasing amounts of time to process additional information. Option number four can be ongoing and, thereby, can reduce the duration time of each option.

In terms of receptor anticipation, the main events of concern are the speed and direction of approach of the player, the ball, or both together. How short a period of time will it take to cover the intervening distance? These two sources of information, receptor and effector, can then be timed or coordinated such that the goalkeeper is able to prevent the ball from entering the goal. A good goalkeeper will always try to perform option number four, "cutting down the angle," because this reduces the required duration times for all movements and allows the use of the preferred option, number two, rather than the more spectacular but less secure third option of diving. When the goalkeeper is standing up, the body provides a second line of defense if the hands miss the ball, but when diving, the hands are the only line of defense.

In performing a dive, it is important to dive sideways and place as wide a barrier as possible across the line of flight of the ball. Diving forward is dangerous as well as unsafe in terms of maintaining possession of the ball. This skill involves performing a set sequence of movements and can, therefore, be facilitated by perceptual anticipation. This applies particularly to the final phase of catching and "wrapping" around the ball. As the player drives off against the ground, this movement should coincide with a rapid movement of the head and arms also being thrown in the direction of the dive. The cue for the initiation of the second movement is the preparatory phase of the first movement, which is a slight flexion of the knees. As a result of this second movement, in addition to the added force generated, the hands are now in the correct position to catch the ball and the head is in the correct position to watch its flight. This latter point is most important, for goalkeepers who wait to feel the ball against their hands before initiating the wrap around strategy are more likely to drop the ball or give

FIGURE 6-18 Wrap-around technique for soccer goal keepers.

rebounds from hard shots. By watching the flight of the ball and taking a cue from it, the goalkeeper can anticipate its arrival and initiate the wrap-around technique at the same time that contact is made; the goalkeeper pulls the ball into the body, wraps the arms around it, and lets the knees come to the chest.

Although these represent only a few of the goalkeeper's skills, they do serve to show how key elements and cues can be identified given an appropriate model to guide the analysis.

Part Four   Motor Control

Chapter 7
Components of Motor Control

Interpreting the pause is their problem
(Prather, 1970)

Three components were identified in the information processing model: the perceptual, decision, and effector mechanisms. So far we have dealt only with the processing of the initial input information, or perceptual mechanism. The next step is to examine, for both individual movements and sequences of movements, those central decision and effector mechanism processes that are involved in the actual control of the motor response. This includes both the decisions made regarding the choice of the movement and the process involved in putting that choice into effect. The role of feedback in the learning and performance of a motor skill and the potential effects of stress will also be considered in this chapter. The discussion of the central components is based on an analysis by Posner and Keele (1972).

The post-war development of computers has led to the realization that there are many similarities between the operations of the computer and the human brain. By manipulating the input information and observing the output or response, we can deduce the internal processes involved. The two key variables that allow us to analyze the mental operations in the control of skilled movements are the concepts of *time* and *space* (Keele, 1973).

Each mental operation performed in the control of a movement takes a certain amount of *time* to process. As either the complexity or the number of mental operations involved in the control of a movement increases, so will the response time for that particular movement. If the information relevant to performing a particular skill must be processed sequentially through a series of processing stages, then the longer the sequence the longer will be the response time. To represent roughly the contributions of the decision and effector mechanisms, we can measure a subject's reaction time or movement time and see what manipulations affect these time intervals. These measurements enable us to make inferences about the processes involved.

The second concept put forward by Keele (1973) was that each mental operation may demand *space* within a limited capacity system. We have already noted some of the limitations of the human motor system. Using the computer analogy, we know that a computer only has a certain number of circuits or a given amount of "computing" space available. If the circuits are all being used, any new information will be delayed until a circuit, or space, becomes free. Therefore, in terms of motor skills, one of the questions is whether two tasks can be performed simultaneously; more specifically, under what conditions can the "computer" process two sets of information at the same time.

If two tasks using different receptor and effector processes interfere with one another, then they can be said to be competing for space in the central processor, the computer or brain. We can walk and talk at the same time, so we could say that walking involves time but little space. The control of walking certainly involves some mental operations, but they appear to involve little of the central processing capacity. To revert to our earlier terminology, because walking is fairly automatic it only engages a minimal depth of processing, freeing the major portion of the "computing" space to handle the second task of talking. The extent to which the performer is successful in completing the two tasks will depend on the nature of the discourse and the depth of processing required by the two tasks. Singing the national anthem while walking down a crowded street, for example, would hardly seem as demanding a task as trying to get a politician to make a simple unequivocal statement on some burning public issue. In fact, if the latter were attempted on the same street, it would engage more attention and increase the likelihood of collisions with other pedestrians.

By using the two concepts of time and space and by observing whether the two tasks interfere with each other or if a certain task manipulation adds a fixed amount of time to the response time, we can divide a skill into a series of mental operations. In Chapter 4 we made a distinction between the structural components of memory, the memory stores themselves, and the control processes that regulate what information gets into and is selected from memory. Thus the two types of manipulation illustrated by the concepts of time and space actually allow us to distinguish between processing and structural interference, respectively. Interference in the time taken to perform a certain task may reflect changes in processing, while two tasks that interfere with one another may imply competition for space within the same controlling structure or store.

Now we will analyze some of the separate mental operations involved in the control of a simple motor skill by using as a base a model put forward by Posner and Keele (1972). The motor task put forward by Posner and Keele to illustrate this model (Figure 7-1) was used later to produce the specific laboratory task in Figure 7-2 (Kerr, 1980). Although the reference task illustrated by this figure is not a "real world" motor skill, it is useful in that its components represent the main elements involved in the learning and performance of almost any motor skill.

For this task the subject grasps a stylus that rests on the home plate (H). The warning light comes on, and a short time later (*e.g.*, one-fourth second) either stimulus light A or B comes on and the subject moves to that target plate. The subjects are told that after a series of practice trials they will be asked to repeat the task blindfolded with a tone cue instead of the lights. Therefore, to be efficient in performing this task, the subjects must prepare themselves, choose the correct direction, perform a precise movement, and store a record of that movement for future use. These processes are represented in Figure 7-1.

The interval between the first stimulus light (S_1), the warning signal, and the second stimulus light (S_2) represents the preparation or anticipation phase. S_2 also acts as the "go" signal, and the time period between S_2 and the initiation of the movement represents the decisional component or reaction time. The final two components are the movement phase—the time taken to complete the movement—and storage, which in an experimental setting is represented (approximately) by the intertrial interval.

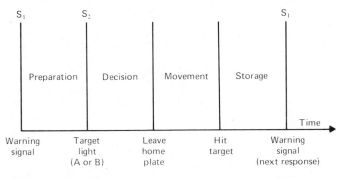

FIGURE 7-1 Mental operations involved in a simple motor task (after Posner & Keele, 1972).

On seeing this task, a very natural question would be, how does this laboratory task relate to a normal gross motor skill? If we look at the task more closely we may see the answer. The preparation phase, which begins with the onset of the warning light, is similar to the swimmer or track runner waiting for the starting gun after being told to "get set." Similarly, the onset of the target light (S_2) indicates the direction of the correct response just as the opponent's return tells a tennis or badminton player where to move. The movement component of this task involves the performance of a very specific movement in the same way that a wide-receiver in football runs a specified pattern to a pre-determined spot. Finally, if any movement is to be repeated accurately in the future it must be stored properly. Consider the tenpin bowler who tries to retain the set of movements necessary to produce a strike. Therefore, if through research we gain insight into the mental operations involved in the control of a specific motor skill by manipulating the components of the task in a laboratory situation, then at the same time we are gaining insight into the overall process of the control of motor skills. In order to understand more clearly the components of the task explained above we will consider them sequentially, as outlined by Posner and Keele (1972).

PREPARATION PHASE

Generally, immediately before an event we subjectively find ourselves "getting ready." Intuitively we feel that when a warning signal is provided the reaction time will be decreased. Experimentally we find that this decrease is

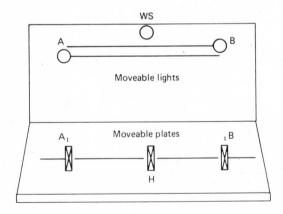

WS – Warning signal
A, B – Stimulus lights
A_1, B_1 – Target plates
H – Home plate

FIGURE 7-2 Apparatus for a simple movement task (based on Kerr, 1980).

greater if the warning signal interval is a constant length, with 200 to 500 msec producing the optimal reaction times (Bertelson, 1967). A constant foreperiod (preparation phase) means that the learner can respond to the warning signal rather than the stimulus, because the subject now "knows" when the stimulus will occur. Consequently, the subject has, in effect, more time to prepare the response. Optimum states of readiness are not easily maintained (Requin, 1969) and, in fact, constant foreperiods that are greater than two seconds show longer reaction times (Klemmer, 1957), reflecting a decreased ability to judge the time interval. The starter in athletics or swimming who holds the racers in the "set" position for any length of time is likely to produce more false starts and is not going to help the sprinters break world records (not that this is the role of the starter).

Normally, when foreperiods are not fixed (as in races with a starter), reaction times tend to be faster if a foreperiod is in or near the middle of the range of the previous foreperiods (Welford, 1976). The tendency to respond to the middle of the range is possibly a reflection of our search for invariance in our perceptual world. Assuming most starters try to be consistent, it should prove most beneficial for an athlete to listen to the starter's cadence on earlier races. Obviously then, the preparation phase is very important in the overall performance of a motor task. Two different factors appear to be involved in this phase; they are referred to as sensory set and motor set (Henry, 1960).

Sensory set

Sensory set refers to a change in the level of alertness such that the subject increases the rate at which target signals can be processed. This change occurs within the central processing mechanism and not peripherally at the level of the receptor.

Sensory set appears to be a general effect because it has been found that subjects who are prepared for a visual cue respond more quickly to an infrequent auditory cue, or at least within the normal reaction time (Posner & Boies, 1971). If the sensory set were a specific effect, then the reaction time to the unanticipated auditory cue should have been slower than normal because the subject expected and was set to respond to a visual cue and not an auditory cue. Thus, the normal or facilitated reaction time to an auditory cue suggests that this central alertness is not specific for one sensory modality.

The effect could be achieved in either one of two ways:

1. By a decrease in the cortical threshold for sensory stimuli. Evidence of changes in brain wave activity shown on an electroencephalogram [EEG] has suggested this possibility (Karlin & Martz, 1973). Therefore, even weak signals could be processed and identified. Not all signals or cues are as obvious as a starting gun. Conceivably, as a spectator in the crowd one could cause a false start by snapping one's fingers before the gun goes off.

2. By an increase in the rate at which the central attentional mechanism receives and processes the signal. There is no preliminary filtering; the subject simply opens all sensory channels.

Motor set

In the reference task (Figure 7-2), there are two possible movements, one to each target, and each has an associated motor program. It has been suggested (Henry, 1960) that at the time of the warning signal, the threshold of these two programs is altered by the subject such that both are highly available in relation to all the other motor programs stored in memory. If one program is more probable, it is given a higher priority and thus it would show a greater decrease in reaction time with an optimum warning signal than the less probable program. We use this foreperiod to select the most probable movement from among all the possible movements that could be made in any situation. Therefore, it seems that the preparatory phase involves the specific preparation of the correct motor response *(motor set)* as well as the increase in central alertness, that is sensory set.

Weiss (1965) fractionated reaction time into motor and premotor components. *Premotor time* represents the interval between the presentation of the stimulus and the onset of the action potential in the responding muscle, while *motor time* is defined as the interval between the arrival of this neural signal at the muscle and the actual contraction of the muscle that initiates the response or the first observable movement.

Studies using this approach (Botwinick & Thompson, 1966) show that the variable foreperiod produced changes in premotor time, with motor time remaining relatively constant. Thus, motor set appears to refer to the preparation within the central mechanism and not to muscle tone. However, evidence suggests the facilitation of alphamotor neuron activity prior to the initiation of a response in a coincidence timing and a reaction time task (Frank, 1978). On the basis of this evidence, Frank argued for a separation between those processes involved in the control of response initiation and in response gain—the strength or size of the response.

DECISION COMPONENT

When the second stimulus light (S_2) occurs, we are "prepared" to select and initiate the appropriate response. The actual time it takes to complete this decisional phase is usually referred to as *reaction time*. By using electrodes placed on the responding muscles, it is possible to signal the arrival of the neural impulse at the muscle and, thereby, measure the premotor and motor components of reaction time. Premotor time is usually related to central processing, and motor time is usually related to peripheral delays in the musculature. Thus, reaction time has both central (the time taken to select the response) and peripheral (the time taken to initiate the response) components. The time from the firing of the efferent signal centrally to the onset of muscular contraction peripherally is relatively constant for any given response.

In a majority of the fractionated reaction time studies, changes in the overall reaction time were mainly a reflection of changes in premotor time (Lagasse & Hayes, 1973). Therefore, reaction time is regarded as a function of how information is processed by the central control mechanisms. However, some studies have shown increases in the motor time component as a result of preliminary muscle tension (Schmidt & Stull, 1970) or local muscle fatigue (Klimovitch, 1977). Kroll and Clarkson (1978) emphasized the point that changes in motor time due to fatigue are found only in resisted reaction time tasks in which the subject has to work against a load. The fatigue apparently reduces the rate of tension development in the muscle, producing increases in total reaction time by increasing the motor time when a certain minimum tension is needed to initiate a movement. Kroll argues that fractionated reaction time tasks that do not require subjects to work against a load cannot provide satisfactory explanations for the performance of motor tasks such as running, lifting, or throwing, all of which involve working against some load or resistance.

Kroll and Clarkson (1978) also made one other interesting suggestion, which involved the fractionation of the premotor time itself by placing electrodes on the scalp to analyze changes in brain wave activity (EEG). The three subdivisions suggested are reception time, opto-motor integration time, and motor outflow time (Figure 7-3). These divisions represent respectively the time between the onset of a visual stimulus and an EEG wave in the visual cortex, the time between the reception at the visual cortex and a second wave at the motor cortex, and, finally, the time needed to conduct a signal to the muscle. Relating to this technique, Kroll and Clarkson (1978) cited a study by Champion (1977) that found differences between the premotor times of power and endurance athletes. The faster times of the endurance athletes could be attributed to differences in opto-motor integration and motor outflow times.

As we have already mentioned, the speed of selection will be influenced by the factor of probability and the number of items, or possible responses, held in memory. An additional factor that must be considered is the question of the compatibility of the stimulus and the response, or the ease with which they are related to one another. Reaction time is found to be fastest when target and light are compatible (Posner, 1966), as in the reference task in which the target is placed directly under the appropriate stimulus light. However, if the stimulus lights are spatially separate from the targets, with the two stimulus lights (A and B) placed directly under the warning signal, the subjects will tend to activate both programs, delaying the selection process. As the degree of stimulus-response compatibility is lost (*e.g.,* if stimulus lights and response targets are arranged randomly), it tends to cause errors and further increases reaction time, since these errors in selection have to be corrected centrally before the correct response is initiated. Note, if these errors are corrected after the initiation of an incorrect response, then they will add to the movement time component and not to reaction time. One important factor here is the natural tendency to react in the spatial direction of the stimulus, suggesting perhaps that starters should be in front of the athletes rather than behind.

Because there is a wealth of information on reaction time, selected aspects of the associated phenomena will be discussed separately. These are (1) the Hick-Hyman Law, (2) the repetition effect, (3) the logogen model, (4) the psychological refractory period, and (5) the effects of movement parameters. It should be noted that while most investigators did not fractionate reaction time, the assumption made was that they were studying aspects of the central processing mechanisms. It is in the context of central processing that the term *reaction time* will be used in the remaining discussion of this topic.

Hick-Hyman law

Clearly, some of the factors that affect our initial perception of a situation will also affect our ability to decide on the appropriate response. The main problems facing a performer are the retrieval of information from memory,

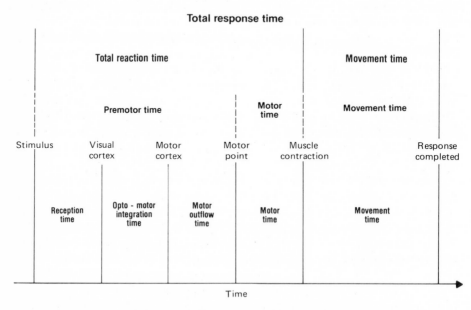

FIGURE 7-3   Fractionated reaction time (based on Kroll & Clarkson, 1978).

choosing between a number of alternatives, and selecting a sequence of responses or more than one response at a time. As mentioned in the section on information processing (Chapter 2) the performer uses information (bits) to reduce uncertainty; the greater the uncertainty (*e.g.*, an increased number of alternatives), the greater the amount of information needed to make a correct decision. As the probability of an event or sequence of events increases, so the level of uncertainty decreases, but so does the amount of information provided by that event. You hear a fire engine and then see the flashing light. The second event (the light) although predictable is redundant and adds little information. It does not tell you whose house is on fire.

To investigate these factors, Hyman (1953) used a serial choice reaction time task in which the subject had to give a different vocal response as rapidly as possible for each one of eight possible lights. As soon as the subject had responded to one light the next stimulus in the series would be initiated, hence the term *serial choice reaction time*. This procedure was continued over an extended number of trials and 40 experimental sessions, during which Hyman varied either (1) the number of alternatives (*e.g.*, two, four or eight), (2) the probability of each light coming on (10% to 50%), or (3) the successive occurrence of any given sequence of lights (sequential dependencies). The latter condition refers to when a certain sequence of lights re-occurs during the testing session. Changing the number of alternatives can be likened to increasing the number of receivers for a play in football. The idea of variable probabilities acknowledges that not all receivers are equally competent at catching the ball and that the quarterback may have certain preferences. The idea of sequential dependencies acknowledges that at the start of each play the center must hike the ball and that any consistency in the quarterback's cadence will act as a cue for the defense. Hyman found that for all three methods of varying information there was a direct link between reaction time and the amount of information. This is expressed graphically in Figure 7-4, in which the reaction time seems to increase as a linear function of the amount of information. The more information a performer must handle, the slower will be the decision process (reaction time).

Hick (1952) looked at this same problem but considered the question of errors. As people speed up their responses they make more errors, and so less information is transmitted (processed). The assumption is that an error occurs because the subject does not use all the available information. When the subject makes only a few errors, the information transmitted is thought to be approximately equal to the stimulus information. The subject is making use of all the information available and, therefore, avoids errors. This relationship between errors and the speed of response is referred to as the *speed-accuracy trade-off*. Hick found results similar to Hyman's in that the key variable in determining reaction time was the amount of information transmitted. The results of these studies combined give the Hick-Hyman law: *all other things being equal, equal information conditions must produce equal overall mean reaction times.* For example, if you increase the number of choices from two to four in a choice reaction time task, you should produce the same increase in reaction time as an increase of four to eight alternatives. This is so because in terms of information theory both increases represent a change of one bit of information. The formula for reaction time using the Hick-Hyman law is as follows:

$$RT = a + b\,(H)$$

where a and b are constants and H is the information transmitted. This is actually a logarithmic relationship in which a doubling of the number of stimuli produces a constant increase in the reaction time (Figure 7-4).

Keele (1973) has suggested that the two constants in Figure 7-4—the intercept (a) and the slope of the line (b)—may represent (1) some measure of the quickness of the sensory and motor systems and (2) the efficiency of information retrieval from memory. More specifically, these can be expressed where the intercept represents the efficiency of stimulus encoding and response execution, processes uninfluenced by the degree of choice (equivalent to simple reaction time), and where the slope of the line represents the efficiency of stimulus identification and response selection. The lower the slope, the better the individual is able to deal with higher levels of information and more difficult choices.

Other research has proposed some limitations to this law. Leonard (1959) used a high compatibility stimulus-response key-pressing task involving tactile stimulation of the responding finger and found no increase in reaction

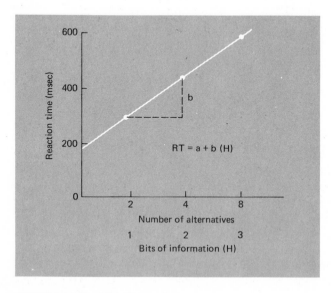

FIGURE 7-4 The Hick-Hyman law.

time as the number of alternatives was increased. Similarly, Mowbray and Rhoades (1959) demonstrated that the incremental rates disappeared with extensive practice, and Kornblum (1975) reported the same lack of variance for repetitions of a response (the same response twice in a row) but did find the incremental rates for non-repetitions. Thus, the Hick-Hyman law would seem to represent how the learner makes decisions dealing with relatively new information that is not repetitive.

In a practical sense, what would this law imply? As the number of possible choices affects the overall response time of the learner, the first step is to reduce the number of alternatives. This can be done through specific instructions ("either pass or shoot") or by simplifying the game (playing two vs one instead of five vs five). Second, because practice can reduce the choice reaction time, the learner needs practice in making decisions. Playing a game in which there is one ball and many players is not the best way to achieve this objective. You must reduce the ratio or perhaps use the tachistoscopic technique referred to in Chapter 4 in which game situations can be presented on slides. Finally, because there appears to be an advantage in repetition, it is important to maximize the benefits gained from practice by emphasizing those decisions or choices that are most essential to the activity or the role of a particular player, and not just practice making decisions about passing in general. The practice must deal with the functions of the players involved.

Repetition effect

In a rapid series of responses, such as a serial reaction time task, the reaction times are faster to repeated signals than to different signals (Hyman, 1953; Bertelson, 1963). Bertelson (1963) suggested that subjects were bypassing the retrieval stage of searching memory by first checking to see if a stimulus was the same as the previous one; only if it were not the same would the subject have to search memory to retrieve the correct response.

However, in some studies using a two-choice reaction time task, the reaction times to repeated responses have been slower, producing an alternation effect. If the first stimulus (S_1) occurred on the first trial, subjects would anticipate that the alternate stimulus (S_2) would occur next. The result of this false anticipation would be a slower reaction time to the repeated stimulus S_1 (Figure 7-5). Kirby (1974) manipulated the subject's expectations in a two-choice task by asking the subjects to focus on either the same signal and response or on the alternative pair. The results indicated that either repetition or alternation effects could be produced by changing the instructional set.

Further research has tried to identify whether this effect occurred in the stimulus identification or response selection phase of decision-making by analyzing the repetition effect in terms of three different transitions:

1. Identical transitions, in which both the stimulus and the response are identical on each repetition
2. Equivalent transitions, in which the same response is made to a new signal
3. New transitions, in which neither the stimulus nor the response is repeated

Rabbitt (1968) found that early in practice, reaction times for equivalent transitions were equal to those for new transitions, with identical transitions

FIGURE 7-5 False anticipation.

producing the fastest reaction times. Later in practice the difference between equivalent and identical transitions was diminished, although not removed. From the research, it appears that changing from one stimulus to another but giving the same response has less effect than changing the response. From these findings, it would appear acceptable to change the signals used to call a particular set play or to have more than one set of signals for the same play, as long as they have been practiced a great deal.

Rabbitt (1965) also found that successive although dissimilar movements with the same hand were faster than successive equivalent movements with alternate hands. Therefore, reaction time appears to be concerned both with expectancies that a certain stimulus will occur, derived from previous signals, and expectancies relating to the response that will be required. If we review our tachistoscopic technique for presenting slides showing situations about which the learner must make a decision, we would suggest now that rather than make a verbal response, the learner should respond by making the appropriate movement. If the slide was presented against a wall, the learner could respond by actually passing or shooting a ball against the wall, thereby tying the responses closer to the decisions.

Logogen model

Certainly reaction time has to involve some search of memory, at least for non-repeated items. Sternberg (1969) has suggested that there is a strong similarity between the rate of search of an external display and of memory. However, his linear (non-logarithmic) relationship between reaction time and the number of items in the list really only reflects the situation in regard to new or unfamiliar items. One model that does account for much of the data derived from reaction time studies is the *logogen model*.

This model is based on the same concepts as signal detection theory (Morton, 1969). *The logogen describes the unit of information that is activated in memory.* As in signal detection theory, the critical assumption is that the activity of the logogen is superimposed on a variable background of activity (noise). If we assume that there is more than one alternative response available, these items will also be partially activated and so we must include in the background noise the activity of other logogens within the set of alternatives. It is the relationship of this noise to the activity of the correct logogen that directly affects reaction time. In this case, how quickly can a new item (logogen) be retrieved from memory? As the levels of activity of all these items can vary over time, there is no fixed retrieval time.

Retrieval is completed based on some criterion level specifying what is sufficient information to initiate a response and how certain we are that an item is the correct one. When the criterion is stringent, more information must be accumulated and a more complete search of memory made; few errors will be made, but reaction time will be lengthened. This idea fits very well with the speed-accuracy trade-off described by Hick. Basketball players caught defending one on one with the team one point ahead are faced with this type of problem. The players can make a quick decision and risk an error or can wait until they are certain what their opponent will do, by which time it may be too late.

The logogen model also suggests that high stimulus-response com-patibility or extensive practice directly strengthens the link between the sensory input and the logogen; it becomes more automatic. We "see" the stimulus, and the related item is automatically activated in memory: 9—nine. As a result, under these conditions, increasing the number of alternatives would not affect reaction time. Normally, however, increasing the number of alternatives will increase the number of competing logogens, because the stimulus that activates one logogen tends to activate logogens associated with a similar stimulus or response. In tennis, when the opponent comes to the net the way is open for a backhand passing shot . . . or a forehand passing shot . . . or a lob. . . . Errors are avoided in this situation by raising the criterion, but this in turn increases the reaction time. The tennis player can check to see whether there is more space on the backhand or forehand side of the court before playing the shot.

In the same manner, low probability logogens would tend to have high criteria to avoid errors and highly probable logogens would have low criteria. For example, you may require less information—lower criterion—to recog-nize the opportunity for a smash than you would for the opportunity for a drop shot. This is the same type of phenomenon we discussed when outlining the models of selective attention. Information activated in memory is compared with information in the environment in order to select the information that will be attended to.

Now we have labeled the unit of information in memory that is activated as the logogen. We note that the item "Joey the dog" may contain more information than just the name; we remember his aggressive disposition and initiate an appropriate response. Thus, the logogen model, while accounting for much of the data on reaction time, also can accommodate some of the variations from the straight logarithmic relationship between reaction time and the information transmitted, deviations based on expectancy, priorities, familiarity, practice, and speed-accuracy set.

Psychological refractory period

Although the discussion so far has dealt with single responses, there are times when an individual must respond to two or more sets of information. In the section on selective attention (Chapter 5) we have seen how people can reduce the information that must be dealt with and we also noted a limited ability to process simultaneous signals (the doctrine of prior entry). Commonly, when separate responses are required for two successive signals, the second signal shows a longer reaction time. The increase in reaction time to the second signal is reduced as the interval between the two signals increases. This phenomenon is known as the *psychological refractory period,* in which an individual is unable to process a second signal until the first response has been initiated (Welford, 1952). It is as if the events related to the second stimulus are frozen in time until the response to the first stimulus has cleared the central mechanism. A subject may be required to react to a visual stimulus by pressing a key with the right hand and to an auditory stimulus by making some simple verbal response. Ordinarily, the reaction time to the tone may be slightly quicker than the reaction time to the light, but when the tone is presented while the subject is still reacting to the light the response is delayed (Figure 7-6). The subject appears unable to process the second signal until the response to the first signal has been initiated. This latency is roughly equivalent to the time between the presentation of the second stimulus and the onset of the first response.

However, the psychological refractory period is not an absolute limitation, particularly if we consider the concepts of time and space. We are able to occupy more than one channel if one set of operations does not take attention. In fact, although the refractory period cannot be eliminated by practice alone (Gottsdanker & Stelmach, 1971), it can be eliminated if the performer knows in advance the stimulus and when it will appear (Reynolds, 1966) or, if the

a)   Simple reaction time: different stimuli and different responses.

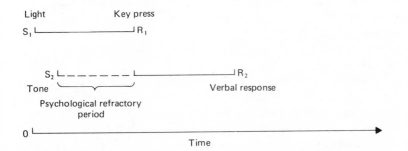

b)   Second response delayed when S_2 presented during reaction time interval to S_1.

FIGURE 7-6 Psychological refractory period.

stimuli occur together, the subject may group them together and respond to them as a single signal. A skilled athlete can take advantage of this refractory period situation by making a quick fake to the right before moving left. If the defender is not expecting the fake, the reaction to the second movement may be delayed and allow the attacking player to break away. Even if the defender recognizes the first move as a fake and resists the desire to react, this process in itself may delay the response to the second movement. Only by being prepared for the fake can the defender cover a skilled opponent. Speed and timing are important in the fake, for if the delay between the two moves is greater than 250 msec they may be reacted to as separate signals without delay (Creamer, 1963). In a practical setting, Marteniuk (1976) suggested the intersignal interval may be as long as 400 msec, but if it was shorter than 100 msec the defender may respond to them as a single signal. The key is to make the fake slow enough for the defender to see it and respond but fast enough that you have made your move while the defender is still dealing with the fake. The advantage is always with the attacking player as that player knows the direction of the movement in advance; the defender can only react. The thoughtful reader might add, "or anticipate."

Effects of movement parameters

Many studies have shown that reaction time is affected not only by the expectancy of a particular response but also by the characteristics of the movement to be produced. Henry and Rogers (1960) showed that reaction time increased with changes in the complexity of the movement, and since that time researchers have endeavored to establish more precisely which movement parameters affect reaction time. An excellent summary of this work was provided by Kerr (1978). In her review, Kerr listed at least five movement parameters that influence reaction time and about which there appears to be some agreement:

1. Reaction times are slower when preceding movements require some degree of terminal accuracy (Glencross, 1972; Laszlo & Livesey, 1977).
2. Reaction times increase as the required movement durations increase (Klapp & Erwin, 1976).
3. Reaction times do not increase as the resistance to movement increases (Glencross, 1973a).
4. Reaction times increase as the number of possible responding limbs increases (Glencross, 1973a).
5. Reaction times are longer for movements that incorporate a pause than for simple forward movements (Norrie, 1967; Glencross, 1972).

Such statements might suggest a more precise analysis of all set plays used in basketball or football. When analyzing the speed with which an athlete reacts prior to performing a specific skill, it would seem important to consider the nature of the movement itself. If in a set play two athletes must react to the same cue but perform different movements, failure to complete the task efficiently may relate to the effect of the different movements on reaction time.

Kerr (1978) noted some disagreement in regard to the effects of movement distance or target width. Unfortunately, in studying both variables and especially the factor of distance, most researchers ignored the potentially confounding effects of duration on distance whereby longer movements take longer to perform. However, Kerr felt that these latter two elements were not primary factors in influencing reaction. Instead she emphasized the critical role of changes in the complexity of the timing requirements. To support her theory, Kerr cited three lines of evidence:

1. Reaction times increase as the number of timed movement segments increases. Sternberg, Monsell, Knoll, and Wright (1978) noted that as the number of letters in a string of letters increases, the reaction time for typing the first letter in the string increases.
2. Reaction time is longer for the longer of two possible durations, as demonstrated by Klapp and Erwin's study (1976) using a Morse code key-press type of response.
3. Reaction time varies in response to the timing requirements of the components of the movement. In particular, movements that require pauses on intermediary targets produce longer reaction times (Henry & Rogers, 1960; Glencross, 1973a).

Recognizing the influence of the timing and number of movement segments, it would appear that practice related to the temporal organization of a skill is essential. Such practice can have a major influence on both the performance of the movement itself and the speed with which related decisions are made. In constructing a set play in any sport, spatially organizing the position of performers would seem less important than determining the time when a particular move should be initiated.

MOVEMENT PHASE

Fitts' law

Having decided when and where to move, the next phase involves the question of how to move. After viewing the reference task (Figure 7-2), it is clear that the farther you have to travel between the home and target plates the longer it will take. This fairly logical relationship was perhaps first demonstrated by Brown and Slater-Hammel (1949), who found that the movement time from a starting point to a narrow line increased as a logarithmic function of the increases in distance, meaning that there was a consistent relationship. Yet we know that we can write our name on a blackboard in about the same time it takes us to sign a check, which is a much smaller movement in terms of the distance covered.

Fitts (1954), in what is now referred to as Fitts' law (Keele, 1968), offered the following explanation for this phenomenon. He predicted that the length of time it takes to complete a movement is a function of both its length and its required terminal accuracy. By asking subjects to move a stylus back and forth between pairs of targets (Figure 7-7), Fitts demonstrated that by either doubling the required distance (A) or halving the size of the target (W), the increase in the movement time was the same. A simplified version of the formula for measuring the difficulty of the task is:

$$ID = \frac{2A}{W}$$

where ID is the index of difficulty, A is the center to center distance (amplitude) between the targets, and W is the target width.

For Figure 7-7, the relative index of difficulty for the three targets is 8 (3 bits), 16 (4 bits), and 16. In Figure 7-7, target *a*, $ID = \frac{2(2)}{\frac{1}{2}}$. The units in the brackets, 3 bits and 4 bits, represent the informational value ascribed to these indices when the complete formula is used. From this example we see that a doubling of the raw score value for the index represents an increase of one bit of information. As long as the index of difficulty is held constant, the movement times should be equivalent for different pairs of targets regardless of changes in movement amplitude or target width. One way to view this concept is through the idea of feedback. Even a single movement to a target can be divided into an initial movement plus a series of even finer corrections as you approach the target. The outcome of such a process would be that a greater proportion of the movement time would be spent near the target. This idea

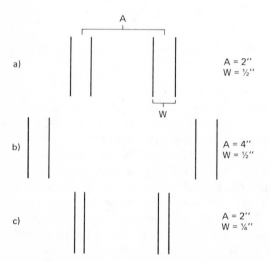

FIGURE 7-7 Pairs of targets used to test Fitts' law.

was confirmed in a study by Annett, Golby, and Kay (1958). To some extent, therefore, movement time depends on the processing time of feedback.

Try this simple experiment on yourself, with a little help from a friend. Make a copy of the pairs of targets shown in Figure 7-7 and borrow a watch with a second hand; your friend can do the timing. First, practice moving back and forth between one pair of the targets for 30 seconds to familiarize yourself with the task. Use the top of a pen so that you make no marks. Next give yourself three 20-second trials, one trial on each pair of targets. Starting with the pen resting on one target, move back and forth between the targets as fast as you can *but ensuring that you hit the targets on each movement.* Without the accuracy component (*i.e.*, the requirement that targets be contacted each time) the law does not hold. You should count the number of hits (movements) for each trial. If you use a pencil, this will give you a record of your errors (misses), which should be less than 5% of your total movements. According to Fitts' law, the number of movements for the target pairs illustrated in Figure 7-7, *b* and *c* should be fairly equal and fewer than those achieved for the targets shown in Figure 7-7, *a*: the actual movement time equals 20 seconds divided by the number of movements. By drawing your own targets you can test the law further.

To summarize, Fitts' law makes movement time constant for any given ratio between movement amplitude and target width, with proportional changes in either factor producing equivalent changes in movement time. By changing the ratio between distance and accuracy, you can make movements less difficult. A simple analysis of the task of the soccer goalkeeper might illustrate this point. The size of the goalkeeper's hands and the ball cannot be changed, so the only factor the coach can manipulate is the distance the hands must travel to meet the ball. If you anticipate a normal distribution of high and low shots, the best ready position for the goalkeeper would be one in which the hands were held at waist height rather than hip height, which would only be good for low shots, or chest height, which would only be good for high shots. Note that it is impossible for anybody less than 7 feet tall to cover all the goal. The ready position is scaled to the player and not the goals; otherwise most goalkeepers would need to hold their hands at chest height.

Moving to a prescribed target requires the continual monitoring of the movement in order to compare the current position with the desired outcome and to make appropriate corrections. Welford, Norris, and Shock (1969), however, felt that two separate controlling processes ought to be distinguished: (1) a faster one concerned with distance-covering and (2) a slower one for "homing in" on the target. This notion gains heuristic support from Adams' closed-loop theory (1971), in which the memory trace selects the initial direction and dimensions of the movement and the perceptual trace guides the completion of the movement. In an attempt to separate these two factors, Kerr (1978*b*) tested subjects (scuba divers) on land and underwater using a reciprocal tapping task—a version of the demonstration experiment you have just read. Testing underwater does not change the basic parameters of the task, target distance and width, but it does put the subjects under informational stress. By changing the viscosity of the medium (working underwater) the subjects were faced with a situation in which a sustained application of force, rather than a ballistic initiation, is necessitated to complete the response, with a concomitant increase in the number of corrections being required. This situation places a greater burden on the central controlling processes in that it requires more information to control the movement.

The results of this study demonstrated the general relationship between movement time and the difficulty of the task as described by Fitts (1954). However, while the contributions of movement precision and distance to movement time were approximately equal on land, this was not the case underwater. Because the contributions of these two factors could be manipulated by changing environments, this supports Welford's dual controlling interpretation of Fitts' law. Taken together, it would appear that under normal circumstances these two processes are balanced or are part of the same higher-order operation, and only in tasks that are loaded in favor of one factor do the two processes operate individually.

Results such as these might make us pause and take a second look at the simple basic skill of passing a ball to a moving target such as another player. For the skilled performer, this involves making simultaneous judgments about the distance of the pass, the required accuracy that depends on the space available, and the timing of the movements of the ball and player so that they may coincide. It would seem logical that to facilitate the learning of the final task we should allow the learner time to establish a means of assessing each element individually and only then begin to build the final task. First we concentrate on the distance factor by making passes of varying lengths, with only minimal constraints on accuracy. Then we focus on precision, but only after establishing these two elements do we bring in the factor of movement. Prior to this, all the passing would be to a stationary target. Once this is established, we can then ask the receiver to move and eventually can put the passer in motion as well.

Movement variability

One pertinent question is whether the peripheral feedback interpretation of Fitts' law applies to fast movements, particularly in regard to the use of visual feedback to make corrections. In an experiment by Keele and Posner (1968), subjects were trained to move to a target at varying rates such that the movement times varied between 150 and 450 msec. On half of the test trials, the room lights were switched off as soon as the movement was initiated and the movement was completed in darkness. It was found that this process only affected the accuracy of movements that took longer than 200 msec. Therefore, it appears that the minimum time in which a movement can be visually corrected is 200 msec; movements faster than this are too quick to be corrected, but the feedback may still be used from one movement to correct a future movement. This is the case in the Fitts' reciprocal tapping task, although at very high speeds the relationship tends to be lost.

Schmidt, Zelaznik, and Frank (1978) offered an alternative explanation of Fitts' law. They suggested that movement variability was a function of the force applied to make the movement. As more force is applied so the potential variability in the end point of that movement will increase, seen as an increase in the number or size of movement errors. If you must make a precise movement, your only way to reduce the variability in the system is to slow down the movement and reduce the force. By the interpretation of Schmidt and his co-workers, Fitts' law represents the conflict faced by a subject when making a particular movement; the subject must balance the amount of force used against the required precision of the movement. However, although this would appear to be an appropriate description for a situation in which movements are to be made in less than 200 msec, the evidence to date would suggest that for slower movements the corrections are visually based. For example, if an individual could accurately pre-program a response based on a judgment of the amount of force needed—assuming that this judgment is the major determinant of the subject's ability to hit the target—then blindfolded movements to a target at speeds between 200 and 400 msec should be as accurate as visually guided movements. This is not the case, because visually guided movements are more accurate, underlying the role of visual feedback in the control of slow movements. What the interpretation of Schmidt and co-workers does is provide us with an explanation of the source of the variability in the system that necessitates the visual corrections.

Many lay people see motor control as a low-level intellectual activity based mainly on automatic reflexes. Thus, the question of the extent to which movements involve conscious attention is very relevant to the role of the central control mechanisms. To investigate the attention demands of a task, a simple experiment was used (Posner and Keele, 1969). In this experiment there were three conditions:

1. Blindfolded subjects moved a lever to a fixed stop position.
2. Blindfolded subjects moved to a previously demonstrated target position, with the stops removed.
3. Sighted subjects moved to wide and narrow targets.

At any time during these tasks the subjects had to react to an auditory probe stimulus by pressing a button with the opposite hand. Under these conditions it was found that the reaction time to the probe was fastest for the first task and slowest for the second, with the time for the third task falling in between. Therefore, when we do not need to make corrections (task one) or when the feedback is predictable, the kinesthetic movement information is not attended to. However, movements that require control from memory (task two) or visual feedback (task three) interfere with the reaction time to a probe. They require attention and central processing capacity and are clearly not automatic. In further examining task three, Posner and Keele found that the probe reaction times were longer around the initiation and completion of the movement and more so for the smaller targets. These increased attention demands would support a visual monitoring interpretation of Fitts' law.

Before leaving our discussion of the movement time component of the reference task, we should consider the work of Glencross (1979), who suggested that the organization of a response could be divided into seven sub-processes. Glencross also identified two general stages in the development of any skill: the timing of the actions of the body in order to make a movement and the timing of the whole movement itself in relation to some external event. His model therefore was designed particularly to deal with these timing elements. The seven sub-processes of response organization were (1) representation and discrimination of response units, (2) sequencing, (3) phasing, (4) gradation, (5) timing, (6) response selection, and (7) motor control.

The first sub-process involves the discrimination and selection of the appropriate response units. This immediately raises the question of how the basic units of action are centrally represented. Glencross favors the explanation of Evarts (1973), who suggests that the basic units by which movements are stored are not representations of muscle action but are representations of force. The process of selection becomes one of choosing the forces that are most appropriate to the task. The selection of inappropriate force units, producing extraneous movements, is one of the characteristics of inexperienced learners (*e.g.*, swimmers who throw their heads from side to side with every arm stroke of the front crawl). Skillfulness is characterized by the efficient use of force. Having selected the appropriate force units, the next stage is to place them in the correct sequence. Glencross (1979) gives the example of the typist who types *CTA* instead of *CAT*, indicating an appropriate selection but an inappropriate sequencing of the response units. Glencross emphasizes that only when the correct sequence of movements has been established can the learner deal with the phasing of the response units.

Phasing refers to the timing or temporal organization of the units within the sequence, referred to by Glencross as a form of internal timing. Looking at the electromyographical analysis of typing, Lundervold (1958) has found evidence that higher skilled performers characteristically use fewer muscles that are active for a shorter period of time. Therefore, the correct phasing of a movement leads to a greater consistency in performance. Glencross (1973*b*) reported that the faster subjects in a hand-cranking task evidenced a greater stability of the organization within a sequence. He also noted that there was a wide variety in the styles of the successful subjects, the obvious implication being that there is no single "right way" of performing any skill. Within any skill there are certain key elements that can be identified, but beyond that there is a large amount of flexibility in how the movement is performed. How the students write their names is irrelevant as long as the reader or teacher can read the name, an *A* is an *a*, is an *A*. Similarly, as long as the lay-up goes into the basket, the majority of the other movements might more accurately be described as secondary factors.

The fourth sub-process is gradation, which refers to the amplification or gradation of the amount of force exerted. Jumping to spike the ball in volleyball involves a far greater exertion of effort than jumping to skip rope, although the response units used in the two movements may be the same. Again, one of the changes that result from learning a skill is a reduction in the amount of force applied. In the fifth element, timing, Glencross addresses his second major stage of skill development, the timing of the whole response in relation to some external event.

We can now label the two types of timing emphasized by Glencross as phasing and coincident timing. The separation is important because the influence of either process will vary with the skill being performed. In cyclical skills such as running, swimming, or riding a bike, in which the same series of movements is repeated rhythmically, the phasing or the serial organization of the response units takes on major importance. Getting to the end of the pool by swimming as efficiently as possible rather than arriving at the same time as another swimmer is the prime aim of the racer. The swimmer is concerned with the internal timing of the skill. However, in a relay race, the second swimmer on the team has to make a special effort to time the start to coincide with the arrival of the incoming swimmer. Obviously the influence of the external time structure is also dominant in most ball games.

In proposing this analysis, Glencross also warns that while a breakdown in skilled performance is often attributed to incorrect judgments in the external timing of a skill, the fault may actually lie in the internal phasing of the components of that skill. As we have seen already, one of the problems faced by the learner involves choosing the correct response. The problem of response selection is one of discriminating between competing responses. When we receive the ball under the basket it is important that something be done very quickly. If we are guarded by a much taller player, the best response is to pass the ball to an unguarded teammate rather than to shoot. We can do either efficiently; the problem is the choice. Taylor (1966) has in fact suggested that in a two-choice situation the delay that results purely from the response selection process could be as much as 50 msec, which in rapidly performed skills is a significant contribution to reaction time.

The seventh sub-process identified by Glencross is motor control. Because we will deal with this aspect in more detail in Chapter 8, it is sufficient for now to say that motor control represents the stage of developing some form of cognitive structure to control actual actions or responses. The capacity demands of this sub-process should be reduced as the skill level increases. Finally, we should note that although a detailed analysis of the relative contributions of all these phases has not been performed, Glencross' model is one of the few that has focused on the actual organization of the response and drawn together the essential ingredients and, if only for that reason, merits our consideration.

STORAGE

Representation

If we are to repeat a movement, we must store some representation of that movement in memory. How do we store motor programs and represent them in memory, and what do we use for a motor code? Some of the possibilities of how we store movement are (1) as a visual representation; (2) as the rate of moving or the time taken to move; and (3) as the amount of muscular effort, which is the one favored by Evarts (1973). In fact, it appears that all these elements may be involved, and it is difficult to separate them experimentally.

As we have noted, if motor information can be coded, it can be rehearsed and should not decay over time. Determining exactly how and in what form it is coded is difficult, but one way to investigate this question is through the processes of structural and capacity interference. *Structural interference* occurs when activities occupy the same mechanism of perception and/or storage. *Capacity interference* occurs as a result of attentional demands on the central control mechanism, that is, when several operations require the use of the limited amount of space available. These are the sorts of problems that face the learner when trying to drive a standard car. Each change of gear involves coordinating the movements of both feet and one hand while still monitoring the external stimuli and steering the car. Even the learner who can handle all this may be overloaded when required to process some additional verbal information, such as, "look out for that police car!"

Structural interference is more specific. For example, if a visual task such as identifying pictures caused structural interference with stored movement information and makes the movement more difficult to recall, then it can be inferred that the movement information was stored in a visual code. In this way, by seeing how different tasks interfere with one another, we can begin to ascertain how the different types of movement information are stored.

We will look at one experiment by Posner (1967), illustrated in Figure 7-8. The subjects were required to reproduce a movement of either a specified distance or a movement to a particular location that had previously been demonstrated to them by the experimenter. In this task, the subject faced a circular disc and was required, by grasping the center dial, to either move the pointer from a given starting position to a specific location, or to move it over a specific distance between 0 and 360 degrees. There were no markings on the subject's side of the disc, but on the reverse side a duplicate pointer allowed the experimenter to make a precise measurement of each movement. The starting position of the movement was always varied for each trial because this allowed a distinction to be made between distance and location tasks. This was possible because moving to a fixed location would always involve traveling a different distance on each trial, whereas moving a specific distance would always produce a different end point location.

The movements were performed either blindfolded or visually guided. In the latter case, the subjects could not see the target but they could see their own hand. This apparatus illustrates how you can have a visually guided movement to a "target" selected by the experimenter without the subject actually seeing the target. The subject must rely on either visual information such as the position of the pointer and hand or on kinesthetic information from the movement of the hand and wrist. The findings for the two main groups are listed below:

1. Blind movements. These showed a decrease in retention as the time increased between the initial execution of the movement and its reproduction, indicating there was a rapid decay of information. If the experimenter prevented rehearsal by distracting the subject's attention, it had little additional effect on the rate of decay.

2. Visually guided movements. These showed less decrease in retention over longer retention intervals, but performance was greatly reduced whenever the subject's attention was distracted during the retention interval.

Also, it was found that under both conditions, location in space (0 to 360 degrees) was retained better than a specified distance.

Clearly, when blindfolded the subjects developed a much poorer representation of the task, which was quickly forgotten if they had to wait before reproducing the movements. Preventing rehearsal had little effect on this group because there was little left to forget. However, the visually guided group performed better even if they had to wait, and it was only if they were

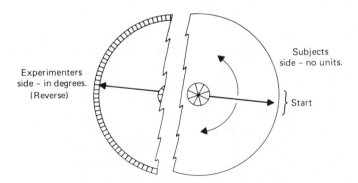

FIGURE 7-8 Apparatus for a short-term motor memory task.

distracted in this waiting period or retention interval that their performance deteriorated. Therefore, because the visually guided group retained the movement better and both groups were better at recalling locations, it was suggested that loci or positions involve some type of visual code that can be rehearsed and maintained. How distance information was stored was unclear. Possibly it might be represented as the relative distance between two loci. The "doubling" of the potential error factor caused by subjects trying to retain two loci rather than one, plus the problem of transferring between different situations because of the continual changing of the starting position, might explain the poorer scores for distance retention.

A neurological explanation has also been offered to support a division between these two types of judgments, specifically that positional information from joint receptors has a direct link to the cortex, whereas muscle spindle information, signaling changes in muscle length, goes to the cerebellum. However, as our discussion of the proprioceptors in Chapter 6 indicated, this explanation would appear to be both inappropriate and inaccurate. Thus, while it was suggested that location information might be stored as an image, because of the possibility of using some sort of spatial map, this interpretation only answered part of the problem.

Posner (1973) later proposed the term of *enactive* or *non-visual codes* as the basis of motor information storage, since it was clear that visual codes could not account for all movement information. He gave the example of the touch typist who could type the alphabet rapidly without error but when faced with a blank diagram of the typewriter keys and asked to fill them in, took much longer and made errors. Clearly, the information regarding the organization of the typewriter keys was not visually coded, but the exact nature of these enactive codes has yet to be determined.

Short-term motor memory

Short-term motor memory research has been one of the most active areas of interest in the recent growth of the field of psychomotor learning, but it has proved to be a most illusive concept. Marteniuk (1976) has estimated the duration of short-term memory as 60 seconds. A short-term memory study by Laabs (1973), using blindfolded subjects, demonstrated that distance information was poorly retained over a 12-second retention interval even if the subjects' attention was not distracted from the task. However, location information, while being better retained over an unfilled interval, was interfered with significantly if the subjects had to count backward to distract their attention during the retention interval.

On the basis of his research, Laabs proposed a two-process model of motor short-term memory. The first component was a central memory that has access to the central processing capacity and where proprioceptive information regarding location can be coded and rehearsed. The other mode of storage would be some type of short-term sensory store where there is spontaneous decay of information to account for the distance data.

Stelmach (1974) cited a study by Stelmach and McClure (1973) that found that resting at the target was the most effective form of rehearsal, indicating, in agreement with Laabs, that location is perhaps the most important cue in movement reproduction. However, Marteniuk (1973), using active movements in which the subject moves to a target and passive movements in which the experimenter moves the subject to a target, found evidence that distance information could be retained over an unfilled retention interval.

Also, Stelmach, Kelso, and Wallace (1975) have demonstrated that distance information can be encoded, provided that the subjects are allowed to pre-select the desired movement length that they will subsequently be required to reproduce. Clearly, distance cues are able to be encoded, and the pre-selected condition is much closer to the normal condition of most motor skills than the experimenter-defined movements commonly used in research studies. The superior reproduction accuracy found when comparing voluntary pre-selected movements with experimenter-defined movements has proved to be one of the most robust effects in recent psychomotor behavior research (Kelso, Pruitt, & Goodman, 1979).

In a practical sense, the active and passive conditions can be compared to the gymnastic coach who lets the gymnast try the movement with a little push or support (active) rather than lifting the gymnast through the complete movement (passive). The use of pre-selection might be seen by allowing students to choose their own distance from a wall in order to practice a wall volley rather than dictating that the distance will be 5 yards for everybody. In track and field, it is important to let athletes select approach runs that are comfortable for them and not allow them to mimic some famous international athlete.

Before leaving this section on storage, we should consider some of the more recent work in verbal learning, particularly that of Tulving and Thompson (1973) and of Jenkins (1977). Although they each have their own approach to memory, one of the main thrusts of their work is to change our concept of storage. In the past, we have studied what happens to information when it is put into the little black box called memory and those factors that affect the time period and quality of the retention. Tulving and Thompson (1973), however, simply regard memory as an intermediary step between encoding and retrieval. Jenkins goes one step further and even titles his paper, "Remember that old theory of memory? Well forget it!" In both cases, the emphasis is placed on the conditions present when the "to be remembered" information is presented, because these conditions will directly influence how the information is stored and, therefore, how it may be retrieved.

Jenkins (1977) refers to the *context* of the situation as the key variable. First he proposes that the instruction given to the learner is one of the most important determiners of what will be remembered. As such, a learner who is required to store each specific example of a "good pass" seen in a game will tend to recognize fewer of those events than a learner instructed to note the relationship between the players in each instance. In fact, the learner who concentrates on abstracting the relationship will be able to accept or reject actual instances not seen before as further examples of the general event being considered. The learner, however, may not be able to say if any particular example was one of those in the original learning. Thus, in terms of verbal learning, Jenkins states: "What is remembered is definitely not verbal and probably not even linguistic, but it plays a key role in determining which linguistic constructions are recognized and recalled."

The work of Tulving and Thompson (1973) is more perceptually oriented. They emphasize the role of the surroundings in which the "to be remembered" item is embedded, for example, trying to recognize the word *pot* as a presented item embedded in the word *hippopotamus,* compared with recognizing *hit* from the word *architecture.* How an item is retained depends very much on how it is presented, and this in turn decides how that item can be retrieved. The idea that the retrieval cues must match some part of the encoding pattern is referred to as the *encoding specificity hypothesis.*

We have, therefore, two separate approaches to memory, one general and the other specific. The two approaches deal with different aspects relating to the recall of specific items or the recognition of relationships and, therefore, are not necessarily mutually exclusive. One idea, the context of the situation, suggests that different instances of an event can become fused together to provide a means of identifying new or old instances as examples of the global event. The second idea, the encoding specificity hypothesis, suggests that the recall of a specific item depends on the circumstances under which the item was first encoded and the extent to which these are matched by the retrieval cues. If, for example, we wish our players to "hit" the "open" player with a pass, we can create many situations that provide examples of the desired response. In providing these examples, it is important that we treat them not as specific instances that have to be remembered but as instances of a particular relationship. In order to find an open teammate, therefore, we look to those areas where there is not a crowd of players. The encoding specificity hypothesis underlines one other point regarding situations in which a specific play or movement has to be retained in order to be recalled at a later date. The process of learning that play should be as close to the retrieval conditions as possible. Few set plays in any sport start with the coach saying "ready, go."

In their discussion, Tulving and Thompson also warned us to recognize the difference between *functional* and *nominal cues.* The nominal cues are those identified by the teacher as being important in a particular situation, whereas the functional cues represent the cues actually used by the learner. The teacher may say "watch the opponent's eye movements," on the theory that the attacking player will look in the anticipated direction of movement before taking the first step, but the learner may actually be watching the opponent's head. As a result, the learner may be misled when the two cues—movement of the head, movement of the eyes—do not match, as is the case in a head fake. Only by establishing what cues the learner is actually using can this type of error be avoided (Figure 7-9). We are a long way from a theory of motor memory storage, but it is still a new field being vigorously pursued.

An alternative model

This look at the storage component completes our analysis of the reference task. The aim of using such a breakdown is to establish more clearly the sub-processes involved in the control of movement. There has been a great deal of research, and, as a result, many models have evolved. We will now close our discussion by outlining a model by Theios (1975), which has tried to take into consideration many of the factors we have discussed. Theios (1975) split the analytical process into six major stages, and these are represented in Figure 7-10. Stimulation refers to the initial peripheral reception of the sensory signals and the firing of the receptors, while the input stage includes the actual encoding or transformation of these signals centrally before being labeled and identified. Theios then breaks the response decision stage into two stages. The first stage, response determination, involves selecting the appropriate response for the stimuli presented, which is response labeling. The second stage, response program selection, involves processing the program that matches the label. This is a little like deciding to drive for the basket and then deciding how you are going to do it.

FIGURE 7-9   This is no time to watch the bull's eyes (functional cue). The Minoan sport of bull jumping, 3000–1100 B.C.

The stage of response output exists to recognize that there must be some minimal delay before any central plan of action can be enacted at the periphery in order to produce or inhibit movement. Renaming the two stages of response decision as response selection and response programming, Clarke (1979) and Dickie (1979) have produced evidence to support this model. As we continue slowly to fill in the many processes, we can become more specific and efficient in our teaching technique by analyzing the various motor skills in terms of these models.

THE ROLE OF FEEDBACK

So far, based on the analysis of the reference task, we have looked mainly at single movements. However, we will now look at the ability to perform more complex skills, such as controlling a sequence of movements, which implies a continual updating of the available information at all levels of processing and not the one-time decision that is typical of a single response. When considering such a subject, we must necessarily deal with the role of feedback in both the learning and performance of motor skills.

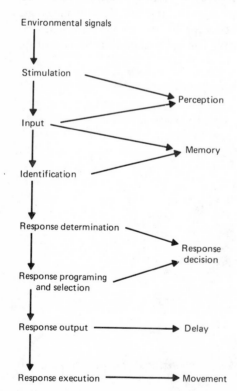

FIGURE 7-10 Components of Theios' model (based on Theios, 1975).

Noble and Trumbo (1967) reviewed the performance of subjects in tracking experiments that require the continual processing of information and decisions about very accurate movements. They suggested that when each movement is relatively independent, that is, when it is not predictable, we rely on closed-loop control, in which the feedback resulting from the first movement becomes the input for the next. With practice and more predictable sequences of movement, there is a shift to some type of internal or open-loop control (Pew, 1966), in which there is a temporary independence of the sequence of movements from external feedback. When performing a lay-up, the skilled player does not watch the ball bounce, although once the ball touches the player's hands it is immediately lifted toward the basket. If we have this switch to some form of internal control, how does it work? There are two main possibilities (Posner & Keele, 1972):

1. Kinesthetic feedback may trigger the next move, providing an internal closed-loop system or a type of stimulus-response chain.
2. A central program in memory exists that initiates the movement independent of kinesthetic feedback; this is the motor program concept.

Motor programs

The stimulus-response chaining theory implies that while early in learning each response in a series is cued by some stimulus in the environment, eventually the response itself, specifically the sensory consequences or feedback from that response, becomes the stimulus for the next response in the series. Lashley (1951) argued against this theory, giving as an example the pianists who can move their fingers at a rate of 16 movements per second. Such movements are too fast for feedback to play a role in the control of movement when a normal kinesthetic reaction time is around 119 msec (Chernikoff & Taylor, 1952). However, in a study by Dewhurst (1967) in which subjects were required to hold a weight in their hand, sudden increases or decreases in the weight produced changes in the electromyographical firing pattern of the biceps muscle within 30 to 50 msec. Sears and Newsom Davis (1968), studying the functioning of the respiratory muscles, also showed evidence of electromyographical activity within 50 msec. Certainly, Lashley's argument taken alone would not be sufficient to challenge the stimulus-response chaining concept.

Although stimulus-response chaining remains a possibility, recent evidence seems to support the motor program concept, in particular the Taub (1977) and Taub and Berman (1968) deafferentation studies. In their experiments with rhesus monkeys, they severed the dorsal roots or sensory fibers to the spinal cord. Consequently, the monkeys had no kinesthetic feedback from their limbs but their motor output was normal. Taub and Berman reported that if only one forelimb was deafferented the monkeys walked on three legs.

If, however, the second forelimb was put in a cast, the monkeys used the deafferented limb, without the kinesthetic feedback. In fact, they could walk and climb with two or even four limbs deafferented. Taub (1977) also gave evidence of deafferented monkeys who could learn to perform various tasks with an unseen forelimb, including pointing, opposing a force, and picking up grapes. Therefore, it appears that the patterning of well-practiced movements may be centrally controlled through some form of motor program.

How well these findings transfer to humans is difficult to assess, but if it takes 200 msec to process a visual correction, then at least the first 200 msec of a movement must be under some central control. Although we now recognize it is not a very strong argument, the speed at which musicians often play would seem to allow little time to make corrections and, therefore, would suggest some type of central control such as a motor program. In humans, there is less direct support for the programming notion, but we find that we can maintain finger tapping with little or no kinesthetic feedback, as is experienced when a blood pressure cuff is used to cut off the proprioceptive feedback (Laszlo, 1967). Although performance is impaired, it does improve with practice, suggesting that simple motor programs may be learnable. Unfortunately, this particular technique has been criticized on the grounds that it confounds sensory and motor impairment (Glencross & Oldfield, 1975).

Some work with an improved variation of this technique (Kelso, 1977) has suggested that while preselected movements are not dependent on peripheral cues, experimenter-constrained movements are. These results would suggest that if the terminal location of a movement is preselected it can be determined centrally and attained without the use of proprioceptive feedback. Under the "blocked" condition, however, subjects would presumably not be able to detect if a movement had been interfered with, that is, stopped, by the experimenter and thus they would report the movement as being properly completed, thereby clearly demonstrating the lack of peripheral feedback.

Monitoring

We have just suggested that we can learn and perform motor skills without feedback. Thus, it would seem reasonable to ask what the function of feedback really is, particularly as we said earlier (Fleishman & Rich, 1963, Chapter 6) that instances have been reported in which subjects with high kinesthetic sensitivity outperform those with low kinesthetic sensitivity. Pew (1966), through his tracking experiments, has suggested that after considerable practice we use visual feedback to monitor progress toward a goal rather than to control individual movements. Feedback appears to serve mainly as a monitoring device for well-practiced movements. If feedback is normal, we ignore it; but if it is different than anticipated, then the difference comes to our attention. For example, if we slip on ice, the kinesthetic feedback will tell us where our foot is as against where it should be in the program; therefore, we can make corrections.

In the Taub and Berman studies, although the deafferented monkeys could still walk and climb, they were much more clumsy. Visual feedback allowed the monkeys to monitor progress toward a goal, such as walking around the cage, but sudden corrections (*e.g.*, when one monkey was knocked off balance by a second monkey) were very difficult. This indicates a continuing role for feedback even in the case of movements under central motor program control.

Efference copy

As a motor task is learned, the role of feedback switches from being the essential ingredient in facilitating learning to one of monitoring the acquired skill. However, before leaving this consideration of the role of feedback, it is necessary to introduce a slightly different concept, that of *efference copy*. Unfortunately this term has been used to describe at least three different processes. The simplest was first postulated by von Helmholz (1925) and later used by Festinger and Canon (1965) to explain the perception of eye movements. This viewpoint suggests that efference copy is nothing more than feed-forward information. In other words, by knowing what the eye has been told to do, it is easier to judge whether it is the eye or the background that is moving. The *feed-forward* is simply a process that readies the system for incoming sensory information. To test this, you can simply place your finger below the eye and gently push upward. You will note that as a result of this passive movement of the eye the image of the world moves downward. Compare this with the stability of the image if you voluntarily rotate your eyes. Teuber (1964) also applied this idea to other types of voluntary movement, suggesting that along with the discharge to the muscles there is, centrally, a simultaneous or corollary discharge from the motor to the sensory systems that presets the sensory system to handle the response-produced feedback.

A second definition, which is a further extension of the feed-forward concept, was described by von Holst (1954) and termed the *inflow model* by Jones (1971, 1974). Von Holst suggested that a person stores, or copies, the efferent information (outgoing motor commands) and then compares this information with the actual feedback or inflow that the subject receives. One problem with this position is that we have one type of information in the language of muscle commands while the other is in the language of sensory information. As in the case of comparing French and German, it may be very difficult to get an exact translation, and this would also appear to require a large scale and unnecessary translation operation. Also, this process only tells people if they did what they intended to do, that is, performed the movement, and not how closely this met the overall goal of the task. Was the arm extension too fast or too slow to put the ball in the basket?

Jones (1971, 1974) also described another possibility, which he called the *outflow model*. Here people would store previous efferent commands, efference copy, and then when asked to reproduce an "old" response they could compare the current efferent commands, outflow, with the expected commands, or efference copy, in order to detect errors. This avoids the language problem and would also allow corrections to be initiated before the actual movement has begun. Such a process is equivalent to the short central feedback loop referred to in Chapter 6.

In eye movements, the load on the muscles is fairly constant and therefore the end location for a given muscular contraction is quite predictable. However, this is not the case with most limb movements, particularly in open skills. It is not always possible to predict the load that the limb will encounter, and as a consequence the same muscle contraction could produce different end locations. As such, this version of efference copy would not seem sufficient by itself to provide a basis for the control of movement because there is still a clear need for proprioceptive feedback to provide information as to the current position of a limb. Under certain circumstances, such as in fairly automated movements, a mechanism like this outflow model could provide a sufficient basis for control. There are still many unanswered questions about these ideas, but they are important in that they show how information can be used to prepare the motor system (feed-forward) as well as to make corrections during or after the completion of a movement.

One intriguing idea that accrues from this work involves the possible relationship between the idea of alpha-gamma coactivation and the accuracy of pre-selection as suggested by Gibbs (1970). The word *pre-selection* is used here although Gibbs referred to this idea in terms of motor programs. The suggestion is that as a pattern of neural impulses is sent to the main muscles a copy of the pattern is sent to the corresponding muscle spindles. If nothing interferes with the movement, the stretch in the muscles and muscle spindles will balance. When there is a slight mismatch, the muscle spindle servo loop can initiate corrections without involving the brain. Large discrepancies would presumably be under central control. For a pre-selected movement, a subject would have more information available to facilitate reproduction of that movement than in the case of an experimenter-defined movement in which the subject responds to the constraints imposed by the experimenter. Hence, the greater accuracy evidenced in the recall of pre-selected movements would not be unexpected.

STRESS

Although at first glance this may seem an unusual topic to include in this chapter, it is not so out of place once we recognize that most motor skills, at least in sports situations, are performed under some form of stress. The most common problem is the limited time available in which to execute a skill. Try your luck at this problem. Before looking at Figure 7-11 and reading the following instructions, make sure you have a watch that you can use to time one minute: this is the total time allowed to read the instructions and solve the problem. If you are ready, start the watch now. Look at figure 7-11. Along with three other people you have been placed on the pool deck (A-B-C-D) on one side of an octagonal pool. Your task is to get to the island in the middle first. The three losers will be thrown into the pool. The prize is $1,000,000. The problem is that the pool is 6 feet deep and is filled to a depth of 5 feet 6 inches with concentrated sulfuric acid. The distance to the island is 15 feet. You are dressed in a swimming suit and are provided with two planks, each of which is 10 inches wide, 2 inches thick and 14 feet long. Good luck, and keep your feet dry.

If you do not happen to find a practical solution, try again in your own time or check the answer at the end of this chapter. In either case you will then realize how a fairly easy problem can be turned into an impossible one by adding a time constraint. Hence, the need to consider the role of stress in motor performance.

An integrated model

Before looking at stress and motor performance we will first try to relate some of the terms that have been used thus far: *motivation, stress, arousal,* and

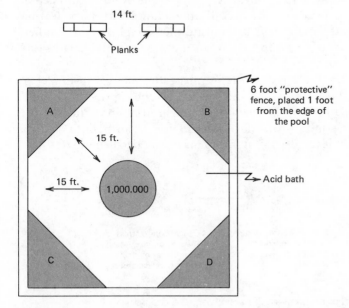

FIGURE 7-11 The acid bath problem.

anxiety. One of the problems in tying these concepts together is that they have been variously defined and the terms used interchangeably. Welford (1976) states that "stress occurs whenever there is a departure from optimum conditions which the organism is unable, or not easily able, to correct," and McGrath (1970) sees stress as a perceived imbalance between demand and the capacity of the organism. The links between these notions of stress and our earlier exploration of motivation in terms of needs and drives seems clear and would appear to justify the suggestion that stress can represent an extreme form of motivation. Increased stress leads to an increase in arousal, and the end product of this process can be represented as an increase in the intensity of behavior. If, in turn, we define anxiety as being a general fear or sense of foreboding (Cratty, 1973*a*), the extent of this arousal will reflect the individual's level of anxiety.

Now using the trait-state distinction put forth by Spielberger (1966), in which trait anxiety describes a general disposition to increased arousal when faced with stressful situations, and state anxiety describes the arousal actually manifested by a stressful situation, we can complete the picture in Figure 7-12. The stimuli that lead to an imbalance in the situation, the stressors, can be almost anything: the presence of spectators, shooting a free throw, needing one point to win when time has run out, or just learning a new skill. The effect of any stressor depends on how it is perceived by the learner. To some, performing in front of any spectators may be stressful; but to others, only the thought of making a mistake in front of the home crowd leads to stress. The degree of arousal or reaction to stress depends on the extent to which the situation is physically threatening or ego involving. The overall point is that the reaction to stress depends on the overall interaction between the learner and the environmental situation. It is a multidimensional process (Endler, 1975), and only by identifying the various mediating variables can a more complete model be developed.

Personality factors, such as those relevant to the interaction model of anxiety, are more the concern of the sports psychologist, so we will concentrate on the relationship between stress and arousal, in particular, the process whereby this relationship may affect motor performance. Welford (1973) has shown how signal detection theory may be used to demonstrate this

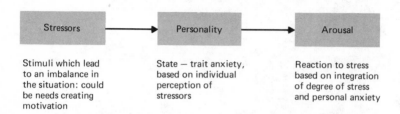

FIGURE 7-12 Integration of motivation, stress, anxiety, and arousal.

relationship. Activation theory, which is concerned with the level of arousal, postulates an inverted U relationship between activation and performance (see Figure 3-13). Arousal here, from an information processing point of view, could be represented by the level of neural or central processing activity. As we have seen from signal detection theory, the detectability of a signal is a function of the signal-to-noise ratio, with the background noise referring to the level of neural activity. Therefore, Welford postulates that an increase in the arousal level leads to a partial depolarization of the brain cells or an increased readiness to fire. The resultant increase in neuronal activity would produce an increase in both the distribution curves for noise and signal plus noise. The signal-to-noise ratio would not be changed, but both the distributions would shift to the right. The results of this process can be seen in Figure 7-13 in which changes in the level of arousal can lead to an increase in the number of errors of judgment even though the criterion or cut-off point set by the individual remains the same.

In Figure 7-13, the "normal" situation described when discussing signal detection theory in Chapter 5 is shown in the center. The two other sets of curves illustrate the two extremes in which the individual is underaroused/

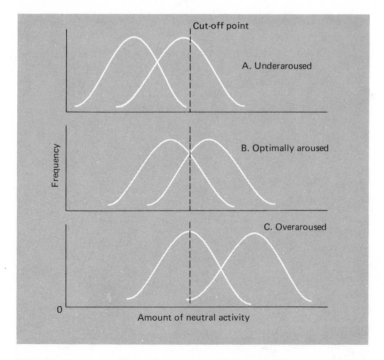

FIGURE 7-13   Activation and signal detection theory (based on Welford, 1973).

relaxed, resulting in a decrease in the baseline level of neuronal activity, or overaroused, producing an increase in the baseline level of neuronal activity. When the individual is underaroused, a majority of the cases of "no signal" will be reported correctly but many of the cases in which a "signal" was presented will be missed; the mistakes will be *errors of omission*. If the individual is overaroused, there will be a tendency to report correctly all cases in which a "signal" was present but the individual will also give many false alarms by reporting a "signal" when none was present; these are *errors of commission*. In the optimal condition, the individual will still make errors (misses and false alarms) but the majority of the decisions will be correct. From this model we can now see how an increase in the level of arousal as a result of stress can produce an increase in the number of judgment errors. If you are 1 point behind with 20 seconds left to play in a championship basketball game and you intend to run a set play that has three options, it is not the time for the coach to emphasize the importance of the play. Unless the players were poorly motivated, it would be the time to calmly outline the three options and the role of each player and to try to "relax" the players for a second.

Having drawn one picture, we will now look at stress in a different manner, in terms of the demand that the environment places on the individual, considered in relation to information overload and environmental stress.

Information overload

Having noted that the limitations of processing capacity on how we can respond only allow us to handle definite amounts of information, the question is how do we react when faced with increased input. It is possible to react in at least three different ways.

1. *We can work faster and let the number of errors increase.* We all see this when we try to type an assignment for a deadline. In this phenomenon, which is sometimes referred to as the speed-accuracy trade-off, a subject may emphasize one factor or the other, depending on the pay off. Unfortunately, making errors is not an efficient way to deal with an overload if the task demands precision; such as playing first violin in an orchestra. The current trend in professional ice hockey is to get as many shots on goal as possible; therefore the emphasis is on getting the shot away quickly. Basketball players also need speed in getting shots away, but it must be balanced with accuracy; in billiards, speed is not a factor at all.

2. *We can filter or disregard certain information,* thereby reducing the total amount of information that must be processed. In one way this is an inappropriate procedure, because an omission may be the same as an error. This problem may be reduced if the filter is selective or based on prior knowledge. In preparing for an exam, you try to select what

is important and disregard the rest and hope you are in tune with the teacher. In sports, the defender tries to "read" fakes by disregarding certain moves.

3. *We can process the information serially.* The first two options mean that some information is missed. The third option is *queuing,* in which we allow the messages to wait in line and we temporarily store the information. By processing the information bit by bit nothing is lost, but this delay may in some cases be equivalent to an error—the other side of the speed-accuracy trade-off. By the time a defender has interpreted all the moves of the attacking player, that player may already be past and attacking the next defender. However, it does allow a more regular and efficient flow of information. Obviously this could not work without some type of short-term memory, and there are limits as to how long the information can be stored.

Welford (1976) points to four other alternatives to deal with the stress of handling large amounts of information quickly:

1. *A more thorough perceptual and response coding of the information* to produce larger "chunks" that can be handled more easily. It is less demanding to read words than letters, which is necessary when proofreading.

2. *The prediction of events* to allow a more efficient deployment of attention to deal with those events. Unfortunately, unexpected events may be missed or reacted to slowly.

3. *The pacing of performance.* How often have we seen the older, experienced player walk casually off the court while the younger, defeated player is "blue in the face?"

4. *The establishment of realistic aims and ambitions in relation to capacity.* Much of the stress we face is self-created by setting ourselves challenges beyond our ability levels.

Environmental stress

Under environmental stress we are not simply concerned with information that affects the decisions made regarding the performance of the skill but with any element in the environment, related or unrelated to the skill, that can affect performance. Here we meet some physiological limits in that an individual's tolerance is much greater for noise and light than for heat and, therefore, the resistance to stress will vary according to the stressor. The second point to make is that the effects of different types of stress are not always additive. To illustrate this point we will deal with stressors common to many students, specifically sleep deprivation, noise, and alcohol, and their effects on the performance of a vigilance task. Although some marathon runners suggest drinking a beer at the end of a race, alcohol is not normally a recommended part of a training routine. However, because there is a strong association between beer and sports in our society, its role should not be ignored. First we should note that a vigilance task is one that requires constant monitoring by the subject over a prolonged period of time, like the forest ranger on firewatch. To perform the task efficiently the subject must be alert, and any loss of alertness due to environmental stress will be shown in a poorer performance.

In a vigilance task involving a five-choice serial reaction time, Wilkinson (1963) had the subjects perform after 32 hours without sleep (sleep deprivation, SD) or after having rested. The groups were further sub-divided depending on whether they performed the vigilance task in the presence of intense noise (noise = 100 decibels) or in quiet conditions. The four groups that were formed and their associated results are shown in Figure 7-14. It appears that when a person is deprived of sleep for 32 hours, noise acts as a stimulus and produces a better performance (SD/N) than the combination of sleep deprivation and quiet (SD/Q), but if you are "active" and have rested normally (S/Q), noise acts as a distractor and performance deteriorates (S/N).

A further experiment by Wilkinson and Colquhoun (1968) with alcohol and sleep deprivation, using the same type of design, appears to suggest an additive effect (Figure 7-15), with the sleep/no alcohol (S/NA) condition producing the best performance and the sleep deprived/alcohol (SD/A) condition the worst. The addition of a single stressor, sleep deprivation or alcohol, produced an intermediary effect, with alcohol having slightly less of an effect. However, when these investigators considered the level of alcohol in the bloodstream after 32 hours for subjects in the sleep deprived/alcohol condition (Figure 7-16), they found a different effect. Those subjects with low levels of alcohol in the blood (less than approximately 0.032%) actually performed better than sleep-deprived subjects with no alcohol, so alcohol can

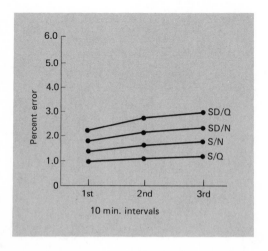

FIGURE 7-14 Sleep deprivation and noise (based on Wilkinson, 1963).

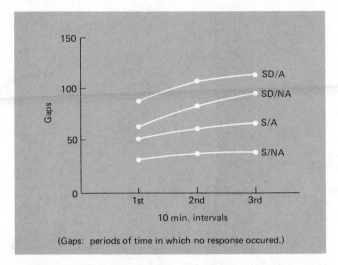

FIGURE 7-15 Sleep deprivation and alcohol (Gaps: periods of time in which no response occured) (based on Wilkinson & Colquhoun, 1968).

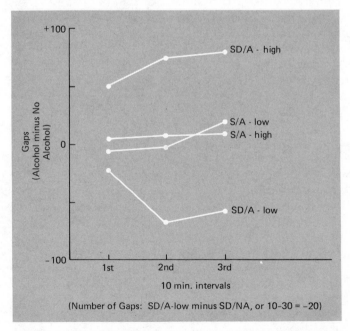

FIGURE 7-16 Alcohol levels in bloodstream of sleep-deprived subjects (based on Wilkinson & Colquhoun, 1968).

apparently have arousing or depressing effects, depending on the concentrations in the bloodstream. (N.B. 2nd analysis uses Gaps in attention, not errors.)

However, perhaps more effective in maintaining alertness than either of the two elements mentioned thus far (low levels of alcohol and noise) is the introduction of variety or periodic rests into the task. Morgan, Brown, and Alluisi (1970) noted that men can sustain a work-rest schedule of four hours work and four hours rest for long periods of time without any serious decrement in performance.

Today, one of the big concerns is ecology and the protection of our environment. From a psychological point of view, one of the questions concerning sport practitioners is to what extent pollution affects performance. This is a very relevant question when we consider the fact that many of our outdoor physical activity and sports programs are conducted in highly industrialized cities. In one experiment (Lewis, Braddeley, Bonham, & Lovett, 1970), subjects were required to breathe polluted air collected near a busy road while performing several tasks, such as rapid addition. These subjects showed a poorer performance compared with scores achieved when breathing normal "pure" air. It has been suggested that a reduction in mental efficiency through air pollution may be a contributing factor to traffic accidents in large urban areas. It would not seem unreasonable to infer that complex motor skills involving fast decisions might be similarly effected.

Optimal stress, or the idea that performance is best at a certain level of stress (the inverted U hypothesis), has already been described in terms of arousal level. This phenomenon, however, can also be related to the difficulty of the task, in which the optimum level of irrelevant stimuli increases as the level of task difficulty decreases. In other words, simple repetitive work may be best done with the radio on while serious work should be done without such an extraneous stimulus. It seems that high levels of stress interfere with the flexibility of behavior necessary to solve complex problems: remember the acid bath?

As a rebuttal to this theory, some might point to schoolchildren who successfully complete homework assignments while working in front of the television or listening to the radio. This author claims to be just such a child, who wrote historical essays, according to my mother, to a non-stop deafening series of Buddy Holly records. While I worked in our dining room, which overlooked our garden and a busy street, my brother watched television in the next room and my parents washed the dishes from the evening meal. The music served the purpose of drowning out or dominating all the other sensory stimuli, functionally isolating me, my music, and my homework. Because all the music was highly familiar, it occupied little of my attention and was very quickly blocked out, leaving me to interpret the domestic policies of Louis XIV.

As one final point, we should also note here that high-anxiety people tend to do better on simple learning tasks than low-anxiety people but may perform worse on more complex tasks. It is this relationship of motivation, stress, and the individual anxiety level that is most significant in determining an individual's level of attainment.

SUMMARY
The analysis of the components of motor control is based on the twin concepts of time and space. Mental operations take a measurable time to complete or require space (*i.e.,* attention) in the limited central processing mechanism or require both time and space. By using these concepts, it becomes possible to infer the actions of the various mental processes associated with a particular stage or mechanism.

Preparation phase
Being prepared for some event helps to reduce the amount of processing necessary to deal with that event.

The term *sensory set* refers to a central change in the level of alertness such that the rate of processing of any sensory signal is increased.

The term *motor set* refers to the preparation of the possible or most likely movements from a given set of responses; by doing this the learner short-cuts the response selection and preparation stages.

Decision component
The decision component is usually measured as the time taken to react to a stimulus, and this reaction time can be broken down into two components: (1) the premotor time, the time from the onset of the stimulus to the arrival of a signal at the responding muscle, and (2) the motor time, the interval between the arrival of the signal and the first observable movement. A majority of the reaction time effects influence premotor time or the central processing component rather than motor time.

HICK-HYMAN LAW. Simply stated this law implies that as the number of alternative choices increases, there is a linear increase in reaction time. However, in cases of high stimulus-response compatibility, extensive practice, or repeated responses, these incremental rates may not apply.

REPETITION EFFECT. The faster reaction time to a repeated response seems to reflect a subject's expectancies related to both the stimulus and the required response. Slower reaction time to a repeated response, the alternation effect, can also be produced by manipulating the subject's expectancies.

LOGOGEN MODEL. The logogen represents the unit of information activated in memory. Any unit will be activated against a background of noise, so retrieval is completed only when the level of activation is sufficient to differentiate it from the background. This process is affected by expectancies, priorities, familiarity, and practice.

PSYCHOLOGICAL REFRACTORY PERIOD. This phenomenon describes the increased reaction time to the second of two stimuli occurring close together in time. This effect cannot be eliminated with practice and represents a basic limitation of the central channel mechanism's ability to consciously process two signals closely spaced in time.

EFFECTS OF MOVEMENT PARAMETERS. The complexity of the response can also influence reaction time, particularly changes in terminal accuracy or if the movement involves a pause. Most important, however, are the timing components of the required movement. Overall, athletes tend to outperform non-athletes in reaction time and speed of movement.

Movement phase

FITTS' LAW. The time taken to make a movement is a function of both its length and its required terminal accuracy. Equivalent changes in the index of difficulty produced by proportional changes in either of these factors should produce equivalent changes in movement time. However, this process may be sub-divided into a ballistic distance-covering movement and homing onto the target.

MOVEMENT VARIABILITY. The minimum time for a visual correction of a movement appears to be around 200 msec. An alternative explanation for Fitts' law suggests it is a function of the amount of force applied. However, studies of the attention demands of movements support a visual monitoring interpretation. A more detailed breakdown of movement control by Glencross emphasizes the separate and interacting roles of the internal timing, phasing, and the external coincident timing of movements.

Storage

REPRESENTATION. How movements are coded has not clearly been determined, and it may vary with the type of movement or stage of processing from a visual image to units of force. The combination of information from different sensory modes may be one of the factors producing the finding that locations are normally retained better than distances.

SHORT-TERM MOTOR MEMORY. While confirming the superior retention of location information, these studies also show that active movements are retained better than passive movements and show the overall superiority of pre-selected movement retention. Also important in how information is recalled is how it was stored in the first place, specifically, the other cues present and the instructions given to the learner. The encoding specificity hypothesis suggests that the cues present at recall must match those present at encoding to retrieve a specific item, while the contextual approach suggests that general relation-ships established at encoding can be used to discriminate between similar or different relationships, including examples not previously encountered.

AN ALTERNATIVE MODEL. Most pertinent in the Theios model is the separation of the response decision stage into the two sub-processes dealing with response selection and response programming (Clarke's terms).

The role of feedback

The role changes from a closed-loop system early in learning to some form of internal control.

MOTOR PROGRAMS. Evidence from deafferentation studies suggests that monkeys can perform and "learn" motor tasks without kinesthetic feedback, suggesting some form of central motor program. Some recent evidence with human subjects also suggests that pre-selected movements are not dependent on peripheral feedback.

MONITORING. Once a "program" is established, the main role of feedback is to serve a monitoring function, knowing where you are compared with where you should be in the program.

EFFERENCE COPY. There are three common uses: (1) that information is fed forward to ready the sensory system; (2) that the outgoing motor commands are compared with the sensory feedback, the inflow model; and (3) that stored copies of previous efferent commands are compared with the current efferent instructions, the outflow model.

Stress

AN INTEGRATED MODEL. Stress is a result of the interaction between the individual and the environment, in particular the extent to which certain potential stressors in a given situation are viewed as threatening, physically or psychologically. An information theory approach suggests that the resulting activity affects performance by shifting the relative distributions of the noise and the signal plus noise curves, producing an effect equivalent to changing the criterion.

INFORMATION OVERLOAD.   An overload can be handled by (1) working faster and creating more errors, (2) filtering the information and risk missing something important, and (3) processing the information serially (queuing), but this slows the whole process down.

ENVIRONMENTAL STRESS.   The effect of any particular stressor depends on whether it acts alone or in conjunction with other stressors and on its intensity. The effects of noise, sleep deprivation, alcohol, and pollution are not always additive and differ according to the complexity of the task and the anxiety state of the learner.

PROBLEM

The acid bath problem: solution
Standing on the pool deck, place one plank across the nearest corner and then place the second plank from the middle of the first over to the island, like a capital T. Don't forget to collect your money on the way out.

Question
Using any sports skill, take the Theios model and illustrate how the different components might influence the performance of that motor skill.

A possible answer
Because the first three steps in the Theios model relate mainly to perception, they will not be dealt with in great detail. Please note, the Clarke terms of response selection and preparation will be used instead of response determination and selection because they are more descriptive of the actual processes involved. The skill is a spike in volleyball during a competitive game. The player who will perform the spike is getting ready while the ball is on its way to the setter. By the time the ball arrives at the setter, the player making the spike should have already begun the approach.

The player is getting ready to act, the preparation phase, and main purpose of this process is to reduce the processing time for the various components of the decision-making process. This preparation is based mainly on previous knowledge and expectancies, although the concept of sensory set would imply a general speeding up of the first three steps from stimulation to identification.

From the work on repetition and alternation effects and from Rabbitt's work on varying the response, we know that expectancies about the sensory input and the response can influence the reaction time. This would affect the response selection (determination) stage in which a response that matches the stimulus is selected. If the player knows which hand is going to be used, has limited the choices regarding the direction of the spike, and has some reasonable expectancy as to whether it will be a quick low set or a high set, then the selection process can be greatly simplified. Through practice and familiarity with the setter, the player may be even more certain and also will not need any additional cues. At a lower level, the setter may give some verbal cue for the player to start to move, but here we may run into the problem of the psychological refractory period if the setter is not consistent. In addition, if the important cue was the movement of the ball and the verbal cue only an extra cue, the idea of functional and nominal cues would suggest a problem for the learner who focused on the verbal cue when that cue is withdrawn or forgotten by the setter.

The response preparation (selection) stage is influenced by the complexity of the movement, in particular the timing of the movement. Glencross has noted the distinction between internal and external timing. The timing can be improved with practice, thereby reducing the complexity of the response and the processing load for the experienced player. For the learner, the timing factor would play a major role; therefore, a high set is essential in order to allow the player the maximum time to prepare the movement. At the onset of the skill the player can only guess the reaction of the opponents in their attempt to block the spike. With a beginner, any unexpected response could not be reacted to, but the experienced player who is aware of different possible responses may be able to out-guess the opponents and produce the appropriate response because of the more efficient operation at these two processing stages. The player may even have time to change the response in mid air.

The response output stage would provide a last check of the selected movement before it was put into action. The efference copy idea would suggest that at this stage errors could be detected and corrections initiated, as in resisting the temptation to rush to the net. The execution stage is when feedback is used to monitor the response and initiate changes. The amount of central computing space that is being occupied to perform this response will influence the ability of the player to utilize this feedback. If there is a gap in the opponent's block, the player could drive the ball through. The size of the gap will determine the required accuracy and the amount of processing involved in changing the response.

The role of memory is pervasive throughout this process. By assigning logogens high or low criteria, it is possible to have an appropriate set of responses ready. Because any logogen will also partially activate competing logogens (noise), this would cause a problem for a learner unless clear-cut alternatives have been provided. Similarly, the surroundings in which the skill has been practiced, embedded, may limit the learner's ability to discriminate the appropriate cues in a game situation when compared with a practice situation in which you work only with the setter, such as a drill in which you throw the setter the ball and spike the return pass. However, if the player has established an understanding between the positioning of the setter, the opponents, and the ball, the context of the situation may facilitate selecting the appropriate response.

It is not practice that makes perfect but practice that identifies the pertinent cues in association with the correct decisions and responses that makes perfect.

Chapter 8
The Process of Motor Control

Sometimes the only way for me to find out what
it is I want to do is to go ahead and
do something. Then the moment I start to act,
my feelings become clear.
(Prather, 1970)

In Chapter 7 we looked at how the process of motor control can be broken down into various components: preparation, decision, movement, and storage. Now we will consider how these processes operate together in controlling skilled performance: if skilled performance depended only on a stimulus-response chain, with feedback used simply to elicit the next step, then learning would involve solely the repetitive practice of that movement. However, as we saw in Chapter 7, the role of feedback can vary according to the stage of learning or the task at hand. Feedback, in fact, is only one source of information. In a great majority of motor skills, the efficient processing of all sources of information—from perception, memory, or feedback—is the key ingredient to effective skilled performance.

By taking the information processing approach to motor skill learning, therefore, we have two main methods of improving skills. First, we can improve the individual components of a skill by decreasing the reaction time and movement time or by increasing the precision of memory. Second, we can develop some form of central motor program to govern the response. Motor programs only become involved when there is a predictable sequence of movements. The aim of such programs is to bypass the time-consuming decision components of closed-loop performance and, by decreasing the attention demands of the task, to free central processing capacity to deal with other aspects of the task. Once you know how to shoot the basketball, for example, the only question is when to make the play.

The final chapter is divided into five main sections: (1) improving components of motor control, which follows on directly from Chapter 7; (2) development of motor programs, which represents one of the main answers to the overall question of motor control; (3) teaching models, which are practical applications derived from an analysis of the control processes; (4) specificity vs generality revisited, which describes one of the oldest conflicts in the field of psychomotor learning and offers a possible answer; and (5) some thoughts on a theory of skill acquisition. At the present time we have no such theory, but a composite of what we do know may mark a solid beginning.

> *The resolution of a jigsaw puzzle lies in the placement of the first piece.*
> (Kerr, McGavern, Booth, Dainty, Gaboriault, & O'Hara, 1979)

IMPROVING COMPONENTS OF MOTOR CONTROL

The process of motor control is seen as an outgrowth of the increasing efficiency of its components. Because the critical components of a motor skill vary greatly from skill to skill, this section will concentrate more on presenting a few examples of how specific skills might be improved rather than on attempting to provide general rules for all motor skills. A detailed discussion of the various sub-processes of motor control has already been presented in Chapter 7. However, two components that were not discussed directly in that section but that were implicit are identified by Klein (1979) as (1) the ability to strategically control the use of limited processing resources; and (2) a store of automated sequences of action whose execution places minimal demands on the limited capacity mechanism.

The former component, which in essence is a description of selective attention, would appear essential in order for the learner to solve problems and generally respond sensibly to the environment. Without the existence of the latter, even the most simple task would place severe demands on the available processing capacity and complex tasks could not be handled. Klein (1976) views attention as a flexible mechanism that can be allocated to various inputs and memory locations, but one that is limited, in that attention given to one task reduces the likelihood that the task will be interrupted and that non-attended tasks or inputs will have access to attention. When one is trying to finish a term paper in a crowded dormitory, the ability to focus on the task of concentrating in order to complete the assignment can be an advantage, but not if someone is shouting "fire."

Klein (1979) summarizes the main functions of this strategic control process in the following manner:

1. Selective attention: the choice of one message over another
2. The selection of certain mental operations to be performed on items held in memory (*e.g.,* rehearsal)
3. The switching or sharing of sensory channels or resources to complete simultaneous tasks (*e.g.,* watching television while doing schoolwork)
4. The resolution between competing response tendencies (*e.g.,* doing the schoolwork during the commercials)

In addition, Klein notes that these allocation processes are not always optimal or voluntary. The former limitation is illustrated by the notion of visual dominance in that when both vision and kinesthesis are present, visual information appears to have priority over kinesthetic information for access to attention (Klein, 1976). Similarly, our tendency to orient to a novel stimulus suggests that the allocation of attention is not always voluntary, but Klein points out that with practice this resource allocation can become automated.

On the practical side, Klein (1979) suggests that when the learner tries to chunk material into higher order units (bits), operations are slowed down and errors increase. Consequently, when the learner is progressing from one level of complexity to a higher one, Klein suggests that it is best to reduce the performance criteria by demanding less speed or accuracy in order to give the learner more time to integrate the lower units into the higher one. When a gymnast is learning a handspring, for example, the lead-up skills of kicking up to a handstand and the approach phase (hurdle) might be taught separately. In mastering these elements, the gymnast may indeed develop some "automated sequences" that permit the "limited capacity mechanism" to focus on the main features of each phase. However, when putting the two phases together the gymnast must now allocate some of the "limited processing resources" to monitor this union. As such, less attention can be given to each individual phase and their execution may suffer. Although it may be logical to state that the performance of phase two is dependent on the successful completion of phase one, at this stage it would be more productive to de-emphasize overall performance criteria and accentuate the transition between the two phases.

While recognizing the pervasive influence of the attentional mechanism as outlined by Klein, the two most important factors for the successful performance of a skill that is not pre-programmed are the speed of decision and the efficiency of the movement (Posner & Keele, 1972).

Speed of decision

Athletes must react accurately in a constantly changing environment. The three principal elements discussed by Posner and Keele (1972) in which improvements can be made are preparation, compatibility, and sequential dependencies.

PREPARATION. As the following example clearly illustrates, in some sports it is not only important to prepare but also to anticipate. Kane (1969) reported that the boxer Muhammad Ali was credited with a reaction time of 190 msec, which is average, but his time to move 16 inches to strike a punch bag was only 40 msec. If an opponent waited to see where the punch was coming from before making a move, Muhammad Ali could conceivably have completed a second punch before the opponent reacted to the first punch. Skillful boxers therefore cannot rely on reacting to an opponent's punch, they must pick up cues before its onset. In addition, the boxer can make the movement more difficult for the opponent by providing as small a target as possible and moving about the ring in an unpredictable manner.

In coaching, we can improve the athlete's performance by either picking out certain cues or by introducing such cues into situations that lack them. Being a good truck driver involves not only performing a whole series of distinct motor skills but also looking ahead to prepare for the next turn. For example, to improve a person's driving skills you could use a driving simulator to develop this ability; in a team sport you might use the same approach with a goalkeeper if you had the appropriate laboratories to build a goalkeeping simulator. Even if you do not have a machine, you can simulate situations that are likely to occur in a game by re-creating on the practice field those situations that a particular player must face (in coaching jargon, these are called functional plays) and the athlete can then experiment with different responses. When your team is watching another team play, assign each of your team one member of the opposition to observe. To aid them in this process, ask them to analyze and keep a written record of such categories as favorite moves and dominant direction of passing. By planning ahead and studying your opponent, you can reduce the number of alternatives that you must consider in the game situation and appropriate "reactions" can be ready to go.

COMPATIBILITY. We have seen from the work on the Hick-Hyman law and the repetition effect that the factor of stimulus-response compatibility can have a major influence on motor skill performance. If responses are incompatible, you should try to change the task. For example, a set play in which you are required to follow your pass may be easier to develop than one in which you pass right and then run left, or in any team sport it will be easier to develop a general principle of play in which players move toward the ball rather than away from it. Alternatively, you may try to reduce the reaction time through mental practice. In learning to type, you may note the special order of the letters on the keyboard in order to help automate selection. Similarly, you can apply this mental practice technique to any organized play or principle. An application of this notion of compatibility, in reverse, can be seen in the fakes that are used in all sports. It is very hard not to move in the direction of the initial fake, particularly if the body and the ball appear to move in the same direction. In this instance, making a response compatible with the stimulus would be an error.

SEQUENTIAL DEPENDENCIES. The third element suggested by Posner and Keele (1972) is based on the idea that most motor skills are at least partially predictable. Using a serial task, Keele (1967) has shown that when subjects are not told a particular sequence may re-occur within the overall series of responses, they will perform no better than if it were a random sequence. You cannot assume the learner will see or pick up such sequences. This assumption describes the fallacy that underlies the idea of learning by playing the game. In fact, important elements must be pointed out. In typing, for example, certain letter combinations are more frequent, and in most sports also there are certain plays or situations that are more common; deal with those first and use them as a base on which to build. Partial sequences are particularly helpful in improving anticipation, because once they are identified the learner can time the response to coincide with the stimulus instead of reacting to an expected signal. In rugby, if the ball is being passed from one player to another and the first player always "telegraphs" the start of the passing motion, then the defender is in an ideal position to make an interception and breakaway.

Movement efficiency

Once a decision is made, a new movement is initiated or an ongoing one is modified. Making this movement as efficient as possible is the second factor relating to the improvement of motor skills. Like the often abused time and motion expert, we must carefully analyze each task and look for "short cuts." A time and motion man (Gilbreth & Carey, 1948) once claimed he could lay bricks faster than any bricklayer. His trick was simply to construct a scaffold such that he could maintain the bricks and mortar at a working level, thereby affording the minimum movement time. By applying Fitts' law to a motor skill, you can try to reduce the movement time by changing either the distance or the precision factor. The ready position of the soccer goalkeeper, with hands held at waist height to be equally prepared for ground balls or high balls, is a simple but important example of where the few milliseconds gained by being equally prepared for either alternative can make the difference between giving up or saving a goal. Movements also take attention, so if you make them more efficient and reduce their complexity you will decrease the attention demands of the task and allow more central "computing" space to be available for controlling other motor tasks.

   To provide an example of analyzing the components of a skill to find ways of changing or improving it, we will review a paper on baseball hitting by Schmidt (1975a). Three basic assumptions were made:

1. That the movement time from the beginning of the swing until the bat crosses the plate is 100 msec for good hitters.
2. That the time taken to initiate the swing averages 200 msec. This reaction time represents the time immediately before the swing starts and is based on the velocity and height of the ball.

3. That the time for the ball to travel from the pitcher's hand to the plate is approximately 600 msec.

Therefore, if it takes 300 msec to react to the ball and swing the bat, the batter must decide on all details of the swing 300 msec before the ball reaches the plate. The anticipation time, or the time available to complete this analysis, is also 300 msec in this example: Total time − movement time − reaction time = anticipation time, or 600 − 100 − 200 = 300 (Figure 8-1). This means that the decision of whether to swing and where must be made before the ball is halfway to the plate and that any changes in the ball's flight that occur after this time (the so-called late breaks) cannot be reacted to. Although the batter often makes some movements prior to the throw, these preliminary movements are more concerned with developing force and occur whether the batter decides to swing or not. As we know from the ice hockey shooting analysis of Salmela and Fiorito (1979), the players can also take cues from the movements made before the release.

As can be seen in Figure 8-1, Schmidt compared the fast and slow swings. Although you would think the fast swing would be the least accurate, the theory suggests the opposite. If a batter speeds up the swing to 80 msec, this allows more time to watch the ball and the possibility of delaying the decision to swing by 20 msec, which represents approximately two more feet of flight time. The increase in anticipation time should lead to increased accuracy in hitting because of better decisions. This hypothesis was supported by a laboratory study conducted by Schmidt (1969). The assumption is that the batter makes use of this additional anticipation time and does not simply concentrate on developing more force.

Obviously, in a real-life situation the ability to hit the ball will be based

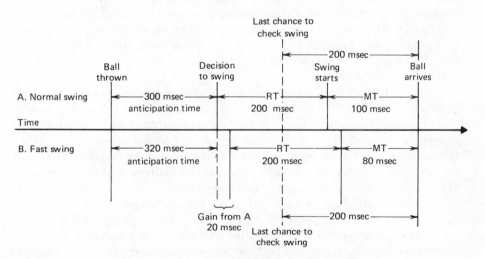

FIGURE 8-1   Timing of a baseball swing (based on Schmidt, 1975a).

not only on the player's ability to interpret cues from the flight of the ball but also on previous knowledge of how the pitcher throws or selects certain pitches. Also, the hitter has less than 100 msec after making the decision in which to change that decision and initiate a second signal to check the swing. In theory, a person's potential ability to perform any task could be predicted by a complete knowledge of that person's capacities on various information processing or psychomotor tests and a complete analysis of the particular task. Unfortunately, in practice we lack an appropriate battery of standardized tests and we must rely mainly on our own analytical abilities.

In an attempt to fill this gap Kerr, Booth, Dainty, Gaboriault, and McGavern (1980) worked with the Canadian Amateur Diving Association to establish just such a battery of tests for competitive athletes. Some of the psychomotor factors identified included balance, kinesthetic rotation, anticipation reaction time, and judging the time to complete a movement. Other factors that showed potential for inclusion in the test battery were field dependency and rhythmic ability. With the continuing advance of the psychomotor learning area, it may now be reasonable to approach this type of research with some expectation of success.

DEVELOPMENT OF MOTOR PROGRAMS

Motor programs are not a new idea but originated with the work of Lashley (1917). Lashley found that a patient suffering from a gunshot wound that had severed the sensory nerves could still accurately perform voluntary movements. Lashley's work represents one of the few deafferentation studies in humans. His work was criticized as being rather subjective and the stimulus-response theory with its closed-loop approach tended to dominate the field of psychomotor learning for many years, however, more recently motor programs have gained renewed interest. The work of Keele (1968), in particular, has provided one of the few counter arguments to Adams' closed-loop theory (1971).

Closed-loop describes a system in which the second movement in a series is only initiated after the feedback from the first movement has been processed and analyzed. The idea is that this feedback is compared with some intended movement or goal. This situation is illustrated by Fitts' law in which the learner monitors the progress toward a goal and initiates corrections to meet the accuracy demands required by the task. The main sources of feedback are visual and kinesthetic, and each source takes a finite time to analyze. As we saw earlier, while visual corrections take about 200 msec, kinesthetic corrections, based on the muscle spindles' contribution to alpha-gamma coactivation, take about 50 msec. In addition, the efference copy concept suggests an alternative short central feedback loop. Therefore, we have an internal kinesthetic feedback system that can correct small unexpected deviations in the movement and an external visual feedback loop for monitoring the overall progress of the movement.

An open-loop system, on the other hand, places the burden of control directly on the central mechanisms and gives the feedback loops only a supplementary role. Keele (1968) defines a *motor program as a set of muscle commands that allow movements to be performed without any peripheral feedback*. Keele's definition was not designed to deny the role of peripheral feedback in controlling motor skills but to explain how very fast movements of less than 200 msec, or a series of movements, can be controlled efficiently while demanding little attention. Schmidt (1975*a*) gives the example of a drummer who must make the second drumbeat exactly 50 msec after the first.

An alternative explanation to the motor program is the motor chaining hypothesis (Gagné, 1970). *A motor chain implies that the response to the first stimulus itself becomes the cue for the next response*. In this way a chain of movements can be built up with each movement being cued by the completion of the preceding movement. Although the motor chaining hypothesis might explain a stage in the learning process—building the motor program—it would not be sufficient to describe the high-speed performance of a skilled drummer. Finally, to summarize, a closed-loop system involves a continuous flow of information feedback; while in an open-loop system the flow is at best discontinuous, with samples taken only from time to time, if at all.

Further evidence: Keele's model

When there are predictable sequences of movements, it is possible to develop motor programs, but most of the evidence for this concept comes from animal studies. Before we look at how motor programs may be developed in humans, we will review some interesting evidence based on research with bird song presented by Marler and Hamilton (1966) and by Nottebohm (1970). At first glance, such research findings appear to be a long way from motor skill performance in humans, but it is simply not possible to perform some of the surgical techniques on humans that are a necessary component of these direct intervention studies.

We know that each species of bird has its own characteristic song, but research indicates that if the young birds from a particular species are raised in isolation and never hear the adult song, then the appropriate song will not be developed. However, this problem is avoided if the young birds hear the adult song for only a few weeks in the summer, even if they are isolated until the next spring. Clearly, the bird song is neither inherited nor instinctual but necessitates the storage of a standard or model of the skill (song) in order for the young bird to develop the proper adult song or motor program.

Further studies indicated that if the young birds are deafened after hearing the song, no song will develop, even though they clearly have a model. When this process of deafening the birds is delayed until they establish their song, then the song is retained. From this research we see that although auditory feedback is necessary to establish the program, it is not essential after the skill has been established. Even if certain muscles are de-innervated, making it impossible to produce certain notes and eliminating parts of the song, the remainder of the song persists even though both auditory and kinesthetic feedback has now been disrupted. These findings clearly indicate that such programs are not just stimulus-response chains or they would not persist after such extreme intervention.

It is a long jump from birds to humans, but these studies now give us some insight into the main ingredients involved in developing motor programs (Figure 8-2). According to Keele (1977), a template or model of the task (what the task looks like, feels like, or sounds like) is first established. Once this template is established, the movements or program must be performed to allow for a comparison of these movements with the stored model. As errors occur, corrections can be made in the motor program until it matches the model. This process is similar to the growth of a perceptual trace except that the motor program is being compared with an internal model rather than experimenter-provided knowledge of results. After the motor program is established, feedback is used only to monitor the execution of the program. In Keele's model the notion of efference copy is included to facilitate the correction process.

If motor programs allow sequences of movements to be performed with a high degree of regularity, it is important to assess the manner in which the sequencing and timing are embedded in the motor program. Keele (1975), in training subjects to respond to a sequence of lights, suggested that events were more closely related to the events that preceded and followed them than to their position in the sequence. If, when performing a gymnastic sequence, for example, you insert a movement from later in the sequence, you will tend to go forward from where you are in the sequence rather than return to the point immediately prior to the movement you omitted. Once you have made an

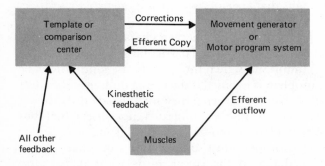

FIGURE 8-2 Keele's model for establishing motor problems
(based on Keele, 1977).

error you will tend to continue with the movement that flows from the one you have just completed rather than return to the correct point in the sequence.

Restle and Burnside (1972) worked with the same sort of task as Keele but used longer sequences of lights. They found that organizing the sequences into sub-units based on simple rules facilitated performance. When similar sequences of lights would recur (the illumination of lights numbered 1-2-1, or 2-3-2, or 3-4-3), grouping parts of the sequence together enabled the subjects to store larger sequences of movements. From these two lines of research (Keele, 1975; Restle & Burnside, 1972), it appears that the sequencing of elements within a motor program can occur as an event-to-event structure, in which a movement is associated with those that immediately precede and follow it, or as a higher order, rule-governed structure, in which longer sequences may be broken into sub-units based on some simple rules.

Another important aspect in the structure of motor programs is the timing of the movements within the sequence. To investigate the aspect of timing, Summers (1975) trained subjects to respond to a series of lights presented with a definite temporal structure. The time intervals between the response to one stimulus and the onset of the next stimulus were fixed at varying lengths to create distinct sequences. Summers found that subjects trained in this manner when simply asked to perform the sequence as fast as possible and to ignore the temporal structure, the fixed time intervals, were still influenced by the established temporal structure. Although the sequences were performed faster, there was still evidence of the original rhythmic structure or timing of the sequence. The implication drawn from this work was that the relative timing of events is an integral part of the motor program.

MacNeilage target hypothesis

An alternative view of motor programs was provided by MacNeilage (1970) in an attempt to handle one of the major challenges to the advocates of motor programs: the storage problem. In considering the production of sounds (phonemes) in speech, MacNeilage and MacNeilage (1973) estimated that, recognizing the various accents and inflections, 100,000 phonemes were required in the English language alone. If all the sounds required a separate motor program for their production, it would create quite a storage problem, particularly as the movements necessary to produce a given sound would vary according to the sounds that preceded and followed it and would thus potentially require even more programs. MacNeilage (1970) attempted to circumvent this problem by proposing that what was stored was the essential features that described the terminal location (target) that is required for the various components of sound production, including the position of the tongue, lips, and jaw. You can test this out yourself by deliberately placing your tongue in different places in your mouth and then trying to sing "La." You will find that in order to say the word properly, the tongue must always finish in the same position.

MacNeilage suggested that movements would be generated as they were required in order for the components to achieve the target location. Relating the MacNeilage hypothesis to a jump shot in basketball would imply that as long as the ball was brought to the correct point of release, given the appropriate direction and amount of force, how the ball arrived at this point was irrelevant and could vary from trial to trial. The essential components in the performance of a jump shot are those that describe the moment of release. Similar crucial moments might be identified for many motor skills. In tennis, for example, the angle of the racket, its direction, and its speed at the moment of contact with the ball will largely determine the outcome of the shot. How the racket arrived at that point is irrelevant as long as the angle, speed, and direction are correct. Movements are thought to be performed not on the basis of specific movement information, how to arrive at a certain point, but on centrally stored spatial location information (Russell, 1976) that defines the relative positions of the essential components at that critical moment. Consequently, the amount of information that has to be stored in memory would be reduced significantly.

Suzuki method

There are not many studies showing clear evidence for motor programs in humans. However, as an example of how the motor program concept might be applied we will look at the Suzuki method of learning music developed over 30 years ago in Japan (Pronko, 1969).

According to the Suzuki method you would begin by playing a particular classical record on the stereo for an infant when it is only a few months old. You would continue to play this record for several months until the infant recognized it, as indicated by a smile or its soothing effect on the child. Once the child recognizes the piece you add a second selection, and this process is repeated until the child is three or four years old when it is time to go to the music school. By this time the child will have been exposed to a large repertoire of music. On entering music school the children are not taught how to read music but given instructions on the basic technique of playing the instrument and then simply encouraged to play by ear. It is assumed that the children, like birds, are using the stored templates to guide their efforts to play along with the teacher. It is only after one or two years of this type of practice that they are taught how to read music and given some more formal instruction. The followers of this method, including several international musicians, claim a high success rate. It is, of course, very difficult to separate the obvious motivational factors involved in persisting with such a technique, but this technique does suggest that perceptual models developed in infancy are very important as adjuncts to learning in general.

The major implication here is not that practice makes perfect, but that it is important to try and instill a perfect model in memory. In sports this model might be achieved through loop films, video-tapes of an expert or oneself, or even through guided movements. Holding (1965) suggested that some types of guidance can actually promote the development of inappropriate "templates". Forced-response guidance, for example, may in some cases be in conflict with the to-be-learned response. These techniques are not designed to build the motor program itself but to provide a model with which to compare feedback resulting from later attempts to build that program. Obviously there are problems with this technique:

1. The learner may not possess the patience to constantly watch the repetitious presentation of the model.
2. The learner may not see or assimilate the critical points.
3. The learner may not be able to relate the performance of others to his own performance. This is the same problem we noted with regard to visual imagery.

One possible solution, at least to this latter problem, might be the use of a split-screen video set-up showing the expert plus learner on separate sides. This would allow the learner to switch back and forth between the two, as is the case in language laboratories.

As yet there is little direct experimental evidence to support the idea of modeling motor skills with human subjects (Keele, 1977). However, most of the studies that Keele presented involved visual models. One sense that most of us have some success at modeling is audition. It does not take long before most of us are humming the latest television advertising jingle. We may not have the tonal qualities of a Maria Callas or a Barbra Streisand, but we can at least get the words and notes in the right places. The floor exercises in women's gymnastics are already performed to music, so it would seem only a short step to trying to develop auditory models to guide the internal timing of a motor skill.

TEACHING MODELS

Gentile's model

We have looked at motor control from the point of view of increasing the efficiency of the individual components of a skill and the role of motor programs. Now we will consider a different model of skill acquisition put forward by Gentile (1972) and its relationship to the role of the teacher or coach (Figure 8-3). The model is divided into two stages. Stage one is when the learner gets a general idea of the movement, while stage two is when refinements and final adjustments are made to the skill (referred to as fixation and diversification by Gentile).

The major assumption of this model is that there is a given set of

	Stage I Initial Skill Acquisition								Stage II Skill Refinement
	Step 1	Step 2	Step 3	Step 4	Step 5	Step 6	Step 7	Step 8	Stage II
	Goal-Directed Behavior / Activated	Population Of Stimuli Established	Selective Attention	Formulation Of Motor Plan	Response Execution	Feedback	Decision Process	Next Response	Fixation Or Diversification
Tasks of the learner		a) non-regulatory (distractors or irrelevant cues) b) regulatory (all cues relevant to task)	Regulatory stimulus subset	Based on temporal organization of spatial components	Initiate plan of action	Process, consolidate and compare to the goal and plan of action	Use KR and KP to correct the plan or modify the goal	Initiate	Refine (closed skill) or extend repertoire (open skill)
Tasks of the teacher	Establish Motivation	Identify all stimuli in subset that control this movement and structure the environment accordingly	Help learner to identify the regulatory stimulus subset	Guide learner in relation to their own limitations	Support and observe	Augment FB when and if needed, focus attention	Guide further adjustments	Organize practice	Structure conditions of practice, provide FB and assist the decision process

FIGURE 8-3 Gentile's stages of skill acquisition (based on Nixon & Locke, 1973).

regulatory stimuli associated with each motor task. The primary role of the teacher is to see that *all* the regulatory stimuli are made evident to the learner in the initial learning stage. Regulatory stimuli may include such factors as the distance from and the angle to the goal and the positions of the defending players. In the initial stages of learning a basketball lay-up shot, however, a defender may distract the learner's attention from the key elements of the technique. The teacher may remove some of the non-regulatory stimuli or distractors to simplify the learning, but at some stage the learner should face the actual situation in which the skill is to be performed. From Gentile's point of view, learning is concerned with focusing on the appropriate cues and their associated feedback. Teaching is concerned with structuring the environment and giving guidance to the learner in accordance with the learner's motor ability and capacity to integrate and organize the relevant movement information. Therefore, in the model in Figure 8-3 we see that each of the steps taken by the learner is paralleled by a description of the teacher's contribution. Nixon and Locke (1973) have taken this model one step further and added a third section that indicates the type of research that is relevant to each step.

Because most movement in the "real" world is goal directed, the first step the teacher has to take in the artificial world of a physical education class is to clearly establish the goals of the movement and induce an appropriate level of motivation. The second step for the learner is to identify the various cues that are present and determine whether they are relevant to the task at hand. The teacher, by controlling the learning environment, can facilitate this process and also the next step of focusing the learner's attention on the regulatory subset of cues that are essential to that task. While the learner formulates a motor plan and responds, the teacher should remember to avoid correcting individual styles of moving when the movement itself is not the goal. Removing individual idiosyncrasies from a motor skill, assuming they do not interfere with the performance of the skill, may actually inhibit learning, particularly if the idiosyncratic movements are tied to an essential element of the motor skill. This comment would not apply to sports like gymnastics in which the goal is to execute a specific movement. The final few steps of the model underline the teacher's role as a provider of relevant information to assist the learning process.

Marteniuk's model

A very straightforward teaching model was proposed by Marteniuk (1976) (Figure 8-4). In particular, he described how the teacher can contribute to the analysis of performance (Figure 8-5). This analysis is based on the assumption that after completing a response, the learner has available in short-term memory four sources of information: (1) the goal of the movement; (2) the result of the just completed response: knowledge of results (KR); (3) the plan of action that was formulated; and (4) the actual manner in which the movement was performed: knowledge of performance (KP). By analyzing the information available from these sources with the aid of the teacher, the learner is now in a position to modify the plan of action, the goal, or both. Overall, Marteniuk (1976) summarized the main concerns of his model as follows:

1. Learning involves the repeated modification of future attempts at a skill by comparing both KR and KP with the goal and the plan of action. Learning proceeds by examining previous errors and successes in order to adjust subsequent efforts.

2. The above analysis is dependent on the short-term storage of informa-

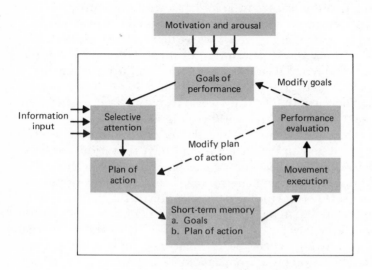

FIGURE 8-4   Marteniuk's teaching model (from Marteniuk, 1976).

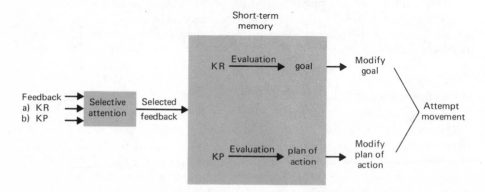

FIGURE 8-5   Role of KR and KP in the evaluation of performance (from Marteniuk, 1976).

tion. Only by having the detailed immediate sensations available can the most judicious decisions be made.

3. Selective attention determines how much of this information actually gets into memory. Normally, far more information is available than can actually be processed.

4. The selection process can be greatly influenced by instructional sets provided by the teacher. Separating relevant from irrelevant cues is perhaps the most important task for the teacher.

5. Sources of feedback not immediately obvious to the learner may have to be augmented by the teacher. What is blatantly obvious to the skilled performer may be obscure to the beginner.

6. Learners should be given some time after each attempt to complete their own analysis before the teacher provides additional feedback. It is self-analysis that opens the door to the higher levels of skill performance.

From these models it would seem that the role of the teacher is to organize carefully, observe attentively, and then instruct.

SPECIFICITY VS GENERALITY REVISITED

We stated at the beginning of Chapter 6 that the selection of the most appropriate teaching method depends on a clear understanding of the process of skill learning. Therefore, before leaving the discussion of the control of motor skills, it is relevant to reflect on the issue of specificity vs generality that has dominated the field of psychomotor learning for a long time (Kerr, 1979). Many of the teaching techniques that are in vogue today are based on these two philosophies. This issue originated at the turn of the century with the study of general motor ability.

General motor ability

Early in physical education research there was an attempt to measure coordination in the same manner as educators had assessed IQ. Athletes were considered to possess a certain amount of innate ability that allowed them to develop specific skills. Note the separation between motor skill and ability. It is their coordination or motor abilities, such as a quick reaction time, that allowed the athletes to develop proficiency in performing specific movements or motor skills. To many observers it seemed clear that athletes good in one sport were often good in several others. Early attempts to measure this general motor ability included the Brace test (Brace, 1927) and the strength index (Rogers, 1925), since strength was regarded as being important in many sports. Other prominent general motor ability tests were established by McCloy (1934) and Scott (1939). These were batteries of skill tests or exercises that were thought to measure the coordination factor. A good score on these tests would predict that the individual would be able to cope with many sports, an ability that distinguished them as athletes. In addition, the Brace test and the Iowa revision of the Brace test (McCloy & Young, 1954) were regarded as tests of motor educability, which were purported to measure the ease with which an individual could learn a new skill.

Memory drum theory

The general motor ability notion was one of the first principles of physical education and as such has been hardest to bury. It has been challenged many times; one example is a study reported by Schmidt (1975a), which had been completed by Henry. This study involved testing particular groups of athletes on selected motor skill tests.

The four groups of subjects were
1. Basketball players
2. Gymnasts
3. Rifle team members
4. Non-athletes

The four types of motor performance tested were
1. Balance
2. Choice reaction time
3. Body sway
4. Kinesthetic sensitivity

All groups performed all the tests and their scores were compared. Henry found no differences between any of the groups on any of the tests, suggesting that there was no general motor ability factor. Remember, one of the groups was composed of non-athletes and the general motor ability idea would lead one to predict that they should have been outperformed by the athletes. One has to wonder, however, what constitutes a non-athlete in a large University where only the elite get to play on the varsity teams.

Henry continued his work and developed the notion of *specificity* of motor skills (1956, 1958): "The evidence from controlled research gives no indication that there is any quantitatively important unitary function that can be called general coordination." Several studies have demonstrated very poor correlations between reaction time, movement time, and strength within the same individual (Clarke & Glines, 1962; Henry, 1960; Lotter, 1960). Therefore, Henry (1958) proposed that these were independent specific factors rather than a function of some general coordination factor: ". . . . it is no longer possible to justify the concept of unitary abilities such as coordination and agility, since the evidence shows that these abilities are specific to the test or activity."

Henry explained the high correlations found in some general motor ability studies by pointing out that some people were probably gifted with many specific abilities while others had only a few. Therefore, a battery of motor skill tests might produce a number of high correlations but these correlations would not necessarily represent a coordination factor; it might only reflect a sample of the specific abilities an individual has. The individual with many specific abilities may be able to play in numerous sports but may lack the key ingredient necessary to excel in any sport. Alternatively, an individual could demonstrate only a few abilities, but if that same individual were 7 feet 8 inches tall, he might be expected to make a good basketball player.

In 1960, Henry (with Rogers) proposed the memory drum theory: a sort of computer or music box analogy. According to this view, the mind is seen as a computer that stores programs ready to function on cue. These programs are stored in an unconscious motor memory on a type of memory drum. The well-coordinated skills are performed without effort once initiated, at a point just above the unconscious level. A complex, or less well learned, skill is performed at the conscious level and is less coordinated, mainly because of the lack of a stored program. In this theory, only specific acts are stored, so even similar movements will not presumably be controlled by the same stored program. For example, an individual's speed of arm movement is specific to the movement tested and there is only a small amount of general ability to move the arm rapidly. So, for Henry, there is no general coordination factor and no transfer of motor skills, unless, of course, two programs are combined to form a larger program.

Support for this theory has been provided by subsequent studies (Singer, 1966; Bachman, 1961). Bachman used two balancing tasks, a stabilometer, and a free-standing ladder. Although both of these tasks would seem to require the same or similar balancing ability, Bachman found almost no relationship between subjects' performance on the two tasks. The correlations between the two tests were very close to zero. This lack of a significant relationship between apparently similar tasks has been demonstrated by many other researchers (Scott, 1955; Wiebe, 1954). However, although the idea of specificity does appear to fit in with similar ideas of specificity in physiology, in which strength training at one joint angle apparently strengthens the muscle only at that angle, it denies the basic flexibility of the human motor system. Most of the work to support specificity comes from two main sources of evidence: (1) Henry's own tests of reaction time, movement time, and other factors and (2) gross motor tasks such as Bachman's (1961) balancing tests.

Marteniuk (1974) has raised some questions about the interpretation of these results. He pointed out that a majority of the studies have relied on correlation techniques, comparing the relative ranking of subjects on two tests, to interpret the data. Marteniuk argued that in a case in which performing the first task facilitated the performance on a second task (transfer of learning) the fact that the rankings or order of the subjects' scores on the second task may have changed could produce a very low correlation. In other words, the subjects who performed best on the first task may be ranked lower on the second task. The conclusion would be that the tasks were not related and represented highly specific abilities.

However, if instead of a correlation the group mean scores were considered, then this facilitatory effect of the first task on the second could be demonstrated. Experimentally, the group scores on the second task would be compared with those of a control group who had not previously performed the first task. If significant transfer could be demonstrated to have occurred, in that experimental subjects performed better than control subjects, the tasks would then be considered to be related. What this point illustrates is that one task can influence the performance of a second task; however, the amount of improvement a particular individual demonstrates may not be predictable.

The emphasis on correlational techniques may have resulted in certain general behaviorial traits being obscured by the lack of individual predictability. To quote Sherlock Holmes (*The Sign of the Four*): "While the individual man is an insoluble puzzle, in the aggregate he becomes a mathematical certainty." While the rank-order correlation reflects individual variation, the only way to determine the influence of one task on another is through transfer-of-learning experiments and group mean scores. If one task can have a facilitatory effect on another task, the two tasks can then be said to be related.

Fleishman's abilities

Perhaps the answer to the dilemma of whether motor skill learning is based on a general motor ability or specific abilities lies somewhere between these two poles. Such was the reasoning of Fleishman (1954, 1964, 1972b), who sought to identify clusters of skills that are related by some basic underlying ability or factor. Although the statistical techniques used by Fleishman have also been criticized, his results must be accounted for by any future theory. Fleishman and his colleagues tested hundreds of subjects on many batteries of psychomotor tests. Then, after inter-correlating these tests, Fleishman "clustered" those test items that demonstrated some relationship and labeled them, based on some common characteristic, as an ability or factor (see Chapter 3).

In his work over the past 20 years, Fleishman has developed a list of 15 to 20 factors or abilities that are most important in motor control, such as rate control and multilimb coordination. He has done this work for both gross and fine motor performance. A further point raised by Fleishman (1972a) is that the abilities important in the performance of a particular skill may change as the level of performance improves (Fleishman & Rich, 1963, Chapter 6). In particular, he noted that task-specific variables become more important as the level of performance rises. Hence, it would seem reasonable that in tests of skill and tests in the later stages of learning, specificity is likely to be evidenced, although perhaps more so with athletes than children, whereas at the early stages of learning some more generalized ability factor might be important. Although the tennis player can play squash, that player may not be very good. Therefore, if the motor skill test used measured the ability of the players to hit a specific target in a squash court, we might support the concept of specificity because hitting a target is a highly specialized skill. If instead we considered only the "underlying" ability to make contact between racket and ball, in which the player has to judge the flight of an object and coordinate the movement of the racket to coincide with its arrival, we might produce a different pattern of results.

It has been this change in research orientation, from considering only the tasks that individuals can perform under certain conditions to trying to outline the underlying controlling processes involved that has produced many interesting new ideas. One of the questions that is at the heart of this dichotomy between specificity and generality is the question of transfer of skill, and one possible answer lies in the development of schema theory.

Schema theory

MOTOR CONCEPTS. The theory of motor concepts was presented by Schmidt in 1975*b*. Basically it proposes that the motor programs we store are not specific records of the movements to be performed but are more a general set of rules to guide performance. The schema theory is in part a recognition that human performance is flexible and variable, not machine-like and rigid. It caters to the two problems that are associated with many other theories. First, humans rarely, if ever, perform exactly the same movement twice, and theories that require a separate motor program for each of these variations create quite a storage problem. Second, if we first need a model in order to develop an appropriate response, how can we account for an athlete's ability to deal successfully with novel situations? If what is stored is a schema, or set of rules, for overhand throwing, for example, we can understand why baseball outfielders can always throw to second base regardless of where they are on the field. For example, the rule might be that for every 10 feet the player should apply 1 pound more of force while maintaining the same movement sequence.

What we are trying to do here is to treat motor programs in the same way as we deal with concepts in verbal learning. If we wished to describe the schema or motor concept for overhand throwing, we could represent it schematically as an area within the central computing space bounded by a certain set of attribute dimensions (Figure 8-6, *a*). Attribute dimensions are certain stimulus characteristics present in the internal and external environment, and the motor concept itself is developed by the abstraction of common properties from a number of specific instances of a movement (based on Saltz, 1971). For example, the four main attribute dimensions concerned with throwing might be (1) distance, (2) muscular force applied, (3) angle of release, and (4) arm speed, where the dimension of distance represents the continuum from very short to very long. The quadrilateral *ABCD* represents the *relationship* between these dimensions necessary to produce a particular throw. To throw a given distance one must apply *X* amount of force, with an arm speed of *Y* and release the object at angle *Z*. Once established, the relationship, or motor schema, enables the individual to select quite accurately the appropriate level of each dimension for a throw of a different distance. If you know the proportions that make up the equation, you can estimate the contribution of each element, like making an omelette for one, two, or ten people when you can increase or decrease the amount of each ingredient.

Now we can understand how the basketball player can shoot accurately from new or novel positions on the floor. It simply involves a little motor mathematics regarding the relationship between the distance to the basket and the angle of release, for example. The more the dimensions that bound a motor concept are clearly defined, the stronger is the concept (Figure 8-6, *b*).

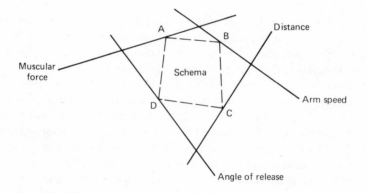

(a) A schema interpretation

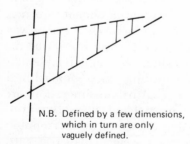

(b) i. Weakly bound concept

N.B. Defined by a few dimensions, which in turn are only vaguely defined.

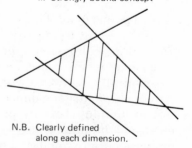

ii. Strongly bound concept

N.B. Clearly defined along each dimension.

FIGURE 8-6 A motor concept, a) a schema interpretation, and b) weakly and strongly bound concepts.

Bound refers to the strength or clarity with which a dimension is defined and differentiated from other dimensions. The dimension of force is signified by an ability to differentiate between a maximum and a minimum force and many points in between.

A particular motor concept is defined by a particular set of attribute dimensions. The problem is that certain of these attributes may be involved in other motor concepts or be close (similar) to another attribute. The strength and separation between competing dimensions will affect the overall clarity of a given motor concept. The more complex a motor concept, in terms of the number or clarity of the attribute dimensions that are required to define it, the more difficult it is to establish that concept and separate it from competing concepts. For example, if the attribute dimension representing the wrist action in the tennis forehand is strongly established, it may be difficult to differentiate a separate but similar dimension concerned with the wrist action in a badminton forehand stroke. The ability to clearly establish separate attribute dimensions would be a key to the development of motor skill.

Saltz (1971) describes intellectual development as involving the "increased differentiation of dimensions and an ability to form more abstract concepts which consist of broad regions of values on relevant dimensions, rather than restricted sets of points on these dimensions." With the development of schema theory, such a definition could easily be applied to motor skill development.

One of the most basic applications of schema theory is that the learning of a skill can be facilitated by providing a variety of movements in practice. Just as we learn the numerical concept of *two* with apples, oranges, and fingers, so we might learn the badminton serve by hitting long, short, hard, and soft. In terms of closed skills that involve the refinement of a particular movement, schema theory operates very much like Adams' closed-loop theory (1971). When we are trying to establish one particular movement, such as a strike ball in bowling, our practice throws will be variations of that movement. In Adams' terms we are building up a perceptual trace, whereas in schema theory each trial is a new example of the rule and we are refining in more detail one particular area along each dimension, thus making it more precise.

The schema approach now also offers some explanation of how we acquire open skills with their inherent factor of uncertainty. In basketball, by practicing from left and right and near and far, we clearly outline each dimension involved in shooting and so the concept, the shooting schema, becomes more clearly bounded. With the rule (schema) to guide us we can handle novel shooting situations on the court, whereas Adams' theory would require us to develop a perceptual trace and practice the correct response before we could be accurate. While Adams' theory shows how we could correct movements, Schmidt's theory shows how we can generate new ones. The two approaches are not entirely competitive, because Schmidt has really only extended the logical approach begun by Adams.

THE SCHEMA. As was indicated earlier, Schmidt suggests that what we store is not just a specific set of motor commands but rather a general set of rules or schema. In order to return the ball to first base after making a diving catch in baseball, the player must select certain pre-structured sequences of muscle commands (*motor programs*)—how to return to the standing position, how to move the arm through the overhand throwing action—and the *parameters*—which direction to face, how much force to use, the angle of the throw, and the moment of release—that will mold these motor programs into the specific response required.

Note, schema theory does not deny the need for motor programs, based on set sequences of muscle actions, but now these are thought of as generalized motor programs that control a class of movements that have the same movement pattern rather than being limited to specific muscles. The two main invariant features that are thought to define a particular generalized motor program are (1) phasing, or the relative timing of the muscle contractions, and (2) the relative forces that are applied by the muscles used in the movement (Shapiro & Schmidt, 1979). These two factors are thought to be capable of producing sets of movements that are quite similar to one another even though the sequences may be speeded up or different muscle groups used.

Every time you write your name it is slightly different, but it involves the same movement pattern whether you hold the pen with your fingers or your toes. To account for this flexibility, schema theory adds the concept of motor schema, which are necessary to execute a particular generalized motor program. *The schema are sets of rules that define both the relationship between the parameters of a particular response and the expected consequences that help to evaluate its outcome.* By modifying the generalized motor program, the motor schema could help to establish a skill with a similar movement pattern. The generalized motor program for the overhand throw, for example, could provide a basis for the overhead smash in tennis.

The schema are based on the *relationship* between four sets of multi-dimensional information related to a given class of movements: (1) the initial conditions, (2) the response specifications, (3) the sensory consequences, and (4) the response outcomes (Figure 8-7). Each dimension in this case represents a whole library of information; they are like miniature concepts that have a special link: the motor schema. Therefore, although we may forget specific instances of a movement, we retain the general rule drawn from these sets of information that enables us to repeat that movement or perform a new variation of it. Looking at our earlier basketball example, the initial conditions represent the distance from the basket and the desired outcome is the goal of the movement to hit the target or basket and score two points. As in Adams' theory, the schema has both recall and recognition functions. The four attributes mentioned have both a sensory element (what should it feel like), which is involved in the recognition function, and a motor element (how should it be performed), which is the recall function.

To apply a dictionary analogy to Adams' theory, the memory trace (MT) is represented by the list of words and the perceptual trace (PT), by their definitions. Recall (MT) involves identifying and selecting the correct word to be used; recognition (PT) involves knowing what meaning the word should convey. Similarly, in terms of motor skills, recall schema in Schmidt's theory are used to specify the instructions and recognition schema are used to specify the expected sensory consequences or feedback from that movement (Figure 8-8). Thus, the motor schema involves two related but independent memory states, the recall and recognition schema. They are related in that they are both concerned with the same task (the same initial conditions and desired outcome), but they are independent because they are based on different sources of information (past response specifications and past sensory consequences). Therefore, once the motor schema is established, given a particular set of initial conditions and a desired outcome, the recall schema can then generate a set of movement instructions. This would be the best guess of the appropriate movement based on the relationship between past outcomes and past response specifications. At the same time, the recognition schema generate a best guess of the sensory consequences of the correct movement, not necessarily the one chosen by the recall schema, but one based on the relationship of past sensory consequences and past desired outcomes.

If an inappropriate response is generated on trial number one, the error will be recognized, the recall schema updated, and different response specifications produced on trial number two. The expected sensory consequences, recognition schema, would remain the same because the desired outcome did: the response didn't "feel" right. From the schema theory we can now explain how individuals can easily transfer their signature from a check to a blackboard with some accuracy despite the fact that it involves a com-

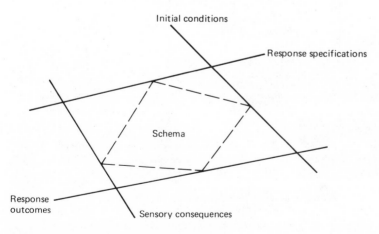

FIGURE 8-7 The motor schema or concept.

pletely different set of muscles. All the subject has done is to magnify the forces involved.

In schema theory, therefore, we have a generalized motor program that governs a given class of movements that require a common movement pattern (Shapiro & Schmidt, 1979). To set the parameters for a particular instance of that class of movements and to evaluate its consequences, two independent but related memory states are required within the motor schema. These are the recall and recognition schema that embody the rules or relationships among the various sources of information associated with a particular generalized motor program. *Learning,* therefore, *is concerned with establishing the rules* or relationships that are *necessary to run the generalized motor program,* a process that appears to be a function of the amount and variability of the practice.

SOME THOUGHTS ON A THEORY OF SKILL ACQUISITION

The schema theory is most important as a potential base for a more comprehensive theory of skill acquisition in that it captures some of the basic flexibility of human motor performance. The schema theory is yet to be fully tested, but it is gaining some support (Kelso & Norman, 1978; Kerr & Booth, 1977, 1978; Kerr, 1977). Kerr and Booth (1977, 1978), working with 7- and 9-year-old children, used an underhand throwing task during which the

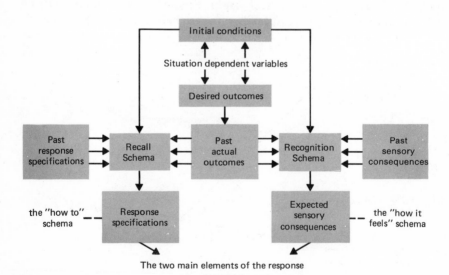

FIGURE 8-8   The relationship of recall and recognition schema (based on Schmidt, 1975b).

children wore a special harness that obstructed their view of the targets or their own hands. It was considered a novel task because although they had the motor abilities necessary to perform the task, it normally would have been visually guided. The children were required to kneel at the restraining line and throw miniature bean bags (1 inch square) at targets designated by the experimenter (Figure 8-9a). The children were divided into two practice groups: (1) specific, that is, throwing to one particular target, and (2) varied, throwing to two different targets. For the learning phase the children were given KR after each throw by being shown where it landed. By turning their upper body and looking sideways they could view the target. If KR was given as the number of inches from the target, it may not have been possible for the children to accurately interpret this information.

As can be seen from Figure 8-9, *b,* while the specific practice group practiced on the criterion (test) targets, the varied practice group did not. According to the concept of specificity, the varied practice group should not be able to perform as well as the specific practice group when KR is withdrawn, because while the latter group would have begun to develop a perceptual trace for the second target the varied practice group would have no such trace. The specific practice group did indeed improve over their 16 trials in the learning phase. However, in the test phase the varied practice group was both more accurate and less variable in their throws.

At first glance the results seem rather improbable and do not fit the concept of specificity, but the data can be interpreted if we turn to schema theory. Put simply, the varied practice group had developed a better concept or model of this novel task; that is, boundaries had been established.

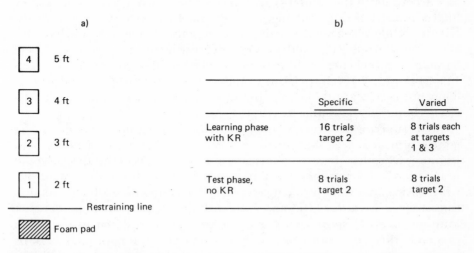

	Specific	Varied
Learning phase with KR	16 trials target 2	8 trials each at targets 1 & 3
Test phase, no KR	8 trials target 2	8 trials target 2

a)

4 — 5 ft
3 — 4 ft
2 — 3 ft
1 — 2 ft

———— Restraining line

▨ Foam pad

FIGURE 8-9 The experimental design of Kerr and Booth (1977), a) simple experimental motor task, and b) design.

Remember, it was a novel task and these represented only the early trails. The varied practice group developed a better model by clearly establishing what was a long or a short throw. Although the specificity group would throw long and short as well, these throws were actually errors that had been initiated as attempts to hit the target and could only be labeled "too long—too short" after the throw when the traces had already begun to decay. On the other hand, the long and short throws of the varied practice group were clearly labeled as such before initiation. Analogously, we might say it is easier to stay in the middle of the road when you know where the two sides are. Clearly, over a longer period of time the specific practice group would also have had sufficient experience with longer and shorter throws to provide themselves with boundaries for the 3-foot target.

Obviously, a stronger test of schema theory would have been to have both groups throw at a 5-foot target to assess the ability of both groups to transfer to a new target outside of the range practiced, but the superior performance of the varied practice group is still a clear challenge to the concept of specificity. Kelso & Norman (1978) conducted a study with 2- to 4-year-old children that further explored the question of transfer. In this study the children pushed cars along a trackway to a target indicated by a stop sign. Specific, varied, and control groups were tested on targets within as well as outside the range of practice targets. The varied practice group used four different targets, while the subjects in the constant practice group only used one of these targets. The constant practice group was subdivided such that three of the subjects practiced on each of the four targets, then all subjects were tested on the same two new targets (Figure 8-10). This particular design was used in order to test the similarity effects hypothesis (Kelso & Norman, 1978).

According to the similarity hypothesis, the varied groups should show higher transfer because all the subjects practiced on targets close to the criterion while only a portion of the constant practice subjects would have this advantage. It would suggest that those subjects who practiced on targets 2 and 3 would perform better on the first test target than those subjects using targets 1 and 4 (Figure 8-10). If true, this would be a serious blow to schema theory. This, however, was not the case and Kelso and Norman's study provided a clear rebuttal of the similarity effects hypothesis.

The superior performance by the varied practice group on both transfer targets provided clear support for a schema interpretation of motor skill learning. Of course the strongest practical implications of this theory would be in the area of elementary school physical education, because it is at this age when basic motor skills are being established. Developing a solid foundation consisting of a variety of motor skills early in life may facilitate the later learning of novel sports skills. Further work with children in recreation programs (Kerr & Booth, 1978) indicates that an exploratory motor skills activity program, including movement education, may enhance schema formation.

Three views of motor control

The three main positions outlined are those of Keele (1968), Adams (1971), and Schmidt (1975b). Keele suggests that at the center of the motor control question is the motor program that is capable of controlling a sequence of movements while being relatively independent of peripheral feedback. Many skills involve movements lasting less than 100 msec; yet this is less than reaction times to kinesthetic stimuli (Keele, 1968), which would appear to refute an internal stimulus-response chaining theory based on kinesthetic feedback. More direct evidence of the motor program concept comes from studies by Wilson (1961), who severed the sensory nerves of locusts and found that they still maintained a rhythmic wingbeat. The deafferentation studies of Taub and Berman (1968) also provide evidence of some central motor program that controls the sequencing and timing of movements in animals.

Adams (1976) refuted the various arguments of Keele. Adams did not accept the deafferentation studies as being evidence of motor programs and saw them only as evidence that skills could be performed in the absence of feedback. He also rejected the traditional piano player analogy that stated that feedback loops are too slow to control a series of fast movements, such as those characteristically used by a pianist. He cited the work of Bowman and Combs (1969), who recorded a response in the cerebellum of a monkey within 4 msec

Groups	Varied				Constant				Control
Total No. subjects	12				12 (3/target)				12
Practice	4 targets				1 target				None
Targets	T_1	T_2	T_3	T_4	T_1	T_2	T_3	T_4	
	30 cm	55 cm	95 cm	120 cm	30 cm	55 cm	95 cm	120 cm	
Transfer A	75 cm				75 cm				75 cm
B	140 cm				140 cm				140 cm

FIGURE 8-10   Overall experimental design for Kelso and Norman (1978).

of stimulating the radial nerve. Of the various efference copy notions, he criticized the corollary discharge theory in which information is fed forward to the sensory system to prepare it for the response-produced feedback, on the basis that we have no idea of what information is actually carried by this mechanism. Finally, while he accepts that there is some supportive evidence for a stimulus recognition schema, the same cannot be said for recall schema, and Adams did not feel research for schema theory would be conclusive until it showed transfer to an original task. Therefore, Adams returned to his own closed-loop theory as the only defensible position, in which the output from the system is fed back to be compared with some reference in order to detect errors and make corrections. With practice, the learner may switch to some internalized mode of control but, for Adams, this does not provide an argument for motor programs, rather it represents a more efficient closed-loop operation.

The most recent theory is that of Schmidt (1975*b*). While noting the physiological evidence that has been presented, Schmidt (1976) argues that the fast loop times demonstrated by Dewhurst (1967) of 50 msec or even the work of Bowman and Combs (1969) does not make motor programs irrelevant. The questions raised are more concerned with the role of feedback in motor control. Schmidt contends that there is a clear difference between corrections made to change the goal of the program, which may require a minimum of 150 msec, and corrections made to change an error in the execution of the program, which would be handled by the very fast kinesthetic loop times. Schmidt also suggests that there is a role for alpha-gamma coactivation and re-defines a motor program as "a set of prestructed alpha and gamma motor commands that, when activated, result in movement oriented toward a given goal, with these movements being unaffected by peripheral feedback indicating the goal should be changed."

Schmidt's re-definition suggests that a motor program must continue to run for at least one reaction time (150 msec) before a new goal can be established, but peripherally based corrections can be made in the execution of the movements, hence underlining the different contributions of feedback to motor control.

Schmidt's motor schema is like a general motor program in which the details of the program are added in accordance with the demands of a particular situation. The notion of the motor schema as an abstraction would gain some general support from the work of Jenkins (1977), Posner and Keele (1970), and Kelso & Norman (1978). Working with verbal information, Jenkins saw the abstraction of relationships as a key element in retention. Posner and Keele (1970), looking at visual long-term memory, showed that subjects could identify previously unseen prototypes of a series of dot patterns, again suggesting the abstraction of some sort of general relationship. Finally, Kelso & Norman (1978) showed that the performance of children receiving a varied practice schedule was superior to that of those receiving limited practice when transferring to new instances of the same movement.

A model of motor control

If we accept that motor programs are general rather than specific in nature, then a model of motor skill learning might be produced by combining elements of both Keele's and Schmidt's models (Figure 8-11). Specificity and schema concepts are not seen as mutually exclusive but as representative of different stages in the development of a model of motor skills. Early in learning, general abilities and general relationships drawn from other schemas are sufficient to complete the new task, but as learning progresses the abilities necessary to perform the task will become more task specific. Furthermore, the need to clearly define the attributes that constitute the schema means that attention must be centered on those instances of the task that best illustrate the concept.

Put simply, as learning advances it becomes more specific and more detailed. For example, early in learning to play racketball, a general forehand stroke borrowed from tennis would suffice whereas the refined racketball stroke incorporates a much greater wrist action. In terms of judging where and how to hit the ball, again early in learning a general understanding of the rebound properties of a tennis ball and the relationship between the orientation of the body and the direction of the stroke may be sufficient to play the game. However, to become a skillful racketball player involves understanding the influence of the confines of the court on the movement of the ball and the proper orientation of the body necessary to complete a successful stroke.

Schema theory describes the process whereby the model of a motor skill is built. The actual model (Figure 8-11) includes the following:

1. Two separate memory states: recall and recognition

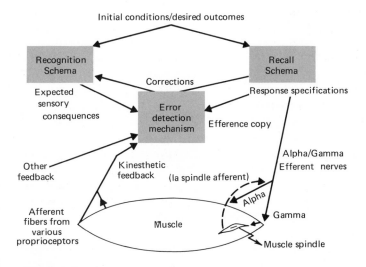

FIGURE 8-11 A model of motor control.

2. An error detection mechanism for the task at hand based on the expected sensory consequences and a copy of the response specifications (efference copy) from past and present responses
3. Alpha-gamma coactivation, which allows fast corrections to be made during the execution of the movement without reference to central control but which records all sensory information available to the central controlling mechanisms

If our aim is to establish a particular version of the movement in a closed skill such as diving, then the variation of practice will be very narrow or specific. The variation is a result of human inefficiency in reproducing movements. Unlike machines we rarely, if ever, perform the same movement twice, so even when practicing a specific variation of a movement there is still a certain amount of variability, but within a fairly narrow range. Similarly, as we become more skilled at open skills, we can narrow down the range of uses for particular skills.

In sports such as basketball it is possible for the coach, by dictating the role of the player, to delineate even further the normal shooting range for each player and coach accordingly. This would include varying how the player received the ball on entering the shooting area, whether there is a defender or not, rather than just shooting from various points on the floor. Likewise the practice of lay-up drills from left, right, and center is limited in value once the basic skill is achieved. In a game a player is often required to perform the lay-up from too far out or too close. By recognizing this, the coach can allow the athlete to practice a more appropriate sample of the individual examples of that particular skill or motor schema. By including as many variables of the real task as possible, it allows a clearer definition of the rule or schema.

At higher levels of performance, practice becomes more specific. The range of variables that has to be dealt with becomes more limited. To the casual observer, therefore, while specificity may describe our external behavior, the schema concept may represent the actual process whereby skills are acquired and refined. To the observer it would seem logical that baseball players would practice throwing the ball to one of the bases (specific practice). Even this specific skill, however, would benefit from varied practice in terms of how the player received the ball (high or low), whether they were standing still or on the move, and the direction of their movement relative to the bases. All these variations, or at least the more common ones, should be practiced in order to develop the one skill of throwing the ball to the bases. Although schema theory itself still needs some refining, it does at least provide the beginnings of a more complete theory of the process involved in motor skill learning. As such, it has some important implications for designing the program best suited to convey the skill to the learner.

The teaching models presented earlier gave some important suggestions for developing a skill learning program, and now we can blend these with some of the concepts from schema theory. According to Gentile's model

(Figure 8-3), it would seem that in the learning phase (Stage I), schema theory has implications for the young child or the beginner in terms of establishing some general relationships between particular movements and their consequences. It has been suggested that in the development of motor skills, such as the manipulation of objects, the young child sees the skill not as a means to an end but as an end in itself. Once an infant has learned to reach out and grasp its bottle, that grasping activity is applied to a variety of objects and is not just used when feeding. The "end" becomes a skill for which the child seeks different uses; therefore, it would seem reasonable that a theory of psychomotor learning should emphasize this concept of movement variability.

In Stage II, schema theory has more implications for open than closed skills. The difference here is whether we are concerned with the means, (*i.e.*, how well we performed the movement), or the end result of that movement. Open skills are concerned with achieving a set goal (*e.g.*, scoring a touchdown in football), whereas closed skills are more concerned with the movement itself (the means), such as a handspring in gymnastics. It is a question of the amount of emphasis placed on the means or on the end result.

Overall, incorporating the schema ideas with Gentile's approach would suggest that children would benefit from a broad range of motor activities to establish a whole range of motor schema. Then when the children are introduced to more specific sport skills they will be in a better position to acquire and apply those skills, but not necessarily to become proficient. Similarly, it suggests that we provide the beginner with a better model of the task by providing a variety of practice experiences. At the more advanced stages of skill, we can continue to take advantage of this broader base of understanding in the process of skill learning. In open skills such as basketball, when trying to establish the motor concept (schema) of a lay-up, we should not simply practice from 5 yards out, for in a game we will have to start the lay-up from all sorts of distances and angles. Also, sometimes we will finish too close or too far from the basket. By contrast, in closed skills we are mainly trying to direct the learner's attention to particular parts of the movement, such as the position of an arm or a leg.

By knowing the sport, the learner, and the process, we can now define the normal range over which the individual will work and can structure our practice to account for all of these factors. You can learn your 12 times table by rote memorization methods or by understanding the concept of numbers. Many athletes may never understand a movement and can only learn it by a rote method as many people did their 3 *R*'s. However, many athletes might learn more, in a far shorter time, and be more flexible in their responses, if they are given a greater breadth of experience in their practice sessions.

Specificity and generality are relative terms, and the methodology implied is dependent on the goal of the task. Schema theory suggests a progression from a general base to more specific concepts, but whether the task is an open or closed skill the internal process is the same. Either the natural variation of human performance or the forced variation due to the practice requirements leads to a process of defining the boundaries of a skill and the rule that associates those boundaries. In practices, an experienced baseball coach would sometimes get the catcher to stand 4 feet either side of the plate to help the pitcher's control. He did it because it worked. Perhaps now we know why it worked and can make similar appropriate analyses of the skills and the problems encountered by the learner and, based on our knowledge, devise programs and practices that will best convey that skill to the learner.

An alternative model

In previous chapters we have underlined the role of perception and how perception is an inter-active process between an individual and the environment. Therefore, if we are to develop a truly composite theory of motor skill acquisition we must adopt a similar approach that describes the behavior of the "actor" (the person performing the action or learning the skill) within the context of environmental constraints. Such is the line of argument put forward by Turvey (1977) and Fowler and Turvey (1978).

The man-machine analogy, on which much of this text is based, is important in that it brings precision to the field of cognitive psychology and provides a basis for more advanced models than the serial processing models offered by the stimulus-response theorists. In fact, the extension of the man-machine analogy toward a process-oriented theory of motor skill performance by Pew (1970, 1974) provided the foundation for the development of schema theory (Schmidt, 1975b). However, while the computer is artificial and passive, humans are real and active. Computers are purposeless, while our behavior is goal directed (Shaw & Bransford, 1977). Even the most complex machine is still simple when compared to a human being. A machine does not reflect the emotional, personal, and social factors that govern a person's behavior. It is important to recognize these limitations of the man-machine analogy in order not to let the analogy restrict our thinking. Underlining the difference between people and machines, Shaw and Bransford (1977) stated ". . . humans . . . are active, investigatory creatures driven by definite intents through a complex, changing environment replete with meaning at a variety of levels of analysis."

Humans seek information; machines need to be fed. Referring directly to the man-machine analogy, Shaw and Bransford state: "In such a sterile model for man, perceiving becomes a passive process and knowing a purposeless one, and as for action (that is, purposive behavior), it remains non-existent." The machine is simply reacting to specific instructions and information fed to it and can only "act" within the limitations of those instructions. For critics of the man-machine analogy, the question should not be one of how information is stored and abstracted from these stores (memory) by some passive device but how people extract the stored information in the real world. Most frequently, when an individual acts, it is on the basis of some information recently abstracted from the environment—the results or anticipated consequences of one's actions—and not purely on the basis of previously stored information.

The main tenet of the ecological approach (which places the actor in the environment) is, to quote Shaw and Bransford once more, ". . . that the nature of humans is inextricably intertwined with the nature of the world in which they live, move and have their being." A proper description of the human "machine" is a model that will function in the real world and not just in the controlled laboratory situation. To survive and function, an individual must adapt to the environment. People cannot function as efficient machines in isolation but only as machines attuned to the vagrancies of the environment, aware of the information it provides and the behavioral consequences of that information. This is the ecological view of the human "machine." As people both perceive and act, an action theory or a realistic theory of motor skill acquisition must both tie perception to action and place the individual back in the environmental niche that affords that individual's existence.

The ecological view, therefore, tries to consider learning not just in terms of the individual but also acknowledges the inter-dependence of the individual and the environment. This approach brings forward several ideas. Here we will focus on (1) the link between perception and action, (2) the level of control or grain size, and (3) the concept of constraints.

PERCEPTION AND ACTION. Because this ecological approach is applied to motor skill acquisition (Fowler & Turvey, 1978), it tries to answer the question of what is actually going on when we say to ourselves, "shoot that ball." From the information processing approach we have gained a considerable knowledge of those processes involved in the perceptual and decision-making components of the model, but little knowledge regarding the organizational and control functions of the effector or output mechanism. If we tie perception to action, however, we are in fact saying that many of those processes involved in perception are also elemental to the effector or action mechanism.

The first step in the discussion is to establish the bond between perception and action. Turvey (1977) presents this quite nicely by pointing to our ability to identify a visually presented capital A regardless of variations in the style or size of the presentation. This perceptual ability is matched by the flexibility of the motor system in writing a capital A, by using only the fingers, by using the whole arm as when writing on a blackboard, or by holding a pen in our teeth. Clearly, this response is not achieved by one set sequence of motor commands, but how is it achieved? One answer is provided by the language concept of deep and surface structures. The deep structure is an abstract system of rules or principles from which the learner can generate an infinite number of movements. The movements that are generated represent the surface structure. Thus the ability to write the capital letter *A* may be regarded as being based on a set of rules abstracted from previous attempts at writing a capital A or other letters. Whether the rule is applied to the movements of an arm or a leg (move up, down, and across), the same basic shape can be produced (Kerr, 1981).

Accordingly we can conceptualize perceptual constancy and action constancy from the same type of abstract concept that allows us to both recognize and reproduce variations of the capital *A*. If there were two separate concepts, one specific to perception and one for action, then we would be dealing with different structures and would need to establish separate theories. However, Turvey (1977) believes that the two processes are directly related in that the factors accounting for constancy in perception also account for constancy of action. Perception is indeed tied to action. In describing a functional level of operation for perception, we must at the same time be describing elements of the action control system.

LEVEL OF CONTROL OR GRAIN SIZE.   In order to explain this alternative approach and introduce the concept of grain size, we will first take a step backward and begin by taking a second look at the words we are reading now.

When you read a text in a new field of study for the first time you often find it very hard reading, and it is tempting to say this is much more difficult than "X," much more advanced. From a motor control point of view it would imply that a higher level of control is needed to handle the more advanced material. In fact, we are not functioning at a higher level but simply at a different focus of control. The shift is caused by the unfamiliar material (in information processing terms, language with less redundancy), and as such a "new" focus of control needs to be established to deal with this information. The abstraction of meaning from the more difficult text requires more processing at the lower levels. To use the heterarchical control system analogy (Chapter 1), we are simply operating from a different center within the same control level. In controlling the lower level operations, the new control center may in turn borrow hypotheses from other centers at the same level. For example, regardless of the advanced nature of the subject matter in front of us, we still try to find and define the key words. The change in processing is not one of moving to a higher level of control but more a question of an increase in the depth of the analysis.

To abstract meaning from the difficult text we must now read all the words, whereas before we could pick out the few key words and ignore the rest. If the text uses symbols we have not previously seen, we will have to pay attention to the various shapes of these symbols. However, this type of fine-detailed analysis will not be necessary for the letters that constitute the majority of the words. Therefore, what the difficult text has done is make us aware of the many perceptual processes that we normally take for granted. In reading, you have established a level of operation whereby whole phrases or sentences could be dealt with at once, but when faced with a new task the detailed analysis requires that the basic unit of analysis be reduced from phrases to words or even symbols.

To express this analogy in terms of motor skills, the letters might be thought of as the basic techniques of shooting and passing necessary for a team sport. The application of these techniques in simple one-on-one and two-on-one situations would be equivalent to the words, whereas applying the same techniques in a game situation would be a level of operation equivalent to whole phrases or sentences. Consequently, even though you may be quite skilled at basketball, switching to a new offense may require the learning of some new techniques. The level of operation will have to change until these new techniques are properly established. Once this is achieved, however, you will try to move as quickly as possible to a more global level of operation. The player who concentrates purely on technique will not have the time to select the best opportunities for applying those techniques.

Reading new material is difficult because of possible variations in word combinations. Similarly, learning a new basketball offense creates a new range of motor responses. To aid in the process of altering our frame of reference we must also change what is termed the *grain size* of our operating vocabulary. *Grain size refers to the size of the basic unit of our analysis.* Just as you can change a chemical filter to allow the passage of larger or smaller molecules, so in our current verbal example we can move from the rather coarse grain level of phrases to a finer grain level of words or symbols. However, to be efficient in our reading, the aim is to return to a coarse grain level of description in order to avoid the time-consuming word by word analysis. By scanning the opposition as they line up, the quarterback tries to read the defense to check the play selection. This is achieved not by observing the stance of every defensive player but by noting the overall defensive alignment and the positions of one or two key players.

In delineating a possible vocabulary for motor control, Fowler and Turvey (1978) suggest that the finest grain level of control would be the individual cells of the body, but even if we were capable of regulating individual cells there would simply be too many possible variations to be controlled in order to deal with the millions of cells that constitute the human body. As a result, this level of control is rejected; however, by dealing with classes of cells as a unit, such as a muscle, the problem is simplified. There are now fewer units, and thereby fewer variations to be controlled. In addition, while regulating the larger unit—the muscle—the components of that unit— the cells—are at the same time also regulated. The point about changing the level of description is important because it implies that at a more abstract level, a coarser grain size, it allows the learner "to know less of the details of the system he controls, but to regulate it more easily and effectively" (Fowler & Turvey, 1978).

In fact, Fowler and Turvey (1978) suggests that a more appropriate level of control would be through groups of muscles. In this manner, various reflexes, involving several muscles, are combined in order to move in a coordinated manner; what Easton (1972) refers to as *coordinative structures*. Certain of these coordinative structures are represented by established reflexes, while others are represented by temporary combinations of specific reflexes in order to perform a more general activity such as walking. These coordinative structures may not in themselves be sufficient to produce the desired movement, but they simplify the problem for the learner in terms of the number of additional controls that must be imposed. When such a set of coordinative structures can be used to control a long sequence of movements, they are said to be nested (Easton, 1972) and as such require minimal control by the learner. The hurdle step used by the springboard diver involves a combination of walking and a hop. Being able to draw on these previously established movements would facilitate the learning of the hurdle step itself, which involves the addition of an exaggerated arm lift and a two-footed landing. Establishing a level of control that operates by utilizing coordinative structures would suggest that a large part of the process of skill acquisition for the learner is involved in ". . . the forming of the relevant coordinative structures" (Fowler & Turvey, 1978).

CONSTRAINTS. When reading familiar material, such as, "The Lord is my _____," each successive word that occurs in the sentence places limitations on the possible words that can follow in order for the sentence to be intelligible. These constraints arise from our familiarity with the material, but for new material the number of possible variations and combinations of words is much greater. This greater degree of freedom to vary, or lack of constraints, means that more attention must be given to each part of a sentence. To insert a motor example, as each succeeding joint angle in a limb is fixed (*e.g.*, shoulder, elbow, and wrist), so the number of possible movements that can be produced is progressively reduced. When the right-handed billiards player lines up a shot, the bridge made by the left hand and the position of the arm is fixed. The position of the head, shoulders, trunk, and right arm and the grip are also fixed. The only part of the body free to move is the right forearm, which swings easily at the elbow. If the shot has been lined up correctly, only one movement can be made and the player can concentrate on the amount of force to be applied. By limiting the variability at each of the joints we impose constraints on the system as a whole.

By knowing the demands of the task the learner has only to add the necessary constraints to a given set of coordinative structures in order to produce the desired movement. There is still a large degree of flexibility because the learner can vary the force applied, the timing, and the sequencing of the components. However, by operating at the level of words and phrases (coordinative structures) rather than letters and symbols (muscles), it becomes easier to communicate successfully (move efficiently). The skilled billiards player has learned through experience to fix the various joint angles in order to produce a single movement of the billiard cue, but the learner will vary the position from trial to trial and may allow movement at other joints, like the shoulder of the cue arm. This is an example of *imposing constraints to limit the number of mechanical degrees of freedom in the system.* An example of the role of reflex-based coordinative structures is provided by Easton (1978), who likens the action and limb positions of the baseball player jumping to catch a fly ball (the leg and arm on one side of the body are stretched while the opposing limbs are flexed) to the movements seen in the tonic neck reflex in the newborn.

From an ecological point of view, the learner is seen as a cognitive being who faces problems and finds solutions, not as a machine that simply responds to stimuli. As such the learner is not separable from the environment and neither is perception from action. When moving through the environment, the learner seeks sources of invariance and notes various transformations in relation to objects within the environment. Through repeated sampling of the environment, the learner is able to build a perceptual framework to describe the moment by moment changes in the environment.

Gibson (1977) further underlines this interaction with the environment in his concept of *affordance,* which relates to the adaptive value of objects for organisms. Put simply, the physical properties of a surface, land or water, will determine whether the surface will afford locomotion by the individual and even, if we compare sand and ice, the type of locomotion. Therefore, part of the process of detection involves identifying the properties of the surface and the types of locomotion it will afford. The problem for the learner is one of assessing the constraints imposed by the environment in order to determine the additional constraints that must be imposed by the learner on the motor system to achieve the desired goal.

The movement of the limbs requires an action plan, given by some executive level of control. One element in that action plan is the coordinative structure, but if the executive does not control the muscles, then how does it express its control? We can hit the cue ball in the correct direction, but how far will it travel? Evarts (1967), working with monkeys in a task that required the monkeys to make a wrist movement to counteract a given force, found evidence in the recordings from cells in the motor cortex that the firing of these cells was related more to the amount of force applied than to the amount of limb displacement, suggesting that movements are represented as forces. The relationship between the learner and the environment can now be described in terms of the forces that each contribute. To every force there is an equal and opposite reaction; when we push against the ground to take off for a jump the earth "pushes" back. Playing tennis on a windy day constitutes a whole set of different problems as opposed to playing on a calm day. Fitting together the automated coordinative structure solves one part of the problem; the learner's task is to complete the plan of action. The ability to do this successfully is derived from experience or, more particularly, from assessing the various sources of information, as we described earlier in schema theory. "Thus, it may be argued that the control of movement is in many respects the reorganization or tuning of the system of segmental interactions . . ." (Turvey, 1977).

To provide a general overview of this ecological viewpoint we should note the following (Fowler & Turvey, 1978):

1. Within limits the learners are able to apply constraints to their muscles or coordinative structures to establish different action systems.
2. Learning a motor skill is regarded essentially as the discovery of the optimal self-organization.
3. Skills are seen as having a structure based on the environmental and mechanical relationships that specify the essential features of the skill. These relationships describe a set of potential constraints that provide boundaries for the skill, and therefore, simplify the learner's search for an optimal self-organization. The restrictions of a squash court will simply not permit the graceful extended backswing and follow-through seen in many tennis strokes.
4. Several different organizations of muscles or coordinative structures may be adequate to perform a particular task, but the theory is that man seeks the organization that is most harmonious. As Fowler and Turvey suggest, we all learn to swim before we learn to swim skillfully.

In an attempt to assess the possible role of coordinative structures in the control of movement, Kelso, Southard and Goodman, (1979) asked subjects to initiate and terminate two disparate hand movements simultaneously. The subjects moved to two spatially separate targets, one with each hand, at the same time. A cinematographical analysis of the data suggested a very close coordination between the two movements in terms of peak velocity and the rate of acceleration. Kelso and colleagues took this as evidence that indeed the optimal solution for this task was the functional organization of the groups of muscles such that they operated as a single unit. In the terminology of Turvey, we would say that the coordinative structures were constrained to act as a single unit.

This approach to skill acquisition is by no means complete, but it does mark an important beginning. Words such as *grain size, constraints,* and *coordinative structures* are new to the field of psychomotor learning, but they provide an important frame of reference for defining and describing the unsolved problems of motor skill acquisition and placing it in the context of the individual performer. The work of Turvey and his followers was presented here not because it provides a definitive answer, a complete theory of motor skill acquisition, but because it asks the next question. Just because schema theory finally seems to make sense of the old specificity vs generality argument does not mean it is the final solution. It is only a solution to the first question of how an individual establishes a motor skill. Now we must ask the second question of what happens to this process of motor skill learning when we place the individual in the real-world environment as contrasted to the more sterile laboratory situation.

A final note

Whether the level of control is represented as a motor program, a set of coordinative structures, a perceptual trace, or a motor schema, the process of learning is one of fitting together the various components in order to meet the demands of the task. This involves imposing constraints on the system to establish the appropriate timing, sequencing and amount of force. Practice may involve improving error detection, refining the schema, automating the motor program and/or tuning the various constraints. However, if we are to place humans in a dynamic environment, we require a flexible system to interact efficiently and in harmony with that environment. Whether we are developing a model, an abstraction, or an optimal solution of several variables, skill acquisition can best be described as a problem-solving process. Hence, this is a textbook on *psychomotor* learning.

SUMMARY

Improvements of motor control

Klein suggested that the most important skill we possess, from an information processing point of view, is that which allows us to strategically allocate our limited processing resources. Although this process is not always optimal, it can be automated with practice.

SPEED OF DECISION.   This is one of the two components proposed by Posner and Keele as being necessary for skilled performance. Involved in this component are the following factors:

1. Preparation. Planning ahead or anticipating in a competitive situation and studying the opponent can reduce the number of alternatives to which the learner must react.
2. Compatibility. Stimulus response compatibility can greatly reduce reaction time and as such is an important factor to consider when planning movement sequences.
3. Sequential dependencies. Most movement sequences are at least partially predictable, and identifying these dependencies can aid the learner.

MOVEMENT EFFICIENCY.   The second component identified by Posner and Keele involves analyzing movements in order to remove or reduce unnecessary elements. The baseball batting example of Schmidt suggests how gains might be made from such an analysis.

Development of motor programs

A closed-loop system describes a situation in which the sensory information from a movement is fed back to be compared with some intended movement or goal, whereas an open-loop system emphasizes central control as being capable of producing a desired movement in the absence of peripheral feedback.

KEELE'S MODEL.   Drawing on observations from bird song research, Keele suggests that a model or template is first established and then movements are produced and compared with that model in order to develop the actual motor program. Thus, while feedback is important in building the motor program, once established, its main role is to monitor the execution of the program. The two main elements that appear to be built into the motor program are the sequencing and the timing of the components.

MACNEILAGE TARGET HYPOTHESIS.   In an attempt to reduce the storage problem created by the notion of fixed motor programs, MacNeilage proposed that all that was stored was the desired spatial location or target, with the actual movements being generated at the moment to achieve a given target position.

SUZUKI METHOD.   One of the few successful applications of the modeling concept involves learning to play a musical instrument by ear after being provided with appropriate auditory models. However, because this is a commercial technique rather than a laboratory-verified procedure, it is difficult to assess its validity.

Teaching models

GENTILE'S MODEL.   This model attempts to link the various stages of skill development to appropriate teaching strategies and emphasizes the teacher's role in structuring and controlling the environment in order to focus the learner's attention on key variables.

MARTENIUK'S MODEL.   This model clearly illustrates the differing roles of knowledge of results (KR) and knowledge of performance (KP) in the learning process and how they relate to the desired goal of the movement and the proposed plan of action.

Specificity vs generality revisited

GENERAL MOTOR ABILITY.   This is a fairly old concept and represents the motor equivalent of IQ, or what is sometimes referred to as coordination, and was generally measured by a battery of skill tests or exercises. General motor ability and IQ are measures of motor and intellectual capacity, respectively, whereas motor educability measures the ease with which an individual can learn a new skill.

MEMORY DRUM THEORY.   As an alternative, Henry proposed that motor abilities were actually very specific to the task at hand. Similarly, individual motor tasks were regarded as having separate stored programs that would operate with little conscious effort. The specificity of skills idea has been supported by many studies, but Marteniuk suggested that the correlational technique used may have limited the findings.

FLEISHMAN'S ABILITIES.   A middle-of-the-road position between specificity and generality is represented by the idea of ability factors. On the one hand, there may be a certain amount of commonality between two skills; but as learning progresses, abilities specific to those skills become more important.

SCHEMA THEORY.   As an answer to the storage problem raised by MacNeilage and the novelty problem ignored by Adams, Schmidt proposed the idea of generalized motor programs and motor schema based on rules abstracted from previous attempts at related movements. This included both sensory and motor information in relation to particular sets of initial conditions and desired outcomes. The strength of such motor concepts is dependent on the clarity with which the various attributes are defined, that is, the boundary strength. Once established, the motor schema are capable of successfully generating original movements.

A theory of skill acquisition

Schema theory has provided a major step toward establishing an overall theory of motor skill acquisition and is quickly gaining research support, as represented by Kelso's work.

THREE VIEWS OF MOTOR CONTROL.   Although Adams, Keele, and Schmidt still defend their separate positions and draw on various sources of physiological evidence to support their cases, the obvious conclusion would seem to be that they are all correct, within limits, and a good starting point would be to emphasize their similarities rather than their differences.

A MODEL OF MOTOR CONTROL.   The main elements in a composite model appear to be (1) two separate memory states, recall and recognition; (2) an error detection mechanism, including efference copy; and (3) alpha-gamma coactivation.

AN ALTERNATIVE MODEL.   The work of Turvey and others emphasizes the view that people function by interacting with the environment not by performing tasks in isolation (the ecological approach). People are seen as problem-solvers who seek optimal solutions for a given task. The task is performed by marshaling sets of coordinative structures and then imposing constraints on the remaining degrees of freedom in the system in order to establish an appropriate action plan. Such a plan must also take into account the forces contributed by the environment as well as those contributed by the learner. What this approach to skill acquisition does is move our theoretical models out of the laboratory to place them and the individual back in the real world.

PROBLEM

Question

In this chapter we have seen several attempts to devise models that describe skill acquisition. What possible teaching model would you design to capture some of the main elements that have been identified?

Possible answer

The answer is based on three sets of ideas. Using Marteniuk's model as a base, it attempts to combine some of the essential elements of both schema theory and the ecological approach.

Skill acquisition is seen as a problem-solving process, and the model presented in Figure 8-12 essentially identifies three sets of operations (environmental inputs, stored inputs, movement related decisions) and two mechanisms that have a dominant influence on the overall process (selective attention and motivation/arousal).

Initially there are two main sources of sensory input represented by the general environmental constraints and task-specific information. Not all this information is environmentally derived, because some of it represents internal feedback, such as proprioceptive information, from the learner. The learner can also draw on stored information, represented here by the recall and recognition schema, that is related to the task at hand to provide models or general rules and targets. From all these various inputs, a general plan of action and specific goals are quickly identified and held in short-term memory. More specific plans are then devised on the basis of this initial assessment.

The movement to be produced is based on a set of available coordinative structures that fit the action plan, with the addition of the necessary constraints and components to establish the correct sequencing and timing of the components. At this stage the feedback loop (a) allows a check to see if the specific action plan fits the general action

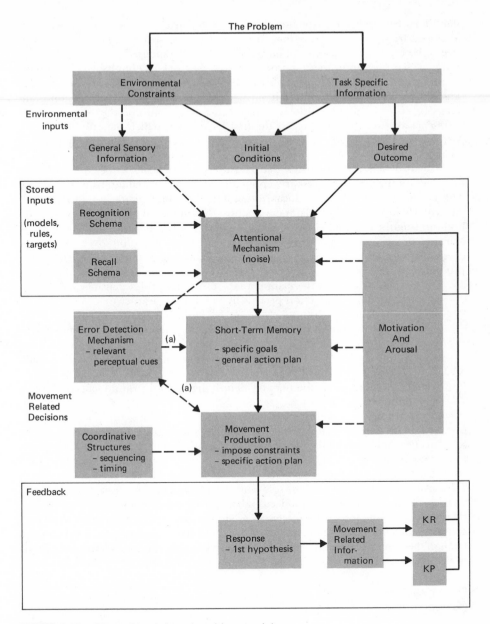

FIGURE 8-12 General basis for a teaching model.

plan. This feedback loop is centered on the error detection mechanism, which is developed from stored information, in particular those perceptual cues that can be used to both guide and assess the movement. Once a response is initiated, the third source of sensory input, the response-produced feedback, is established. The movement-related information most useful is the KR (knowledge of results) and the KP (knowledge of performance) which influences both goal-related and action-plan-related decisions. Because this is a problem-solving process, the response only represents an overt attempt to test the first hypothesis, which may not be correct, particularly with a beginner, and the process must be repeated and the hypothesis revised.

The two major mechanisms that can exert a general facilitory or inhibitory influence on the overall process are represented by attention and motivation/arousal. The ability to strategically allocate attention is essential to the overall process, particularly in the context of dampening down the amount of noise in the system and highlighting the essential elements. The factor of motivation/arousal is basic to the learning situation and can either help by increasing the attention given to relevant cues or hinder by increasing the level of noise and interfering at all stages in the process.

For teachers or coaches there are perhaps three main roles that they can fill:

1. They can aid the selection process by helping the learner to
   a. Focus on the key points of the initial input information
   b. Identify the important cues that occur during the movement to form an error detection mechanism
   c. Build a general action plan by providing models of the skill (visual, auditory)
   d. Form a specific action plan by identifying the basic components of the new movement.
2. Practitioners can aid the analytical process that follows a response by trying to make the KR as precise as possible and by augmenting the KP when possible.
3. They can control the balance between motivation and arousal. This means maintaining sufficient interest for the learner to continue at the task but at the same time avoiding overarousal.

For the detail of what each of these roles entails we would have to return to the relevant sections of the text. However, if indeed skill acquisition is a problem-solving process, then the main function of the teacher is to aid learners in establishing a method for solving problems, rather than just teaching them specific answers. If we memorize enough theorems we may pass our geometry test, but a better approach would be for us to try to solve the problems with a little help from a friend.

Dux Vitae Ratio
(Reason is the guide to life)

Glossary

absolute frequency (of knowledge of results): total number of knowledge of results trials.

absolute judgments: judgments that are made on the basis of some standard stored in memory; the standard is implicit.

activity-set hypothesis: the preparation to perform involves not the specifics of a skill but the preparation of the underlying sub-systems (*e.g.*, the level of arousal or the appropriate feedback channels).

adaptation level: the size, or level, of the difference between the object and its background and the extent to which this difference is influenced by past experience.

adaptive system: a system with no fixed goal and that changes with the situation.

afferent pathways: the peripheral nerve pathways that bring sensory information into the brain via the spinal cord; the ascending tracts.

affordance: the adaptive value of objects for organisms. The physical properties of a surface will determine whether the surface will afford locomotion and even the type of locomotion.

association stage of learning: when an association is made between the correct response and what it feels like to make that movement.

association theories: the development of the association between a given stimulus and response through repetition, with reinforcement used to help elicit the response.

attention: taking possession by the mind of one of what seem several simultaneously possible objects or trains of thought.

attenuation: the strength of the signal is weakened, rather like adding a muffler to a car's exhaust system.

autonomous stage of learning: the final stage of skill refinement in which skills are performed with little conscious effort, requiring minimal attention.

backward masking: see masking.

bilateral transfer: transfer from one limb to another or, for example, the ability to learn more easily a skill with one hand after learning it first with the opposite hand.

binary digit (bit): the amount of information that is needed to choose between two equally probable alternatives.

binocular cues: when both eyes work together to judge depth.

binocular parallax: because the two eyes are set approximately 2½ inches apart the brain receives two different views of the world; this disparity provides cues for depth perception.

capacity interference: the result of attentional demands on the central control mechanism (*i.e.*, when several operations require the use of the limited amount of space available).

ceiling effect: when there is a maximum performance score for a test (*e.g.*, 10 of 10).

central channel mechanisms: in information processing models it is equivalent to the central nervous system, particularly the brain.

channel capacity: the maximum amount of information, or number of items, that can consciously be attended to at one time (7 ± 2 bits).

chunks: groups of related bits of information.

closed motor skill (Poulton, 1957): skills in which the environment is "fixed" and the individual can concentrate on internal feedback related to the skill (*e.g.*, diving).

closure, law of: the learner tends to complete the field or fill in missing parts.

cognition: the process of knowing, involving both awareness and judgment.

cognitive level: a sense of knowing what the movement feels like and the circumstances under which it is normally produced (Rappaport, 1971).

cognitive stage of learning: when the learner evolves strategies, makes many errors, and often shows large improvements.

cognitive theories: the individual's interpretation or perception of the environment is emphasized.

coincident timing: the integration of effector and receptor anticipation.

communication skills: those skills essential for further development in terms of meeting educational needs (*e.g.*, writing, reading).

comparative judgment: comparison of the signal with previous information from the same sensory modality (*i.e.*, a new stimulus vs a standard).

conceptual level: when the percepts are categorized and generally organized to produce associated concepts or general groupings of motor tasks.

concurrent feedback: feedback evident during the movement

constraints: imposing constraints limits the number of mechanical degrees of freedom in the system.

context: secondary sensations based on past experience; it is based on one's relationships with other objects (core-context theory).

continuous motor skill (task): skills that involve a continuous or repetitive series of movements with no distinct end points (*e.g.*, swimming).

coordinative structures: various reflexes, involving several muscles, are combined in order to move in a coordinated manner.

core: the group of immediate sensations aroused by the stimulus, which is fairly stable for different individuals (core-context theory).

critical flicker frequency: when a light is flashed on and off at an increasing rate, eventually the person sees it as a steady light.

desired goal: see goal.

discrete motor skills (task): skills that have a distinct beginning and end, involving a single effort of short duration (*e.g.*, a baseball throw).

distributed practice (within a practice session): when the rest interval is equal to or greater than the trial length.

disuse, law of: no practice weakens the stimulus-response bond.

doctrine of prior entry: humans are limited in their ability to process two simultaneous signals from more than one sensory source. When signals arrive simultaneously from two different sources, a person will process them in serial order.

drive theory: high levels of arousal tend to elicit the dominant response.

ecological approach: learning is considered not just in terms of the individual but of the inter-dependence of the individual and the environment.

effect, law of: if the response is satisfying, the subject will repeat the response and consequently strengthen the S-R bond.

effector anticipation: anticipation in which the performer must predict the time it will take to perform a movement.

efference copy: feed-forward information, in which outgoing motor commands are compared with sensory feedback (inflow model) or with stored copies of previous efferent commands (outflow model).

efferent pathways: the peripheral nerve pathways by which motor responses are carried from the brain to the skeletal musculature; the descending tracts.

encoding specificity hypothesis: the retrieval cues must match some part of the encoding pattern. The recall of a specific item depends on the circumstances under which the item was first encoded and the extent to which these are matched by the retrieval cues.

error detection mechanism: a mechanism for comparing current performance with previous attempts.

errors of commission: when a signal is reported as being present when in fact there was no signal.

errors of omission: when "no signal" is reported when in fact a signal was present.

exercise, law of: see use and disuse.

extinction: the gradual loss of a response due to repetitions of the response without any reward.

extrapyramidal tract (or extracorticospinal tract): this tract sends fibers to the basal ganglia and the reticular formation of the brain stem (pons and medulla), thereby providing a less direct means of controlling movement.

extrinsic feedback: feedback that is artificially added and is not a direct consequence of performing the movement.

feedback: the information that the performer receives while performing a task or as a result of performing the task.

field items: the non-target items in the array of stimuli.

Fitts' Law: movement time is constant for any given ratio between movement amplitude and target width.

floor effect: when there is some minimum time beyond which performance cannot improve.

forgetting: the reverse of retention, or the failure to retain information; the gradual loss of a response over a long period of time.

functional cues: the cues actually used by the learner.

functionalism: an approach taken in much physical education research that emphasizes seeking practical solutions to practical problems.

generalized motor program: controls a class of movements that have the same movement pattern rather than being limited to specific muscles.

Gestalt: an organized pattern or form.

goal (desired):   the consequence or outcome of a particular activity.

Golgi tendon organ: receptor situated in the muscle tendon close to the junction with the muscle that signals the amount of tension in the tendon as a result of muscle contraction.

Golgi tendon type of organ: type of receptor in the ligament that is not affected by the muscle tension at the joint and therefore may signal a more exact joint position as well as direction.

gradation: the extent to which the amount of force exerted is amplified.

graded response: a motor skill is a response that may be guided and determined by feedback received from the various sensory receptors.

grain size: the size of the basic unit of the analysis.

habit: some relatively stable internal state.

habitual skills: those skills involving automated stimulus-response chains necessitating repeated practice but requiring little decision-making (*e.g.*, gymnastics).

heterarchical system: the idea that for a particular response the level of control needed may not be the highest level. It is also quite possible for a lower level of control to take a dominant role and both draw from and manipulate higher levels of control. This system acknowledges the basic flexibility of the human motor system.

Hick-Hyman law: all other things being equal, equal information conditions must produce equal overall mean reaction times.

hierarchical system: the idea of a series of levels of control with each succeeding level having control over all the previous levels. Each level of control has its own responsibilities.

higher-order reinforcement: the use of some neutral reinforcer that has acquired its power through learning is involved.

inflow hypothesis: a person stores, or copies, the efferent information (outgoing motor commands) and then compares this information with the actual feedback.

information: the psychological concept of stimuli and cues. A stimulus can be almost any item present in the environment.

information overload: this theory relates particularly to the limited capacity of short-term memory. As you increase the amount of information entering short-term memory you must eliminate some of the information previously stored; therefore, the information is lost and it cannot go into long-term memory.

information reduction: reduction of the mass of incoming sensory information to a manageable size.

intermittent reward schedule: not all responses are rewarded; the reward is simply not predictable.

intertask transfer: the possible transfer of learning from one task to a second different task (*e.g.*, as from handball to squash).

intratask transfer: the possible transfer between variations of the same task.

intrinsic feedback: feedback that is a direct consequence of performing the movement.

just noticeable difference: the smallest amount of stimulus change that can be detected.

kinesthesis: the awareness of body position and movement based on proprioceptive information.

knowledge of performance (KP): the quality or efficiency of the pattern of movement.

knowledge of results (KR): the extent to which some external goal is achieved.

latency period: in visual search, for example, the delay between the presentation of the array and the onset of the response indicating the subject has located the target item.

latent learning: the idea that learning may have occurred but is not immediately evident in terms of performance.

learning: a relatively permanent change in performance resulting from practice or past experience.

learning sets: learning how to learn or the idea of learning a technique for solving a particular type of problem.

level of aspiration: the concept of goal setting, one's personal expectations of performance based mainly on the interaction of the individual's self-concept and prior success and failure.

limited channel capacity: see channel capacity.

logogen: the unit of information that is activated in memory.

masking (backward): if a stimulus is followed immediately by a second more intense stimulus, the first stimulus may not be identified.

massed practice (within a practice session):   when the rest interval is less than the trial length.

memory span: the amount of information that can be handled at one time.

memory trace: a recall function to select and initiate the appropriate response. It is like a short open-loop motor program.

monocular cues: when one eye is used to judge depth.

motivation: a state of being aroused to action, of mobilizing resources in order to move toward some goal.

motor chain: the response to the first stimulus itself becomes the cue for the next response. In this way a chain of movements can be built up with each movement being cued by the completion of the preceding movement.

motor learning: a relatively permanent change in the performance of a motor skill resulting from practice or past experience.

motor program: a set of muscle commands that allow movements to be performed without any peripheral feedback.

motor set: in the preparation phase when the most probable movement from among all the possible movements that could be made in any situation is selected.

motor skill: any muscular activity that is directed to a specific objective.

motor time: the interval between the arrival of the neural signal at the muscle and the actual contraction of the muscle that initiates the response or the first observable movement.

noise: any neuronal activity in the brain that is going on within the system regardless of whether it is a result of some sensory input or a decision being made.

nominal cues: those cues identified by the teacher as being important in a particular situation.

ontogenetic skills: those skills peculiar to an individual. Sometimes referred to as a combination of communication and recreational skills.

open-loop system: the output or the consequences of that output are not fed back directly into the system. There is no means of obtaining feedback, and each response is separate.

open motor skill (Poulton, 1957):   skills in which the situation or environment is constantly changing and the individual must respond within an unpredictable environment (*e.g.*, tennis).

operant: the set of acts that constitute the response. An individual operates on the environment and as such generates consequences.

operational short-term memory: a descriptive concept referring to the combination of short-term memory and information retrieved from long-term memory for use in the current task.

outflow model: previous efferent commands are stored, efference copy; when asked to reproduce an "old" response they could compare the current efferent commands, outflow, with the expected commands, or efference copy, in order to detect errors.

overgeneralization: the process of taking a finer discrimination and transposing it into a simpler form (*i.e.*, the tendency to simplify relationships).

overlearning: the continued practice after the skill is learned. The theory states that we continue practice once a skill is established not so much to improve the skill itself but to "set" or reinforce the learning.

paciniform corpuscles: type of receptor that probably responds primarily to acceleration and may be capable of detecting very small movements.

patterning: the timing or temporal patterning of the skill and the sequencing or spatial organization of the task.

perception: the active, not the passive, process of interpreting sensory stimuli. It is a function of the brain itself. Perception involves the conscious organization of incoming information, and it is this perceptual organization that provides the basis for learning.

percepts: the combination of related information from different sensory modalities (mental images).

perceptual anticipation: anticipation in which the performer identifies some regularity in the approaching event based only on past experience.

perceptual skills: skills in which an individual is reacting to a changing environment. It involves acquiring the basics of the skill and then learning to apply them according to the situation, thereby emphasizing the element of decision-making.

perceptual trace: a recognition function to check out each response. It is a record of a given movement based on all the sensory information from previous attempts at that movement.

performance: a temporary occurrence fluctuating from time to time, something that is transitory; also refers to the actual score achieved on a task.

phasing: the timing or temporal organization of the units within the sequence; a form of internal timing.

phi phenomenon: if two lights are sequentially switched on and off in a darkened room in a synchronized manner, the light will appear to move.

phylogenetic skills: those skills developed in early life that are primarily dependent on maturation and are common to all mankind (*e.g.*, crawling, walking).

plateau: the leveling off in the performance curve that is not necessarily indicative of a halt in the learning process.

preception: the labeling process of integration in which various bits of kinesthetic or auditory information are recognized as being associated with some event.

premotor time: the interval between the presentation of the stimulus and the onset of the action potential in the responding muscle.

preparation phase: the specific preparation of the correct motor response as well as the increase in central alertness.

primary effect: the phenomenon of normally recalling best those items presented early in the list. The primacy effect seen in the short-term retention curve is attributed to information entering long-term memory.

primacy reinforcement: the satisfaction of some basic biological need such as hunger.

proactive transfer: looking at transfer in terms of how an "old" skill affects the learning of a new skill.

progressive part learning: P_1; P_2; $P_1 + P_2$; P_3; $P_1 + P_2 + P_3$. . . . The components of the skill are combined additively in sequence.

proprioceptive level: first level of Rappaport's perceptual model, which provides for the initial organization of all incoming information within any sensory modality.

proximity, law of: the learner associates, or groups, those stimuli that are close together in time or space.

pseudodiscrimination: when a person makes a finer discrimination than warranted.

psychological refractory period: the individual is unable to process a second signal until the first response has been initiated.

psychomotor learning: learning that is concerned with observable behavior as well as those central controlling processes that guide and produce that behavior.

pure part learning: P_1; P_2; P_3; $P_1 + P_2 + P_3$. . . . All the components of the skill are practiced independently and then joined together.

pursuit speed: the ability to follow or track a target.

pyramidal tract (or corticospinal tract): this tract provides a direct link from the sensorimotor cortex to all levels of the spinal cord and is thought to be involved in the more precise control of individual muscle groups.

queuing: processing of information in serial order.

rate of search: the rate at which the key element in the visual field or memory can be found.

reaction time: represents the latency period from the presentation of the stimulus to the initiation of the response.

reactive inhibition (I_r): the psychological reluctance to sustain work. It is a function of practice. As the amount of practice increases so does the level of I_r and, as a result, performance deteriorates.

readiness, law of: if a person is "ready" to respond (learn), then it is pleasant to respond.

recall: one of the most common techniques for assessing retention, although the least precise. The person is either right or wrong; you know the answer or you do not.

recency effect: improved retention of the final one or two items in a list.

receptor anticipation: anticipation in which the performer must also assess the duration of certain external events.

recognition: one of the most common techniques for assessing retention. The chances of producing the correct answer are somewhat greater, because the correct answer is made available.

recreational skills: those skills learned for oneself (*e.g.*, painting, gymnastics).

regulator system: one that works in relation to a fixed goal (*e.g.*, a thermostat).

rehearsal: see type I and type II.

relative frequency (of knowledge of results): the number of trials between knowledge of result trials.

relearning: retention is measured as the degree of savings (%) economy in the effort to learn.

reminiscence: the apparent improvement in performance over a period of no practice.

retention: the persistence of a skill over a period of no practice.

retroactive transfer: looking at transfer in terms of how the learning of a new skill can affect the performance of an acquired skill.

Ruffini endings: type of receptor that appears to signal the speed and direction of movement. Because they are affected by muscle tension at the joint, they may also signal the resistance to movement or discriminate active from passive movements.

running hypothesis: the learner can compare what is actually present in the environment with expectations based on prior learning or experience.

running memory span: a running account of changing events in the perceptual field and the continuous presentation and retrieval of information.

schema: sets of rules that define both the relationship between the parameters of a particular response and the expected consequences that help to evaluate its outcome.

selective attention: the process whereby humans can selectively attend to a specific stimuli; the individual can concentrate on one specific feature while ignoring other simultaneously presented stimuli.

sensory: the input from the object and its background (sensory-tonic theory).

sensory analysis: the operations that may be performed on the sensory information and that represent both the extent and the limitations of the perceptual mechanism.

sensory information store (SIS): the phenomenon that general information provided by the senses is available not only for the duration of the event but also a short while afterward.

sensory modality: the combination of receptor, nerve pathway, and reception area of the brain.

sensory set: a change in the level of alertness, such that the subject increases the rate at which target signals can be processed. This occurs within the central processing mechanism. This central alertness is not specific for one sensory modality.

serial choice reaction time: as soon as the subject has responded to one stimulus the next stimulus in the series is initiated.

serial task: a given set of movements must be performed in sequence to complete the final task (*e.g.*, the pole vault), which has an identifiable starting point and finishing point.

servomechanism: a type of closed-loop system in which there is a direct link between output and input based on continual feedback. It can function as either a regulator or an adaptive system.

shaping: the gradual molding of the desired response from the behavior emitted. The clinical application of shaping is commonly referred to as behavior modification.

short-term memory: a memory store that can only hold information for a short period of time in the absence of rehearsal.

similarity, law of: homogeneous groups are easier to identify than heterogeneous groups.

Skaggs-Robinson hypothesis: the effect of transfer is a function of the degree of similarity between the skills involved.

span of apprehension: all you can absorb in a glance.

spatial awareness: this concept consists of three main elements representing stages in the development of spatial awareness in children: spatial relations, spatial orientation, and spatial visualization.

spatial orientation: the making of judgments about the positional changes of objects in space.

spatial relations: the ability to discriminate direction with one's self as a reference point.

spatial visualization: the mental manipulation of objects in space.

speed-accuracy trade-off: the relationship between errors and the speed of response.

speed of vision: the ability to monitor accurately a constantly changing environment. This is especially important because of the large amount of information that the system can absorb.

state anxiety: the arousal actually manifested by a stressful situation.

structural interference: when activities occupy the same mechanism of perception and/or storage.

target item: the specific stimulus in the array of stimuli.

task complexity: the demands the task places on memory and the information processing capacity: the number of bits of information.

task organization: the number of separate components and the inter-relationships of these components within the task: their timing and sequencing.

taxonomy: an orderly classification according to presumed natural relationships.

terminal feedback: feedback available at the completion of the response or shortly afterwards.

threshold value: the minimum amount of information or stimulation needed to make a positive identification, and thereby activate some item in memory.

time sharing: the performance of two tasks at the same time, both of which demand attention.

tonic: the input from inside the body (sensory-tonic theory).

trait anxiety: a general disposition to increased arousal when faced with stressful situations.

transfer: the effect of learning one skill on prior or future learning.

transformations (over time):   as a person moves then so does the perceptual field. The items you can see and the angle at which you view them changes as you move through the environment.

type I rehearsal: rehearsal that serves only to maintain the information at that particular stage of processing.

type II rehearsal: rehearsal that involves the continued analysis of the information and, as such, requires more attention and puts greater demands on the individual's limited processing capacity. It is the active organization of information.

use, law of: practice strengthens the stimulus-response bond.

visual-field: the mass of stimuli that we can see in the environment at any one time.
von Restorff effect: if one of the items to be remembered is notably different from any
   of the other items, this item tends to be retained better.

warm-up decrement (WUD):   mental or physical preparation aids subsequent
   performance.
Weber's law: the ability to make comparative judgments between some standard and
   a second signal allows us to distinguish between large numbers of alternatives. It
   is expressed as

$$K = \frac{\text{just noticeable difference}}{\text{intensity of the standard}}$$

where K is a constant.
whole learning: practice on the whole task.
whole-part learning: whole; P_1; whole; P_2; . . . . Practice between each part and
   the whole skill is alternated.

Yerkes-Dodson law: simple skills are facilitated by a high drive, or level of motivation, but for complex skills a low drive is better.

References

Adams, J.A. Some mechanisms of motor responding: An examination of attention. In E.A. Bilodeau (Ed.), *Acquisition of skill.* Academic Press: New York, 1966.

Adams, J.A. A closed-loop theory of motor learning. *Journal of Motor Behavior,* 1971, *3,* 111-150.

Adams, J.A. Issues for a closed-loop theory of motor learning. In G.E. Stelmach (Ed.), *Motor control: Issues and trends.* New York: Academic Press, 1976.

Adams, J.A., & Reynolds, B. Effect of shift in distribution of practice conditions following interpolated rest. *Journal of Experimental Psychology,* 1954, *47,* 32-36.

Agranoff, B.W. Memory and protein synthesis. *Scientific American,* 1967, *216,* 115-122.

Annett, J., Golby, C.W., & Kay, H. The measurement of elements in an assembly task— the information output of the human motor system. *Quarterly Journal of Experimental Psychology,* 1958, *10,* 1-11.

Armstrong, C.W., & Hoffman, S.J. Teaching experience knowledge of performer competency and performance outcome as determinants of proficiency in performance error identification. In P. Klavora & J. Flowers (Eds.), *Motor learning and biomechanical factors in sport.* Toronto: Publications Division, School of Physical and Health Education, University of Toronto, 1980.

Arnold, M. Physiological differentiation of emotional states. *Psychological Review,* 1945, *52,* 35-48.

Atkinson, J.W. The main springs of achievement-oriented activity. In J.A. Krumboltis (Ed.), *Learning and the educational process.* Skokie, Illinois: Rand McNally & Co., 1965.

Attneave, F. *Applications of information theory to psychology.* New York: Holt, Rinehart & Winston, 1959.

Atwood, G.E. Experimental studies of mnemonic visualization. Unpublished doctoral dissertation, University of Oregon, 1969.

Averback, E., & Coriell, A.S. Short-term memory in vision. *Bell System Technical Journal,* 1961, *40,* 309–328.

Bachman, J.C. Specificity versus generality in learning and performing two large motor tasks. *Research Quarterly,* 1961, *32,* 3–11.

Bahrick, H.P., Noble, M.E., & Fitts, P.M. Extra-task performance as a measure of learning a primary task. *Journal of Experimental Psychology,* 1954, *48,* 298–302.

Baker, K.E., Wylie, R.C., & Gagné, R.M. Transfer of training to a motor skill as a function of variation in rate of response. *Journal of Experimental Psychology,* 1950, *40,* 721–732.

Barker, D. The structure and distribution of muscle receptors. In D. Barker (Ed.), *Symposium on muscle receptors.* Hong Kong: Hong Kong University Press, 1962.

Barnett, M.L., Ross, D., Schmidt, R.A., & Todd, B. Motor skill learning and the specificity of training principle. *Research Quarterly,* 1973, *44,* 440–447.

Bartlett, F.C. The measurement of human skill. *Occupational Therapy,* 1948, *22,* 83–91.

Barton, J.W. Smaller versus larger units in learning the maze. *Journal of Experimental Psychology,* 1921, *4,* 418–429.

Battig, W.F. Transfer from verbal pretraining to motor performance a function of motor task complexity. *Journal of Experimental Psychology,* 1956, *51,* 371–378.

Beisman, G.L. Effect of rhythmic accompaniment upon learning of fundamental motor skills. *Research Quarterly,* 1967, *38,* 172–176.

Belbin, E. The influence of interpolated recall upon recognition. *Quarterly Journal of Experimental Psychology,* 1950, *2,* 163–169.

Bernstein, N. *The coordination and regulation of movement.* New York: Pergamon Press, 1967.

Bertelson, P. S-R relationship and reaction times to new versus repeated signals in a serial task. *Journal of Experimental Psychology,* 1963, *63,* 478–484.

Bertelson, P. The time course of preparation. *Quarterly Journal of Experimental Psychology,* 1967, *19,* 272–279.

Bies, S., & Kerr, R. Intersensory integration and motor control. Paper presented to North American Society of Psychology of Sport and Physical Activity, Ithaca, 1977.

Bigge, M.L. *Learning theories for teachers.* New York: Harper & Row, 1971.

Bilodeau, E.A., & Bilodeau, I.McD. Variable frequency of knowledge of results and the learning of a simple skill. *Journal of Experimental Psychology,* 1958, *55,* 379–383.

Bilodeau, E.A., Bilodeau, I.McD., & Schumsky, D.A. Some effects of introducing and withdrawing knowledge of results early and late in practice. *Journal of Experimental Psychology,* 1959, *58,* 142–144.

Bilodeau, E.A., & Ryan, F.J. A test for interaction of delay of knowledge of results and two types of interpolated activity. *Journal of Experimental Psychology,* 1960, *59,* 414–419.

Blais, C. An EMG and cinematographic analysis of schema theory as applied to the transfer of learning of a novel task. Unpublished manuscript, University of Ottawa, 1979.

Bliss, J.C., Crane, H.D., Mansfield, P.K., & Townsend, J.T. Information available in brief tactile presentations. *Perception and Psychophysics,* 1966, *1,* 273–283.

Blodgett, W.C. The effect of the introduction of reward upon the maze performance of rats. *University of California publications in psychology,* 1929, *4,* 113–134.

Boring, E.G. A new ambiguous figure. *American Journal of Psychology,* 1930, *42,* 444–445.

Boring, E.G. *History of experimental psychology.* New York: Appleton-Century-Crofts, 1950.

Botwinick, J., & Thompson, L.W. Premotor and motor components of reaction time. *Journal of Experimental Psychology,* 1966, *71,* 9–15.

Bowman, J.P., & Combs, C.M. Cerebellar responsiveness to stimulation of the lingual spindle afferent fibers in the hypoglossal nerve of the rhesus monkey. *Experimental Neurology,* 1969, *23,* 537–543.

Brace, D.K. *Measuring motor ability, a scale of motor ability tests.* New York: A.S. Barnes Co., 1927.

Brantly, W. The similarity of factors in transfer and inhibition. *The Journal of Educational Psychology,* 1938, *29,* 145–157.

Briggs, G.E., Fitts, P.M., & Bahrick, H.P. Transfer effect from a single to a double integral teaching system. *Journal of Experimental Psychology,* 1958, *55,* 135–142.

Briggs, G.E., & Waters, L.K. Training and transfer as a function of component interaction. *Journal of Experimental Psychology,* 1958, *56,* 492–500.

Broadbent, D.E. *Perception and communication.* London: Pergamon Press, 1958.

Broer, M. Effectiveness of a general basic skill curriculum for junior high school girls. *Research Quarterly,* 1958, *29,* 379–388.

Brown, J. Some tests of the decay theory of immediate memory. *Quarterly Journal of Experimental Psychology,* 1958, *10,* 12–21.

Brown, J. Evidence for a selective process during perception of tachistoscopically presented stimuli. *Journal of Experimental Psychology,* 1960, *59,* 176–181.

Brown, J.S., & Slater-Hammel, A.T. Discrete movements in the horizontal plane as a function of their length and direction. *Journal of Experimental Psychology,* 1949, *39,* 84–95.

Brown, R.W. Comparative study of the whole, part and combination method of learning piano music. *Journal of Experimental Psychology,* 1928, *11,* 235–297.

Bruner, J.S. *The process of education.* New York: Vintage Books, 1960.

Bruner, J.S. Organization of early skilled behavior. *Child Development,* 1973, *44,* 1–11.

Bruner, J.S., Oliver, R.R., Greenfield, P.M. et al. *Studies in Cognitive Growth,* New York: John Wiley & Sons, 1966.

Caskey, S.R. Effects of motivation on standing broad jump performance of children. *Research Quarterly,* 1968, *39,* 54–59.

Champion, C.L. The effects of specific fatiguing exercise regimens on the spatio-temporal dimension of sensori-motor performance. Unpublished doctoral dissertation, University of Massachusetts, 1977.

Chapman, D.W. Relative effects of determinate and indeterminate Aufgaben. *American Journal of Psychology,* 1932, *44,* 163–174.

Chernikoff, R., & Taylor, F.V. Reaction time to kinesthetic stimulation resulting from sudden arm displacement. *Journal of Experimental Psychology,* 1952, *43,* 1–8.

Cherry, E.C. Some experiments on the recognition of speech. *Journal of Accoustical Society of America,* 1953, *25,* 975–979.

Church, R.M., & Camp, D.S. Change in reaction time as a function of knowledge of results. *American Journal of Psychology*, 1965, *78*, 102–106.

Ciszek, I. A study to determine the relationship between tachistoscopic and baseball batting ability. Unpublished doctoral dissertation, Boston University School of Education, 1968.

Clarke, H.M., & Glines, D. Relationships of reaction, movement and completion times to motor, strength, anthropometric and maturity measures of 13 year-old boys. *Research Quarterly*, 1962, *33*, 196–201.

Clarke, J.E. Compatibility and complexity in response decision processing. In G.C. Roberts, & K.M. Newell (Eds.), *Psychology of motor behavior and sport—1978*. Champaign, Illinois: Human Kinetics Publishers, 1979.

Clarke, L.V. Effect of mental practice on the development of a certain motor skill. *Research Quarterly*, 1960, *31*, 560–568.

Colville, F.H. The learning of motor skills as influenced by knowledge of mechanical principles. *Journal of Educational Psychology*, 1957, *48*, 321–327.

Connolly, K., & Jones, B. A developmental study of efferent-reafferent integration. *British Journal of Psychology*, 1970, *61*, 259–266.

Cook, R.W. Studies in cross-educational mirror tracing the star-shaped maze. *Journal of Experimental Psychology*, 1933, *16*, 144–160.

Corbin, C.B. Effects of mental practice on skill development after controlled practice. *Research Quarterly*, 1967, *38*, 534–538.

Craik, F.I.M., & Lockhart, R.S. Levels of processing: A framework for memory research. *Journal of Verbal Learning and Verbal Behavior*, 1972, *11*, 671–684.

Cratty, B.J. Effects of intra-maze delay upon learning. *Perceptual Motor Skills*, 1962, *15*, 14.

Cratty, B.J. *Perceptual and motor development of infants and children*. New York: Macmillan, 1970.

Cratty, B.J. *Movement behavior and motor learning*. Philadelphia: Lea & Febiger, 1973. (a)

Cratty, B.J. *Teaching motor skills*. Englewood Cliffs, New Jersey: Prentice-Hall, 1973. (b)

Creamer, L.R. Event uncertainty, psychological refractory period, and human data processing. *Journal of Experimental Psychology*, 1963, *66*, 187–194.

Cross, R.J. A comparison of the whole method, the minor game method, and the whole part method of teaching basketball to ninth grade boys. *Research Quarterly*, 1937, *8*, 49–54.

Cureton, K. Physical training helps to regulate and improve glandular functions. A review of research. *Research Quarterly*, 1959, *30*, 266–281.

Damron, C.F. Two and three-dimensional slide images used with tachistoscopic training techniques in instructing high school football players in defenses. *Research Quarterly*, 1955, *26*, 36–43.

Daniels, D. Transfer of training and retroactive inhibition existent in learning of a selected tennis and badminton skill. Unpublished master's thesis, North Texas State University, 1968.

Darwin, C.J., Turvey, M.T., & Crowder, R.G. An auditory analogue of the Sperling partial report procedure: Evidence for brief auditory storage. *Cognitive Psychology*, 1972, *3*, 255–267.

Davis, D.R., & Sinha, D. The effect of one experience upon the recall of another. *Quarterly Journal of Experimental Psychology*, 1950, *2*, 43-52.

Davis, R.C. The pattern of muscular action in simple voluntary movement. *Journal of Experimental Psychology*, 1942, *31*, 347-366.

Dawes, R.M. Cognitive distortion. *Psychological Reports*, 1964, *14*, 443-459.

Deci, E.L. Effects of externally mediated rewards on intrinsic motivation. *Journal of Personality and Social Psychology*, 1971, *18*, 105-115.

Deese, J. Skilled performance and conditions of stress. In R. Glaser (Ed.), *Training research and education*. New York: John Wiley & Sons, 1965.

Denny, M.R., Allard, M., Hall, E., & Rokeach, M. Supplementary report: Delay of knowledge of results, knowledge of task, and the intertrial interval. *Journal of Experimental Psychology*, 1960, *60*, 327.

Deshaies, P., Pargmen, D., & Thiffault, C. A psychobiological profile of individual performance in junior hockey players. In G.C. Roberts & K.M. Newell (Eds.), *Psychology of motor behavior and sport—1978*. Champaign, Illinois: Human Kinetics Publishers, 1979.

Deutsch, J.A., & Deutsch, D. Attention: Some theoretical considerations. *Psychological Review*, 1963, *70*, 80-90.

Dewhurst, D.J. Neuromuscular control system. *IEEEE, Transactions on Biomedical Engineering*, 1967, *14*, 167-171.

Dickie, D.A. The effect of perceptual or motor practice on reaction time and movement time. Unpublished masters thesis, University of Ottawa, 1979.

Diewert, G.L., & Stelmach, G.E. Perceptual organization in motor learning. In G.E. Stelmach (Ed.), *Information processing in motor learning and control*. New York: Academic Press, 1978.

Dillon, E.K. A study of the use of music as an aid in teaching swimming. *Research Quarterly*, 1952, *23*, 1-8.

Easton, T.A. On the normal use of reflexes. *American Scientist*, 1972, *60*, 591-599.

Easton, T.A. Coordinative structures—the basis for a motor program. In D.M. Landers & R.W. Christina (Eds.), *Psychology of motor behavior and sport—1977*. Champaign, Illinois: Human Kinetic Publishers, 1978.

Elkind, D., Koegler, R.R., & Koegler, E.G. Studies in perceptual development: II. Part-whole perception. *Child Development*, 1964, *35*, 81-90.

Endler, N.S. A person-situation interaction model for anxiety. In C.D. Spielberger & I.G. Sarason (Eds.), *Stress and anxiety* (Vol. 1). Washington, D.C.: Hemisphere, 1975.

Evarts, E.V. Representation of movements and muscles by pyramidal tract on the perceptual motor cortex. In M.D. Yahr & D.P. Purpura (Eds.), *Neurophysiological basis of normal and abnormal motor activities*. New York: Raven Press, 1967.

Evarts, E.V. Brain mechanics in movement. *Scientific American*, 1973, *229*, 96-103.

Eysenck, H.J. On the dual function of consolidation. *Perceptual Motor Skills*, 1966, *22*, 273-274.

Fantasia, T.J. The effect of mental and physical practice upon gross motor learning within selected period patterns. Unpublished doctoral dissertation, Boston University, 1969.

Festinger, L., & Canon, L.R. Information about spatial location based on knowledge about efference. *Psychological Review*, 1965, *72*, 373–384.

Fitts, P.M. The information capacity of the human motor system in controlling the amplitude of movement. *Journal of Experimental Psychology*, 1954, *47*, 381–391.

Fitts, P.M. Factors in complex skill training. In R. Glaser (Ed.), *Training research and education.* New York: Wiley, 1965.

Fitts, P.M., & Posner, M.I. *Human performance.* Belmont, California: Brooks/Cole Publishing Co., 1967.

Fleishman, E.A. Dimensional analysis of psychomotor abilities. *Journal of Experimental Psychology*, 1954, *48*, 437–454.

Fleishman, E.A. *The structure and measurement of physical fitness.* Englewood Cliffs, New Jersey: Prentice-Hall, 1964.

Fleishman, E.A. On the relation between abilities, learning and human performance. *American Psychologist*, 1972, *27*, 1017–1032. (a)

Fleishman, E.A. Structure and measurement of psychomotor abilities. In R.N. Singer (Ed.), *The psychomotor domain: Movement behavior.* Philadelphia: Lea & Febiger, 1972. (b)

Fleishman, E.A., & Hempel, W.E., Jr. Changes in factor structure of a complex psychomotor test as a function of practice. *Psychometrika*, 1954, *19*, 239–252.

Fleishman, E. A., & Parker, J.F., Jr. Factors in the retention and relearning of perceptual-motor skills. *Journal of Experimental Psychology*, 1962, *64*, 215–226.

Fleishman, E.A., & Rich, S. Role of kinesthetic and spatial-visual abilities in perceptual-motor learning. *Journal of Experimental Psychology* 1963, *66*, 6–11.

Fowler, C.A., & Turvey, M.T. Skill acquisition: An event approach with special reference to searching for the optimum of a function of several variables. In G.E. Stelmach (Ed.), *Information processing in motor learning and control.* New York: Academic Press, 1978.

Fox, M.G., & Lamb, E. Improvement during a nonpractice period in a selected physical education activity. *Research Quarterly*, 1962, *33*, 381–385.

Fox, M.G., & Young, V.P. Effect of reminiscence on learning selected badminton skills. *Research Quarterly*, 1962, *33*, 386–394.

Frank, J.D. Recent studies in the level of aspiration. *Psychological Bulletin*, 1941, *38*, 218–226.

Frank, J.S. Temporal prediction in motor responding, what's the "gain"? A paper presented at the Congress of the Canadian Society for Psychomotor Learning and Sport Psychology, Toronto, 1978.

Gagné, R.M. *The conditions of learning.* New York: Holt, Rinehart & Winston, 1970.

Gagné, R.M., & Foster, H. Transfer to a motor skill from practice on a pictured representation. *Journal of Experimental Psychology*, 1949, *39*, 342–354.

Gallahue, D.L. The relationship between perceptual and motor abilities. *Research Quarterly*, 1968, *39*, 948–952.

Gentile, A.M. A working model of skill acquisition with application to teaching. *Quest*, 1972, *17*, 3–23.

Gentile, A.M., Higgins, J.R., Miller, E.A., & Rosen, B.M. The structure of motor tasks. *Movement 7.* Actes du 7e symposium en apprentissage psycho-moteur et psychologie du sport, Quebec City, 1975.

Gibbs, C.B. Transfer of training and skill assumptions in tracking tasks. *Quarterly Journal of Experimental Psychology*, 1951, *3*, 99–110.

Gibbs, C.B. Servo-control systems in organisms and the transfer to skill. In D. Legge (Ed.), *Skills.* Middlesex: Penguin, 1970.

Gibson, E.J., & Walk, R.D. The visual cliff. *Scientific American,* 1960, *202,* 64–71.

Gibson, J.J. *The perception of the visual world.* Boston: Houghton-Mifflin, 1950.

Gibson, J.J. The theory of affordance. In R.E. Shaw & J. Bransford (Eds.), *Perceiving, acting and knowing: Toward an ecological psychology.* Hillsdale, New Jersey: Erlbaum, 1977.

Gilbreth, F.B., Jr., & Carey, E.G. *Cheaper by the dozen.* New York: Bantam Books, 1948.

Glencross, D.J. Latency and response complexity. *Journal of Motor Behavior,* 1972, *4,* 251–256.

Glencross, D.J. Response complexity and the latency of different movement patterns. *Journal of Motor Behavior,* 1973, *5,* 95–104. (a)

Glencross, D.J. Temporal organization in a repetitive speed skill. *Ergonomics,* 1973, *16,* 765–776. (b)

Glencross, D.J. Output and response processes in skilled performance. In G.C. Roberts & K.M. Newell (Eds.), *Psychology of motor behavior and sport—1978.* Champaign, Illinois: Human Kinetics Publishers, 1979.

Glencross, D.J., & Oldfield, S.R. The use of ischemic nerve block procedures in the investigation of the sensory control movements. *Biological Psychology,* 1975, *2,* 227–236.

Goldfarb, J.M. Motivation psychology in coaching. *Scholastic Coach,* February, 1968, 54–59.

Goodenough, F.L., & Brian, C.R. Certain factors underlying the acquisition of motor skills by pre-school youngsters. *Journal of Experimental Psychology,* 1929, *12,* 127–155.

Goodwin, G.M. The sense of limb position and movement. In J. Keogh & R.S. Hutton (Eds.), *Exercise and sport sciences reviews* (Vol. 4). Santa Barbara, California: Journal Publishing Affiliates, 1977.

Goodwin, G.M., McCloskey, E.I., & Matthews, P.B.C. Proprioceptive illusions induced by muscle vibrations: Contribution by muscle spindles to perception? *Science,* 1972, *175,* 1382–1384.

Gordon, R.A. An investigation into some of the factors that favour the formation of stereotyped images. *British Journal of Psychology (General Section),* 1949, *39,* 156–167.

Gottsdanker, R., & Stelmach, G.E. The persistence of psychological refractoriness. *Journal of Motor Behavior,* 1971, *3,* 301–312.

Gould, R. Some sociological determinants of goal striving. *Journal of Social Psychology,* 1961, *13,* 461–473.

Gregory, R.L. *Eye and brain, the psychology of seeing.* New York: McGraw-Hill, 1971.

Guthrie, E.R. *The psychology of learning* (rev. ed.). New York: Harper & Row, 1952.

Guyton, A.C. *Basic human physiology: Normal function and mechanisms of disease.* Philadelphia: W.B. Saunders, 1971.

Halverson, L.E. A comparison of three methods of teaching motor skills. Unpublished master's thesis, University of Wisconsin, 1949.

Harlow, H.F. The formation of learning sets. *Psychological Review,* 1949, *56,* 51–65.

Harmon, J.M., & Johnson, W.R. The emotional reactions of college athletes. *Research Quarterly*, 1952, *23*, 391–397.

Harmon, J.M., & Miller, A.G. Time patterns in motor learning. *Research Quarterly*, 1950. *21*, 182–187.

Hartman, E.B. The influence of practice and pitch-distance between tones by the absolute identification of pitch. *American Journal of Psychology*, 1954, *67*, 1–14.

Held, R. Plasticity in sensory motor systems. *Scientific American*, 1965, *213*, 84–94.

Helson, H. (Ed.), *Theoretical foundations of psychology*. New York: D. Van Nostrand, 1951.

Helson, H. *Adaptation level theory*. New York: Harper & Row, 1964.

Hempel, W.E., Jr., & Fleishman, E.A. A factor analysis of physical proficiency and manipulative skill. *Journal of Applied Psychology*, 1955, *39*, 12–16.

Hendrickson, G., & Schroeder, W.H. Transfer of training in learning to hit a submerged target. *Journal of Educational Psychology*, 1941, *32*, 205–213.

Henneman, E. Organization of the motor system - a preview. In V.B. Mountcastle (Ed.), *Medical physiology* (13th ed.). St. Louis: C.V. Mosby, 1974.

Henry, F.M. Coordination and motor learning. *Proceedings of the College Physical Education Association*, 1956, *59*, 68–75.

Henry, F.M. Specificity vs generality in learning motor skills. *Proceedings of the College Physical Education Association*, 1958, *61*, 126–128.

Henry, F.M. Influence of motor and sensory sets on reaction latency and speed of discrete movements. *Research Quarterly*, 1960, *31*, 459–468.

Henry, F.M., & Rogers, D.E. Increased response latency for complicated movements and a "memory drum" theory for neuromotor reaction. *Research Quarterly*, 1960, *31*, 448–458.

Hershberger, W.A., & Terry, D.F. Typographical cuing in conventional and programmed texts. *Journal of Applied Psychology*, 1965, *49*, 55–60.

Hick, W.E. On the rate of gain of information. *Quarterly Journal of Experimental Psychology*, 1952, *4*, 11–26.

Holding, D.H. *Principles of training*. New York: Pergamon Press, 1965.

Horowitz, L.M., Lampel, A.K., & Takanishi, R.N. The child's memory for unitized scenes. *Journal of Experimental Child Psychology*, 1969, *8*, 375–388.

Howell, M.L. Influence of emotional tension on speed of reaction and movement. *Research Quarterly*, 1953, *24*, 22–32.

Howell, M.L. Use of force-time graphs for performance analysis in facilitating motor learning. *Research Quarterly*, 1956, *27*, 12–22.

Hull, C.L. *Principles of behavior*. New York: Appleton-Century-Crofts, 1943.

Hyden, H. Activation of nuclear RNA in neurons and glia in learning. In D.P. Kimble (Ed.), *The anatomy of memory*. Palo Alto, California: Science and Behavior Books, 1965.

Hyman, R. Stimulus information as a determinant of reaction time. *Journal of Experimental Psychology*, 1953, *45*, 188–196.

Ittleson, W.H., & Cantril, H. *Perception, a transactional approach*. New York: Doubleday, 1954.

Jable, J.T. The relative effects of training with basketballs of varying weights upon free throw shooting accuracy. Unpublished master's thesis, Pennsylvania State University, 1965.

James, W. *Principles of Psychology* (Vol. 1). New York: Holt, 1890.

Jenkins, J.J. Remember that old theory of memory? well forget it! In R.E. Shaw & J. Bransford (Eds.), *Perceiving, acting and knowing: Toward an ecological psychology.* Hillsdale, New Jersey: Erlbaum, 1977.

Johnson, R. Wicks, G., & Ben-Sira, D. Practice in the absence of KR: Skill ac-acquisition and retention. In G.C. Roberts & D.M. Landers (Eds.) *Psychology of motor behavior and sport.* Champaign, Illinois: Human Kinetics Publishers, 1980.

Jones, B. Is there any proprioceptive feedback? Comments on Schmidt (1971). *Psychological Bulletin,* 1971, *79,* 386–390.

Jones, B. Is proprioception important for skilled performance? *Journal of Motor Behavior,* 1974, *6,* 33–45.

Jones, J.G. Motor learning without demonstration of physical practice under two conditions of mental practice. *Research Quarterly,* 1965, *36,* 270–276.

Judd, C.H. Movement and consciousness. *Psychological Review,* 1905, 7, 199–226.

Judd, C.H. The relationship of special training to general intelligence. *Educational Review,* 1908, *26,* 28–42.

Kane, M. The Art of Ali. *Sports Illustrated,* 1969, *30,* 48–57.

Karlin, L., & Martz, M.J. Response probability and sensory-evoked, potentials. In S. Kornblum (Ed.), *Attention and performance IV.* New York: Academic Press, 1973.

Katz, L. Effects of differential monetary gain and loss on sequential two-choice behavior. *Journal of Experimental Psychology,* 1964, *68,* 245–249.

Kay, W. Information theory in the understanding of skills. *Occupational Psychology,* 1957, *31,* 218–224.

Keele, S.W. Compatibility and time-sharing in serial reaction time. *Journal of Experimental Psychology,* 1967, *75,* 529–539.

Keele, S.W. Movement control in skilled motor performance. *Psychological Bulletin,* 1968, *70,* 387–403.

Keele, S.W. *Attention and human performance.* Pacific Palisades, California: Goodyear Publishing, 1973.

Keele, S.W. The representation of motor programs. In P.M.A. Rabbitt & S. Dornic (Eds.), *Attention and performance V.* New York: Academic Press, 1975.

Keele, S.W. Current status of the motor program concept. In R.W. Christina & D.M. Landers (Eds.), *Psychology of motor behavior and sport* (Vol. 1). Champaign, Illinois: Human Kinetics Publishers, 1977.

Keele, S.W., & Posner, M.I. Processing of feedback in rapid movements. *Journal of Experimental Psychology,* 1968, *77,* 353–363.

Kelso, J.A.S. Motor control mechanisms underlying human movement reproduction. *Journal of Experimental Psychology: Human Perception and Performance,* 1977, *3,* 529–543.

Kelso, J.A.S., & Norman, P.E. Motor schema formation in children. *Developmental Psychology,* 1978, *14,* 153–156.

Kelso, J.A.S., Pruitt, J.H., & Goodman, D. The generalizability of preselection. In G.C. Roberts & K.M. Newell (Eds.), *Psychology of motor behavior and sport-1978.* Champaign, Illinois: Human Kinetics Publishers, 1979.

Kelso, J.A.S., Southard, D.L., & Goodman, D. On the coordination of two-handed movements. *Journal of Experimental Psychology: Human Perception and Performance,* 1979, *5,* 229–238.

Kelso, J.A.S., & Stelmach, G.E. Central and peripheral mechanisms in motor control.

In G.E. Stelmach (Ed.), *Motor control: Issues and trends*. New York: Academic Press, 1976.

Kerr, B. Task factors that influence selection and preparation for voluntary movements. In G.E. Stelmach (Ed.), *Information processing in motor learning and control*. New York: Academic Press, 1978.

Kerr, B.A. Weighted and velocity factors in kinesthetic learning and transfer of training. *Journal of Motor Behavior*, 1970, *3*, 195-205.

Kerr, R. Motor skill learning and schema theory. *Canadian Journal of Applied Sport Sciences*, 1977, *2*, 77-80.

Kerr, R. Project your way to success. *Coaching Review*, 1978, *1*, 13-15. (a)

Kerr, R. Diving, adaptation and Fitts law. *Journal of Motor Behavior*, 1978, *10*, 255-260. (b)

Kerr, R. Specificity vs generality revisited: Implications for the practitioner. In *Proceedings of 6th Commonwealth Conference*, 1979, *2*, 148-154.

Kerr, R. Development of motor skills in children. Unpublished manuscript, University of Ottawa, 1980.

Kerr, R. Getting into the scheme of things. In N.L. Wood (Ed.), *Coaching Science Update 1980-81*. Ottawa: Coaching Association of Canada, 1981.

Kerr, R., & Booth, B. Skill acquisition in elementary school children and schema theory. In D.M. Landers & R.W. Christina (Eds.), *Psychology of motor behavior and sport* (Vol. 2). Champaign, Illinois: Human Kinetics Publishers, 1977.

Kerr, R., & Booth, B. Specific and varied practice of motor skill. *Perceptual and Motor Skills*, 1978, *46*, 395-401.

Kerr, R., Booth, M., Dainty, D., Gaboriault, R., & McGavern, D. Talent identification for competitive diving. In P. Klavora & K.A.W. Wipper (Eds.), *Psychological and sociological factors in sport*. Toronto: Publications Division, School of Physical and Health Education, University of Toronto, 1980.

Kerr, R., McGavern, D., Booth, M., Dainty, D., Gaboriault, R., & O'Hara, T. Motor skill analysis of the prerequisite abilities for diving. In *Proceedings of 6th Commonwealth Conference*, 1979, *2*, 297-302.

Kimble, G.A. Performance and reminiscence in motor learning as a function of the degree of distribution of practice. *Journal of Experimental Psychology*, 1949, *39*, 500-510.

King, R.A. Consolidation of the neural trace in memory: Investigation with one-trial avoidance conditioning and ECS. *Journal of Comparative Physiology and Psychology*, 1965, *59*, 283-284.

Kirby, N.H. Sequential effects in serial reaction time. Unpublished thesis, University of Adelaide, 1974.

Klapp, S.T., & Erwin, I. Relation between programming time and duration of the response being programmed. *Journal of Experimental Psychology: Human Perception and Performance*, 1976, *2*, 591-598.

Klein, R.M. Attention and movement. In G.E. Stelmach (Ed.), *Motor control: Issues and trends*. New York: Academic Press, 1976.

Klein, R.M. Automatic and strategic processes in skilled performance. In G.C. Roberts, & K.M. Newell (Eds.), *Psychology of motor behavior and sport—1978*. Champaign, Illinois: Human Kinetics Publishers, 1979.

Klemmer, E.T. Simple reaction time as a function of time uncertainty. *Journal of Experimental Psychology*, 1957, *54*, 195-200.

Klimovitch, G. Startle response and muscular fatigue effects upon fractionated hand grip reaction time. *Journal of Motor Behavior*, 1977, *9*, 285-292.

Knapp, B.N. Simple reaction time of selected top-class sportsmen and research students. *Research Quarterly*, 1961, *32*, 409-911.

Knapp, B.N. *Skill in sport: The attainment of proficiency*. London: Routledge & Kegan Paul, 1963.

Koffka, K. *Growth of the mind*. New York: Harcourt, Brace & World, 1929.

Kohler, W. *The mentality of the apes*. E. Winter. (Trans.) New York: Harcourt, Brace & World, 1925.

Kornblum, S. An invariance in choice reaction time with varying number of alternatives and constant probability. In P.M.A. Rabbitt & S. Dornic (Eds.), *Attention and performance V*. New York: Academic Press, 1975.

Kroll, W., & Clarkson, P.M. Fractionated reflex time, resisted and unresisted fractionated time under normal and fatigued conditions. In D.M. Landers & R.W. Christina (Eds.), *Psychology of motor behavior and sport—1977*. Champaign, Illinois: Human Kinetics Publishers, 1978.

Krus, D.M., Werner, H., & Wapner, S. Studies in vicariousness: Motor activity and perceived movement. *American Journal of Psychology*, 1953, *66*, 603-608.

Laabs, G.J. Retention characteristics of different reproduction cues in motor short-term memory. *Journal of Experimental Psychology*, 1973, *100*, 168-179.

Lafuze, M. A study of the learning of fundamental skills by college women of low motor ability. *Research Quarterly*, 1951, *22*, 149-157.

Lagasse, P.P., & Hayes, K.L. Premotor and motor reaction time as a function of movement extent. *Journal of Motor Behavior*, 1973, *5*, 25-32.

Langley, L.L., Telford, I.R., & Christensen, J.B. *Dynamic anatomy and physiology* (3rd ed.). New York: McGraw-Hill, 1969.

Lashley, K.S. The accuracy of movement in the absence of excitation from the moving organ. *American Journal of Physiology*, 1917, *43*, 169-194.

Lashley, K.S. The problems of serial order in behavior. In L.A. Jeffress (Ed.), *Cerebral mechanisms in behavior: The Hixon symposium*. New York: John Wiley & Sons, 1951.

Laszlo, J.I. Training of fast tapping with reduction of kinesthetic, tactile, visual and auditory sensations. *Quarterly Journal of Experimental Psychology*, 1967, *19*, 344-349.

Laszlo, J.I., & Livesey, J.P. Task complexity, accuracy and reaction time. *Journal of Motor Behavior*, 1977, *9*, 171-177.

Leonard, J.A. Tactual choice reactions. *Quarterly Journal of Experimental Psychology*, 1959, *11*, 76-83.

Lewin, K. *Principles of topological psychology*. F. Heider & G.M. Heider. (Trans.) New York: McGraw-Hill, 1936.

Lewis, D., McAllister, D.E., & Adams, J.A. Facilitation and interference in performance on the modified Mashburn apparatus: I. *Journal of Experimental Psychology*, 1951, *41*, 247-260.

Lewis, J., Braddeley, A.D., Bonham, K.G., & Lovett, D. Traffic pollution and mental efficiency. *Nature*, 1970, *225*, 95-97.

Locke, E.A. Toward a theory of task motivation and incentives. *Organic Behavior and Human Performance*, 1968, *3*, 157-189.

Locke, E.A., Cartledge, N., & Koeppel, J. Motivational effects of knowledge of results:

A goal-setting phenomenon? *Psychological Bulletin*, 1968, *70*, 474–485.

Logan, T.H., Wodthe, K.H. Effects of rules of thumb on transfer of training. *Journal of Educational Psychology*, 1968, *59*, 147–153.

Lordahl, D.S., & Archer, E.J. Transfer effects on a rotary pursuit task as a function of first task difficulty. *Journal of Experimental Psychology*, 1958, *56*, 421–426.

Lotter, W.S. Interelationship among reaction times and speed of movement in different limbs. *Research Quarterly*, 1960, *31*, 147–154.

Lundervold, A. Electromyographic investigations during typewriting. *Ergonomics*, 1958, *1*, 226–233.

Luria, A.R. *The mind of a mnemonist.* L. Solotaroff (Trans.), New York: Basic Books, 1968.

MacNeilage, P.F. Motor control of serial ordering of speech. *Psychological Review*, 1970, *77*, 182–196.

MacNeilage, P.F., & MacNeilage, L.A. Central processes and controlling speech production during sleep and walking. In F.J. McGuigan (Ed.), *The psychophysiology of thinking.* New York: Academic Press, 1973.

Mandler, G. Transfer of training as a function of degree of response overlearning. *Journal of Experimental Psychology*, 1954, *47*, 411–417.

Marler, P.R., & Hamilton, W.J. III. *Mechanisms of animal behavior.* New York: John Wiley & Sons, 1966.

Marteniuk, R.G. Retention characteristics of motor short-term memory cues. *Journal of Motor Behavior*, 1973, *5*, 249–259.

Marteniuk, R.G. Individual differences in motor performance and learning. In J.H. Wilmore (Ed.), *Exercise and sport sciences reviews* (Vol. 2). New York: Academic Press, 1974.

Marteniuk, R.G. *Information processing in motor skills.* New York: Holt, Rinehart & Winston, 1976.

Maslow, A.H. A preface to motivation theory. *Psychosomatic Medicine Monograph*, 1943, *5*, 370–396.

Mathews, D.K., & McDaniel, J. Effectiveness of using golf-lite in learning the golf swing. *Research Quarterly*, 1962, *33*, 488–491.

May, R.B., & Duncan, P. Facilitation on a response-loaded task by changes in task difficulty. *Perceptual and Motor Skills*, 1973, *36*, 123–129.

McCloy, C.H. The measurement of general motor capacity and general motor ability. *Research Quarterly*, 1934, *5*, Suppl, 46–61.

McCloy, C.H., & Young, N.D. *Tests and measurements in health and physical education* (3rd ed.). New York: Appleton-Century-Crofts, 1954.

McGrath, J.E. A conceptual formulation for research on stress. In J.E. McGrath (Ed.), *Social and psychological factors in stress.* New York: Holt, Rinehart & Winston, 1970.

McLuhan, M., & Fiore, Q. *The medium is the message—An inventory of effects.* Toronto: Bantam Books, 1967.

Melnick, M.J. Effects of overlearning on the retention of a gross motor skill. *Research Quarterly*, 1971, *42*, 60–69.

Melton, A.W. Implications of short-term memory for a general theory of memory. *Journal of Verbal Learning and Verbal Behavior*, 1963, *2*, 1–21.

Miller, G.A. The magical number seven plus or minus two: Some limits on our capacity for processing information. *Psychological Review*, 1956, *63*, 81–97.

Miller, G.A., Galanter, R., & Pribram, K.H. *Plans and the structure of behavior*. New York: Holt, Rinehart & Winston, 1960.

Miller, G.A., Heise, G.A., & Lichten, W. The intelligibility of speech as a function of the context of the materials. *Journal of Experimental Psychology*, 1951, *41*, 329–335.

Mohr, D.R., & Barrett, M.E. Effect of knowledge of mechanical principles in learning to perform intermediate swimming skills. *Research Quarterly*, 1962, *33*, 574–580.

Moray, N. *Attention: Selective processes in vision and hearing*. London: Hutchinson, 1970.

Morgan, B.B., Brown, B.R., & Alluisi, E.A. Effects of 48 hours of continuous work and sleep loss on sustained performance. Army THEMIS contract, Interim Technical Report Number ITR-70-16, 1970.

Morrell, F. Lasting changes in synaptic organization produced by continuous neuronal bombardment. In J.F. Delafresnaye (Ed.), *Brain mechanisms and learning*. Oxford: Blackwell, 1961.

Morton, J. Interaction of information in word recognition. *Psychological Review*, 1969, *76*, 165–178.

Mowbray, G.H., & Rhoades, M.U. On the reduction of choice reaction times with practice. *Quarterly Journal of Experimental Psychology*, 1959, *11*, 16–23.

Mowrer, O.H., *Learning Theory and Behavior*. New York: John Wiley & Sons, 1960.

Mumby, H.H. Kinesthetic acuity and balance related to wrestling ability. *Research Quarterly*, 1953, *24*, 327–334.

Murdock, B.B. The immediate retention of unrelated words. *Journal of Experimental Psychology*, 1960, *60*, 222–234.

Murdock, B.B. A test of the "limited capacity" hypothesis. *Journal of Experimental Psychology*, 1965, *69*, 237–240.

Murray, J.F. The activity-set hypothesis for warm-up decrement in a movement balance task. *Journal of Motor Behavior*, 1980, *12*, 262–269.

Namikas, G., & Archer, E.J. Motor skill transfer as a function of intertask interval and pre-transfer task difficulty. *Journal of Experimental Psychology*, 1960, *59*, 109–112.

Naylor, J.C., & Briggs, G.E. Effects of task complexity and task organization on the relative efficiency of part and whole training methods. *Journal of Experimental Psychology*, 1963, *65*, 217–224.

Neimeyer, R. Part versus whole methods and massed versus distributed practice in learning of selected large muscle activities. Unpublished doctoral dissertation, University of Southern California, 1959.

Neisser, U. Visual search. *Scientific American*, 1964, *210*, 94–104.

Nelson, J. Analysis of the effects of applying various motivational situations to college men subjected to a stressful physical performance. Unpublished doctoral dissertation, University of Oregon, 1962.

Neumann, E. Frequency and usefulness of verbal and nonverbal methods in the learning and transfer of a paired-associate serial motor task. *Journal of Experimental Psychology*, 1960, *60*, 103–110.

Newell, K.M. Knowledge of results and motor learning. *Journal of Motor Behavior*, 1974, *6*, 235–244.

Newell, K.M. Motor learning without knowledge of results through the development of a response recognition mechanism. *Journal of Motor Behavior*, 1976, *8*, 209–217.

Newell, K.M., & Boucher, J.P. Motor response recognition: Two processes. *Journal of Motor Behavior*, 1974, *6*, 81–86.

Newell, K.M., Shapiro, D.A., & Carlton, M.J. Coordinating visual and kinesthetic memory codes. *British Journal of Psychology*, 1979, *70*, 87–96.

Nixon, J.E., & Locke, L.F. Research on teaching physical education. In R.M.W. Travers (Ed.), *Second handbook of research on teaching*. Chicago: Rand McNally, 1973.

Noble, M., & Trumbo, D. The organization of skilled response. *Organizational Behavior and Human Performance*, 1967, *2*, 1–25.

Norman, D.A. Toward a theory of memory and attention. *Psychological Review*, 1968, *75*, 522–536.

Norman, D.A. *Memory and Attention*. New York: John Wiley & Sons, 1969.

Norman, D.A. (Ed.), *Models of human memory*. New York: Academic Press, 1970.

Norman, D.A. *Memory and attention: An introduction to human information processing* (2nd ed.). New York: John Wiley & Sons, 1976.

Norrie, M.L. Practice effects on reaction latency for simple and complex movements. *Research Quarterly*, 1967, *38*, 79–85.

Norrie, M.L. Number of reinforcements and memory trace for kinesthetically monitored force reproduction. *Research Quarterly*, 1969, *40*, 338–342.

Nottebohm, F. Ontogeny of bird song. *Science*, 1970, *167*, 950–956.

O'Hara, T.J. A demonstration of the relationship between cognitive experience and performance debilitation in high evaluation conditions. Proceedings of the 9th Canadian Psychomotor Learning and Sport Psychology Symposium, Banff, Alberta, 1977.

Olsen, E.A. Relationship between psychological capacities and success in college athletes. *Research Quarterly*, 1956, *27*, 79–89.

Oxendine, J.B. Generality and specificity in the learning of fine and gross motor skills. *Research Quarterly*, 1967, *38*, 86–94.

Oxendine, J.B. *Psychology of motor learning*. New York: Appleton-Century-Crofts, 1968.

Pascuale-Leone, J. A mathematical model for the transition rule in Piaget's developmental stages. *Acta Psychologia*, 1970, *32*, 301–345.

Pavlov, I.P. *Conditioned reflexes*. G.V. Anrep. (Trans.) London: Oxford University Press, 1927.

Pavlov, I.P. The reply of a physiologist to psychologists. *Psychological Review*, 1932, *39*, 91–127.

Penfield, W., & Roberts, L. *Speech and brain mechanisms*. Princeton, New Jersey: Princeton University Press, 1959.

Pepper, R.L., & Herman, L.M. Decay and interference effects in short-term retention of a discrete motor act. *Journal of Experimental Psychology*, 1970, *83*, 165–172.

Peterson, L.R., Hillner, K.H., & Saltzman, D. Supplementary report: Time pairings and short-term retention. *Journal of Experimental Psychology*, 1962, *64*, 550–551.

Peterson, L.R., Saltzman, D., Hillner, K., & Land, V. Recency and frequency in paired associate learning. *Journal of Experimental Psychology*, 1962, *63*, no. 4, 396–403.

Pew, R.W. Acquisition of hierarchical control over the temporal organization of a skill. *Journal of Experimental Psychology,* 1966, *71,* 764–771.

Pew, R.W. Towards a process-oriented theory of human skilled performance. *Journal of Motor Behavior,* 1970, *2,* 8–24.

Pew, R.W. Human perceptual-motor performance. In B.H. Kanbowitz (Ed.), *Human information processing: Tutorials in performance and cognition.* New York: Erlbaum, 1974.

Phipps, S.J., & Morehouse, C.A. Effects of mental practice on the acquisition of motor skills of varied difficulty. *Research Quarterly,* 1969, *40,* 773–778.

Piaget, J. *The psychology of intelligence.* New York: Harcourt Brace, 1950.

Pittuck, D., & Dainty, D. The effects of a modified ball on the mechanics of selected water polo skills in novice children. In J. Terauds & E.W. Bedingfield (Eds.), *Swimming III, international series on sport sciences* (Vol. VIII). Baltimore: University Park Press, 1979.

Pollack, I. The information of elementary auditory displays. *Journal of Acoustical Society of America,* 1952, *24,* 745–749.

Pollack, I., Johnson, L.D., & Knaff, R.P. Running memory span. *Journal of Experimental Psychology,* 1959, *57,* 137–146.

Posner, M.I. Components of skilled performance. *Science,* 1966, *152,* 1712–1718.

Posner, M.I. Characteristics of visual and kinesthetic memory codes. *Journal of Experimental Psychology,* 1967, *75,* 103–107.

Posner, M.I. *Cognition: An introduction.* Glenview, Illinois: Scott, Foresman & Co., 1973.

Posner, M.I., & Boies, S.J. Components of attention. *Psychological Review,* 1971, *78,* 391–408.

Posner, M.I., & Keele, S.W. On the genesis of abstract ideas. *Journal of Experimental Psychology,* 1968, *77,* 353–363.

Posner, M.I., & Keele, S.W. Attention demands of movements. *Proceedings of the Seventeenth Congress of Applied Psychology.* Amsterdam: Zeitlinger, 1969.

Posner, M.I., & Keele, S.W. Time and space as measures of mental operations. *Proceedings of the 78th Annual Convention of the American Psychological Association.* Miami Beach, 1970.

Posner, M.I., & Keele, S.W. Skill learning. In R.M.W. Travers (Ed.), *Handbook of research on teaching.* Washington, D.C.: American Educational Research Association, 1972.

Posner, M.I., & Konick, A.F. Short-term retention of visual and kinesthetic information. *Organizational Behavior and Human Performance,* 1966, *1,* 71–86.

Posner, M.I., & Rossman, E. Effect of size and location of informational transforms upon short-term memory. *Journal of Experimental Psychology,* 1965, *70,* 496–505.

Poulton, E.C. On prediction in skilled movement. *Psychological Bulletin,* 1957, *54,* 467–478.

Prather, H. *Notes to myself: My struggle to become a person.* New York: Bantam Books, 1970.

Pronko, N.H. On learning to play the violin at the age of four, without tears. *Psychology Today,* 1969, *2,* 52–53, 66.

Prudy, B.J., & Lockhart, A. Retention and relearning of gross motor skills after long periods of no practice. *Research Quarterly*, 1962, *33*, 265–272.

Rabbitt, P.M.A. Response-facilitation on repetition of a limb movement. *British Journal of Psychology*, 1965, *56*, 303–304.

Rabbitt, P.M.A. Repetition effects and signal classification strategies in serial choice-response tasks. *Quarterly Journal of Experimental Psychology*, 1968, *20*, 232–240.

Rappaport, S.R. *Foundations and practice in perceptual-motor learning: A quest for understanding.* An American Association for Health, Physical Education and Recreation publication, 1971.

Requin, J. Some data on neurophysiological processes involved in the preparatory motor activity to reaction time performance. *Acta Psychologica*, 1969, *30*, 358–367.

Restle, F., & Burnside, B.L. Tracking of serial patterns. *Journal of Experimental Psychology*, 1972, *95*, 299–307.

Reynolds, D. Time and event uncertainty in unisensory reaction time. *Journal of Experimental Psychology*, 1966, *71*, 286–293.

Rhoades, W.M. Effects of variations and number of strokes taught and equipment used on tennis achievement by college women. Unpublished doctoral dissertation, Indiana University, 1963.

Rogers, C.A., Jr. Feedback precision and postfeedback interval duration. *Journal of Experimental Psychology*, 1974, *102*, 604–608.

Rogers, F.R. Physical capacity tests in the administration of physical education. *Contributions to Education* (no. 173). New York: Teachers College, Columbia University, 1925.

Rosen, B.C., & D'Andrade, R. The psycho-social origins of achievement motivation. *Sociometry*, 1959, *22*, 185–218.

Rowan, R. Thoughts and other dreams. Unpublished manuscript, 1980.

Rushall, B.S., & Pettinger, J. An evaluation of the effects of various reinforcers used as motivation in swimming. *Research Quarterly*, 1969, *40*, 540–545.

Russell, D.G. Spatial location cues and movement production. In G.E. Stelmach (Ed.), *Motor control: Issues and Trends.* New York: Academic Press, 1976.

Sage, G.H. *Introduction to motor behavior, a neuropsychological approach.* Reading, Massachusetts: Addison—Wesley Publishing Co., 1977.

Salmela, J.H., & Fiorito, P. Visual cues in ice hockey goaltending. *Canadian Journal of Applied Sport Sciences*, 1979, *4*, 56–59.

Saltz, E. *The cognitive bases of human learning.* Homewood, Illinois: Dorsey Press, 1977.

Schmidt, R.A. Proactive inhibition in retention of discrete motor skill. Paper presented at the Second International Society of Sports Psychology, Washington, D.C., 1968.

Schmidt, R.A. Performance and learning a gross motor skill under conditions of artificially induced fatigue. *Research Quarterly*, 1969, *40*, 185–190.

Schmidt, R.A. *Motor skills.* New York: Harper & Row, 1975. (a)

Schmidt, R.A. A schema theory of discrete motor skill learning. *Psychological Review*, 1975, *82*, 225–260. (b)

Schmidt, R.A. The schema as a solution to some persistant problems in motor learning theory. In G.E. Stelmach (Ed.), *Motor Control; Issues and Trends.* New York: Academic Press, 1976.

Schmidt, R.A. Control processes in motor skills. In J. Keogh & R.S. Hutton (Eds.),

Exercise and sport sciences review (Vol. 4). Santa Barbara, California: Journal Publishing Affiliates, 1977.

Schmidt, R.A., & Stull, G.A. Premotor and motor reaction time as a function of preliminary muscular tension. *Journal of Motor Behavior*, 1970, *2*, 96–110.

Schmidt, R.A., & White, J.L. Evidence for an error detection mechanism in motor skills: A test of Adams' closed-loop theory. *Journal of Motor Behavior*, 1972, *4*, 143–153.

Schmidt, R.A., & Wrisberg, C.A. Further tests of Adams' closed-loop theory: Response produced feedback and the error detection mechanism. *Journal of Motor Behavior*, 1973, *5*, 155–164.

Schmidt, R.A., Zelaznik, H.N., & Frank, J.S. Sources of inaccuracy in rapid movement. In G.E. Stelmach (Ed.), *Information processing in motor control and learning*. New York: Academic Press, 1978.

Scott, M.G. Assessment of motor ability of college women through objective tests. *Research Quarterly*, 1939, *10*, 63–83.

Scott, M.G. Measurement of kinesthesis. *Research Quarterly*, 1955, *26*, 324–341.

Scott, R.S. A comparison of teaching two methods of physical education with grade one pupils. *Research Quarterly*, 1967, *38*, 151–154.

Sears, R.A., & Newson Davis, J.N. The control of respiratory muscles during voluntary breathing. *Annals of the New York Academy of Sciences*, 1968, *155*, 183–190.

Seymour, W.D. Transfer of training in engineering skills. *Perceptual Motor Skills*, 1957, *7*, 235–237.

Shannon, C.E. & Weaver, W. *The mathematical theory of communication*. Urbana: University of Illinois Press, 1962.

Shapiro, D.C., & Schmidt, R.A. The schema theory: Recent evidence and developmental implications. Paper presented at CIC Symposium on Motor Development, Iowa, 1979.

Shaw, R.E., & Bransford, J. Introduction: Psychological approaches to the problem of knowledge. In R.E. Shaw, & J. Bransford (Eds.), *Perceiving, acting and knowing: Towards an ecological psychology*. Hillsdale, New Jersey: Erlbaum, 1977.

Shay, C.T. The progressive part vs the whole method of learning motor skills. *Research Quarterly*, 1934, *5*, 62–67.

Shepard, R.N., & Teghtsoonian, M. Retention of information under conditions approaching a steady state. *Journal of Experimental Psychology*, 1961, *62*, 302–309.

Singer, R.N. Transfer effects and ultimate success in archery due to degree of difficulty of the initial learning. *Research Quarterly*, 1966, *37*, 532–539.

Singer, R.N. Physical characteristics, perceptual-motor and intelligence differences between third-grade and sixth-grade children. *Research Quarterly*, 1969, *40*, 803–811.

Skinner, B.F. *The behavior of organisms: An experimental analysis*. New York: Appleton-Century-Crofts, 1938.

Skoglund, S. Joint receptors and kinesthesis. In A. Iggo (Ed.), *Handbook of sensory physiology, somatosensory system* (Vol. II.). Berlin: Springer-Verlag, 1973.

Slater-Hammel, A.T. Comparison of reaction time measures to a visual stimulus and arm movement. *Research Quarterly*, 1955, *26*, 470–479.

Smith, H.M. Implications for movement education experiences drawn from perceptual-motor research. *Journal of Health, Physical Education and Recreation,* 1970 (April), 30–33.

Smith, J.L. Fusimotor loop properties and involvement during voluntary movement. In J. Keogh & R.S. Hutton (Eds.), *Exercise and sport sciences reviews* (Vol. 4). Santa Barbara, California: Journal Publishing Affiliates, 1977

Smith, K.U. Cybernetic theory and analysis of learning. In E.A. Bilodeau (Ed.), *Acquisition of skill.* New York: Academic Press, 1966. (a)

Smith, K.U. Feedback theory and motor learning. Paper presented at the North American Society of Sports Psychology, Chicago, 1966. (b)

Smith, K.U., & Smith, W.M. *Perception and motion.* Philadelphia: W.B. Saunders, 1962.

Smith, L.E., & Harrison, J.S. Comparison of the effects of visual, motor, mental and guided practice upon speed and accuracy of performing a simple eye-hand coordination task. *Research Quarterly,* 1962, *33,* 299–307.

Smith, O.W. Developmental studies of spatial judgements by children and adults. *Perceptual Motor Skills,* 1966, *22,* 3–73, monograph supplement I-V22.

Soule, R.G. The effect of badminton and handball on tennis ability of inexperienced players. Unpublished master's thesis, University of Illinois, 1958.

Sperling, G. The information available in brief visual presentations. *Psychological Monographs,* 1960, *74,* 1–29.

Spielberger, C.D. Theory and research on anxiety. In C.D. Spielberger (Ed.), *Anxiety and behavior.* New York: Academic Press, 1966.

Stallings, L.M. *Motor skills development and learning.* Washington, D.C.: Wm. C. Brown, 1973.

Stelmach, G.E. Retention of motor skills. In J.H. Wilmore (Ed.), *Exercise and sport sciences review* (Vol. 2). New York: Academic Press, 1974.

Stelmach, G.E., & Kelso, J.A.S. Memory processes in motor control. In S. Dornic (Ed.), *Attention and performance VI.* Hillsdale, New Jersey: Erlbaum, 1977.

Stelmach, G.E. & McClure, S. Rehearsal methods in STM. Unpublished manuscript, 1973.

Stelmach, G.E., Kelso, J.A.S., & Wallace, S.A. Preselection in short term motor memory. *Journal of Experimental Psychology: Human Learning and Memory,* 1975, *6,* 745–755.

Sternberg, S. Memory scanning: Mental processes revealed by reaction time experiments. *American Scientist,* 1969, *57,* 421–457.

Sternberg, S., Monsell, S., Knoll, R.L., & Wright, C.E. The latency and duration of rapid movement sequences: Comparisons of speech and typewriting. In G.E. Stelmach (Ed.), *Information processing in motor control and learning.* New York: Academic Press, 1978.

Strong, C.H. Motivation related to performance of physical fitness test. *Research Quarterly,* 1963, *34,* 497–507.

Stroup, F. Relationship between the field of motion perception and basketball ability in college men. *Research Quarterly,* 1957, *28,* 72–76.

Summers, J.J. The role of timing in motor program representation. *Journal of Motor Behavior,* 1975, *7,* 229–241.

Swets, J.A. *Signal detection and recognition by human observers.* New York: John Wiley & Sons, 1964.

Swets, J.S., Tanner, W.P., & Birdsall, T.G. Decision processes in perception. *Psychological Review*, 1961, *68*, 301–360.

Swift, E.J. Memory of skillful movements. *Psychological Bulletin*, 1906, *3*, 185–187.

Tanner, W.P., & Swets, J.A. A decision-making theory of visual detection. *Psychological Review*, 1954, *61*, 401–409.

Taub, E. Movement in nonhuman primates deprived of somatosensory feedback. In J. Keogh, & R.S. Hutton (Eds.), *Exercise and sport sciences reviews* (Vol. 4). Santa Barbara, California: Journal Publishing Affiliates, 1977.

Taub, E., & Berman, A.J. Movement and learning in the absence of sensory feedback. In S.J. Freedman (Ed.), *The neurophysiology of spatially oriented behavior*. Homewood, Illinois: Dorsey Press, 1968.

Taylor, D.H. Latency components in two-choice responding. *Journal of Experimental Psychology*, 1966, *72*, 481–487.

Teuber, H.L. Comment on E.H. Lenneberg's paper—Speech as a motor skill with special reference to nonphasic disorders. *Acquisition of Language, Monographs of the Society for Research in Child Development*, 1964, *29*, 131–138.

Theios, J. The components of response latency in simple human information processing tasks. In P.M.A. Rabbitt & S. Dornic (Eds.), *Attention and performance V*. New York: Academic Press, 1975.

Thorndike, E.L. *Animal intelligence*. New York: Macmillan, 1911.

Thorndike, E.L. *Educational psychology* (Vol. 1). New York: Teachers College Press, 1913.

Thorndike, E.L. *Fundamentals of learning*. New York: Teachers College, 1935.

Tichner, E.B. *A beginner's psychology*. New York: Macmillan, 1916.

Tolman, E.C. Theories of learning. In F.A. Moss (Ed.), *Comparative psychology*. Englewood Cliffs, New Jersey: Prentice-Hall, 1934.

Tolman, E.C. *Collected papers in psychology*. Berkeley: University of California Press, 1951.

Treisman, A.M. Contextual cues in selective listening. *Quarterly Journal of Experimental Psychology*, 1960, *12*, 242–248.

Treisman, A.M. Monitoring and storage of irrelevant messages in selective attention. *Journal of Verbal Learning and Verbal Behavior*, 1964, *3*, 449–459.

Triplett, N. The dynamogenic factors in pacemaking and competition. *American Journal of Psychology*, 1897, *9*, 507–533.

Trowbridge, M.H., & Cason, H. An experimental study of Thorndike's theory of learning. *Journal of General Psychology*, 1932, *7*, 245–258.

Tulving, E. The effect of order of presentation on learning of "unrelated" words. *Psychonomic Science*, 1965, *3*, 337–338.

Tulving, E. Subjective organization and effects of repetition in multitrial free-recall learning. *Journal of Verbal Learning and Verbal Behavior*, 1966, *5*, 193–197.

Tulving, E., & Thompson, D.M. Encoding specificity and retrieval processes in episodic memory. *Psychological Review*, 1973, *80*, 352–373.

Turvey, M.T. Preliminaries to a theory of action with reference to vision. In R.E. Shaw & J. Bransford (Eds.), *Perceiving, acting and knowing: Toward an ecological psychology*. Hillsdale, New Jersey: Erlbaum, 1977.

Tweit, A.H., Gollnick, P.D., & Hearn, G.R. Effect of a training program on total body reaction time of individuals of low fitness. *Research Quarterly*, 1963, *34*, 508-513.

Twinning, W.E. Mental practice and physical practice in learning a motor skill. *Research Quarterly*, 1949, *20*, 432-435.

Ulich, E. Some experiments in the function of mental training in the acquisition of motor skills. *Ergonomics*, 1967, *10*, 411-419.

Underwood, B.J. Interference and forgetting. *Psychological Review*, 1957, *64*, 49-60.

Vickers, D. Perceptual economy and the impression of visual depth. *Perception and Psychophysics*, 1971, *10*, 23-27.

Von Helmholz, H. *Treatise on physiological optics* (Vol. 3, 3rd ed.). J.P.C. Southall (Ed. & Trans.). Menasha, Wisconsin: Optical Society of America, 1925.

Von Holst, E. Relations between the central nervous system and the peripheral organs. *British Journal of Animal Behaviour*, 1954, *2*, 89-94.

Wapner, S., Werner, H., & Chandler, K.A. Experiments on sensory-tonic field theory of perception: I. Effect of extraneous stimulation on the visual perception of verticality. *Journal of Experimental Psychology*, 1951, *42*, 341-345.

Weinberg, D.R., Guy, D.E., & Tupper, R.W. Variation of past feedback interval in simple motor learning. *Journal of Experimental Psychology*, 1964, *67*, 98-99.

Weiss, A.D. The locus of reaction time change with set, motivation, and age. *Journal of Gerontology*, 1965, *20*, 60-64.

Welford, A.T. The psychological refractory period and timing of high speed performance: A review and a theory. *British Journal of Psychology*, 1952, *43*, 2-19.

Welford, A.T. Perceptual selection and integration. *Ergonomics*, 1970, *13*, 5-23.

Welford, A.T. Stress and performance. *Ergonomics*, 1973, *16*, 567-580.

Welford, A.T. *Skilled performance: Perceptual and motor skills*. Glenview, Illinois: Scott, Foresman, & Co., 1976.

Welford, A.T., Norris, A.H., & Shock, N.W. Speed and accuracy of movement and their changes with age. *Acta Psychologica*, 1969, *30*, 3-15.

Welsh, R.L. Transfer of training in the scissor and frog kick. Unpublished master's thesis, University of Illinois, 1962.

Werner, H., & Wapner, W. Sensory-tonic field theory of perception. *Journal of Personality*, 1949, *18*, 88-107.

Werner, P. Integration of physical education skills with the concept of levers at intermediate grade levels. *Research Quarterly*, 1972, *43*, 423-428.

Wertheimer, M. *Productive thinking*. New York: Harper & Row, 1959.

Whiting, H.T.A. Training in a continuous ball-throwing and catching task. *Ergonomics*, 1968, *11*, 375-382.

Whitley, J.D. Effects of practice distribution on learning a fine motor task. *Research Quarterly*, 1970, *48*, 576-583.

Wiebe, V.R. A study of tests of kinesthesis. *Research Quarterly*, 1954, *25*, 222-230.

Wiener, N. *Cybernetics*. New York: The M.I.T. Press and John Wiley & Sons, 1961.

Wilberg, R.B., & Salmela, J.H. Information load and response consistency in sequential short-term memory. *Perceptual and Motor Skills*, 1973, *37*, 23-29.

Wilkinson, R.T. Interaction of noise with knowledge of results and sleep deprivation. *Journal of Experimental Psychology*, 1963, *66*, 332-337.

Wilkinson, R.T., & Colquhoun, W.P. Interaction of alcohol with incentives and sleep deprivation. *Journal of Experimental Psychology*, 1968, *76*, 623-629.

Willcutt, H.C., & Kennedy, W.A. Praise and blame as incentives. *Psychological Bulletin*, 1964, *62*, 323–332.

Williams, H.G. The perception of moving objects by children. Unpublished study, Perceptual-Motor Learning Laboratory, University of California, 1967.

Williams, J.M., & Thirer, J. Vertical and horizontal peripheral vision in male and female athletes and nonathletes. *Research Quarterly*, 1975, *46*, 200–205.

Wilson, D.M. The central nervous control of flight in a locust. *Journal of Experimental Biology*, 1961, *38*, 471–490.

Woodworth, R.S. The accuracy of voluntary movement. *Psychological Review*, Monograph Supplement, 1899, *3*.

Woodworth, R.S. *Experimental psychology*. New York: Holt, Rinehart & Winston, 1938.

Woodworth, R.S., & Schlosberg, M. *Experimental psychology*. New York: Holt, Rinehart & Winston, 1954.

Wright, E.J. Effects of light and heavy equipment on acquisition of sports-type skills by young children. *Research Quarterly*, 1967, *38*, 705–714.

Wrisberg, C.A., & Ragsdale, M.R. Cognitive demand and practice level: Factors in the mental rehearsal of motor skills. *Journal of Human Movement Studies*, 1979, *5*, 201–208.

Yerkes, R.M., & Dodson, J.D. The relation of strength of stimulus to rapidity of habit formation. *Journal of Comparative Neurology and Psychology*, 1908, *18*, 459–482.

Young, O. Rate of learning in relation of practice periods in archery and badminton. *Research Quarterly*, 1954, *25*, 231–243.

Youngen, L. A comparison of reaction time and movement times of women athletes and nonathletes. *Research Quarterly*, 1959, *30*, 349–355.

Author Index (first author only)

339

Subject Index

sensory information store, 109, 110, 239
store, 41, 239
Short-term motor memory, 103, 237, 238, 257
Short-term retention, 100, 101
Short-term storage and teaching model, 273
Signal detection theory, 142, 171, 225
  assumptions of, 143, 171
  criterion, 144
  level of arousal, 248
  probability theory, 145
Sign Gestalt, 31, 35, 48, 153, 178, 206, 308
Similarity, 33, 68, 286, 313
  and field items, 153
Skaggs - Robinson hypothesis, 70, 74, 313
Skill,
  general motor ability, 275
  nature of, 105
Skill acquisition, 293, 301
  learning, 126, 261, 271, 284
Skinner, 26
Space perception theory, 138, 171
Spacing, 114, 120
Span of apprehension, 187, 314
Spatial awareness, 177, 197, 204, 206, 208, 314
  characteristics, 162
  map, 238
  orientation, 177, 206, 314
  organization, 105
  patterning, 169
  relations, 177, 206, 314
  visualization, 177, 206, 314
Specificity
  vs generality, 275, 276, 298, 301
Speed-accuracy trade-off, 221, 250, 251, 314
Speed of decision, 262, 299
  compatibility, 262, 263, 299
  preparation, 262, 263, 299
  sequential dependencies, 262, 264, 299
Speed of vision, 187, 207, 314
Spontaneous decay of information, 239
S-R chaining theory, 243, 287
Stages of learning, 90, 126, 169
Stimulation (Theios), 241, 242
Stimulus generalization, 76, 95
Stimulus-response compatibility, 202, 222
Stimulus-response theories, 21
State anxiety, 248, 314
Storage, 236, 256, 260
Stress, 89, 246, 248, 257
  environmental, 251, 257
  optimal, 254
Stretch reflex, 195
Structural interference, 195, 215, 236, 314
Suzuki method, 270, 300

Target items, 153, 314
Task,
  type of, 105, 119
Task complexity, 60, 314
Task organization, 60, 314
Task structure, 59
  part learning, 59
  whole learning, 59
Teaching models, 271
  Gentile's model, 271, 290, 300
  Marteniuk's model, 273, 300
Temporal discriminations, 187
Temporal patterning, 105, 169
Terminal feedback, 78, 314
Thalamus, 190
Theios' model, 241, 257
Thorndike, 22, 47, 68, 102
Threshold value, 142, 164, 173, 314
Time sharing, 314
Timing, 105, 234, 265, 268
Total body transport, 11
Tote unit, 29, 48
Trait anxiety, 248, 314
Transactional theory, 137, 170
Transfer, 67, 314
  bilateral, 69, 95
  cross education, 69, 95
  intertask, 70, 95
  intratask, 75, 95
  negative, 72, 95
  proactive, 69
  retroactive, 69
Transfer of learning,
  and memory drum theory, 277
Transformations over time, 184, 314
Translator, 202
Transposition theory, 69
Treisman's model, 162, 173
Type I and II rehearsal, 158, 314

U (inverted hypothesis), 249
Unconditioned stimulus, 21
Use, (law of), 23, 314
Utricle, 193

Variability, 139
Vestibular apparatus, 188, 191, 192, 193, 208
Vision,
  peripheral, 187
  speed of, 187, 207
Visual,
  complexity, 177
  cues, 200
  field, 153, 183, 315
  perception, 206
  practice, 64